D0842952

ECONOMICS AND MARXISM

ECONOMICS AND MARXISM

Volume I

THE RENAISSANCE OF THE MARXIAN SYSTEM

Karl Kühne

Translated by Robert Shaw

St. Martin's Press   New York

Originally published in Germany under the title *Ökonomie und Marxismus* © 1972 Hermann Luchterhand Verlag, Neuwied. English translation © The Macmillan Press 1979

St. Martin's Press, Inc. 175 Fifth Avenue, New York, N.Y. 10010
Printed in Great Britain
First published in the United States of America in 1979
LC 9–5149

ISBN 0–312–23436–8

Contents

Foreword

Mao Tse-tung criticised the content of the Soviet textbook on Political Economy:

> The effects of principles and laws must be subjected to analysis and thorough study; only then can principles and laws be derived. Human knowledge always encounters appearances first. Proceeding from there, one searches out principles and laws. The text does the opposite. Its methodology is deductive, not analytical. According to formal logic, 'People all will die. Mr Chang is a person. Therefore Mr Chang will die.' This is a conclusion derived from the premise that all human beings die. This is the deductive method. For every question the text first gives definitions, which it then takes as a major premise and reasons from there, failing to understand that the major premise should be the result of researching a question. Not until one has gone through the concrete research can principles and laws be discovered and proved.[1]

The method of arguing from definitions is prevalent not only among economists in the USSR but also amongst some sects of Western Marxists. In the Soviets, no doubt, strict adherence to officially approved slogans was a protection against personal danger; in the West, it provided a shibboleth by which members of a cult could recognise each other and present a united front in a hostile environment. This attitude has made it only too easy for 'mainstream' economists to isolate the Marxists, to refuse to enter into any serious argument with them and to counter their verbal formulations with slogans even more empty than their own. In this book, Dr Kühne shows that, when mainstream teaching is beginning to emerge from the cocoon of static equilibrium, it can find in Marx the basis for dynamic analysis of the development of capitalism. I have been making the same point ever since 1942;[2] while trying to draw the attention of my academic colleagues to the importance of Marx's main ideas, I have proposed some detailed amendments to his formal analysis. This has caused me to be treated by the dogmatists as an enemy. Perhaps it is worthwhile now to open up the argument afresh.

The Labour Theory of Value. The concept of labour *value* operates on two planes. It is a grand philosophical conception which carries a strong charge of political ideology and it is a particular unit of measurement of industrial output. The ideology has been fused with the analysis so that to criticise *value* as a unit of measurement is taken to be a rejection of the philosophy. I have caused great offence by saying that the 'labour theory of value' is a metaphysical concept. But I did not mean that metaphysical concepts are unimportant. I took the example of the statement: All men are equal.

In a logical view what does it mean? The word 'equal' applies to quantities. What—are all men the same weight? Or do they all get the same marks in intelligence tests? Or—to stretch the meaning of quantity a little—do I find them all equally agreeable? 'Equal' without saying in what respect is just a noise. In this case, the equality is just in respect of equality. Every man is equally equal.

*   *   *

Yet metaphysical statements are not without content. They express a point of view and formulate feelings which are a guide to conduct. The slogan 'All men are equal' expresses a protest against privilege by birth. In an egalitarian society no one would ever have thought of saying any such thing. It expresses a moral standard for private life—that it is wrong to be snobbish about class or colour; and a programme for political life—to create a society where all have the same rights; to refuse to accept a state in which some are more equal than others.

Metaphysical propositions also provide a quarry from which hypotheses can be drawn. They do not belong to the realm of science and yet they are necessary to it. Without them we would not know what it is that we want to know.[3]

Mixing ideology with logic creates an obfuscation of points that analytically are quite simple. The 'transformation problem' is a case in point.

The statement that only labour produces *value* does not mean that a man can produce anything with his bare hands. To produce physical output workers require a pre-existing stock of means of production to work with. One of the strong points in Marx's formal scheme is the distinction between gross and net output, which is often blurred in mainstream teaching.

The flow of output of industry, say per week or per year, is written: $c + v + s$. The flow of net output, $v + s$, divided between wages and net profit, is measured by the total flow of work being performed (reckoned in man-hours). This work, as well as accounting for net output, is also replacing elements of means of production (stocks of materials and wear and tear of plant) used up in the process, represented by c, which is added to the flow of *value* being produced.

Piero Sraffa, in *Production of Commodities by Means of Commodities*, provided a simplified and tightly specified model in which these relationships are quite clear cut. The relation of net to gross output and of replacements (c) to the stock of means of production are physically determined, and it is possible to distinguish the labour time directly and indirectly required to produce a unit of each commodity.

When these relationships are specified, governed by technical conditions, we can express them in terms of any numeraire we please. Sraffa uses a physical unit of output—the standard commodity. I prefer to fix the money wage for a representative man-hour of work and reckon in terms of money.

The main point of Sraffa's analysis is to show that neither prices nor the rate of profit on capital are determined by technical conditions. There are no 'marginal products'. If the rate of profit (uniform throughout the system) is given, all prices and the share of wages in net output are determined and if the ratio of exploitation (s/v) is given, the share of wages, the rate of profit and all prices are determined.

In a special case where the capital to labour ratio (organic composition) is the same in all lines of production, the prices of commodities, at any rate of profit, are proportional to their *values*, but this is of no particular interest. The important relationship, the overall ratio of prices to wages, is not governed by *values* but by the rate of profit, which entails the ratio of exploitation, or by the ratio of exploitation which entails the rate of profit.

The so-called 'transformation' is the relationship between prices proportional to *values* and 'prices of production' corresponding to a uniform rate of profit. This is a mathematical calculation, not an historical process.

In 1942, I argued that there is no reason to treat the ratio of exploitation (net profit over the wage bill) as 'either logically or historically prior' to the rate of profit on capital.[4] I now think that this was a mistake. The forces which govern the distribution of the product of industry between wages and profits are the central features of a capitalist economy. Marx was right, quite apart from ideology, to put the ratio of exploitation into the centre of the picture, while leaving the relative prices of commodities and the overall rate of profit somewhat hazy.

Of course, in real life, relationships are not so clear and definite as in a Sraffa model. The distinction between gross and net output cannot be reduced to physical terms when technical development is going on so that inputs used up are replaced by something different. Insofar as there is a tendency to the equalisation of the rate of profit in a competitive economy, it works through investment, guided by expectations of future profit, and is never exactly achieved. But the share of wages in value added is always an actual ratio, here and now; it can be more or less satisfactorily exhibited in statistical terms and compared between industries, between countries and between periods of time, while the overall rate of profit on capital is not easy to define and still less easy to calculate.

Thus it seems to me that, whether it is expressed in terms of *value* or not, the Marxian theory provides the best foundation that is available for a system of analysis to be elaborated and applied to actual problems.

The value of labour power. There are some points where measurement in terms of *value* obscures rather than illuminates the argument. Marx treats employment at wages as the sale of labour power. As all commodities are exchanged at *values*, the wage must represent the *value* of labour power, in the sense that it provides for the maintenance of the employable labour force. It contains a moral and historical element depending on the prevailing standard of life in the pre-capitalist economy. The amount of *value*, labour time, that an employer gets for the wage that he pays depends upon the length of working hours that he can impose.

Nowadays, in so-called developing economies, growth of population keeps up the supply of labour for industry even when the level of real wages (and the individual expectation of life) is depressed, while in successful capitalist social-democratic nations the level of real wages rises progressively. Dogmatists maintain that a rise in the actual standard of life raises the *value* of labour power, which saves the definition but does not explain the phenomenon.

Socially necessary labour. To keep in touch with common sense, Marx had to show that a batch of goods produced by a labour-intensive technique does not contain more *value* than a similar batch which required less labour time to produce. The *value* embodied in commodities is that of *socially necessary* labour time.

This was sufficient for Marx's broad treatment of the historical development of capitalism but if we are looking for a theory of prices, we must examine the proposition more closely. In Sraffa's simple model, there is no ambiguity about *values* for there is only one set of methods of production in use, but when technical development has been going on continuously, many techniques, for each type of commodity, may be in use simultaneously. Some of the workers are operating the latest best-practice technique; the capitalists employing them have made successful innovations and are enjoying the advantage in the form of a higher than average mark-up on their wage bill. Successively older techniques are successively less profitable (in competitive conditions) while the least productive technique still in use can barely cover its running costs and is just about to be scrapped. Which technique represents socially necessary labour time for each sector of industry? Even if it was possible to pick out a representative or dominant technique in any phase of development we should still want to know what proportion of the labour force is operating it.

Marx usually attributes a higher level of productivity per unit of labour to a higher 'organic composition' of capital—that is, a more mechanised technique. When 'prices of production' rule—that is when there is a uniform rate of profit—the higher mark-up corresponding to a lower **wage** bill per unit of output is just what is required to yield profits at the ruling rate on the cost of the equipment. Expressing all this in terms of *value* is just a rigmarole that adds nothing to an understanding of the relationships involved.

There is another set of complications involved in the concept of *value*. According to the Marxian definition, labour employed in industry and in transport produces *surplus value*, while commercial and financial activities merely reallocate a share in the surplus to capital devoted to non-productive operations. From the point of view of the determination of the ratio of exploitation, this distinction is of no interest. The actual prices at which commodities are sold cover the costs and profits required by wholesale and retail trade, advertising, etc., and it is these actual prices which enter into the determination of real-wage rates.

It seems that in order to find out the *values* of commodities we need full information about the physical conditions of production and the flows of money payments. If we had that information, calculations in terms of *value* would add nothing to it and where information is inadequate, *value* cannot supply the lack.

The importance of the Marxian theory does not lie in the calculation of *value* but in Sraffa's demonstration that the rate of profit on capital is determined by the technical conditions of production and the ratio of exploitation (correlative to the share of wages in value added). This disposes at a single blow of the mainstream argument that profit measures the contribution of capital to production.

The question of what influences affect the ratio of exploitation and how they interact with technical conditions cannot, as Mao Tse-tung observed, be answered by adopting definitions but should be the subject of research.

Value of Capital. In Marx's formal scheme, the inputs used up in a flow of production (represented by c) is treated as a quantity of *value*, put into the materials and equipment when they were produced and now released as they are brought into current production. Here reasoning in *value* conceals a problem which is now topical—the distinction between the inputs that are replaced and those which are destroyed in the process of production.

The stock of means of production in existence is represented by its *value*, that is, the quantity of labour time that went into building it up.

To represent a stock of physical capital in terms of labour time is evidently a crude simplification (like Professor Samuelson's surrogate production function). Marx did not anticipate the subtleties of modern Anglo–Italian capital theory, but the drafts which appear in Volume II of *Capital* show that he was wrestling with the problems of turn-over periods and the time pattern of production. In any case, his measure of capital makes more sense than the neo-neoclassical concept of 'malleable machines'.

However, his notation is confusing. In the formula, c, v and s are flows per unit of time, but Marx writes c + v for the stock of capital and c/v for organic composition, the ratio of physical capital to current employment which corresponds to what is now called the degree of mechanisation of technology. Here v, the wage bill, say per annum, appears in a double role, partly as an element in working capital and partly as a representative of labour currently employed. It would be better to represent the total stock of physical means of production (measured by labour time) by C. Then C/c is the average turnover period of the whole stock—fixed and working capital together—in the time unit in which c, the rate of replacements of inputs, is reckoned. But how can we interpret v, the wage bill, as a measure of current employment? It would be better to write L for the labour force required to operate C at the normal capacity of plant and other inputs. Then organic composition is represented by C/L.

There do not seem to be any analytical or ideological problems involved in this change in notation, only a pious objection to tampering with the text of the scriptures.

The dogmatists often talk glibly of the 'relation between dead and living labour' without seeming to realise that to change the amount of 'dead labour'—that is, the stock of means of production in existence—requires an expenditure of finance to employ living labour in schemes of investment.

The great merit of *Capital*, as compared to mainstream textbooks (in spite of confusing terminology), is that it keeps constantly in mind the dual nature of capital, as a stock of produced means of production and as a command of finance which permits businesses to organise the employment of labour in such a way as to make profits for themselves.

The falling rate of profit. There was one point at which reckoning in terms of *value* led Marx astray, that is in connection with technical progress. Marx believed that innovations were generally capital using, that is that an older technique is replaced by another which requires more investment per man employed—a higher organic composition of capital. (This I propose to represent as a rise in C/L.) He proceeded to argue that if the ratio of exploitation is constant, this must cause the rate of profit on capital to fall. He often observes that higher organic composition is associated with a higher productivity of labour, but he had no symbol, say, o, for the flow of output in terms of physical commodities, so he failed to observe that innovations which require a rise in C/L generally raise o/C; that is, they raise output per unit of investment as well as output per man employed. A misguided attempt has sometimes been made to rescue Marx's proposition by associating it with neoclassical 'diminishing returns'. But even if innovations represent only partial improvements, so that they require a rise in the capital output ratio (C/o), as well as in the capital labour ratio (C/L), they still do not depress the rate of profit, for no capitalist would switch to a new technique that requires more investment per man (a rise in

C/L) unless he expected it to raise output per man (o/L) by more than enough to compensate.

The origin of the prediction of a falling rate of profit is usually traced to the passage in the *Grundrisse* where Marx describes how the ever-growing mechanisation of production will continually reduce the *value* of commodities (by reducing the labour time needed to produce them) and so reduce the surplus value accruing to the capitalists. It is absurd to suppose that when the capitalists are enjoying more and more goods, and money and power, that they should be worried at getting less *value*.

The argument can be interpreted in a moral sense. When the mechanisation of production has been completed, there is no more use for exploitation and accumulation. Society should take over the means of production and see that they are used in a rational manner to reduce toil and increase consumption for the benefit of all.

Effective Demand. The model from which Marx mistakenly derived the theory of the falling rate of profit was set up in long-period terms, that is to say that the output to capital ratio was fixed by technical conditions and could not vary with the level of utilisation of plant. Similarly, the schema of expanded reproduction, in Volume II of *Capital*, which laid the foundation for modern growth theory, imply a technically determined output to capital ratio. There is plenty of short-period argument in *Capital* accounting for booms, crises and depressions, but the two levels of the analysis are not brought into a coherent scheme. The missing link was supplied by Michal Kalecki.

While Keynes was making his 'long struggle to escape' from Marshallian orthodoxy, Kalecki was sorting out the tangle of Marxian theories. Both arrived together at pretty much the same diagnosis of the great depression of the 1930s, and advocated similar policies for dealing with it.

Keynes's version of the theory of effective demand is the more elaborate, and Kalecki's the more robust. In the central simplified argument, Kalecki divides the whole economy into two classes, workers and capitalists. A year's national income consists of wages and gross profits. Expenditure consists of workers' consumption, equal to wages, capitalists' consumption and gross investment. Workers each week spend last week's wages but capitalists' expenditure is not confined by their income for they can borrow or draw upon financial reserves. It is the expenditure of the capitalists which collectively determines their profits. A given stock of means of production can be used to employ more or fewer workers (in a boom or a slump) and to yield a greater or smaller flow of profits.

The existence of intermediate classes, international trade, taxation and the welfare state complicate the argument without altering the essential point.

Now, it is obvious that if we want to find what the return on an investment has been, we must look over its history to see how far it has enjoyed periods of high profits (booms) or suffered periods of stagnation. But when investment is being planned it is the expectations of future profits which guides its amount and its form.

Marx emphasised the instability of capitalism; Kalecki explains its mechanism. When the rate of investment has been rising, the flow of profits is greater, say this quarter than last. Employment and the utilisation of plant are higher. This means that both prospects of profit seem brighter and finance for further investment is more easily obtainable. Plans for investment are speeded up, and as they are carried out, profits rise all the more. Meanwhile the stock of equipment is being expanded. When the acceleration of investment begins to taper off, utilisation of plant will cease to keep up with the growth of capacity. As soon as excess capacity emerges, the realisation of profits begins to be disappointing, the rate of investment slackens and prospective profits decline all the more. Kalecki summed up the analysis: 'The tragedy of investment is that it causes crisis because it is useful. Doubtless many people will consider this theory paradoxical but it is not the theory which is paradoxical but its subject—the capitalist economy.'[5]

Kalecki's analysis also illuminates the formation of the ratio of exploitation. In manufacturing industry, prices are formed by adding a gross margin to direct costs to cover overheads and yield net profits. Costs have to be calculated on the basis of a standard level of utilisation of plant. The more timid or the more greedy are the firms, the lower the standard that they choose and the higher the gross margins that they claim to be necessary. The setting of margins has a direct influence on the ratio of exploitation, for it governs the relation of prices to money-wage rates, but the flow of profits which are actually realised depends upon the flow of expenditure. When sales exceed the standard utilisation, profits turn out to be greater than was allowed for in the calculation of prices, and contrarywise.

To find out whether the overall realised rate of profit on capital had been falling over any particular period would need very elaborate detailed research and the result would depend more upon the behaviour of investment during the period than upon the bias of technology towards raising or lowering the capital to output ratio.

Dynamic analysis. Marx believed himself to be finding out the laws of motion of the capitalist system and Volume I of *Capital* ends with a great apocalyptic vision of its overthrow, but he was not satisfied that his work was completed. The tortured drafts that were thrown together in Volumes II and III leave many problems unresolved. It was his dogmatic disciples who felt obliged to believe in the predictions about the future that could be drawn from his writings, and so had to reinterpret them from time to time to keep them in line with experience.

Mainstream economists also claim to be making testable predictions, though they are usually concerned only with minor details of the behaviour of a market economy. When physics was the model, it was supposed that the aim of science is to discover laws from which reliable predictions can be drawn. Now that the centre of interest is in biology, the uniqueness of history has come to be recognised. Professor J. Z. Young writes in *Programs of the Brain*:[6]

> There is nothing peculiar about the individual chemical components of a living system but no two organisms contain precisely the same set of them. Every creature begins with an endowment of varied possible actions. We can never be sure what these are because they are continually subject to mutation so that the genetic make-up of an organism cannot be known with the same 'certainty' as the composition of a chemical substance.

If this is true of any individual living organism, it is all the more true of human society. Economics and sociology can never aspire to the condition of physics and chemistry; Marx opened up the questions required for them to be developed as part of human biology, but he did not provide ready-made answers. As Mao Tse-tung observed, there is a great deal of research that still needs to be done.

JOAN ROBINSON
Cambridge 1978

1. *A Critique of Soviet Economies* (Monthly Review Press, 1977).
2. *An Essay on Marxian Economics* (Macmillan 1942; 2nd ed. 1960).
3. *Economic Philosophy* (Penguin Books), pp. 2–3.
4. *Essay on Marxian Economics*, p. 16.
5. *Essays in the Theory of Economic Fluctuation* (Allen and Unwin, 1939), p. 149.
6. Oxford University Press, 1978.

Preface

Since the 1930s, the name of Marx has acquired a new significance. The discovery of the manuscript 'Nationalökonomie und Philosophie' ('Political Economy and Philosophy') by S. Landshut and J. P. Mayer in 1930 opened the way for this new development. This and other writings of the young Marx permitted a reappraisal of his overall conception. It was, perhaps, no mere coincidence that this event took place on the eve of the spiritual catastrophe that was to engulf the whole of Germany.

Today, though this epoch is behind us, there still persists in Germany a sullen hostility to Marx, which can best be described by the saying, 'A prophet is not without honour, save in his own country and in his own home.' Nowhere has Marx remained so unknown as in his own country.

We ought not, therefore, to be surprised that the renaissance of Marxism remained within philosophical and sociological confines until the 1960s. This seems to be paradoxical, because Marx in his mature years considered his work, which is of universal character and multidisciplinary in a modern sense, essentially as economic in conception.

As far as the sociological and philosophical discussion is concerned, quite a number of summaries written by competent authors exist. A decade and a half ago, an essay written by J. P. Mayer (1954) exercised such a decisive influence on me that I undertook to attempt to supplement and deepen Mayer's survey by examining the economic aspects (Kühne, 1955). This led to the publication of four articles which examine various aspects of Marx's writings, ranging from the process of concentration to economic dynamics.

In 1970 these attempts resulted in a survey (Kühne, 1970) prepared as an introduction to Marx's *Ökonomische Schriften* (*Economic Writings*), published by Kröner (Stuttgart). That contribution, drawn from my work on the economic aspects of Marx, was no more than a sketch; the present work, of which the foundation was laid in the 1960s, represents, by contrast, a comprehensive attempt to bring to a conclusion a study of Marx which has stretched over thirty years.

Some of the most important representatives of neo-Marxist economics belong geographically to the outer fringe. I thank especially Professor Shigeto Tsuru (Tokyo), who was of help in obtaining the necessary documentation, including articles, and with whom I took counsel. The study must necessarily remain somewhat fragmentary; it can, nevertheless, be maintained that it is at least a fairly comprehensive survey of the relevant literature, even though certain contributions are examined in rather a concise manner.

Although an attempt has been made to cover as much ground as possible, this is far from being an exhaustive survey of Marxian theory in its total development since Marx set it down: Marxist literature as well as non-Marxist work will only be used to illustrate the various attempts at an overall interpretation of the work of Marx. Furthermore, I do not regard myself as competent to deal with the philosophical and sociological issues, other than by way of a brief introduction from the viewpoint of an economist.

I hope, nevertheless, that I have made a contribution to viewing the work of Marx in a new light. Hitherto, academic economists have generally indulged in the triumphant and somewhat condescending attitude of a matador, who believes he is delivering the final deadly thrust. This attitude is particularly conspicuous in Böhm-Bawerk's work *Zum Abschluss des Marxschen Systems*, published in 1896 (English edition: *Karl Marx and the Close of his System*, 1966), and has ever since been repeated by generations of 'conquerors of Marx'.

The present work may perhaps be of use in rehabilitating the work of a man who, outside his home country, is generally considered as one of the decisive founders of modern macroeconomics, and who – in his rather sporadic visions of the future – not only foreshadowed the rise of big business, but also its transition towards planned technology and auto-mation, and who dared to draw conclusions directed at the social transformation of the existing society.

I wish to thank all those who have assisted me with help or suggestions, especially Gerda Kühne who, besides assisting in the preparation of the rough text and typing the first volume, tracked down and inserted English versions of most of the quotations, thus lending a helping hand to the translator, who in only a few cases – mostly where quotation was from the early writings of Marx – had to supply his own version; Mr Robert Shaw, the translator, who undertook the task, in face of the almost insuperable difficulties interposed by terminology and language, of giving this English edition its present shape; and Mrs. Ranavalona Lise Iva, who typed the second volume and prepared the bibliography.

The quotations from *Das Kapital* in the German version of this work are from the 1953 (Dietz, Berlin) edition, which I have used for the last twenty years while working on the subject; those from *Theorien über den Mehrwert* are taken from the text in *Marx-Engels-Werke* (1961–8); those from the *Grundrisse* are from the 1953 edition; and those from other writings of Marx are from the *Karl Marx–Friedrich Engels Historisch-Kritische Geramtausgabe* (1927–35) (*MEGA*).

The English translations used in the present edition are: *Capital*, 3 vols (London: Lawrence and Wishart, 1974); *Theories of Surplus Value*, 3 vols (London: Lawrence and Wishart, 1969); *Grundrisse, Foundations of the*

Critique of Political Economy (Harmondsworth: Penguin, 1973); *Critique of the Gotha Programme* (Posthumous), *Marx–Engels, Selected Works* (London, 1968) II; *The Poverty of Philosophy* (*La Misère de la Philosophie*), ed. Charles H. Kerr (Chicago, 1920); *Wage Labour and Capital*, ed. Charles H. Kerr (Chicago, 1948); and 'Wages, Price and Profit', in *Marx–Engels, Selected Works* (London, 1968). (See also Bibliography in Vol. II).

As to the literature in other languages, the original publication has, wherever possible, been used. In most cases, I have relied on texts which are part of my own library.

In essence, this book is an attempt to give in a concise manner a comprehensive survey of, and informed commentary on, the opinions expressed by 'academic' economists and by the most important Marxist economists. Beyond that, I have tried to arrive at a modern interpretation, free of all traces of dogmatism, of the overall Marxist conception, so as to provide some suggestions for a new formulation of Marxian categories and theses while preserving the dialectic dynamics on which Marx and Engels strove to base their scientific work. For that reason polemics have been deliberately avoided.

Brussels,   KARL KÜHNE
10 August 1972 and
November 1977

Introduction: Marx and Economic Science

With only few exceptions there has been a tendency, especially in the German sphere, to characterise the position Marx holds in modern economics in a rather stereotyped and sterile manner. This is all the more regrettable as at the international level it is more and more recognised that Marx furnished important and basic elements for the interpretation of macroeconomic phenomena which, in the evident sense of the term, may be called dynamic.

In the field of sociology there are available numerous central works ensuring the continuation of the work of Marx. In this area especially, sociologists of German origin or who write in the German language have made considerable contributions. This is above all true of the 'Frankfurt School', consisting of men such as Horkheimer, Adorno and Habermas; it is also true of Marcuse. In the context of modern sociological discussion, however, not only have the economic achievements of Marx been pushed into the background, but in addition there is a general impression that they are of secondary importance. The underestimation of these components leads to a relative neglect of the achievements of Marx in the economic field.

At the same time one cannot deny that in political economy the analysis of Marx's theories has been exposed to the general danger of fossilisation and rigidity. On the occasion of the Twentieth Party Congress of the Communist Party of the Soviet Union, in spring 1956, Mikoyan complained about the lack of creative conceptions in modern Marxism.

In English-speaking as well as in Latin countries, 'academic' economics has in fact begun to rediscover Marx. For Marxist economists as well this could be a suitable occasion to re-examine their relationship with 'academic' economics. For a long time the two schools have coexisted without communicating. It is high time that this hermetic separation, which has done little good on the Marxist side in particular, was overcome.

In an era which is witnessing the beginnings of co-operation between East and West, it would be appropriate for at least a common terminological denominator to be sought for economic concepts. This is all the more important as there exists a noteworthy relationship between the two approaches, as emphasised by Oscar Lange (1934–5). The Polish doyen of Marxist economics has expressed the opinion that 'academic' economics can offer countries belonging to the socialist system much that Marxism itself cannot provide: 'It is obvious that Marshallian economics offers more for the current administration of the economic system of Soviet Russia than Marxian economics does' (ibid., p.191). According to Lange this applies especially to the field of industrial economics, but also to the related areas of microeconomic analysis, including allocative efficiency and investment analysis: ' "Bourgeois" economics is able to grasp the phenomena of the everyday life of a capitalist economy in a manner that is far superior to anything the Marxists can produce.' In the Soviet Union during the period of the 'take-off', for instance, too great a deference to economic rationale may have been disruptive: basic planning often tends to ignore pure economic calculus. This perhaps explains the fact that rigorous theory was pushed into the background during an epoch when physical quantity was granted priority over efficient economic allocation. With the attainment of a certain level, the trend has now gone the opposite way. In the Soviet Union industrial economics has seen new developments since Kantorovich and Liberman.

On the other hand, Lange thought that Marxist analysis was of the greatest importance for the prediction of the future development of 'capitalist' countries. It is true that capitalist countries have recently again become very conscious of their problems of stability, and, as Joan Robinson has said, the questions posed by Marx are of obvious importance for the whole range of macroeconomic problems.

THE RENAISSANCE OF MARXISM

Neisser coined (1931, p. 72) a bitter phrase: 'Any two Marxists will always slay a third.' In view of the retreat by orthodox Marxism since the 'mutiny' by the revisionists, the present work will rely, in its reappraisal, on the classic texts, without developing what might be called a catholic interpretation of Marx. After all, Marx himself once told Lafargue in a rather abrupt way, 'One thing is certain – I myself am no Marxist' (Rubel, 1968, p. 161). In so saying Marx pointed to the danger of fossilisation and to the necessity for constant further development of his concepts. This attitude can, indeed, be inferred from the dialectic character of his own method.

In this context the reader must be warned not to view Marx's writings as fixed in total concept from the very beginning. In a recent essay Kurucz (1970, p. 291) states with some justification, 'Since Marx argued in the "Paris Manuscript" in a different way from in *Capital*, those who took pains to interpret his work believed themselves to be right in asking what really were his thoughts and intentions. They do not realise that in doing so they develop a sort of personal cult.' The 'Paris Manuscript' was written in his youth, whereas *Capital* is the work of his later years.

The answer to the question of the value of Marx's work from his earliest writings onward is to be found in the mature Marx, which is essentially concerned with economic issues. We must not commit the error of supposing that, because his intellectual development began with philosophy and continued with history and sociology, before concluding with economic analysis, we can divide up Marx's works into exclusive compartments. No one showed more clearly than he the strong unity that exists between different disciplines. It is not without good reason that Bronfenbrenner has called him (1967, p. 62) 'the greatest social scientist of all times'.

If, in Part I of this volume, Marx is nevertheless considered first as a 'materialistic' philosopher, then as a humanist, a historian, a sociologist, a revolutionary, and finally an economist, it has to be stressed that the object is not to divide up the whole Marx, but rather to show that, at various stages of his life and thought, one or other of these aspects predominated, though they were all subordinate to his desire for revolution, and all contributed to the economic quest for the laws of capitalist motion, which were to provide the basis for revolution.

In its general conception the economic theory of Marx must be considered as essentially dynamic. Even those parts of his theory that appear primarily static have been examined with an eye on their dynamic consequences. This is true, for instance, of the whole analysis of surplus value. In older exegeses of Marx, 'absolute' surplus value, which goes with the rather static concept of distribution as well as with the labour-value theory, which is of special importance in Marxist literature, has often been granted a predominant position and the dynamic concept of 'relative' surplus value has been underrated. It must be said of Schumpeter that in his later work he took the latter concept as his point of departure.

The essential dynamic approach of Marx's theory is even more apparent in the case of his business-cycle analysis and growth analysis, both of which are based on the idea that capitalism is subject to continual revolutions from within. Here an attempt must be made to appreciate the towering importance of Marxism for the basic ideas of modern business-cycle analysis.

Today, there appear to be three different reasons why it is justified to speak of a 'renaissance of Marxism'. First, there is the fact that the general debate about Marx, by friend and foe, has become much more alive at the present time. Secondly, 'academic' economics has begun to incorporate certain ideas developed by Marx, especially in the field of growth theory. Thirdly, new, unorthodox developments within modern economics itself are beginning to advocate a 'higher stage' (in the Hegelian or 'post-Marxian' sense) Marxism – to quote a term introduced by the Indian Marxist Bose (1975) – which not only presents 'academic economics with serious competition, but even threatens at times to surpass it in vision.

Here is not the place for a thoroughgoing examination of these new tendencies, which the author has surveyed elsewhere (Kühne, 1970). It must, however, be emphasised that Marx is beginning to be freed from the short-sighted judgement which has prevailed even in the narrower circle of his own partisans. If 'academic' economics with its bias tried to stamp him as an economic historian or as a sociologist and to belittle him as an economist, there was likewise in Marxist circles a tendency to let his rôle as an economist recede into the background. This happened partly in veneration of the master, for certain Marxists thought economics to be a trivial discipline as compared to sociology. On the other hand, the sociological achievements of Marx were emphasised in spite of the fact that many of his apparent sociological categories were really economic ones. Added to this, the prophetic and eschatological vision of Marx has been given undue prominence, although the master, as Oscar Lange has stressed, has left next to no pronouncements about the future of state and society. In consequence, it has happened that what was most important to Marx himself – the analysis of the laws of capitalist change, i.e. of its economic dynamics – has received very little attention. It is from this point that a real 'renaissance of Marxism' must take its departure.

THE THEME

This work sets out to demonstrate three things. The first is that it was Marx who created the basis for modern macroeconomic theory. As has been pointed out by Kurihara (1959, pp. 17–18): 'This Marxian theory of capitalistic development anticipates many modern long-run theories, namely, the stagnation theories of Keynes and Hansen, the dynamic theories of Harrod and Domar, the "cyclical growth" theories of Schumpeter, Kalecki, Kaldor, and Goodwin, and Mrs. Joan Robinson's theory of structural underemployment.' Klein has supported this statement with the remark (1968, p. 54) that Marx's theory was 'probably the origin of macro-economics'. Boulding in his turn has stated (1946, p. 223) that Marx 'attempted a task of synthesis which previous economists had neglected; he tried to build up a picture of economic life and relationships as a whole, not merely as a collection of individual phenomena but as an organic unity'.

The second point to be demonstrated is that Marx was not simply a precursor of all these different theories, but laid the foundations for a continuous development of his own concepts. In the framework of Marxist analysis itself this continuous development has received only partial treatment. Bronfenbrenner has succinctly summarised the macro-economics of Marx as follows (1965, p. 206):

To whatever incomplete extent Marx's theoretical economic system is separable from the remainder of his social philosophy, it may be regarded as a system of moving equilibrium at less than full employment. In this respect it anticipates Keynes. It also goes beyond Keynes, in deriving an employment position which deteriorates over time. . . . This level will eventually become impossible to maintain. . . . This is the dilemma which drives the system to stagnation and eventual breakdown. . . . This dilemma is at once an economic 'contradiction of capitalism' and the 'law of motion' of the capitalist economy. . . .'

In short, it can be said that as a 'character reader' of capitalism (Leontief, 1938) Marx showed great prophetic insight into its *Götterdämmerung*. This view is attributable to Horowitz (1968, p. 17), who thinks that for this reason a profound abyss separates the Marxian from the 'orthodox' school. However, the principle of *Götterdämmerung* has been accepted by some authorities of 'orthodox' economics, such as Schumpeter, who, however, provides a different motivation. In the Marxian vision the primary rôle is played by economics, and it is on the degree to which economic trends are correctly interpreted that the realisation of the way that sociologists and philosophers wish things to be depends.

The third point to be demonstrated is that, despite his reticence on the future of socialist society, Marx in the *Grundrisse* did at least sketch the transformation of the social system as far as the era of automation. Here a reference to Tucker is appropriate, for he said (1963, p. 311) that, although Marx died more than three-quarters of a century ago, it seemed that an adequate judgement on his ideas would have to wait till some time in the future. That future, however, has already begun and has taken on a variety of aspects.

Despite the more or less permanent realisation of a new socio-political conception, attention is still focused on its weaknesses. Discussion of the rationality of a socialist system has now been going on for several decades. As to its outcome, we may perhaps follow Oscar Lange in stating that the problems of the new system lie less in economic rationality and possible difficulties in the 'allocation of resources' than in the danger of a general fossilisation brought about by the rise of bureaucracy as a new class.

A century ago this danger had already been acknowledged by the black banners of anarchism. Today, communist dissidents such as Djilas (1957), left-wing socialists such as Paillet (1971) and Guiducci (1971), and Maoist cultural revolutionaries try to counteract such a development by word and deed. Even liberal economists such as Halm admit (1968, p. 224) that modern oligopolistic capitalism cannot avoid the phenomenon. The idea of a 'managerial revolution', which was conceived by the Italian socialist Rizzi (1939) and usurped and popularised by the one-time Trotskyite and later US-chauvinist Burnham (1941), is a pointer in this direction. Marx, who foresaw the process of social transformation as such, must be succeeded by thinkers who see his conception as a sort of inheritance from the Age of Enlightenment and develop it. For therein lies the only hope refuting the bitter saying of Hegel that the owl of Minerva only begins to fly at dusk. In other words, it is not until *post festum* irrevocable damage has already been done and a new darkness has begun to crowd in that science feels that its hour has come.

Part I
The General Importance of Marx

1 The Philosophical Foundations and Dialectical Materialism

Marxian philosophy has its roots in Hegel in the teleological idea of human development, in which the 'spirit' manifests and realises itself. For Hegel, the instrument of such self-realisation consists in the phenomenology of this 'spirit', i.e. in the incessant continuation of intellectual history and in the further development of ideas. These ideas transpose themselves into real social and national life. Marx accepted the Hegelian idea of the teleology of history. His entire system is Hegelian in so far as it results in socialism and communism: History unfolds itself stage by stage in the progress of man to higher social systems.

Marx's philosophy took a decisive change of direction for two reasons. First of all, the driving force is no longer the 'spirit' but the real social structure, which makes use of technology and is itself dependent upon this technology. According to Engels, Marx turned Hegel upside-down: the substratum (the socio-technological infrastructure) determines the super-structure, while both advance according to the rules of Hegelian dialectics – i.e. by mutations, as they have been known in natural science since de Vries.

The conclusion which Marx draws from the Hegelian theory of evolution is this: the leaps of the 'world spirit' are the revolutions (literally rotations or transformations), which, however, emanate not from the intellectual sphere but from the substratum, in a development process which makes them a necessity for society. It is a case no longer merely of political revolution, but of an appointed class in a particular environment undertaking the general emancipation of society. (*Frühschriften* [Early Writings], p. 219.)

What need then is there for 'general emancipation' as opposed to a purely political emancipation? Moderate interpreters of Hegel are satisfied with the latter, since Hegel himself in his philosophy of history never went that far, and even left open the possibility that the *status quo* might be justified.

For this reason Hegel has even been regarded as the patriarch of a reactionary *status quo*, as if the 'world spirit' could find its final manifestation in the omniscience of Prussian and Russian autocracy, according to

the principle that 'what exists, can be justified'. In recent times Karl
Popper (1966, II, pp. 61, 177), with a shot of nineteenth century
materialism, has endeavoured to make Hegel responsible for the fascist
form of political reaction, while, on the other hand, accusing Marx of
Platonic idealism.

The basis and justification of Marx's revolutionary aspirations were not
simply the necessity for emancipation of intellectual man and the pressure
for spiritual freedom, but, by contrast, the ever-increasing bondage of man
in the material sphere, with his alienation culminating in the materialis-
ation of social relationships in capitalism: 'Man as worker, as commodity,
is the product of the whole movement' and, instead of realising himself in
congenial work, becomes (and this applies to the worker as well as to the
capitalist) spiritually and physically an object of capital, which leads to a
'dehumanised being, both spiritually and physically' (*Frühschriften*,
pp. 302–3).

Even in his early analysis of Hegel, whom he wants to turn upside-down
by turning a purely intellectual process into real historical development,
Marx adumbrates his later concepts, as when he says that 'what is
important in the phenomenology of Hegel' and its 'dialectic, the negativity
as the creative and moving principle', resides in the fact that 'Hegel
considers the self-realisation of man as a continuous process . . ., as
alienation and as neutralisation of this alienation', and that he sees 'labour
as the proved essence of human existence'. At this juncture Marx sees the
point of departure for the shaping of the history of mankind in man's self-
realisation through real work. For him the history of mankind is no longer
what it is for Hegel, for whom it is 'the history of the abstract spirit of
mankind'. (Ibid., pp. 269, 322.)

In the last stage of development of the social conditions of production in
capitalism, endogenous forces must develop that will turn capitalism
upside-down and awaken inherent contradictions, giving rise to a new
order. This new order will allow man to find his better self, after passing
through the purgatory of various forms of dehumanisation. Marx, in his
Grundrisse der Kritik der Politischen Ökonomie (Foundations of the Critique of
Political Economy – generally known simply as the '*Grundrisse*') envisages
such a possibility for liberation as lying in the development of productive
forces based on automation, which he sees as freeing labour from the depth
of drudgery and making possible to man the highest fulfilment of himself in
the sphere of free creative work.

This is the philosophical vision of Marx, and it is fundamentally
optimistic even if teleological. In order to verify his vision, Marx is obliged
thoroughly to examine economic conditions and their dynamic movements, which leads him into the realm of political economy.

Many authors have taken the rudimentary sketch in Marx's preamble to
his *Critique of Political Economy* as their starting point. One of the most
important is Labriola, who distinguishes sharply (1969, p. 57) between the

economic interpretation of history and the materialistic conception of it. The latter, he believes, embraces the 'organic conception of history', the 'totality and unity of social life', but qualifies the importance of the economic factor and allows for ideologies which harden into tradition and develop a certain life of their own, as has been stressed by Croce.

The theory of 'dialectical materialism' goes well beyond the historical framework, and it even embraces natural science. According to Carrit (1934, p. 134) its inherent principles are the following: There is a real perceptible physical world subject to permanent transformation and moving from contradiction to contradiction. Human institutions and social relationships are subject to the same changes; man's conscience is shaped by the material substratum. Into this conscience there also enters the idea of the need for redundant social forms to be replaced.

According to Bernal (1934, p. 112), 'dialectical materialism' in the sense of Marx is more than a concept for explaining the universe, for thought and action form an inseparable unity. This conception of 'dialectical materialism', however, is rather a product of Engels as he developed it in *Anti-Dühring*. Lichtheim was right in saying that 'Marx wisely left [human] nature alone.' According to Lichtheim, 'Engels ventured where Marx had feared to tread, and the outcome was dialectical materialism: an incubus which has not ceased to weigh heavily upon his followers.'

Lichtheim offers two further criticisms. First, it is not clear 'how in the absence of normative standards ("eternal truths") it is possible to qualify the long-term development as "progressive", Engels does not trouble to explain. . . .' Secondly, 'his evolutionary scheme is basically Darwinian. . . . His appeal to "inner, hidden laws" recalls Hegel's "Cunning of Reason" . . . . What is missing from this picture is just what constituted the originality of the young Marx: the "coincidence of the changing of circumstances and of human activity" whereby history is "brought to itself".' (Lichtheim, 1967, pp. 247–9.)

It is, therefore, upon the younger Marx that we must keep our sights, not to develop a contradiction between his humanistic and philosophical era and the Marx of maturity, but in order to understand the answers given by the latter to the questions of the former.

2 Marx as a Humanist: Reification and Alienation in Capitalism

Marx as a thinker travelled a long way: from the humanistic philosophy of Hegel, who conceptualised world history as the realisation of the 'world spirit', to a more profound analysis of the basic elements of the economic system. In so doing he took the way of 'historical materialism', in which he turned Hegel upside-down by stressing the real foundations of society as opposed to its idealistic reflection. The expression 'materialistic conception of history' was not coined by Marx himself and can easily be a source of error. Marx knew very well what weight to give to thought, ideas and 'conscience' and their capacity to induce change (Schütte, 1954, p. 34).

Deep down in Marx's essential thought we encounter a tragedy and a paradox. A thinker whose chief interest was to overcome the self-alienation of modern man became an analyst of the economic system, which rules our existence today in a way that it never had under any previous great civilisation (Toynbee's interpretation). For Marx this 'self-alienation' resides ultimately in the fact that human work, which originally had been the essence of and the means for the self-fulfilment of man, has been reified and materialised. It is imposed upon him as a soulless, 'external' relationship between him and production, overpowering social relations and symbolised by money.

Whereas Aristotle and antiquity, as also the British gentleman of the nineteenth century, had looked down on chrematistics as an obsession with money, classical economists held it to be a valuable science. Marx criticised this attitude. He considered this 'fetishism of commodities' a sin against the holy spirit, for the economists reduced economic ties to relationships between commodities, when properly speaking they are relationships between people.

This downgrading of people to commodities applies, however, to both sides of any relation, for the property-owning bourgeoisie and the proletariat represent for Marx the two sides of the coin of alienation (*Frühschriften*, p. 317). In a certain sense Marx here continues the work of Aristotle with his contempt for chrematistics. In this context a French sociologist, Cuvillier, has even asked (1956, p. 393) whether Marx is not in a certain sense advocating a kind of 'economic spiritualism'.

Marx was, indeed, inspired by the desire to overcome the domination of material things and to re-establish the whole man. In seeking to do so, he was searching for Hegel's 'cunning of Reason', which would provide the starting point in historical development for the renewed self-realisation of man on a higher plane. It is from this point that Marx the revolutionary historian and economist takes his departure.

To discover the 'laws of motion' within capitalism it is necessary to pierce the 'veil of money' inherent in the flow of capital in the cycle money–commodity–money and in the reinvestment of capital. This 'money obsession' has been made acceptable by capitalism, which has turned it into the dominating element of our times, but not without creating a new, paradoxical distortion. The obsession with money is not paramount only because money is the key to consumption. Yet the signs of our times are that consumption is being renounced in favour of building-up investment funds for growth purposes. 'Accumulate, accumulate! That is Moses and the Prophets!' This is the slogan coined by Marx to symbolise the victory, in modern civilisation, of the obsession with investment over the desire to consume.

A Russian economist, Tugan-Baranowsky, starting from a Marxist position, has apotheosised this very pursuit of investment in a scenario in which consumption as good as disappears in the face of an overwhelming propensity to invest, even in the construction of a new Tower of Babel. Hilferding, indeed, has dubbed this as ' "madness", but still Marxism – Marxism gone mad!' In a parable from the Age of Enlightenment, the king of England was the sole 'worker' in his country, and by turning a lever he could make the whole economic machinery of the country work. One could regard this as a fool's paradise of the future, but the disappearance of the work force, marking the apotheosis of automation, could be accompanied by the disappearance of consumption, and perhaps even by the suppression of man as a creative being; machines would have supplanted man. Marx, however, in the *Grundrisse* (pp. 582–594) saw automation as providing the possibility of a new conception of value and of the liberation of man from the slavery of work.

Marx saw capital as holding a dominating position in the society in which he lived. It resulted in a particular configuration of the relations of production and this in turn had a determining effect on the social structure. According to Marx (*Theories*, I, pp. 389–90) capital is '*materialised* labour, of the material conditions of labour – which, having assumed this independent form, are personified by the capitalist in relation to living labour', and the '*productivity* of capital consists . . . in the *compulsion to perform surplus labour*, labour beyond the immediate need; a compulsion which the capitalist mode of production shares with earlier modes of production, but which it exercises and carries into effect in a manner more favourable to production'.

Marx here puts the emphasis on the 'more favourable' way. Capitalism constitutes in this respect a social framework well adapted for rational production. According to Marx (*Theories*, III, pp. 467, 461, 456–7), 'Capital is not only the result of, but the precondition for, capitalist production', is 'self-expanding, self-maintaining and self-increasing value', and 'The characteristic movement of capital is the return of the money or commodity to its starting point – to the capitalist.'

Marx further defines capital as a power relationship, based upon 'past labour', that subjugates 'free' but propertyless workers. This conception is closely related to other, simpler ones, such as Blanc's ingenuous definition of capitalism (1850, p. 161) as 'the acquisition of capital by one group to the exclusion of others'. Modern writers on distribution who wish to overcome capitalism through the formation of property on behalf of workers ignore that this very lack of property is the basis of the capitalist structure and of its social discipline.

3 The Historian: The Rôle of Capitalism in History

Marx himself used the word 'capital' for whát we today understand as 'capitalism'. A number of leading economists, following up Marx, have further enlarged the notion of capitalism. Passow (1927) pointed out that the term 'capitalist' was first used towards the end to the eighteenth century, for instance by Krünitz (1776, p. 637) and by Mirabeau, although in both cases it was used to mean a rentier living on interest. Passow, in elaborating upon the Marxian definition, lists the economy with money and interest, economic calculation in money terms, and the predominance of capital and capitalists. In addition, he sees (fifty years before Galbraith!) the large corporation as the really decisive factor. Sombart (1922, p. 693) regards the division of the factors of production into different groups as the precondition for private enterprise and the market economy. Among liberal economists of the same period a moralising and deprecatory undertone prevailed. Stephinger, for instance, stressed (1918, p. 253) that capitalism was not just a matter of the possession of capital and of the profit motive, but also one of holding a position of unlimited power, which he calls 'mammonism'. Ehrenberg (1910, p. 34) connected the term with exploitation, while von Mises (1922, p. 110) emphasised the self-accusatory and critical elements in it. Pöhle (1910, p. 6) thought that it was a term not of perception but of censure, and Röpke (1943, p. 193) thought that this made it a term of doubtful usefulness so for as economics is concerned.

One of capitalism's apologists, Dunstan (1967, p. 158), has imputed to Marx the desire to see the beginning of the capitalist mode of production in the development of the trade in cloth in Mediterranean cities in the fourteenth and fifteenth centuries. Dobb would have remarked on that that Marx could also have mentioned in this context Flanders and the Rhineland. It is true that Marx argued that

> merchant's capital appears as the historical form of capital long before capital established its own domination over production. Its existence and development to a certain level are in themselves historical premises for the development of capitalist production (1) as premises for the concentration of money wealth, and (2) because the capitalist mode of

production presupposes production for trade, selling on a large scale, and not to the individual customer. . . .

He nevertheless adds, 'Yet its development is incapable by itself of promoting and explaining the transition from one mode of production to another.' According to Marx, the merchant's capital 'functions only as an agent of productive capital' in high capitalism. 'The special social conditions that take shape with the development of merchant's capital, are here no longer paramount. On the contrary, wherever merchant's capital still predominates we find backward conditions.' And he adds a note saying that, 'in modern English history, the commercial estate proper and the merchant towns are also politically reactionary and in league with the landed and moneyed interest against industrial capital'. (*Capital*, III, ch. 20, pp. 358–9.)

It is clear, then, that Marx's concept of capitalism is not based principally upon merchant capital. Dobb, indeed, simply denied (1946; 1967, p. 10) that we could talk of a period of 'merchant capitalism'. The thesis, therefore, that capitalism already existed several centuries before the Industrial Revolution cannot be conclusively traced to Marx, nor to his disciple Dobb; as Dobb emphasises, it must rather be ascribed to 'academic' economic historians such as Cunningham and Lipson.

Dobb himself has divided the definitions of capitalism (ibid., pp. 8–10) into three major categories. The first is that of Sombart, whose fundamental idea in his great work is that capitalism is not principally characterised by its 'economic anatomy or physiology' (Dobb), but rather by a certain spirit of rationality and economic calculus. Weber and his school, who identified capitalism with the Protestant or Calvinist ethic of 'élite' by reason of success, are in this akin to Sombart. To Weber, the American thinking on business has close affinities with Calvin's teaching on predestination. (Sombart, 1922, I, p. 25.)

The second category is that in which capitalism is identified, following the German 'historical school' of economics, as the 'organisation of production for distant markets', linked with a money economy and subject to the profit motive and the urge to invest (the 'animal spirits' of Keynes). As protagonists of this version, Dobb mentions Bücher, Hamilton (1929, p. 399), and Pirenne (1949, p. 163). Pirenne wanted to place the origins of capitalism in the nascent money economy of the twelfth century.

Dobb contrasts these two categories with his third, that of Marx, to whom capitalism is not simply the system of production (for instance, of merchandise) for the market, but is a régime in which the labour force has itself become a marketable commodity.

The historical conditions for such a development are the concentration of the means of production in the hands of a small minority and the development of the proletariat. According to Dobb, 'It is clear that . . . the definition of Capitalism in actual use in historiography has moved increasingly towards that which was first adopted and developed by Marx.'

In the meantime, Oppenheimer (1911, pp. 680–8) has tried to unite hatred and love, in that he has tried projecting the evil in capitalism back upon its predecessor, feudalism:

> the responsibility for all distortions of the social economy can be laid at the door of the 'political element' in its perverted form of large-scale land-ownership. Capital is only a derivative, secondary centre of power; it can operate to exploit and to produce surplus value only where through the presence of large estates in the same economic system there exist social monopoly conditions which throw more free workers onto the urban labour market than can be employed by existing capital. . . . Capitalism is a bastard arising from the unnatural union of two forces which are inimical to each other and whose struggle fills the world's history or is even synonymous with world history: on one side the ancient domination founded upon conquest, which created the feudal state and its first and most important institution, the denial of access to land through the creation of large estates; and on the other side the freedom to choose one's place of domicile, the original and most important of human rights, won after a long struggle. We understand now why capitalism is an abortion of filth and fire and possesses a strange 'double personality'. The worthy citizen coupled to the gruesome criminal. . . . all the curses which capitalism has inflicted on mankind are inherited from its mother, primeval violence, which has made man the object of a strange despotism, while all the blessings are inherited from its father, the spirit of freedom.

These words are not very far from the dithyramb that Marx and Engels sang, in the *Communist Manifesto*, in praise of the positive achievements of capitalism. Nor are they far from the savage atmosphere of 'original accumulation' in chapter 24 of Volume 1 of *Capital*. Nevertheless, it seems that Oppenheimer sees the 'worthy citizen' in too one-sided a manner and overlooks the new super-disciplinary element of coercion that big business, with its stopwatch, has introduced into the life of mankind.

The denial of access to land – Oppenheimer's 'foreclosure' – is no longer of any practical importance in Europe, given that peasants are leaving the countryside in ever-greater numbers. This exodus is being consciously encouraged, for instance, in the new Mansholt plan. To the extent that the problem does persist, however, it is in the immigration of foreign workers from quasi-feudal areas. Here we find an affinity to the ideas of Rosa Luxemburg, who emphasised the importance of pre-capitalist elements in reinforcing capitalism.

'Marx's bitter hatred of oppression' (Joan Robinson, 1949) has not impaired his scientific analysis in the least. In fact the adversary often has the sharpest eye for the advantages and weaknesses of the object of his hatred. De Man expressed this (1931, pp. 67–8) very convincingly:

> How is it possible, and what does it mean that the severest critic of capitalism, the most powerful prophet of its cataclysm, was at the same time its most gifted and path-breaking theoretician? . . . He understood capitalism in the same way as he hated it. Every act of comprehension is an act of passion, and there is, as we well know, a clairvoyance of hatred, which can compete with the clairvoyance of love. Only he can hate intensely who can also truly love, and whose hatred derives from injured love, as Marx's hatred derived from the injured love of mankind. . . . Wherever these three conditions – moral greatness, ingenious acumen and demoniac passion – are fulfilled, as was the case with Marx and some other gifted and exceptional men, the rare combination of opposition and comprehension can be realised. Nobody understood Israel better than Jeremiah. Nobody understood the Roman Empire better than St Augustine. Nobody understood the Middle Ages better than Luther. Nobody has understood capitalism better than Marx.

It has been said of Marxism that it is wrong, though common, to view it only as economic theory. Theimer (1950, p. 7) has argued that Marxism contains an 'entire system of humanistic and social sciences', and Barion (1959, p. 11) has emphasised that Marxism is 'not only a system of economics or of sociology or of politics, or a distinct conception of history (it is all of these things), but must, first of all, be considered as a philosophy, from the point of view of the classic German philosophy of the nineteenth century'. This means that Marxism has to be explained through Hegel; but is not this to neglect the economist in Marx?

According to Lenin (1947, p. 11), Marx and Engels saw 'the greatest achievement of this philosophy in Hegelian dialectics, as the most comprehensive, most fruitful and deepest theory of development'. It nevertheless remains true that the starting point of Marx was by no means world history in its abstract totality, but its concrete emanation at that time, in capitalism. For Marx, understanding capitalism meant, in the first instance, examining its economic structure; and Engels even spoke of Hegelianism as a 'colossal miscarriage'.

It is typical that some of his enemies wanted to dismiss Marx by declaring him purely an economic historian, as, for instance, Kerschagl did, in his rather unfair attack. It cannot be denied that Marx has an enormous achievement to his credit in economic history, but one may doubt whether this is in fact his strongest side. Croce at a very early date underlined the 'confusion' introduced by the rigid historical schemes of slavery, feudalism and capitalism in Marxist works. He pointed out (1900, p. 128) that a 'feudal Middle Age' can be said to have existed under both the Egyptian culture of old and the ancient Mediterranean culture of the Greeks.

An amusing modern controversy rages between Soviet and Chinese authors. The latter are embarrassed when asked to demonstrate the existence of a purely slave society before the undoubtedly feudal epoch of the Chou dynasty or the time of the unification of the Empire (221 BC). (See, for instance, Fan Wen-Lan, 1958, pp. 114–15, and Rubin, 1959, p. 3.) It is true that Marxist economists from Cunow to Mandel have always harboured the ambition to deal with economic history. To the extent that they have, they continue the work of the German historical school of economics, so that we might almost call 'historical materialism' an offshoot of this school. This, however, presents both a strength and a weakness.

On the rise and fall of civilisations Marxists could learn much from Ibn Khaldun (1382/1967), whose 'biological' theory of history was taken up first by Breysig and then ornamented by Spengler in an almost baroque style. Ibn Khaldun was not only a great historian but also an economist and discovered the labour theory of value (Mandel, 1962, II, p. 391). The work of Breysig (1918) is much more original than that of Spengler (1923). Breysig, like Ibn Khaldun (but without reference to the great Tunisian), formulated around the turn of the century, and about twenty years before Spengler, the idea of the 'general similarity in the pattern of the development of nations', but did not arrive at the almost biological theory of Ibn Khaldun, with its sequence of childhood, youth, maturity and old age in every civilisation. By comparison with this theory, the Marxist conception of history is optimistic, for it sees the condition of maturity as still in the future.

It is a further sign of Marxist vitality when economic historians of the quality of Mandel try to lead us away from a purely European interpretation of history, which, for instance, leads Marx's so-called 'Asiatic mode of production', which occurs in the original form of village community in the most diverse cultures, to be seen in a narrow, geographical context (Sofri, 1969, p. 175). Melotti has recently emphasised (1972, p. 77) that it should be seen not as something local but as a historical stage, as a system of 'village exploitation' or group slavery. Similarly, Marx in his *Poverty of Philosophy* (1847) criticised the classical British economists for holding an ahistorical and abstract conception of capitalist society. Modern Marxists such as Althusser (1968, pp. 150, 225) have maintained, however, that the historical element does not prevail in Marx, and by the same token they wish to diminish the influence of the humanistic element.

The revolutionary consistency and the will to intervene in the historical development of the economy constitute the particular contributions of Marx. Other authors, too, have explained history from the economic point of view: for instance, without any reliance upon Marx, the Englishman Rogers (1888) and the Frenchman d'Avenel (1920); and, taking account of Marx, the American Seligman (1903). None of these authors saw the teleological dialectics of history, which moves on through revolutions (i.e. in the proper sense of 'revolution': revolving motion).

For Marx, capitalism is a transition, a sort of purgatory cleansing society of the slags of feudalism. It kindles a fire under the gigantic cauldron of modern industrial production, thereby creating the conditions for a deployment of productive forces such as should bring about the socialist society of the future, about which Marx himself says hardly anything.

With this social transformation we arrive at a social structure, the antagonisms in which provide the lever for the dénouement. This lever is the class of martyrs chosen by history, namely the proletariat.

4 The Sociologist: The Problem of the Class Struggle

There are at least two (diametrically opposed) opinions about the rôle of Marx as a sociologist. There is first the view that Marx was principally a sociologist. This view was probably first proposed by Gurvitch (1948, p. 5), who especially regretted that British economists had had such a great influence on him. The same opinion was expressed by Marchal (1955, p. 211), who went so far as to regret that Marx had not remained a pure sociologist, as he had been during the first years of his intellectual life. Others, especially French sociologists, came to the conclusion that only the really bold conception of economic life as portrayed by Marx, namely the study of the whole man, was in keeping with the spirit of sociology; this was the opinion of Cuvillier (1956, p. 393). In general it can be said that Marx's economic theory required a sociological approach, and this has provided certain foundations for modern sociology.

Hegel developed sociological categories only in a sporadic manner: for instance, in his thoughts on the 'creation of the rabble' and the framework of the 'degradation of the large mass of people below a certain level of subsistence' (Conze, 1954, p. 9). This category corresponds in the Marxian theory to 'pauperism' or *Lumpenproletariat*.

The severest criticism of Marx as a sociologist has been levelled not by sociologists themselves, but rather by eminent economists, such as Schumpeter, acting *ultra vires*. After recognising the achievements of Marx in economic history, saying that he brought to bear on his task 'an extensive command over historical and contemporaneous fact', and despite his admission that 'hardly any historical work of his time that was of any general importance or scope escaped him', Schumpeter maliciously remarked (1947, p.10) that Marx had been too 'bookish' and had not read enough newspapers.

Some authors tend to stress Marx's early writings to explain the antagonism between 'two inimical classes of people' both of whom are self-alienated (Barion, 1954, p. 19). According to Marx, the 'realisation of the world of commodities leads in direct proportion to the depreciation of the world of man' (*MEGA*, III, p. 83). Here one must beware of any one-sided interpretation: If Marx emphasises this conflict, he does so in order to elaborate the dialectics of the two essential 'agents' (namely, the 'property-owning class' and the 'proletariat') in their pure form, and not to sketch sociological categories as such.

In Marx's early writings the philosophical component prevails over sociological analysis. On the other hand, it is true that here Marx already recognises the decisive antithesis which conditions the class struggle at the economic level (*MEGA*, III, p. 206). In this case the transition from the philosophical to the economic plane is defined without any deviation into purely sociological categories. It was certainly Marx's intention to represent this opposition between antagonistic classes as a consequence of history and as capable of being overcome; socialism was supposed to usher in the era of the classless society and the victory over alienation.

The social and historical vision of Marx, therefore, leads us to his prophecies for society. His sociological analysis encompasses a series of prophecies, which are scattered all over his works and are more implicitly than systematically formulated. The class struggle will intensify; the 'chosen' class, the proletariat, will become conscious of the dynamics of history; this class will play the rôle of midwife in the birth of a new society through revolution; the means of production will be socialised and the 'expropriators will be expropriated' to establish the classless society of the future.

In the meantime a 'new class' has come to power in the countries of the socialist bloc. The question is, to what extent does the proletariat live on in this new class? This class, as first Trotsky and Rakowsky, and in more recent times Rizzi and Djilas, have recognised, is the bureaucracy.

Mention should be made of the influence exercised by Marx upon Veblen in America. Veblen's 'concept of the relationship between knowledge and society reflects the influence of Marx'. This is the conclusion reached by Davis (1945, p. 143), who, however, warns us not to be drawn by this to overrate Veblen.

It is a matter of dispute whether the notion of class in Marx's work really represents a sociological category. It is fundamentally an economic definition, according to which a business executive who owns no shares in his company is considered just as much a member of the proletariat as is the last worker employed by the firm. The polarisation into three classes for which Zweig (1950, p. 39) reproaches Marx is nothing but an economic simplification. This very same critic had to admit that Marx derived it from the distribution theory of Ricardo and Adam Smith.

From a sociological point of view, the notion of 'class' depends not only on the economic situation of people but also on their consciousness. Halbwachs (1912) has even declared that it would be self-contradictory to assume that a class could exist without being 'conscious of its existence'. On the other hand, there have been objections to this argument on the grounds that such a clear 'consciousness of class' can result only from a ripening process: for instance, it was not until the July monarchy that the French working class reached such a state (Cuvillier, 1956, ii, p. 433).

The problem of class consciousness is so decisive because, as Marcuse has formulated it (1940, p. 47), Marx's ideas, according to which the liberation of the working class must be its own work, presuppose that such a class consciousness has already been developed into a common ideology: 'Socialism must become reality with the first act of the revolution because it must already be in the consciousness and action of those who carried the revolution.'

In modern sociology attempts have been made to interpret the concept of class: 'those who are not part of it themselves', writes Dahrendorf (1968, p. 111), 'like to doubt the fact that there is any working class left in Germany'. He then goes on to coin the term 'false middle class', which

> includes those nominal white-collar workers whose peculiar position and mentality is responsible for the fact that the term 'new middle class' has lost nearly all meaning. Basically, the false middle class consists of the workers of the tertiary industries, that is, those who occupy subordinate positions in the ever-growing service industries: the waiter and the salesgirl, the conductor and the postman, the chauffeur and the petrol-station attendant.

Marcuse and others have defended the thesis that, with the disappearance of the identifiably antagonistic figure of the capitalist, the working class has to a certain extent lost its catalyst. The objection has, however, been raised (for instance, by Vacca in his criticism of Marcuse – 1969, p. 257) that the class struggle was long ago translated to the level of political strife.

The distinction according to method of payment (monthly salary or weekly wage) is no longer decisive in determining membership of the proletariat in an economic context, for the distinction has vanished over wide stretches of the world.

Zweig was wrong in reproaching Marx for extreme polarisation. In fact Marx distinguished in the *Poverty of Philosophy* seven different classes: high and low aristocracy, industrial and other bourgeoisie, landowners, tenants and workers. In his 'Eighteenth Brumaire of Louis Bonaparte' (1852) Marx enumerates at least eight classes: aristocracy, bureaucracy, bourgeoisie, retailers (*épiciers*), working proletariat and sub-proletariat (*Lumpenproletariat*), peasants and part-peasants (*paysans parcellaires*). On the other hand, modern sociology distinguishes, at most, nine classes (Geiger, Moore and Kleining, and others; Warner and Lunt list six, Wright only five, and Sorokin not more than four – Dahrendorf, 1968, pp. 110–12). It can be concluded, therefore that Marx differentiated classes and their structure to a greater degree than many modern authors have done.

For the general public, Heilbroner (1955, pp. 135–6) in a biographical study has given a positive judgement on Marxian social economics: capitalism is characterised by an unending search for new technology. Technological progress leads to more and more imperfect forms of competition, which throw sand into the works of society. Giant firms dominate business life. All this is

> an extraordinary bit of foresight. . . . For all its shortcomings, . . . the Marxist model of how capitalism worked was extraordinarily prophetic. . . . In the end, Marx's 'pure capitalism' *collapsed*. . . . Let it be said at the outset that this prediction as well cannot be lightly brushed aside. In Russia and Eastern Europe capitalism has disappeared; in Scandinavia and Britain it has been partially abandoned; in Germany and Italy it drifted into fascism and emerged from its bath of fire in less than perfect health. Indeed, almost everywhere except in the United States capitalism is on the defensive. . . . Why did it break down? Partly because it developed the instability Marx said it would. A succession of business crises, compounded by a plague of wars, destroyed the faith of the lower and middle classes in the system. But that is not the entire answer. . . . European capitalism failed not so much for economic as for *social* reasons. And Marx predicted this too!

Heilbroner goes on to say that Marx did not consider the economic difficulties of the system to be insurmountable. It is true that there was not yet any anti-trust legislation or business-cycle policy, but one could imagine such measures. On the whole it can be said that the real remedy for the evils of capitalism rests with a 'government [that] would have to rise above the interests of one class alone'; capitalism threatens to founder because of the lack of social flexibility. 'The Marxist prediction of decay was founded on a conception of capitalism in which it was *socially* impossible for a government to set wrongs right.' However, Heilbroner ends up on a hopeful note: he thinks that political democracy can save capitalism.

> The laws of motion which his model of capitalism revealed may still be visible, but they are faced with a set of remedies, which spring from social attitudes quite beyond his imagination. . . . But shorn of its overtones of inevitable doom, the Marxist analysis cannot be disregarded. . . . For all its passion, it is a dispassionate appraisal.

According to Marcuse (1970), in the developed industrial society white-collar groups are not likely to develop an independent political consciousness and take independent action. It must be asked whether this situation has not changed recently. In many countries, group consciousness, trade-unionism and readiness to strike extend even to civil servants. The conception of the proletariat as developed by Marx on the economic plane seems here, after its long suppression by corporative ideas, to gain new vitality in the social struggle over distribution.

One must be careful not to fall into the very common error of assuming that the economic situation of the 'chosen' class is decisive in determining whether or not it will struggle against the ruling class. This has been confirmed by Aron (1964, p. 48):

> The ultimate reason for a definite polarisation into two camps is not of an economic character; one can envisage an improvement in the situation of the working class without upsetting in the least the basic idea of Marx, that in the end the conflict must be between two classes, and only two. We here arrive at the political concept of Marx: he thinks that every society is defined by domination exercised by one particular class.

At this juncture, the relationship between the class struggle and revolution needs to be defined.

5 The Revolutionary: Automatism or Voluntarism in Revolution

The absolute position in social or income terms of different classes is not the decisive factor in the question of how far any class will form an explosive mass for revolutionary purposes. This depends not only on the relative situation between classes, but also upon timing.

> Whenever the 'contestation' includes not only the 'sons of the bourgeoisie' but also highly-placed officials, civil servants and judges (as has been seen in Italy), it will be possible to gauge the degree of agitation of a class against higher classes as a function of its position on the social ladder, of its normal growth of income in relation to the growth of the social product, and finally as a function of the development of the social product itself and of its fluctuations. The working class, in so far as it gains self-awareness, tends to be revolutionary; it does not deserve to be called the proletariat if it is not revolutionary in character – for if it is not, it is not conscious of its own struggle, i.e. it has no consciousness of itself. And finally it is significant to summon the workers to revolt, because the development of history is such that the working-class will fundamentally transform the organisation of social life.

This interpretation by Aron (1964, p. 50) is certainly most spirited and would do justice to Marx at about the time of 1848. The mature Marx, however, must be seen as the proponent of a more 'down to earth' kind of revolution, containing fewer idealistic and more realistic elements.

The vulgarised, primitive interpretation of Marxism is based on the hypothesis of growing poverty consequent on the malfunctioning of capitalism – a malfunctioning viewed partly in the framework of the 'myth of collapse' and partly as the result of increasing unemployment of labour. The growing misery should drive the proletariat into revolution.

This exaggerated and crude version is not to be found in Marx. Counter-arguments lie ready to hand.

There never existed a 'theory of growing poverty' in Marx, but only a theory of the pauperisation of the dregs of the proletariat. A refined version of the Marxian theory of revolution starts from the idea of growing consciousness of exploitation. This version is put forward by Aron, who links it to the formula, 'The proletariat will be revolutionary, or it will cease to be' – a phrase coined by Sartre. Aron sees it as having three possible interpretations. First, the industrial working class (!) should be designated the 'proletariat' only if it is revolutionary. Aron rejects this interpretation, because the formula would be tautological. Second, as soon as the working class becomes conscious of its class position, it will automatically become revolutionary. Aron criticises this on the grounds that 'in Western countries there are numerous examples of working classes which have a certain consciousness of their unity and which do not wish to bring about a revolution. They wish reforms, which is normal. . . .' Third, the formula can be seen as invocatory, i.e. as a sort of moral appeal, a summons exhorting people to prove worthy of their historic vocation. Aron thinks that 'The strength of Marx as a prophet and the weakness of Marx as a sociologist lie in the fact that we can interpret this formula as well in one way as in another. Marx as a dialectician thinks that the three formulas are simultaneously true.' (Ibid., pp. 50ff.)

In modern society the threat of revolution seems to emanate from the specialised industrial worker, who possesses the necessary minimum both intellectual and materialistic; this has been the case, for instance, in Spain since 1965, but was not so there before 1955. A genuine revolution, as distinct from a putsch, is a luxury: society must be able to bear the interruption of production for more or less prolonged periods. Only rich countries can afford that.

On the other hand, even specialised workers and 'white-collar' workers can be defined as slaves within the context of the soulless modern giant enterprise, as has been argued by Perroux. According to him (1958, p. 600), slavery 'cannot be defined with reference to obedience or hard work, but only on the basis of status: man becomes a mere instrument to be depressed to the condition of an object'. It is significant that his formula found acceptance by Marcuse (1970, p. 41).

The coming revolution as seen by Marx was in no way an immutably bloody upheaval. It is significant that he thought it possible for the only country which had been fully developed by the middle of the nineteenth century, namely England, to be capable of a peaceful revolution towards socialism. Later, he added the Netherlands to the list.

At the meeting of the American Economic Association on the occasion of the centenary of the *Communist Manifesto* it was asked whether Marx would not perhaps be only too right, more than he would himself like, in his view that class struggles would persist, even in the society of the future. It was said that he believed, after all, that the dialectic principle, which was to bring about the socialist state, would remain effective at least in the non-economic realms of social relationships. The question was even raised of whether Marx really believed that it was possible to have a society without any conflict whatsoever (McConnell, 1949, p. 39).

One thing is clear: Marx underwent a protracted development from being in favour of revolution at any price to seeking analytically to etablish the preconditions for it and advocating it only if these were fulfilled. He saw the revolution to some extent as the executioner of a downtrodden and bankrupt capitalism. Basso (1969, pp. 37, 107–8, 125) has described this evolutionary process in Marx in a most detailed way. He pointed out that the break with the 'classic' revolutionary tradition, as represented by Blanqui, was not formally completed until 1869, when Marx removed from his 'Eighteenth Brumaire' the phrase 'revolutionary communists', which in the first edition of 1852 was supposed to honour the 'Blanquists'. In fact, however, the change of which this gave notice took place much earlier.

In his funeral oration at Marx's burial in Highgate on 17 March 1883, Engels declared that the scientific economist was not even one-half of Marx, who was primarily a pure revolutionary. As early as his stay in Paris (1843–4), the transition from democratic radicalism to revolutionary communism was complete, as a result 'not of the fruit of scientific analysis, but, rather, of moral indignation clothed in philosophical speech' (Basso, 1969, p. 39).

It is true that Marx divested himself of the 'abstract idealistic form of Hegelian dialectics' (Basso) as early as 1859, in his Preface to the *Critique of Political Economy*, but he nevertheless adhered to the precepts of the French Revolution and its successors for some time. Marat, the 'Society of Equals', Roux, Babeuf and Buonarroti, and finally Blanqui, as the leader of the Jacobin tradition of revolutionary force, stood as symbols of the idea of a 'conspiratorial' élite. This alliance with the Blanquists remained intact until shattered in the revolution of 1848–9.

In the meantime, Engels in his *Condition of the Working-Class in England* (written in 1844–5), had completed the transition to conceiving revolutions primarily as economic phenomena. At almost the same time, in his letter to Annenkov on 28 December 1846, Marx formulated his ideas about the connexion between the forces of production and the conditions of production. He was bound, in this way, to break through to a deterministic concept of revolution, as evident in *The German Ideology*; according to this new concept, communism is identical with a real transformation in things, and the revolutionary can reach his goal only in so far as he follows the laws of development. In this way, revolution is transformed into science. (Basso, 1969, pp. 54–5.)

In general the statement by F. C. Mills (1949, p. 14) that 'Marx the scholar was driven by the purest instinct of workmanship' remains valid. This judgement recalls a statement to similar effect by Schumpeter (1947, p. 10). It is just this pure scientific instinct that induced Marx to formulate a transcendental notion of 'class' going beyond the word's original, teleological meaning. If this concept was originally the outcome of the search for the dynamic factors in capitalist society, its inbuilt centrifugal forces or its gravediggers, it has certainly undergone change in the clash between economics and sociology in Marx's writing. In this context Onofri says (1967, p. 29), 'The initial sociological approach of Marx (which primarily saw the conflict or the struggle between classes) moved gradually in contradiction into the economic field, with the aim of finding the objective basic foundations for the existence of class, before conflict has arisen or before classes exist in a sociological sense.' In this way, the preponderance of the economic concept over sociological analysis becomes evident. The focus of the social transformation process lies in economic dynamics and not in the sociological sphere of consciousness. Revolution occurs *malgré les révolutionnaries*.

Certain Italian Marxists such as Gramsci, however, protested against such an interpretation. According to Althusser (1968, 1, pp. 151–2) Gramsci has

> led a revolution against *Capital* and has brutally stressed that the anti-capitalist revolution of 1917 had to fly in the face of Marx's *Capital*, arising as it did from the spontaneous and conscious action of men, of the masses and of the Bolsheviks, and not on account of a book from which the Second International could read, as from a Bible, of the predestined arrival of socialism.

It cannot be denied that Gramsci was in some measure the predecessor of the young 'voluntarist' revolutionaries of the 1960s and 1970s when he wrote (1957, pp. 149–58), 'No, mechanical forces are never victorious in history: it is men, consciousness, spirit. . . .'

There can be no doubt that social democrats at the turn of the century were in danger of seeing revolution only in terms of automatic forces. 'When conditions are so fully ripe that there merely needs to be removed the chance constraint and everything runs smoothly, as Marx and Engels believed at the end of the nineteenth century, when they hourly awaited the great collapse, then understandably no force would be required.'

This is the way Bloch (1970, pp. 9–10) criticised the later interpretation of the revolutionary idea of these two great socialist writers. Bloch even thought that the eighteenth-century Utopian Novel of Mercier may have played a rôle in this deterministic set-up: Mercier, with reference to a letter written by Leibniz in 1702, tried to develop a social-revolutionary prognosis on the basis of the 'Law of Mariotte', which held that gas under pressure would finally burst a container. By contrast, Bloch recommended a state of voluntary preparedness for Utopia, a voluntary asking after the way to a better future, to the rainbow Münzer had seen.

There can be no doubt that in general Marx passionately believed in revolution, although it is not always quite clear whether he saw in it only the necessary instrument to overcome the remnants of feudalism – for instance, when he recommended in Germany a 'new version of the

Peasant's War' – or whether he considered it the instrument for the
realisation of socialism as a transitional stage on the way to communism.
Nevertheless, the question must be asked whether Marx was ever
'voluntarist' in the way that Bloch was. Dennert has pointed out (1969,
p. 24) that Marx

> was clear, at the very latest at the time of writing the *Communist
> Manifesto*, that revolution cannot be a single act. . . . Here is . . . the
> notion of a period of transition, which is also found elsewhere, although
> it is defined as a limited period of time. During this period history is truly
> a free act of man, while before it had been a deterministic process.

We find several varieties of the argument in Marx (letter to Kugelmann on
12 April 1871, speech in Amsterdam on 8 September 1872, interview with
the *Chicago Tribune* on 5 January 1879), and Engels took up the theme in his
Preface to the 1886 English edition of *Capital*. He states there (1953, p. 28),

> Surely, at such a moment, the voice ought to be heard of a man whose
> whole theory is the result of a life-long study of the economic history and
> condition of England, and whom that study led to the conclusion that, at
> least in Europe, England is the only country where the inevitable social
> revolution might be effected entirely by peaceful and legal means. He
> certainly never forgot to add that he hardly expected the English ruling
> classes to submit, without a 'pro-slavery rebellion', to this peaceful and
> legal revolution.

Logically this must hold for all countries that today find themselves in the
state England had then attained; this would mean almost all of Europe and
North America, as well as a great number of semi-industrialised countries
with a standard corresponding to that of England in those days.

In 1917 Lenin tried to diminish the impact of this argument by pointing
out (xxi, p. 447, of the German edition of his works) that even England had
become 'bureaucratised and militarised' – thus contradicting Karl
Kautsky's interpretation. The general principle here is one about which
there is still great controversy between socialists and communists, though
some communists of Western Europe now seem to be getting near to
applying to their countries the later views of Marx and Engels on the
matter.

6 The Economist: The Verification of Vision

There is, then, not just one Marx: He appears in many forms – as philosopher, sociologist, historian, revolutionary, prophet and economist (Schumpeter, 1947, p. 10). All of these, however, are united in that 'moralistic and rationalistic thinker, who is completely and coherently a humanist' (C. W. Mills, 1962, p. 2). There can be no doubt that it is difficult, if not impossible, to split up this Marx, many-faceted as he is. The facet of the economist may, perhaps, seem the dullest, but is the one that, towards the end of his life, shone most brightly, a fact of which Marx himself was conscious.

The delimitation of what Marx himself regarded as the proper economic element in his work is rather difficult. There has often been attributed to him a conception which is total, a *Weltanschauung* comprising the totality of social processes, as Dobias has written (1970, p. 301):

> For Marx all social fields were interdependent, so that 'political economy' was to him still a unified, undifferentiated social science. . . .
> If sociological and political relationships were endogenous elements for Marx, they are today data for us, but this is certainly consistent with our requirement of formal theoretical elegance – even if it is at the expense of material relevance. . . .

Against this, it should be stressed that Marx, despite all his achievements, still maintained an obvious predilection for the 'formal elegance' of Ricardian economics, which he considered to be the outstanding example of political economy, as opposed to the 'eclectic salad with historical sauce' of one such as Roscher.

As in the case of his teacher Ricardo, it was the intellectual honesty of Marx that made him an economist: it was a matter of definitively testing the possibilities of realising his revolutionary aspirations in real life. Economics was, logically, the last stage of his mission: it was a matter of checking the pulse of capitalism, in which he had already discovered the germs of disease. It is, at any rate, true that we should remember, as Gordon has stated (1967, p. 639), that 'overwhelmingly the largest part of his intellectual work was in economics, not other social sciences'.

Marx himself saw his aim as the study of the capitalist mode of production and its conditions of production and exchange, i.e. of the natural laws of capitalist production; he wanted to understand 'these tendencies working with iron necessity towards inevitable results' (*Capital*, 1, p. 19) in the analysis of the 'contradictions inherent in the movement of capitalist society'. He wanted to find the 'law of their variation', 'the special laws that regulate the origin, existence, development, death of a given social organism and its replacement by another and higher one' ('Afterword to Second German, Edition', *Capital*, 1, pp. 17—18).

The general connexion between the historical and specifically economic analysis of Marx within the framework of 'historical materalism' has been described by the Japanese historian Tsuru with concise clarity. He asserts (1967, p. 322) that

> Marx's contention was that, under capitalism, as productive forces make progress they are bound to have their social character enhanced. This comes into conflict more and more with the *private* character of ownership of the means of production, and according to Marx this conflict will finally be resolved through 'bursting asunder of the capitalist integument'.

The failure of 'academic' economics to analyse economic development went so far that de Man, within the framework of a series of lectures given for the German Association for the Advancement of Political Science in 1930, could in the midst of the Great Depression pay the compliment (1931, pp. 65–6) that Karl Marx, 'if he were still alive, would with a part-satisfied and part-bitter laugh take notice of the fact that the Association had made capital and capitalism the subject of a study course in 1930'. He observed that even in 1905 it did not 'advance one's career' in German universities to employ such terms ('The smell of sulphur still lingered over the place'), that it was not until after the First World War that the term 'capitalism' appeared in the German manual of political sciences, that it made its first appearance in *Encyclopaedia Britannica* in 1926, and that in 1930 it had still not reached the British *Dictionary of Political Economy*!

The attitude has changed in recent times in connexion with the rise of the literature on growth and development, which, paradoxically, received some of its main stimuli not from the analysis of the development of highly industrialised capitalist countries, but from the study of pre-capitalist conditions in modern developing countries. Indeed, Rostow (1952), the author of the notion of 'take-off' (the threshold between underdevelopment and industrialisation) considered it expedient to present his ideas in the form of an 'Anti-Manifesto' to the *Communist Manifesto* by Marx and Engels and to their analysis of development.

The rediscovery of the economist Marx by unorthodox Marxists is still awaited. Here the field has largely been left to those whom Varga describes as 'dogmatists'. It would be possible, in terms of Hegelian dialectic, to conceive of the 'classic' theory of Marxism and of its opponent, revisionism, as 'thesis' and 'antithesis'. Indeed, according to its own logic, even Marxism must undergo a dialectical process, and it must, therefore, end up in a 'synthesis'. But such a synthesis can be found only in a 'broad-minded' or 'enlightened' Marxism which spans the seemingly unbridgeable gap between Marxism and 'orthodox' economics and integrates Marxism with those advances in economic thought that were seen at the outset by its creators.

It is a matter of controversy whether and how far the partial nationalisation of investment (direct or indirect) in the context of modern fiscal policy or as a result of a Keynesian policy of compensation already constitutes 'socialism'. It can hardly be denied that the era of purely private capitalism is over; the reasons for such a development are partly to be found within capitalism itself and its oligopolistic structure, and partly outside, through the independence which the state sector has acquired relative to the rest of society.

There remains, however, one important question: what are the limits to this process of nationalisation, which is inherent within our society? The answer to this question depends on the solution to another problem. How far will the nationalised sector be able to prevent excessive economic fluctuations, which are inherent in the system as long as a large private investment sector continues to exist? State intervention, as the answer to the tendency towards monopoly, is repeatedly mentioned by Marx himself (see, for instance, *Capital*, III, ch. 27, p. 438).

The management of modern capitalism depends on how successfully the state can walk the tightrope between the dangers of investment cycles, which are becoming more rather than less explosive, as the result of the ubiquitous oligopoly structure, and the progressive ossification of rigid schemes of control based on the modern state of knowledge, which might impede progress. A thoroughgoing transformation of capitalism will be essential. Marx has sketched the outlines of such an alteration.

Part II
Marx's Position in Economics

7 Classical Harmony of Interests and the Economic Process in Marx's Vision

Though it is true that economics soon became the monopoly of professors, the share of the self-made man was, from the very beginning, a large one. Besides, some of the most important impulses for the new science originated from authors who were not representatives of the university world (this was not only true of the classics, but remains valid right up to modern times). Marx (an editor, journalist and writer) and Engels (a factory-owner) were typical outsiders, and both were strongly imbued with the metaphysical philosophy of Hegel. All the more important, then, is Schumpeter's judgement (1947, p. 10) that 'Nowhere did [Marx] betray positive science to metaphysics.' He turned not only Hegelianism but also Philosophy on its head and effected the transition to economic reasoning.

The fate of outsiders is never very enviable in the history of economic doctrines, which generally is written by professors . If outsiders are not totally rejected, their theories are frequently represented by clichés, which only in very few cases derive from original material and which mostly represent a rehearsal of the arguments of opponents – not always those whose intellectual strength and integrity are the most incisive. Marx has not been spared this fate.

ACADEMIC ORTHODOXY AND THE HARMONY OF INTERESTS

Academic doctrine initially attacked Marx violently, then haughtily attempted to ignore him, only to rediscover him in recent times and to liberate him from his followers' maze of views, which on their side had produced a counter-orthodoxy of many varieties and containing many colourful facets of heresy. No one has better sketched the contrasts and the similarities between Marx and the orthodox economists than has Joan Robinson (1949, pp. 1–2). The 'harmony of interests' theory, as developed by orthodox economic thought, stands in sharp contrast to the idea of class struggle.

Orthodox economists started from the hypothesis of a 'polypolistic' multiplicity of producers; 'they were apt to project the economics of a community of small equal proprietors into the analysis of advanced capitalism' (ibid.). By contrast, Marx's theory of concentration, and, less remarked, his thoughts in the *Poverty of Philosophy* on 'competitive monopoly' provided a powerful stimulus for analysis of our modern oligopolistic structure.

In the theory of wages, orthodox economics harboured the idyllic illusion of the existence of the 'marginal disutility' of an additional hour of work, a concept 'which has its origin in the picture of a peasant farmer leaning on his hoe in the evening and deciding whether the extra product of another hour's work will repay the extra backache' (Robinson, loc. cit.). Marx, by contrast, saw the proletariat in the real labour market as chained to machinery.

For orthodox economists, capitalism was the best of imaginable systems, even if subconsciously they felt inclined to offer apologies. For Marx it was not so much a question of 'good or bad': for him, capitalism had to complete its historical task. In the course of one century it had built up tremendous productive forces, more than in all previous generations. Capitalism, nevertheless, is nothing more than a transitional stage on the way to a better world. While orthodox economists preach 'only the gloomy doctrine that all is for the best in the best of all *possible* worlds', Marx, 'at the same time, is more encouraging than they, for he releases hope as well as terror from Pandora's box' (ibid., p. 5).

THE DISTURBANCE CONCEPT IN CONTRAST TO THE IDEA OF EQUILIBRIUM

Marx's fundamental idea is that the contradictions which express themselves in the business cycle, will rend the capitalist system asunder and lead to a 'superior' system, in the Hegelian sense.

In the meantime, Marx's general dynamic analysis has acquired its own importance for economic science within the framework of those themes which are relevant to his general work: the question of the laws of capitalist motion leads to the further question of the laws of economic change in general, always bearing in mind that any economic form that is assumed is historically determined. In this sense the methodology of Marxian analysis is not bound to any time period. His questions have even influenced his adversaries, the representatives of 'academic' or 'orthodox' economics.

As Myrdal has emphasised, these adversaries suffer an intense conflict, the conflict between the conservative 'postulate of liberty', which seems to find its economic underpinning in the theory of perfect competition, as a modern version of the 'harmony of interests', and 'the revolutionary theory of real value', which Marx inherited from the fathers of economic liberalism, Adam Smith and Ricardo. Myrdal says (1963, p. 75), 'Marx exposed this conflict by pursuing the premise to its logical conclusion. He thus touched a sore point of economic theory, and it is probably for this reason that he caused so much irritation among economists.' We shall quote some examples of this irritation, for they explain why it was on the subject of value theory that the dispute started.

The general picture has its source in the analysis of 'classical' economics, but it is – especially in view of the fact that the original impulse was provided by Hegel's philosophy – dialectically opposed to the doctrine of harmony *à la* Smith, for it is a theory of the historical and (in a humanistic sense) fruitful consequences of disharmony, as a step towards a higher harmony.

One Neo-Keynesian authority, Joan Robinson, declares (1949, p. 95),

> Marx was mainly concerned with long-run dynamic analysis, and this field is still largely untilled. Orthodox academic analysis, bound up with the concept of equilibrium, makes little contribution to it, and the modern theory has not yet gone much beyond the confines of the short period. . . . Marx, however imperfectly he worked out the details, set himself the task of discovering the law of motion of capitalism, and if there is any hope of progress in economics at all, it must be in using academic methods to solve the problems posed by Marx.

In another passage (ibid., p. 5), Joan Robinson says that 'the movement of modern academic teaching' [goes] 'away from orthodoxy in the direction of Marx'.

VISION AND PREDICTION

The founder of input–output analysis, Leontief (for many years Adviser to US President Franklin D. Roosevelt), formulated (1938; 1968, p. 98) what might be called an apotheosis of Marx's general conception: 'The significance of Marx for modern economic theory is that of an inexhaustible source of direct observation. Much of the present-day theorizing is purely derivative, second-hand theorizing. . . .'

In a similar vein, F. C. Mills declared (1949) at the meeting of the American Economic Association organised in honour of the centenary of the *Communist Manifesto*,

> However, that somber figure, Marx, is no more to be ignored by the student of economic life and thought than by the student of social change. . . . The boldness of his conceptions impressed a new dimension on economics – the dimension of time. The concept of sequence, of process, of cumulative change which stems from Marx is basic in

economic thought today. He was an empiricist in the details of his work,
if not in the application of his findings. He gave a place to evidence in
economic analysis that was granted by few among his contemporaries.

Leontief, and in a certain sense Mills as well, have laid the main stress on
the vision and on the dynamic element in the theory of Marx, namely on
his analysis of economic growth.

Was Marx really a 'prophet' – at least in his economic work? It is
possible to distinguish at least three prophetic functions in Marx's works:
short-run and long-run economic prophecy, and the vision of a socialist–
communist society of the future.

Marx has not been very lucky in his short-run economic predictions.
There is the famous example of the crisis of 1857–8, which he certainly
overrated in its effects. It was nevertheless just this event which guided
Marx as an economist: he felt that his economic ideas were far from being
mature, and this drove him to the gigantic efforts which led to the
manuscript of the *Grundrisse*, the first volume of *Capital*, and the *Theories of
Surplus Value*. The second series of 'prophesies' concerns the general long-
run vision of Marx as an economist:

> The record is really impressive: increasing concentration of wealth,
> rapid elimination of small and medium-sized enterprise, incessant
> technological progress accompanied by the ever-growing importance of
> fixed capital, and, last but not least, the undiminishing amplitude of
> recurrent business cycles – an unsurpassed series of prognostications
> fulfilled, against which modern economic theory with all its refinements
> has little to show.

That is the judgement of Leontief (1938; 1968, p. 94).

THE PRACTICAL APPROACH AND THE DANGER OF OSSIFICATION

The visionary but fleeting glimpse into the future of capitalism and beyond
does not apply to economics alone. There is the problem of the practical
applicability of the theory to the new economic structure, and especially to
such economic systems as are based on the principles professed by Marx.
Here a paradox is encountered.

F. C. Mills, though declaring that Marx was one of the great economists,
pointed out certain weaknesses in his system: it does not permit of an
expansion of its conceptions, and it is too much of a closed intellectual
system, with a 'frightening imperviousness', built in by the founder
himself, 'to the usual methods of scientific review and modification' (1949,
p. 14). As a result of this, the theory became dogma and was used for

propaganda, so losing a vital part of its scientific value and becoming an incomplete, distorted instrument.

But it is precisely this theory that is violently contested in 'academic' circles. To quote Leontief (1938; 1968, p. 98)

> If before attempting any explanation one wants to learn what profits and wages and capitalist enterprises actually are, he can obtain in the three volumes of *Capital* more realistic and relevant information than he could possibly hope to find in ten successive issues of the United States Census, a dozen textbooks on contemporary economic institutions, and even, may I dare to say, the collected essays of Thorstein Veblen.

Finally, Marx's vision of future society is only briefly indicated, in a few passages in *Capital* and in the *Critique of the Gotha Programme*.

8 The General Judgement of 'Academic' Economists on the Work of Marx

Within the framework of 'academic' economics, two basic attitudes can be distinguished. The first consists in 'reproaching Marx with some mistakes, which in retrospect are easy enough to find, so that he can be disposed of as quickly as possible' (Güsten, 1960, p. 61). The second, by contrast, treats the Marxian system as deserving of serious discussion. Even within this framework, however, there has crept in a tendency to follow the work of others, and many authors who believe they are analysing the theories of Marx do not themselves resort to the original texts but rely on certain standardised formulations produced by others. These formulations, even if they still resemble the basic Marxian thesis, are at least strongly simplified.

Scarcely any other economic theorist has had his works subjected to such furious analysis and such crass misrepresentation as has Marx. The reactions range from the sharpest rejection to the most exaggerated enthusiasm, and this applies on the economic as well as on the political level. One of the first to reject Marx's theory was the Frenchman Leroy-Beaulieu, about whom it can at least be said that he broke (in 1884) the silence that he and his colleagues had previously maintained on the subject. An example of overenthusiasm is the Italian economist Loria, who tended to plagiarise Marx. Engels, in the introduction to the third volume of *Capital*, took up arms against the flattery of this author.

An examination of the critiques of Marx that reject his theories outright demonstrates that very often the motive for rejection is not the economic content of those theories, but, rather, their sociological and political implications. Marx's economic contribution has, naturally, been appreciated only by those who have kept largely outside the 'academic' framework and have known how to penetrate to the kernel of Marx's economic theorems.

It is true that a prophet has very little honour in his own country: in the case of Marx, the verdict on him by 'academic' economics in the German-speaking world makes this very clear. As a typical example, the following comment by the Austrian anti-Marxist Kerschagl (1960, p. 189) may be cited. It exemplifies very well the 'irritation' of which Myrdal writes.

A man who addresses his scientific adversaries as 'vulgar economists', as 'fools', as 'paid scribblers' and as 'bought pseudo-scientists' could not be considered by anyone of his time as a proper person with whom to start a scientific discussion. This explains why, if *Capital* was not simply ignored, most economists of his time refused to see Marx as a possible partner for scientific discussion. It is very characteristic that the first serious critic of him, namely Böhm-Bawerk, appeared only many years after his death. Debates on him during his time, if they occurred at all, largely exhausted themselves in abusive language.

At any rate, it was no mark of glory for the professional economists of the nineteenth and early twentieth century to try to ignore Marx (and even the much more conciliatory Engels). After all, the name and ideas of this man were to outlive by far those of his competitors. Laudable exceptions to the general rule are Schäffle (1874) and von Bortkiewicz (1971). The latter's articles on Marx are still of great importance today; the former's have recently been appreciated by Thiemeyer (1970).

The attempt to ignore Marx was not made by really great economists. For instance, Schumpeter, Leontief and Marchal expressed great admiration for Marx's achievements, as they deserved.

'Academic' economists can be divided into four groups, according to their attitude to Marx. First there are those economists who discuss Marx's work in order to refute him and to expose his 'mistakes'. The most important figures here are Böhm-Bawerk, Leroy-Beaulieu, Pareto (1898), and the Russian Simkhovitch, who wrote in the United States; but even Aftalion (1923) and Veblen (1906), as well as Pohle (1919), Muhs (1927) and Wicksteed (1950) belong in this category.

The second group consists of those who took to heart Joan Robinson's comment (1960, p. 2) that 'To learn from the economists regarded as scientists it is necessary to separate what is valid in their description of the system from the propaganda that they make, overtly or unconsciously, each for his own ideology.' This group, while rejecting Marx's principal tenets, particularly in the sociological and political sphere, endeavour to use many stimulating suggestions derived from the arrangement and structure of his ideas. We may call them the sober critics and count among them Piettre, Burchardt, Croce's school in Italy, Henry Smith, Wilson, Güsten, Klatt and Gruber.

The third group goes further, for its members adopt the basic questions raised by Marx, and, therefore, a large part of his ideas, without becoming Marxists in the proper sense. Among them are Leontief, Klein and Kurihara in the United States, and Jean Marchal, Lecaillon and Fourastié in France.

Finally, there is a fourth group, which derives from Marx but has developed in other directions and become 'estranged'. Croce, in particular, followed this pattern of development, but some (around the turn of the century, Lexis, von Bortkiewicz and Oppenheimer; and, in recent times in Germany, Dobias, Gerfin and others) have gone through such a development and remained quite close to Marx. We may also count in this group Joan Robinson and Bronfenbrenner, Bartoli and other Catholics (such as the Jesuits Bigo and Calvez in France), and sometime-Marxist authors such as Tsuru in Japan and Meek in Great Britain.

In this context it must be noted that Marxian ideas have had certain repercussions in conservative circles. The great conservative von Hayek has had the courage to admit that he has been influenced by Marx *via* Tugan-Baranowsky and Spiethoff. Finally, it can be said with justice of Schumpeter that he was a disciple of Marx, although one who accepted the conclusions of the master without being prepared to accept the methods by which Marx reached them.

Among the conservatives there are a great number of outright opponents of Marx whose criticism of him is unworthy of investigation in detail, for the simple reason that it sets out from the premise that Marx is absolutely unacceptable. As examples of this literature may be cited the large work by the former Belgian Minister van Overbergh (1949), who wrote in French; a work by the Frenchman Dognin (1970); and the collection of quotations with commentary by the German Pentzlin (1969), who cannot help wondering at the 'renaissance of Marx'. This whole literature – mostly of a low scientific standard – reflects a tendency which is widespread even among the professional economists of the first of the four groups detailed above, a tendency that Myrdal (1963, p. 75) has encapsulated in the words, 'They often tried not so much to prove him wrong, which would not have been too difficult [here one must ask Myrdal why, then, the process of "refutation" has been going on for a century] as to show that he was an utter fool, a bungler, misguided by those despised German philosophers. They felt it impertinent of him to dare tamper with classical theory.'

What, in fact, is the general judgement on Marx by the authorities of modern economics?

There is certainly no lack of negative judgement on Marx among leading economists. The most famous such judgement is that of Keynes, who, in his article 'A Short View of Russia', written in 1925, characterised *Capital* as 'an obsolete economic textbook which I know to be not only scientifically erroneous, but without interest or application for the modern world'. Yet at the same time Keynes curiously declared that he 'sympathises with those who seek for something good in Soviet Russia' (Keynes, 1933, p. 300).

It is well known that Keynes also ignored or passed unfair judgements on other authors, such as Johannsen, who in reality were his predecessors or forerunners. At any rate, twelve years later he took Marx seriously enough to quote him at the very beginning of the *General Theory* (1936) as the author of the phrase 'classical economists', against whom he at that time fulminated. Also in the *General Theory* (eighth edition, 1949, p. 355), he extolled a really obscure book, that of the 'free money' advocate Gesell, from whom he thought the future would learn more than from Marx, whose real importance he never appreciated.

A similar antipathy is evident in many statements by Samuelson (1967, pp. 617, 621–3):

> Marx did, in his posthumous Volume ii, innovate two-sector models of reproduction and growth. . . . Marx's model of expanded reproduction is perhaps the first example of those golden-paths of compound interest . . . [but] the labor theory of value breaks down even before complications of capital enter into the model. . . . [It is claimed that] its inferior statics can be forgiven considering its much superior dynamics . . . .

And Samuelson adds that 'Marxism was the Opium of the Marxists.'

These statements by Samuelson, made in 1967 at the meeting of the American Economic Association, were, however, somewhat friendlier than was his Presidential Address before the Association in 1961. In this he spoke of Marx 'as a minor post-Ricardian . . . a not uninteresting precursor of Leontief's input–output analysis of circular interdependence'. At the same time he stated (1966, p. 1510) that political economy as we see it today is 'the mere cap of Karl Marx's iceberg. Marx's bold economic or materialistic theory of history, his political theories of the class struggle, his transmutations of Hegelian philosophy have an importance for the historian of "ideas" that far transcends his façade of economics.'

The general trend of opinion on Marx among leading economists in recent times has overwhelmingly been to emphasise the value of the dynamic elements of his theory.

A large number of 'academic' economists who have examined the Marxian system have certainly done so with preconceived opinions, and, among earlier generations of economists, those who display a sympathetic judgement are not very numerous. It is curious, though, that almost every generation of economists since Böhm-Bawerk has felt it necessary to refute Marx. Bartoli has pertinently written (1950, pp. 12–13),

> As long as liberal science was taught as dogma in our faculties there was hardly room for Marxism. It was pushed into the background, and no attempt was made to find the grain of truth which is intrinsic in every error. Marxism was rejected, annihilated, done to death, but nevertheless remained sturdy and more alive than ever. . . . Only recent progress in the theories of full-employment, of market firms, of industrial organisation, of economic welfare, and of economic maturity, and the analyses and attempted explanations of capitalist development have led

many contemporary authors to discover the Marxian analysis of capitalism, which is of a power that is without equal.

French economists, however, were not the worst offenders. Leroy-Beaulieu (1884), despite his negative attitude, did deal fairly with Marx shortly after his death, and Bourguin (1904) and Aucuy (1908), who dealt with Marx in a more descriptive manner, were also quite fair. Furthermore, in one of the most important French-language histories of economic doctrines, that by Gide and Rist (1921), it was recognised, despite the rather negative attitude of Rist, that Marx's prediction in his theory of concentration was fully borne out.

Another leading French economist, Marchal (1955, pp. 200–1), while stressing his non-Marxist position, classed the famous criticism by Böhm-Bawerk as a 'misunderstanding':

> as a macroeconomic conception . . . Marx's approach seems to be superior to the microeconomic approach of the neo-classicals, especially with regard to the problem of distribution. . . . Marx was quite right when he advanced the thesis that the economist has to examine the living relations or, if he prefers it the other way round, to rely on the study of social behaviour. . . . Marx's method is original and fertile.

Marchal, jointly with Lecaillon, has provided, in a monumental three-volume work (1958) devoted to the topic, an exhaustive evaluation of the Marxist theory of distribution.

In Germany, one of the leading authorities on distribution, Preiser, has declared (1964, p. 14), 'We retrace our steps to the classical economists themselves, to Marx . . . and we do not wish to be led astray by the ominous term "theory of class monopoly" nor by the fact that the accent lies on supply, to the neglect of demand.' Similarly, Schneider (1958, 1, p. 134) returns to Marx on the question of the importance of circular-flow analysis for the modern economy: 'The second important stage in the development of schemes of macroeconomic circular-flow analysis is represented in Marx's work on the reproduction and circulation of the total social capital.'

The modern theory of economic development is more or less based upon circular-flow analysis. In this context Schumpeter has stated (1959, p. 574),

> Marx's performance is still the most powerful of all. In his general schema of thought, development was not what it was with all other economists of that period, an appendix to economic statics, but the central theme. And he concentrated his analytic powers on the task of showing how the economic process, changing itself by virtue of its own

inherent logic, incessantly changes the social framework – the whole of society, in fact.

Modern development theorists also recognise the primacy of Marx. For instance, Higgins writes (1959, pp. 107–9),

> Marx's theory of development was the core of his system . . . no book on economic development with any pretensions to generality can ignore the Marxist theory. . . . Marx never underestimated the capacity of the capitalist system for economic expansion. . . . He saw more clearly than his predecessors – and most of his contemporaries – that there is a two-way relationship between investment and technological progress. . . .

Almost all the authors who specialise in development theory deal extensively with Marx. This is true of Lewis (1960, pp. 18, 21, 88, 100, 288, 297, 337), one of the leading authorities in this field, and it applies also to later writings on this subject (for instance, Brenner, 1966). The inventor of the notion of 'take-off', Rostow, even felt obliged to call his main work (1952) an 'Anti-Communist Manifesto', because he considered it to be in the nature of a reply to Marx's early publication. In practice, Ott's comment, in his great work on dynamics (1963), that Marx was 'one of the most important predecessors of modern growth theory' is simply a restatement of what is widely accepted as fact.

Marx's achievement, however, went beyond this, as Schumpeter states in his 'testamentary' principal work (1947, pp. 10, 21, 43), where he devotes no fewer than four introductory chapters to Marx:

> Nowhere did he betray positive science to metaphysics [see above, ch. 7]. . . . [He had] an extensive command over historical and contemporaneous facts. . . . The whole of Max Weber's facts and arguments fits perfectly into Marx's system. . . . As an economic theorist Marx was first of all a very learned man. . . . nothing in Marx's economics can be accounted for by any want of scholarship or training in the technique of theoretical analysis. . . . a theory that in nature and intent was truly scientific. . . . though Marx was often – sometimes hopelessly – wrong, his critics were far from being always right. . . . [He made] contributions, both critical and positive, to a great many individual problems . . . [as, for instance,] his treatment of the business cycle [and the] theory of the structure of physical capital. . . . For there is one truly great achievement to be set against Marx's theoretical misdemeanours . . . the idea . . . of the economic process as it goes on, under its own steam, in historic time, producing at every instant that state which will of itself determine the next one. . . . [He] was also the first to visualise what even at the present time is still the economic theory

of the future. . . . And he not only conceived that idea, but he tried to carry it out.

This explains why one of the authors who has continued the work of Keynes, namely Joan Robinson, finally devoted a whole book (1942/49) to the subject, a book which is certainly one of the most important publications on Marx, if not a *magnum opus*.

9 Strengths and Weaknesses of Marxist Literature

The basic weakness of Marxist literature lies in a slavish adherence to the terminology of the master. The effect of this has been in many cases not only to bar the way to fruitful discussion but also often to prevent the recognition of where the master had effectively acquired a superior position and where he had long anticipated essential elements of academic economics.

Bauer warned against imitating Marx's 'imaginative language' too closely. Even Hilferding fell a victim to the temptation to imitate the master, and he has quite rightly been rebuked for this by Preobrazhensky. Bauer (1909–10, p. 392) has drawn attention to the fact that there is a tendency in modern economics to develop presentations in such a way that colourful images are renounced in favour of abstract concepts:

> Marxism must not shun this tendency . . . less because Marx's imagery, strongly influenced by the images of Hegel, has misled many authors into interpreting Marxism in the sense of idealistic metaphysics, as because this method of presentation is not in general use in economics today and the use of it therefore forms an impediment to the victorious advance of the Marxian system.

Bauer has been much criticised for this statement, especially by Rosdolsky (1968, II, pp. 673–4), who thought (on not very firm grounds) that Bauer wanted completely to do away with Marxian dialectics.

It is important, if the 'Marxian renaissance' is to take permanent root among younger economists, in particular, for the ideas of Marx to be presented in the scientific language of our times. At the same time, it should not be forgotten that a large part of the world uses Marxian terminology in its original form. Something has therefore to be done to overcome the Babel of confusion between East and West, if a fruitful dialogue is to take place. Compromises are possible in this respect, and this is proved by the fact that certain terms, such as 'capitalism', 'creation of value' and 'value added', have become common to both sides.

The need for a dialogue between East and West has been perceived by no less an authority than Oscar Lange, the doyen of the Polish Marxists, if not of Eastern economists in general. He has written (1934–5, p. 191) that

Marxism neglects large areas not only in microeconomics but also in macroeconomic theory:

> But this superiority of Marxian economics is only a partial one. There are some problems before which Marxian economics is quite powerless, while 'bourgeois economics' solves them easily. What can Marxian economics say about monopoly prices? What has it to say on the fundamental problems of monetary and credit theory? What apparatus has it to offer for analysing the incidence of a tax, or the effect of a certain technical innovation on wages? And (irony of Fate!) what can Marxian economics contribute to the problem of the optimum distribution of productive resources in a socialist economy?

He goes so far as to declare (p. 191), 'It is obvious that Marshallian economics offers more for the current administration of the economic system of Soviet Russia than Marxian economics does, though the latter is surely the more effective basis for anticipating the future of capitalism.'

It may be that in the end each of the two systems will, paradoxically, prove of advantage to its competitor.

Lange's judgement appears to be somewhat one-sided. Even in the field of microeconomics quite a number of elements can be quoted in favour of Marx: he made some important contributions to the development of microeconomic categories such as entrepreneur's salary, interest, risk premium and the definition of depreciation. Marx's analysis of competitive processes has affinities to the modern theories of imperfect competition and oligopoly, and it is not for nothing that it ends up with the thesis of increasing concentration. After all, Marxism in our time has given rise to a new school of industrial economics, as represented by the Russians Kantorovich, Liberman and Trapeznikov.

In the area of national accounting, we owe to Marx such concepts as value added and the clear distinction between net and gross national product.

There can be no doubt that his macroeconomic contributions are decisive. The principal features of Marxian analysis are the identity between, on the one side, investment, and, on the other, capitalist consumption plus the share of profits in the social product; and the identification of the form of capitalist growth as the interplay in the cycle between the spontaneous propensity to invest and the tendency to hoard. The danger of lack of proportionality between large sectors of the economy is noted, and variations in the rate of profit, in the short run in the cycle and in the long run in the tendency towards stagnation, are emphasised.

We also find in Marx one of the first formulations of the growth process. This formulation, which is still stimulating, includes all 'data' and contains elements of fundamental instability – in anticipation of Harrod. Following the Second World War and up till the early 1970s we were living through a great international capitalist boom, which was interrupted only by weak recessions or in some countries merely by fluctuations in the growth rate. In the wake of this boom there was a tendency to neglect the forebodings of the Marxian vision. The Marxist ghost, which appeared menacingly on the horizon in the 1930s, seemed to have been dispelled by the quantitative and qualitative extension of state activity, Keynesian analysis and policy, and the neoclassical thesis of the stabilising function of the capital coefficient. It remains to be seen what impact the recent slowdown in growth and especially the 1974/5 recession will have on contemporary economics; very probably it will lead to a renaissance of business-cycle theory and perhaps of the 'breakdown controversy'.

It is strange that in recent years Marxist analysts have made very few specialist contributions to the discussion of these problems. Most of what there has been has been Hungarian in origin, as witness the pioneering work which Varga has tenaciously been carrying out over several decades, and the contributions by Molnár and Erdös. Of authors of other nationalities, mention should be made of the Russian Konyus (whose name seems to be Hungarian) and the Pole Kalecki.

Looking at the subject in detail, Oscar Lange (1934–5, p. 190) sees the superiority of the Marxist conception in the discovery of the tendency towards an ever-increasing scale of production, the tendency towards concentration and the accompanying oligopoly capitalism, the tendency towards protectionism on the one hand and the encroachment into the non-capitalist world on the other, and, finally, the tendency towards an increase in the instability of the total system. All these processes have been played down by a 'petty-bourgeois' attitude within 'academic' economics, 'until the monopolistic (or oligopolistic) character of the basic industries became so obvious that a special theory of limited competition had to be developed to supplement orthodox economic theory'.

On the eve of the great world crisis of 1929, Lange stressed, academic economists were still clinging to the idea that cyclical fluctuations were bound to decrease in amplitude. He could have quoted the classic example of Sombart, who expressed such an optimistic hope in his principal work in 1927*b* (III/2, p. 587). He also could have referred to certain statements by Marxists such as Hilferding (1947, p. 403) on the hoped-for effects of cartelisation. The general optimism of the 1950s seemed to have been contagious even for Marxists such as Mandel (1962, II, p. 189), and Schmidt (1967). In the meantime, however, the business cycle has returned: it was felt in 1957–8 and in 1966–7, but much more severely in 1974–5. Recent analysis showed that leading authorities on the business cycle are not at all convinced that it is obsolete; the question of whether it is had already been answered in the negative, well in advance of the 1975 cataclysm, in a collection of essays edited by Bronfenbrenner (1969).

Assertion of the superiority of Marxist theory, especially in macroeconomic growth analysis, no longer passes as unconditionally valid. A certain retreat can be witnessed from the original Marxist analysis, which only recently has begun to experience a gradual revival.

In general, the flood of publications by Marxist authors has yielded very unequal results, even if we do not confine ourselves to macroeconomics. Schumpeter has remarked (1947, p. 45) that, out of any three Marxist authors, at best only one would be a professional economist, and even he would pay only lip-service before the altar before passing on and using quite different methods. Schumpeter was certainly not wrong in pointing out the high percentage of non-economists or self-made men in Marxist literature. However, a large number of Marxist publications deal purely or predominantly with philosophical, anthropological, philological or sociological problems.

If we limit our investigation to economics, the share of economists is considerably higher. It should, though, be clear from what has been said above that, for each Marxist economist, there are certainly several economists who have been influenced by Marx and who at least partially apply his categories, either unconsciously or without being ready to admit to such a thing. There may be legions of such voluntary or involuntary 'crypto-Marxists'. Engels was not far wrong when, on the appearance of the third volume of *Capital*, he saw such a person in Lexis. We must not forget, however, that certain heretics such as Hobson, who was no Marxist but a predecessor of Keynes, and important enough to inspire Lenin in his theory of imperialism, adopted Marx's ideas without referring to him directly. Hobson lost his post as a lecturer because he did not want to recognise 'Say's Law'. Even in the 1920s, as de Man relates (in Harms, 1931, 1, p. 65), unorthodox thinking was dangerous for academic lecturers.

We must not, therefore, be astonished that the share of non-professional economists in the ranks of Marxists remains relatively large. Neither should we make the mistake of limiting the term 'economist' to university lecturers.

10 Statics and Dynamics in 'Academic' Economics and in Marxism

Samuelson has stated that Marx had 'inferior statics' but 'vastly superior dynamics'. Such a statement requires a clear delimitation of both notions in Marx's work. But what really are 'statics' and 'dynamics'? This is the first question we have to answer.

Harrod begins his *Towards a Dynamic Economics* (1948) by considering (pp. 10 ff.) the precise definition of the two terms. He first underlines that both terms tend to be applied rather vaguely. Statics, for instance, is interpreted as a description of short-term phenomena; it is supposed to denote a state of rest. But we must not confound statics in economics with statics in physics, for in the latter case nothing happens at all. Statics in economics, on the contrary, presupposes that certain values – for instance, quantities and prices of factors of production – may be taken as given. According to Harrod, the static state is in a proper sense an active process, but one that does not undergo any changes.

This condition is synonymous with 'simple reproduction' in Marxian literature. The introductory chapter of the first volume of *Capital* can be considered as being devoted to the static condition: the prices of factors of production and goods remain unaltered, although they are expressed in 'values' of labour hours of equal efficiency.

Schumpeter has described Marxian dynamics in its all-pervading splendour. First, Marx understood the essence of capitalism to be an evolutionary process. Secondly, and this is the actual superdynamics of the Marxian system, Marx 'subjects those historical events and social institutions themselves to the explanatory process of economic analysis or . . . treats them as variables'. Further, for Marx, 'economic process . . . under its own steam [produces] at every instant that state which will of itself determine the next one . . . [until] capitalist evolution destroys the foundations of capitalist society'. (Schumpeter, 1947, pp. 47, 42–3.)

In sum, Marx's development theory within the framework of his 'mega-dynamic methodology' is to be seen as a combination of philosophical, sociological, historical and economic elements, which constitute the

53

essence of the total complex of Marxian ideas. Is it possible, though, despite this 'mega-dynamics', which combines general evolution and the methodology of macroeconomic change in a 'dynamic analysis' in the higher sense, to distinguish in a strictly economic sense between static and dynamic methodology in Marx's work?

In this context, we had best follow the definitions given by Harrod (1948, p.18). He stresses that it is not change as such which represents the essence of dynamics in the economic sense. In order to delimit statics according to Harrod, we must analyse conditions of equilibrium. For instance, a once-for-all change in the position of equilibrium – for example, in prices and quantities, or even in profits – is part of statics. Harrod even considers once-for-all changes in expectations to be part of statics, basing himself on Hicks, who proceeds in a similar way and only aims, as an ultimate objective, at the delimitation of the table equilibrium. Hicks himself calls statics simply 'those parts of economic theory where we do not trouble about dating' . . . (but only about) 'factors' (or) 'quantities of products' . . . (1939; 1950, p. 115)

In this sense Marxian surplus value analysis would typically be part of 'static analysis'. This would be in accordance with Piettre, who considers the notion of exploitation to be part of 'static' analysis, and its inner contradictions, which destroy the system of exploitation, to constitute the dynamics in Marx's work (1962, p. 37).

Harrod (1948, p.19) refuses to accept the definitions of Hicks. To him the essence of statics is not the reduction to a single point in time, but the permanence of equilibrium. As soon as one gets to continual and lasting change one reaches dynamic theory. To Harrod, dynamics is a question of knowing 'what the steady lines of advance would be . . .' Harrod, therefore, classifies essential macroeconomic concepts, for instance, the theory of profits, of employment (of Keynesian inspiration) and of foreign trade as part of statics. According to Harrod, saving and accumulation are emphatically not part of statics.

For him, the political economy of the classics, with its intersection of saving, accumulation, demographic factors and growth processes, is the real nucleus of 'old dynamic theory', which, since Marx, has fallen into oblivion. The nucleus of this 'old' dynamic theory was effectively 'the theory of motive power, and the theory of progressive redistribution'. Keynes did not deal with either of these two problems, and therefore Harrod (1948, pp. 27–9) holds that 'the idea that Keynes is more dynamic than Ricardo is the exact opposite of the truth'.

In so far as Marx goes to the bottom of the 'motive power' in his analysis of the class struggle, and of the 'theory of distribution' in his analysis of surplus value and profits, he continues 'classical' dynamics. But he does more than that: he also thoroughly investigates the 'propensity to accumulate', which 'may be identified with what we regard as saving, and is rightly treated by Richardo as a dynamic concept. He is not guilty of the error which has crept into text-books up to the present day of bringing saving into a static system of equations.'

Because Marx makes surplus value, or saving and accumulation by capitalists, the focus of his analysis, he is fully in accord with Harrod. This, then, is the explanation for the fact that both authors reach a fundamental concept of instability that calls into question the existence of the capitalist order in principle.

Marx's theory of wages (especially in its historical and sociological content), his extension of the analysis of profit (particularly the thesis of the tendency of the profit rate to fall), his business-cycle analysis and the theory of expanded reproduction, with which he equates the growth processes and in which the savings function appears, are essentially dynamic. Here we truly reach the dynamic stage of Marxism. An attempt has been made in the present work to treat the notions of static and dynamic economics apart from each other. It is clear that a watertight separation cannot be achieved, for the boundary will always be somewhat blurred.

Part III
Value and Surplus Value

11 Value and Surplus Value Theory in the Presentation of 'Academic' Economics

There can be presented here only a short general survey of what the 'academic' school and its authors have drawn from Marxian value theory. There are left aside the many distortions, which in most cases arise from a great reluctance to read the original texts and from a tendency for one author to copy another. We shall therefore examine only the texts of serious critics of Marx, letting them speak, wherever possible, in their own words. We shall begin by trying to provide a picture of Marx as he is seen by the 'academic' economists, and then carry out an examination of the proper content and sense of Marxian analysis, taking into account Marxist interpretations.

Let us begin with the first great 'academic' critic of Marx, namely Böhm-Bawerk, who in particular dealt (1931, I, pp. 367–71) – with the problem of value and with microeconomic aspects (in the following extracts references are to *Capital*, vols I and III, in the German edition of 1872 and 1894, respectively).

Marx takes as his point of departure the principle that the value of all commodities is controlled exclusively by the amount of labour that their production costs. . . . It is a sort of conceptual distillate of exchange value. . . . From these statements we can deduce the content of the great 'law of value' which is 'inherent in the exchange of commodities' (I 141, 150) and which controls exchange conditions . . . that commodities are exchanged on the basis of the average amount of socially necessary labour which they embody (e.g. I, 52). The same law is expressed in other terms, such as the statement that commodities are exchanged at their values (I, 142, 183; III, 167) or that one equivalent is exchanged for another (I, 150, 183). Of course, under the influence of transient fluctuations in supply and demand prices appear that are higher or lower than those values. But, these 'constant oscillations of market prices are self-compensatory, they cancel each other out, and finally resolve themselves into the average price which is the essential rule' (I, 151). In the fortuitous and constantly fluctuating conditions of exchange however, it will in the long run always be true that 'the socially necessary labour time will find enforcement as the controlling natural law' (1, 52). . . . The deviations themselves [are] 'violations of the law of exchange of commodities'.

Böhm-Bawerk then presents a sketch of the Marxian theory of surplus value:

> Marx finds the solution to this problem "(of the origin of surplus value)" in the fact that there is one commodity the use value of which possesses the peculiar faculty of being the source of exchange value. That commodity is the capacity for labour, or labour power. . . . By trading in this commodity the capitalist acquires his surplus value. . . . The value of the commodity 'labour power' is regulated, as is that of any other commodity, by the labour time necessary to reproduce it. . . . If he had him work only just so many hours a day as are embodied in the labour power itself, and just so many as he had been compelled to pay for when he made the purchase, then no surplus value would arise. . . . The work day of the worker thus comprises two distinguishable parts. In the first part, that of the 'necessary labour time', the worker produces his own sustenance, or the value thereof, and for that part of his work he receives an equivalent in wages. During the second part, the 'surplus work time', he is 'exploited'; he produces the 'surplus' without receiving any equivalent of any kind of it (1, 205 ff.). . . . 'The secret of capital's ability to create values out of itself resolves itself into its control over a certain amount of unpaid work performed by others' (1, 554).

Pareto's criticism (1926), which appeared shortly after, was less profound, although it was based upon the same microeconomic analysis. Pareto limits himself to attacking Marx's predictions, criticising his theory of value, the idea of 'transformation of prices', and so on, and thinks that Marx in most cases 'only translated the theories of British political economy into his own phraseology'. He concludes that Marx's ideas 'are not much more false than those of many other economists' (!), and thinks that, in spite of its obscurity and ambiguity, the labour theory of value, in particular, is only a sort of symbol, a 'showing of the flag' for the socialist movement.

Many critics have tried to go back to the very roots and have denied that labour is a 'commodity'. In modern times, for instance, Kruse has declared (1953, p. 117) that 'Here Marx committed a grave mistake. Because the only common quality of commodities is supposed to consist in the fact that they are all the product of labour, labour power itself cannot be a commodity, as it is not the product of labour'. In our time, services are gaining in importance; but in services the creation of the 'commodity' and its consumption coincide. This argument of Kruse does not, therefore, appear to be absolutely sound, for, whenever services are provided, the services of the labour power and its maintenance are directly paid for. Both, therefore, directly become a 'commodity'.

Similar objections have, nevertheless, been raised by Marxist authors. Mondolfo for instance, denied (1917, p. 420) that one can recognise in labour power the character of a commodity as soon as one acknowledges that surplus value itself results from unpaid labour. Labour power, moreover, has the property of being able to reproduce itself and to produce a surplus at the same time, a quality which is not shared by any other commodity.

One question that has not been resolved in the debate is as follows. The commodity produced by the worker has a price on the market. Surplus value, it may be said in anticipation, finds its expression as part of this price, in money. The question is, why is the surplus value not eliminated by competition? This question has been asked again and again, especially in English-language works. Whittaker, for instance, in one of the leading American books on the history of doctrine, wrote (1947, p. 429), 'except that [Marx] referred to a tendency toward monopoly, he gave no convincing explanation of why it did not happen that competition caused the surplus value to disappear'.

It is curious that this question was first asked, in all clarity, by a moderate Marxist, Lederer. He put it thus (1922, pp. 158–9); 'Why or when does the entrepreneur not compete for the worker up to the point where he produces "without any profit"?' Lederer partially answers his own question by referring to elements of imperfect competition, which have the consequence that 'competition . . . cannot completely compete away profits'.

Following Lederer, this simple basic criticism has been repeated by 'academic' economists – for instance, by Gestrich (1924, p. 95) in the twenties – and, after the Second World War, the same question was asked by Schumpeter (1947, p. 28):

> Moreover, it can be shown that a perfectly competitive equilibrium cannot exist in a situation in which all capitalist employers make exploitation gains. For in this case they would individually try to expand production, and the mass effect of this would unavoidably tend to increase wage rates and to reduce gains of that kind to zero.

Schumpeter also took up Lederer's answer, urging that it might be possible to appeal to the theory of imperfect competition, frictions and institutional obstacles; but Marx would have despised such special pleading.

This seems doubtful, however, for the Marxian theory of 'temporary monopoly' enjoyed by innovation-loving capitalists comes really very near the theory of imperfect competition. Schumpeter himself admitted, 'surplus values may be impossible in perfect equilibrium but can be ever present because that equilibrium is never allowed to establish itself.'

Further, in his great *History of Economic Analysis* (1959) he wrote (p. 1051), 'Marx's process, as he did not fail to notice, must in strict logic lead to monopolies or oligopolies of those firms that have once gained an initial advantage.'

In conclusion, note should be taken of the criticism advanced by Samuelson at the meeting of the American Economic Association on the centenary of the publication of the first volume of *Capital*. He stated (1967, p. 620) that Marx's labour theory of value might be excused if, as in 'Value, Price and Profit', he had made it quite clear that it was only a working hypothesis from which he had set out. 'I suggest that much ink and blood would have been spared if he had done likewise in *Capital*.' He further gave it as his opinion that 'Most of volume I would stand up if Marx stipulated, purely for expository simplicity, that the organic composition of capital (or, as we would say, labour's fractional share of value added) were the same in all industries.' By arguing in this way, Samuelson repeats a line of attack which has been pursued by a great number of authors since Böhm-Bawerk. Halm (1960, p. 130) has asserted of the value theories of both Ricardo and Marx that they represent a 'misconstruction'.

Unfortunately, it appears that neither Samuelson nor Halm had read the papers of a meeting of the American Economic Association in the previous decade. At that meeting, Gordon (1959, pp. 465–9) said with unmistakable clarity, 'Marx's analysis of Volume I presumes that capital–labour ratios are the same in all industries.' This means that Marx made exactly the assumption that according to Samuelson would have made his analysis respectable. In his study Gordon reached the conclusion that there, 'never was a labor theory of value in that sense of the phrase', but at the most in Ricardo a '93-percent labor theory'.

Similar statements have also been made by Marxists: 'There is no Marxian labour theory of value, but only an investigation of the historical method of production and of the social conditions which accompany it.'

This statement by the Italian Banfi (1967, pp. 169, 173) offers a logical transition, which may appear surprising, from the modern 'academic' to the modern Marxist interpretation of Marxian theory, which here, after generations of Marxist authors have exhausted themselves in defending a (vulgarised) theory of value, passes through a 'purifying purgatory'.

In the discussion at the aforementioned meeting of the American Economic Association, Baldwin stated (1958, p. 495), 'In the case of the labor theory of value, however, recent commentators are surprisingly unanimous. They agree that neither Smith nor Ricardo nor even Marx held a labor theory of value. Indeed, so obvious does this conclusion seem to be that the interesting question becomes not whether these writers did maintain a labor value theory but how anyone could ever have thought they did.'

We must now examine, what the real content of Marxian value theory is.

According to Banfi, the overvaluation of the theory of value is nothing but a 'misunderstanding. *Capital* begins with an analysis of commodity . . . not with a theory of value.' It cannot be denied, though, that Marx devoted much space to the analysis of value and consequently paved the way for such a misunderstanding, all the more so as it has never been clear what rôle he assigned to pure 'value', as opposed to 'use value' (or 'utility') and 'exchange value' (or 'price').

12 The Theory of Value and of Surplus Value

For Marx, the value of commodities has two parts: use value and exchange value. Use value does not necessarily imply exchange value; this is true, for example, of air. On the other hand, exchange value must imply use value for at least one of the parties to the exchange. In his further analysis Marx tacitly presumes opposition between owners of the means of production and those without property.

Labour power, whenever the absence of 'free' land precludes the possibility of independence, confers on its owner no unequivocal use value, if it cannot serve as the basis for his subsistence. He is forced to sell his labour, as he himself has no need for it as long as his own subsistence is not secured. (The application of labour power to 'hobbies' has scarcely any meaning.) It therefore is possible under capitalism for the exchange value of labour power temporarily to fall even below the minimum for subsistence. On the other hand, labour power represents use value to capitalists only for as long as it permits the creation of surplus value.

Exchange values are the basis of capitalist society. They are created by labour. Labour power as the potential source of production offers the basis for the creation of exchange values. Exchange value embodies the 'socially necessary' quantity of labour or labour time for the economic commodity in question.

Marx derived this theory of exchange value from Ricardo, whom according to Schumpeter (1947, p. 22) we may consider in many respects Marx's teacher. Ricardo sharply distinguishes between 'value', which is nothing other than a measure for labour content, and product, which for him represents not 'value' but 'wealth'. Marx adhered to this distinction.

The French economist Piettre has, however, stressed (1962, p. 42) that the theory of value cannot be regarded merely as borrowed from the classics, and in particular from Ricardo. Marx set out from the philosophical premise that the essence of man is to be found in his deeds and in his work.

THE MEANING OF THE CONCEPT OF 'SOCIALLY NECESSARY LABOUR TIME' AS A BASIS FOR DEMAND

For Marx, as for Adam Smith, Ricardo and their predecessors, labour was the common basis for the existence of a commodity: 'If then we leave out of consideration the use value of commodities, the common element in the exchange value of commodities consists in the human labour crystallised therein' (*Capital*, I, ch. I, p. 45). Marx's predecessors, however, referred to a more or less abstract notion of average labour. The new and original contribution of Marx resided in the fact that he defined labour power as the measure of a commodity's value and simultaneously quantified the average amount of 'socially necessary' labour (Piettre, 1962, p. 44).

There are three problems associated with this formulation. First of all, some authors see a problem in the 'reduction' of qualified or highly skilled work (for instance, artistic labour) to 'average labour' (Rosdolsky, 1968, I, p. 153). Can one agree with Marx that this reduction takes place on the labour market every day, in processes of evaluation based on money? Even some Marxists, such as Labriola (1910, p. 145), have not been satisfied with this: 'From individual to individual there is no common measure. . . . As yet no one has found the means for comparing the labour done by one with that of another.' One can try to dispose of this problem, which is considered by some authors to be a serious difficulty, by examining the situation not of an individual labourer, but of groups of similarly qualified labourers, by sectors. One then reaches a notion of 'labour groups' within which the individual qualification groups have different shares.

The second problem built into a general attack on Marxian theory by the marginal-utility school. According to this school, labour expended represents the cost aspect of the commodity, but there must also be taken into account the value that the commodity has to the consumer. Labour effort embodied in a product for which there is no demand cannot have any exchange value. The belief that Marx has missed something here appears unjustified, for with the words 'socially necessary labour' he has already made the assumption that the possession of the good in question is desirable and justified in the context of the given social system – a guarantee of demand! This was early recognised by Lederer, who interpreted as follows (1922, pp. 137–8) the notion of 'socially necessary labour':

If human labour is the only and decisive commodity necessary for economic activity, then human labour, even in the competitive struggle of workers each of whom is aiming to satisfy his needs to the maximum, will be expended only to satisfy equivalent needs, because labour, directed by the mechanism of economic interest as well as of re-munerative use is guided to the most urgent unsatisfied need. To the outside observer it looks as if products are exchanged at the rate of labour time contained therein. . . .

This idea had earlier been put forward by Labriola (1910, pp. 147–8), who wanted to see in the notion of 'socially necessary labour' a relationship between effort and remuneration, between what is desired and the actual commodity itself, and, therefore, between supply and demand. In this case what is socially necessary is also identical with what is demanded by society, i.e. by the totality of consumers.

The third problem concerns the definition of 'socially necessary labour': not every exertion of labour can be considered as 'socially necessary'. The notion is implicitly related to the state of technology. Where obsolete technical methods are applied, it may be that out of, say, twelve hours of labour only six are hours of really 'social (necessary) labour time', given the current state of technology. Marx stressed this point in several places (*Theories*, I, ch. 4, p. 232; II, ch. 8, p. 38).

Given that the notion of 'socially necessary labour' can be filled out in this way, the attacks of the marginal-utility school are fundamentally without justification. It must, however, be admitted that detailed quantification of what is socially necessary for particular products has not been forthcoming.

THE ANALYSIS OF SURPLUS VALUE

The premise for the origin of surplus value is that a man can produce more products than he requires for himself and his family. 'In a slave economy and also in the system of compulsory labour in the feudal period, man becomes unmistakably the source of labour for alien requirements. It is possible to distinguish clearly between labour for the worker himself and labour for his master. Here, "exploitation" appears clearly to arise from the relationship of domination' (Kühne, 1970, p. xxviii).

In capitalism, by contrast, the claim to domination becomes quite objective: it is linked to the possession of the means of production. The labourer is free, in principle, but submits to those in possession of the means of production, for he is obliged to sell that perishable commodity, his potential labour. If he does not do so, he must starve. The process of 'exploitation', however, remains in principle the same. The labourer is always obliged to work more than is necessary simply to supply his own needs.

What are the needs of the labourer himself? Marx sees in the concept more than the minimum of subsistence for the labourer and his family. He recognises that there is in the level of wages a 'historical' element, which tends to increase as civilisation develops, over time and technically. According to Steindl (1952, p. 230) this is 'a very cautious definition of the "subsistence-level" which is *historically* determined'.

This is only logical, for if, as Marx demonstrates, bourgeois society has created more productive forces in a few generations than all other societies since the civilisation of man have done, it is clear that the enormous forces of production, when unchained, must find their expression in enormous quantities of goods. The small group of capitalists, which Marx saw as shrinking, cannot by itself consume this rapidly growing quantity of goods. Furthermore, Marx anticipated Weber's thoughts on the relation between capitalism and Calvinism by imputing to capitalists a mania for 'accumulation' and a renunciation of the joys of life. The consequence is that the level of real wages must grow. This, however, is a consideration that already forms part of dynamic analysis.

Within the framework of static analysis we must start from the supposition that the sum of value added remains constant.

Marx sees the 'mechanism of exploitation', which is typical of capitalism, as decisive in the division of value created, between workers and capitalists. The lower limit to the worker's wage is set by the minimum required for subsistence (as defined above). Marx, however, emphatically refused to accept the 'iron law of wages', which Lassalle derived from Ricardo's teaching. According to Lassalle, wages tend always to sink to the minimum under the pressure of increasing population. Marx does not recognise an upper limit to wages in value created, at least not in the context of static analysis, because he rejects the Malthusian theory of population. Pressure on wages is exercised only by the 'industrial reserve army' in the field of dynamics.

Once the worker is equipped with tools or even 'machinery' and raw materials, his work must also provide for the replacement of worn-out plant and accessories and replenishment of the stock of raw materials. What remains after meeting these requirements is the value created and is available to be divided between capitalists and workers. From the value created expressed in labour hours, the wage, also in labour hours, must be subtracted.

From 1859 at least, Marx distinguished between, on the one hand, labour power and its capacity for production, which are sold to capitalists, and, on the other, the product of labour, which the capitalist gains by employing this labour power. It is for this reason that in the 1891 version of *Wage Labour and Capital*, first published, in article form, in 1849, the expression 'labour power' was frequently used in place of the original's 'labour'. Engels, in his Introduction explained the need for the change. The worker receives in exchange for his labour power the amount required to produce and sustain it. But at the same time he produces a greater value. If four hours of work are required to provide for the wage, which corresponds to the 'wage goods' bought by the worker, the product of the four remaining hours of the working day is available as surplus value to the capitalist, for he sells the whole product. This is 'exploitation', but Marx always stresses that this is an objective factor and is not to be considered as a moral problem, for the worker receives exactly what his labour power 'is worth'. Marx emphasised this especially in his *Critique of the Gotha*

Programme. The difference between the quantity of wage goods the labourer receives and the total product is the 'surplus value'.

It must be noted that Marx generally starts from the hypothesis of a rate of surplus value of 100 per cent. This means that surplus value per worker is practically equivalent to the wage per worker. Difficulties arise from the fact that the appearance of fixed capital presupposes the existence of earlier stages of production in the analysis. Ricardo circumvented this difficulty by the hypothesis that the means of subsistence of the worker and his means of production should be identical: both consist of 'corn', which is consumed by the worker and used as seed by the enterprise. (This has some affinities with the modern models of von Neumann and Sraffa, where 'input' includes wages.)

In this case it is easy to measure the 'surplus value': it is the quantity of corn that remains at the disposal of the capitalist after deduction of the means of subsistence (= 'variable capital') and of corn required for seed (= 'constant capital'). The capitalist can then either entirely consume this surplus of corn (this would be 'simple reproduction') or he can consume only part of it, using the other part for the employment of additional labourers (this would be 'extended production, which belongs to the field of growth theory). Here, three remarks would seem to be appropriate.

First of all, the argument presupposes that the state of technology allows for the satisfaction of all these requirements within a working period of less than the working day. In this way capitalism builds upon the foundations laid by earlier social systems, which had developed techniques of work and means of production such that it was no longer necessary for the labourer to devote all his time to himself and his family to secure his existence.

Secondly, Marx explicitly starts from the hypothesis of a living standard determined by historical circumstances and containing elements of a standard once reached in history. He therefore refutes the idea – propounded by Lassalle and still lingering on in the minds of some latter-day vulgar Marxists – that the worker will permanently vegetate at starvation level, or that the system has an inherent tendency, owing to some 'iron law of wages', periodically to depress him to this minimum. For this reason it is erroneous to suppose that Marx ever held a 'theory of growing poverty'. The reason for this misconception lies in a misinterpretation of the word 'pauperisation'.

Thirdly, the Marxian standard of living is variable. It is therefore within its nature to increase as the productivity of the economic system as a whole rises. This is implicit in the assumption of the constant ratio between wages and surplus value, but it is also compatible with the assumption of a rising rate of surplus value.

It must be stressed that the notion of 'value' in Marx does not completely coincide with the exchange or use value of labour power. On the contrary, it is a term *sui generis*.

Von Bortkiewicz has emphasised (1907a, pp. 107 ff.) that (use and exchange value apart) 'value', for Marx, has basically two different forms: namely relative and absolute value. In the first case, 'value is merely the index of an exchange relationship . . . which indicates how many units of the good serving as a measure of value are obtained in exchange for a commodity or for a unit of this commodity'. In the second case, value is a matter of the 'quantity of labour employed in [the] production' of a commodity. We must add that this is the socially necessary quantity of labour. According to von Bortkiewicz, Marx applies the notion of 'value' in the latter sense when he speaks of 'real value' or 'immanent value', and in the former sense when he specifically says that he is doing so (as when he writes of 'value, respectively the price of labour itself or as wages').

As an instrument of measurement, labour suffers from a basic defect: its productivity changes, and it is therefore a variable measure. The same applies to labour power. 'Socially necessary labour time' is a sort of 'efficiency unit' (to be considered later) the content of which changes, and which with regard to any particular product can also be variable. Finally, the concept of absolute value which von Bortkiewicz sees in Marx can be considered as identical with the minimum subsistence wage required for the labourer from the sociological point of view, or with the socially necessary labour time to be expended on it.

It must be stressed that, if commodities are measured by an index, the same sum of 'value' can represent different or growing quantities of products in a physical sense. One is tempted to develop a parallel to the famous 'laws of Gossen': with increasing productivity (and the same qualitative composition of the work-force) larger quantities of a good represent the same 'value' for Marx, because for the production of the same quantity a smaller social provision of work is necessary.

13 Interpretations of the Theory of Value

Marxian value theory, as a continuation of that of the classics, has been interpreted in at least eight ways: (1) as a kind of historical stage theory; (2) as a theory of basic prices, to which market prices bear a certain relationship; (3) as a purely intellectual aid; (4) as a theory of a socially justified or ethically just measurement of income; (5) as a theory of the forces that determine the 'proper' division of labour among the various branches of the total economy; (6) as a theory of 'efficiency units'; (7) as an interpretation of microeconomic costs, especially in distribution theory; and, finally (8), as a macroeconomic theory of distribution. For the moment we limit ourselves to examining the first five versions.

THE HISTORICAL INTERPRETATION

According to the first version, value theory is nothing but a theory of the historical stages in which value comes to be expressed. This interpretation was formulated immediately after the appearance of the first volume of *Capital* by sagacious observers in 'academic' economics. Its clearest formulation is to be found in an interpretation given by the Viennese professor Grünberg (1907, p. 917): 'Exchange value . . . is the proportion in which use value of one kind is exchanged for use values of another kind . . . a use value or commodity has . . . a value only because it represents abstract human labour . . . of an average social power. . . .' Therefore, 'socially necessary labour time' is the working time that is aimed at 'in order to produce any use value by employing the existing normal social conditions of production and the average social degree of skill and work intensity. Of course, labour means not only manual labour but also . . . any directing and organisational activity within the production process.' If we adhere to this interpretation, it follows that

> commodities . . . that can be produced in the same labour time . . . have the same values, and that, on the other hand, differences in value find their measure in the quantitative difference in the labour time required for the production of the commodities.

In exchange transactions prices, i.e. quantities of value expressed in

70

money, 'gravitate towards values determined in this way and oscillate around these values'. It is better to say 'gravitate', for, according to Engels's interpretation, they did so for the 'whole period of simple commodity production', i.e. 'from the beginning of the exchange of commodities by barter right up to the fifteenth century'.

Böhm-Bawerk objected (1896; English trans. in Sweezy, 1966, pp. 47ff.) that even in 'simple commodity production', where all profits accrue to the independent labourer, who owns his means of production, the owner would have to calculate a rate of interest in his pricing to compensate him for the time which he might possibly have spent in producing more complicated tools. Sombart (1894, pp. 571ff.) criticises Marx from a historical point of view: he objects that capitalism did not establish itself first in branches of industry that were predominantly the preserve of artisans and that, according to the Marxian hypothesis, should have produced high surplus values, because of the high value of the labour expended. On the contrary, he argues, capitalist production began not among artisans but in the new capital-intensive branches of industry, such as mining, where the workers were in most cases 'de-classed elements'.

In contrast to Böhm-Bawerk, Hilferding (1904; English trans. in Sweezy, 1966, pp. 172ff.) has tried to defend the Marxian concept. He objects that,

> in the case of the laborer who works on his own account, . . . the means of production are tools of a comparatively simple kind . . . and there is no very notable difference in value between the tools used in the different spheres of production. . . . Speaking generally, in pre-capitalist conditions dead labor plays a modest part as compared with living labor.

He then goes on to stress that under the mediaeval system of guilds there were quasi-monopolistic barriers to entry. These would have ensured large quantities of surplus value while permitting very different rates of profit. This argument is reminiscent of certain statements by Lexis, according to whom the large quantities of surplus value in wage- and labour-intensive branches should cause the disappearance of the middle classes, which exploit the consumer in a monopolistic manner.

None of the participants in this debate saw the analogy between the disappearance of profit or interest as economic categories in the so-called 'simple reproduction' of Marx and the same result in Schumpeter's stationary economy. Today it can be asserted that Marx in fact spoke of the same situation as did Schumpeter: in his 'pre-capitalist' world such a 'stationary' situation was effectively in existence.

On the other hand, it is not admissible simultaneously to point, as Hilferding does, to the monopolistic elements of the guilds system. If the rate of interest is to be non-existent in this world, then this is to be explained by the lack of dynamic growth elements. Monopolistic guild elements would permit the creation of monopoly-like receipts and, therefore, profits, which in turn would justify the reappearance of the rate of interest. (See Sweezy 1966, pp. 38–41, 163–72.)

But we must ask ourselves if Marx would really have devoted so many pages to a 'historical' theory of value. If he in fact did so, certain critics of his (for instance, Kerschagl) who wanted, with some bias, to stamp him as an economic historian would be right. Besides, Marx uses in many contexts a hypothetically rigid ratio between 'variable capital' and 'surplus value' – for instance, in his theory of the 'tendency of the rate of profit to fall'. Here, as in other passages, one cannot really gain the impression that Marx had rejected the use of value theory as an explanation for the reality of the capitalist world.

If this first interpretation were right, the entire debate about the application of the theory to capitalism would be devoid of interest, for the theory would apply only to pre-capitalist conditions, in which provision of the means of production is insignificant, so that the problem of whether an investment of capital receives a reward or not can be neglected. This was true at least of Schumpeter's stationary economy.

Incidentally, according to Joan Robinson (1954/60, p. 53), even in such a stationary society differential wages and prices would exist, and would depart from average values because of 'natural skill and inherited lore', supply and demand for particular products and 'barriers to entry' in professions in which the wage is driven upwards by 'the need to provide a relatively heavy investment in equipment'.

In any case, the 'historical' interpretation is not satisfactory. Joan Robinson declared,

> There is a curious strand of thought in the Marxist doctrine – the notion that in a pre-capitalist economy of peasants and artisans, where each worker owns his own tools, the prices of commodities must be proportional to *values*. . . . Actual artisan economies are dominated by caste or guild rules, and their prices are influenced by accepted notions of what is fair or pleasing to the gods.

THE 'BASIC PRICE SYSTEM' INTERPRETATION AND THE RÔLE OF CAPITAL REMUNERATION WITHIN THE FRAMEWORK OF PRICE FORMATION

The second interpretation, according to which values represent 'basic' or 'fundamental' prices, has two versions, a 'primitive' and a 'refined' one.

The 'primitive' argument presupposes that Marx (and before him

Ricardo) actually presumed that the only proper measure for the alteration of prices lay in the alteration of the quantity of labour necessary for production. Such a version was put forward quite early by Ernst Lange (1897, pp. 553, 573). In a somewhat modified form this argument was taken up by Masaryk (1899, p. 256), who thought that Marx in the first volume of *Capital* had formulated his law of labour value without sufficiently considering the facts, and that in the third he found himself constrained to admit that these facts simply did not conform to his 'law'.

Later, Günther (1905, p. 33) wanted to improve upon this theory; he claimed that Marx foundered in the desperate attempt to bring about a reconciliation between theory and practice. This argument has been repeated again and again in later criticisms of Marx.

In the face of this 'primitive' version von Bortkiewicz (1906, 1, p. 2) emphatically pointed out that, at the time when he was writing the first volume, Marx was already fully aware of the so-called 'contradiction'. Von Bortkiewicz therefore presupposed that Marx had envisaged the 'solution', as given in the third volume, from the very beginning. He remonstrated with Masaryk in particular that Marx knew very well of Ricardo's statements in view of the necessity to postulate a uniform rate of profit in the economy as a whole, about the deviations from the law of value.

Von Bortkiewicz's hypothesis was later confirmed by Hilferding (1904; English trans. in Sweezy, 1966, p. 155) and Boudin (1912, p. 133) prior to the First World War: both emphasise that the third volume of *Capital* was written long before the first. This fact has been corroborated by modern research on Marx and is now beyond any doubt (cf. Rubel, 1963; 1968, p. 94). In this way the 'primitive' version collapses.

Böhm-Bawerk, however, developed a 'refined' version of the 'theory of basic prices'. According to this (1921, 1, p. 370), 'human labour is accumulated in the means of production. It is a sort of conceptual distillate of exchange value.' The 'great law of value provides . . . that commodities are exchanged on the basis of the average amount of socially necessary labour that they embody.'

According to Marx, however, in the long run 'the socially necessary labour time will find enforcement as the controlling natural law'. It is here that Böhm-Bawerk and the marginal utility school offer criticism: for him 'value' is to be seen not in labour expended but rather on the demand side, in the utility a commodity represents to the consumer.

Adam Smith had already admitted that there were two sides to the coin, and that utility together with labour requirements determined values. Marx himself says that commodities, 'on the other hand, . . . must show that they are use-values before they can be realised as values. For the labour spent upon them counts effectively, only in so far as it is spent in a form that is useful for others. Whether that labour is useful for others . . . can be proved only by the act of exchange' (*Capital*, 1, p. 91). It can therefore be said that Marx himself saw the dualism in the determination of value.

Böhm-Bawerk's objections to the labour theory of value are as follows: first, it completely neglects the demand side; secondly, it does not recognise that the use of capital merits remuneration, i.e. that compensation is justified for the owners of capital who choose roundabout ways of production; and thirdly, it contradicts the relation between prices. When the amount of capital used in the process of production is different in different activities, commodities do not exchange in proportion to their labour value, for their prices will be higher or lower than their values if more or less capital has been used in their production. According to the labour theory of value, high surplus values and high profits should be possible in activities where much labour and little capital are used. Reality shows that the reverse is true, as Marx admits quite clearly. According to Böhm-Bawerk (1921, pp. 393–4), Marx also recognised that

> the amount of surplus which can be produced with a given capital can be in direct proportion to the variable part of the capital, but not to the total capital . . . if the degree of exploitation is equal or the rate of surplus value is equal, then capitals of varying organic composition must yield unequal 'rates of return'. But experience says that . . . capitals will bear equal 'rates of return' without regard to their composition.

As regards the first point of this criticism, we have already stated that demand is taken into account in the Marxian system through the notion of 'socially necessary labour time'. This is also underlined in recent Marxist studies by Kende (1969, p. 237) and others. We must nevertheless admit that this notion is a rather unwieldy one.

A 'value' arises only when the market recognises the necessity of the labour time by accepting the price. This has been stated by Marx himself (*Capital*, 1, ch. 2). But this is known only *a posteriori*. Value is already laid down beforehand, for prices oscillate around it. How is it possible to distinguish whether such a price variation corresponds to the correction of the value *a posteriori* or to a deviation from the original value? Or does each deviation represent such a correction? In this case value would lose its character as a lodestar.

This, however, should be the very purpose of value theory itself: in a world where prices can be manipulated – for instance by advertising, (i.e. by increasing costs – paradoxically, from the side of supply!) – demand itself is no longer independent of supply and can no longer be directly determined. In this case it would indeed be of some importance to acquire an independent point of departure, and it is at this that the labour theory of value is aiming.

With regard to Böhm-Bawerk's second point, the return to capital, it can be said that the labour theory of value would be correct if capital could be obtained for nothing or without any claim to a 'minimum payment' or 'minimum rate of interest' or 'minimum profit'. But such a situation certainly does not exist in real life: there are, indeed, numerous enterprises, some run by artisans and some in retailing, that yield to their respective proprietor practically nothing more than the 'entrepreneur's wage'. Even in ascertaining the 'average profit' in the economy, the considerable losses suffered by some enterprises have to be deducted from the profits made by others. Marx himself believed in the existence of an average profit the sum of which must correspond to the sum of surplus value. This last idea has been contested by Bortkiewicz (1907b, p. 197) and, in modern times, also by Sweezy. Both have argued that in the Marxian calculation values and prices are insufficiently distinguished. Böhm-Bawerk did not realise this weakness of his adversary. He and, before and after him, many economists who have dealt with the problem of the rate of interest have postulated the existence of an 'original rate of interest' and, therefore, of a 'minimum remuneration' of capital.

At the same time, Marx did not deny that surplus value could not sink to zero. Indeed, he has been criticised just because he did not take into account the possibility that competition could lead to the disappearance of surplus value. In introducing the notion of 'absolute surplus value', Marx in fact postulated that there would be a permanent reward to capital. He does not derive this from mysterious 'roundabout methods of production' (Böhm-Bawerk) or 'liquidity preference' (Keynes), but, rather, justifies this minimum yield by the social power relationship between workers and capitalists. For Marx the rate of interest is part of the surplus value and is to be explained by the fact that the ownership of capital makes surplus value possible. Lederer has said (1922, p. 96) that the conundrum of the rate of interest will be solved as soon as it is realised that it is possible to create values that exceed the value of the labour power employed. In the Marxian system a return to capital is, therefore, ensured. It springs from two sources: first, as 'absolute surplus value', from the general monopoly of means of production held by capitalists (this has been stressed by Graziadei); and, secondly, as 'relative surplus value', from the continuous improvement in methods of production (as suggested by Schumpeter).

Some Marxists, however, have tried to prove that capital need not be remunerated. This idea is already embryonic in Marx, for he regards the drive to accumulate as innate in capitalists, for in his view they deny themselves consumption, which brings no utility, in order to save and to increase their power. In other passages, however, Marx speaks of profit losing its sting, but such profit need not be used only for luxury consumption. In similar fashion, Keynes (1919, pp. 18–21) gave a description of the readiness of capitalists before 1914 to save at all costs.

A disciple of Croce, Pietranera, has made an attempt (1966, pp. 96ff.) at a *reductio ad absurdum* by applying the methods of Böhm-Bawerk. Pietranera examines the relationship between capital-owners and capital-users, in order to ascertain whether in fact 'time preference', which furnishes one of Böhm-Bawerk's chief arguments for the rate of interest, does in fact exist. He comes to the conclusion that in the majority of conceivable cases there would be either no positive or even a negative rate of interest, because one or other of the two parties or both of them *ex definitione* value their future receipts more highly than those in the present. This is possible either because their needs will be greater in the future or because the future is uncertain! Even Joan Robinson (1953–4, pp. 81 ff.) has argued in this way.

One could now argue that Marx and Keynes overrated the capitalists' propensity to save, and that Marshall is nearer the truth, for he emphasised the necessity of compensating the capitalists for their waiting, while tacitly assuming that this would also justify a high standard of living.

> Marshall's analysis can [paradoxically] be used to show why socialism is necessary. . . . For society to pay for saving by permitting a great inequality in consumption is a very wasteful and expensive method of getting the job done. It would be far more economical to dispossess the capitalists. . . . In order to be able to have a more economic distribution of income it is necessary for saving to be collective, and if the saving is done collectively, capital must be owned collectively. – If the capitalists fully lived up to Marx's description and really invested the whole surplus there would be no need for socialism. It is the rentier aspect of profit as a source of private wealth, which Marshall emphasises, that makes the strongest case for socialism. . . .

Thus Joan Robinson sketches (1955/60 pp. 10/11ff.) the irony of the reversal in positions.

The question of whether capital ought to be remunerated cannot be answered solely by an appeal to macroeconomic expediency. Beyond this a problem of allocation arises: how, independently of the question of ownership, are scarce means of production to be allocated to various branches and firms?

The question resolves itself into one of the rationality of a system which has no place for the rate of interest. In socialist systems the question has long been decided in favour of using a rate of interest (often camouflaged) in making allocative decisions. (Cf. Lavigne, 1961, pp. 165–8; Vaag, 1969; Thornton, 1971, pp. 546 ff.) The necessity of economic calculus is no longer denied in economic analysis even in the Soviet Union. But there remains another question to be solved: who receives the eventual interest payment, a private owner of capital or the community?

The allocation of capital to techniques of production, which are capital-intensive in different degrees, requires the rate of interest as an instrument for rationing. But in this case the labour theory of value no longer supplies an immediate clue for the determination of relative prices. Marx himself recognised this fact.

Lederer has tried to give an answer to the third of Böhm-Bawerk's objections to the labour theory of value, the contradiction between value and prices. He recognises (1922, p. 99) that 'according to the labour theory of value the surplus in each firm would be determined by the number of workers employed in the respective firm. . . . But this is obviously not the case.' What is really decisive is 'costs, and the entrepreneur relates the surplus to total costs'. This is what Marx explicitly did in setting out his theory in the third volume of *Capital*.

Joan Robinson has commented (1954/60, p. 49), 'This is Marx's theory of "prices of production"; and in fact it is everybody's theory of prices . . . the normal price of any commodity is given by the wages cost of the labour plus a margin sufficient to provide profit at the ruling rate on the capital devoted to its production.'

How does Lederer solve the contradiction between values and prices? He argues that Marx's labour theory of value was not satisfied with the statement that

commodities are sold sometimes above and sometimes below their value without providing an exact measure of such deviations. But there exists a measurement; it is indicated in a precise way by the organic composition of capital in the individual firm. Sales above or below value constitute a deviation, a distortion, the dimensions of which can be determined theoretically. This formula of production prices, therefore, constitutes a solution and not, as Böhm-Bawerk thought, only a sham solution.

This solution seems, indeed, to be a most plausible one as long as one remains within the framework of microeconomic analysis, but it has not completely satisfied many economists, even those who can be regarded as wellwishers.

Joan Robinson, for instance, says (1954/60, p. 53) that Marx 'means by the *value* of a commodity, not its price in terms of labour time, but what its price would be if the share of labor in net output were the same for this commodity as for output as a whole'. This can also be expressed in another way: for Marx the existence of labour time expended (v) was an indicator for measuring value added. He started from the assumption of proportionality between the value of v and the surplus, and he then went on to apply this proportionality in the whole economy, or the average situation, to the individual firm. If competition led to a reduction of this surplus value in labour-intensive firms through pressure on prices, this was considered to be a sort of 'punishment' for the fact that they had remained too labour-intensive.

'Value calculation means to determine the exchange relationships of goods according to the law of value. Price calculation means to determine the same exchange relationships according to the law of the equal rate of profit.' This is the interpretation of von Bortkiewicz (1907a, p. 35), who found the clearest formulation with regard to these questions. In the same essay he wrote (pp. 12–13),

> The rate of surplus value s/v is assumed to be the same in all spheres of production. It follows that the rate of profit $s(c+v)$ varies in the different spheres of production: it is higher or lower according to whether constant capital is more weakly or more strongly represented in the sphere of production concerned. . . . The capitalist economy, however, cannot tolerate this consequence and removes it in the following manner: the total surplus value . . . created in all spheres of production is distributed among the separate spheres of production in proportion to the total capital $(c + v)$ invested in each.

It has to be admitted that this recalculation raises a number of problems that have not fully been solved by Marx.

THE 'INTELLECTUAL AID' INTERPRETATION

The thesis that the labour theory of value represents an 'intellectual aid' probably originated with Bernstein. He states (1920, p. 42) that

> surplus value . . . is an empirical fact that can be proved by experience and which does not require any deductive proof. It is completely irrelevant for the proof of the existence of surplus labour whether the Marxian theory of value is correct or not. In this respect this thesis does not furnish any proof but is only a means of analysis and illustration.

A similar opinion was held by Sombart, who thought (1894, pp. 571ff.) that such an 'intellectual aid' was indispensable for reducing qualitatively different commodities, e.g. consumers' goods, to a common denominator. One must start much more from 'value', i.e. goods should be regarded simply and solely as the products of abstract human labour. Sombart thought that the notion of the productivity of labour found its economic expression in the concept of value.

Von Bortkiewicz, by contrast, argued that a theory that regards work as the most important factor of production has nothing directly to do with the Marxian theory of value. He pursued (1906, pp. 23–5) this interpretation of the Marxian notion of value into the realms of abstract money philosophy, as developed by Simmel (1900, pp. 51–2). Simmel, indeed, compared the notion of value to that of existence or essence and related it to Kantian metaphysics.

The interpretation of the labour theory of value as merely an intellectual aid does less than justice to Marx, especially in view of the strong emphasis on reality of his work as a whole. One can speak of the theory as an intellectual aid really only in the sense in which it used in the first volume of *Capital*, where Marx presupposes that the organic composition of capital, i.e. capital intensity, is the same in all lines of activity, so that values and prices coincide.

THE THEORY OF THE 'SOCIALLY JUSTIFIED' OR 'ETHICALLY JUST' INCOME DISTRIBUTION

In examining the theories of Simmel, von Bortkiewicz mentioned another philosophical concept that is justified in its own right: it is the one outlined by Koppel, who sees a normative function in the notion of value. (See von Bortkiewicz, 1906, pp. 28–9.)

Koppel takes up Simmel's antithesis between value and essence but stresses that Marx wanted to examine the distribution of profits in the capitalist system. The Marxian system is seen in a proper light only when it is realised that under it the law of value does not apply and profits are not distributed in proportion to the participation of labour. This is the proper conclusion from the Marxian analysis of capitalism. According to Koppel, all earlier interpretations have overlooked this.

Von Bortkiewicz admitted that there were certainly connexions between pricing and distribution. It would be possible to ask whether a distribution according to values would not be 'socially more just', in the sense that the workers involved in the production and not the owners of capital would obtain the benefit of the social product thus distributed.

Koppel wanted to see in the non-realisation of the law of value the source of the unequal distribution of income, and at the same time the reason for over-production, the production of luxury goods and under-consumption. Von Bortkiewicz, however, held that such an interpretation would contradict Marx, who thought that it was not the responsibility of socialism to bring to fruition the law of value. On the contrary, under the socialist system the law of value would no longer apply.

In this context von Bortkiewicz quoted a study of Stammler's (second edition, 1926), but he did not think it worthy of analysis, although Stammler develops an ethical concept in his particular interpretation of the notion of 'socially necessary labour time'. Stammler sees in labour time the expenditure of labour necessary in a society organised on the principles of justice. In the view of von Bortkiewicz (1906, note 98), Diehl killed off this rather daring interpretation of the Marxian terminology by declaring it, offhand, as inadmissible, because there is no trace of it to be found in Marxian analysis.

The idea of labour value as the measurement for an ethically just distribution of income was next taken up a quarter of a century later, without reference to Koppel, by Lindsay (1925, pp. 57–8, 61). Lindsay recognises that the labour theory of value could at first sight create the impression that Marx wanted to provide a theory of 'market pricing'. In considering the theory more closely, one has to recognise that the prices are such as would prevail 'under highly abstract conditions'. According to Lindsay, these prices would be valid in 'a society where a man gets what he is worth'. The labour theory of value is 'concerned not with actual but with ideal prices . . . [It is] primarily interested in what a man ought to get in reward for his labour'.

From this angle Lindsay criticises Marx's historical approach to the problem of value. He sees in the labour theory of value a natural rights theory and historical method which do not go well together. In his interpretation he takes his cue from, in particular, the following passage in the first volume of *Capital* (Ch. 1, p. 65): 'The secret of the expression of value, namely, that all kinds of labour are equal and equivalent, because and so far as they are human labour in general, cannot be deciphered, until the notion of human equality has already acquired the fixity of a popular prejudice.'

Meek (1956a, p. 218) has criticised Lindsay's approach and thinks that the passage quoted has been taken out of its general context in Marx's work, for Marx was really only giving a commentary on Aristotle. Meek goes on to argue that Marx would never have taken such pains in developing his theory of value if he had wished to do nothing other than furnish a theory of an ethical claim to the product of labour, or, as one must say today, to the complete value added. Meek also points to the fact that Croce had taken up some of these formulations long before Lindsay – who, indeed, wrote a preface to the English edition of Croce's studies (1914), and was no doubt influenced and inspired by them. It was, strangely enough, Croce who rejected the idea of making the identity between value and labour an ideal of social ethics.

THE THEORY OF THE 'CORRECT' DISTRIBUTION OF LABOUR POWER IN THE ECONOMIC SYSTEM

In consequence of the many interpretations of the labour theory of value, the simplest and most plausible explanation was overlooked. This interpretation can indeed be found in the Marxian formula for the composition of production prices. It consists in the fact that 'values' within the framework of the general economy represent the allocation of disposable labour power to various 'socially necessary' branches of production.

In modern times, the link between these elements has been recorded by Meek (1956, pp. 31, 44ff.). According to his theory, 'value is a social phenomenon, derived from the division of labour in society', and thus 'a quantitative measure of value might be expected to be related in some measure to this social process'. In other words, value is the reflection of the quantitative input of labour power in society; it represents that fraction of the potential macroeconomic labour power which is crystallised in the individual work-performance within the framework of a given technical standard. When the technical standard rises, labour potential is increased and the output of one hour of labour time is greater, but the fraction of the social potential labour power which is manifested in one hour of labour time remains the same, provided we assume that the technical efficiency of such labour time increases proportionately. The difficult question of answering how 'value' in this sense is related to the notion of an 'efficiency unit', as developed in modern growth analysis, will be dealt with later.

According to Meek (ibid., p. 39), if society is regarded

> as consisting in essence of an association of separate producers who live by mutually exchanging the products of their different labours, we may then think of the exchange of these products as being in essence the exchange of quantities of social labour. And if we begin thinking in these terms, we may well eventually conclude that the value of a commodity – i.e. its power of purchasing or commanding other commodities in exchange – is a quality conferred upon it by virtue of the fact that a certain portion of the labour force of society has been allocated to its production.

This is the thesis, which may be called the theory of correct distribution of labour power. It appears to be the only theory which can offer sound reasons why a value calculation ought to be retained alongside a price calculation. The theory can be augmented by a new concept based on old 'productivity ideas', and one which does not discriminate against the provision of services. Such discrimination is in any case somewhat paradoxical from the point of view of the protagonists of the labour theory of value, as opposed to those who would make a 'fetish of commodities'. This new concept may lead to an 'evaluation' of socially positive and socially negative uses of labour. Basically it is owing to the possibilities in this direction, as Dickinson remarks (1957, p. 501) in a review of Meek's book, that

> there are economists, not all dogmatic Marxists, who regard [the theory] as something more, as a theory of value that is, in a way, more fundamentally true than the 'demand' or 'equilibrium' theories that have enjoyed a vogue during the last seventy years. Dr. Meek's argument in its favour is based upon its social significance. . . . But the marginal theories have tried so resolutely to banish from economics any sort of social significance – first insisting on the purely private and personal nature of utility and then expelling utility itself from economics in favour of indifference curves, or of pure equilibrium, or revealed preference – that they have made it impossible for seekers after social

significance to find any *point d'appui* in the structure of orthodox theory.

If there is a revival of Marxian economics, it is largely the reaction from the view that 'there is no penumbra of approbation round the Theory of Equilibrium': 'equilibrium is just equilibrium', and from the successive 'New Welfare Economics' which has progressively stripped the concept of welfare of every element that could conceivably relate it to social reality. . . .

The consequences of Meek's thesis are very far-reaching and go beyond the realm of economics into the sociological sphere and the arena of social reform.

It is conceivable that in a new concept of society of a 'collectivist' kind a reconciliation could be effected between, on the one side, what could be called a labour theory of value based on the notion of a co-operative claim to a share in the total product, and, on the other, the 'normal' theories of imputation of business-oriented economics, retaining the rate of interest as an instrument of calculation.

If this approach is adopted, a rate of interest would have to be calculated proportionate to the capital retained by society, such capital being scarce by definition. It is assumed that the ideal situation as depicted by Keynes and Robinson – i.e. that of an unlimited availability of capital – has not yet been brought about.

The rate of interest is being used, as Joan Robinson demands, for rationing scarce resources in order to direct them to those activities in which they are liable to increase their productivity most. This would seem to be an application of the principle of the 'marginal benefit to society'. The income that would arise from the payment of interest would then accrue to the members of society in proportion to the labour expended by them, unless it were used for public goods or collective activities. This would mean that all working members of society, including housewives, would receive a kind of social dividend, a thirteenth salary in the year or a 'holiday bonus', or whatever formula is preferred. Such a concept would approximate to the French idea of 'participation' and could be improved by notions of joint decision-making, which might effect a reconciliation between the principle of the 'functional' and that of the 'personal' distribution of income.

Such questions must necessarily remain controversial, all the more so as the total supply of capital in a collectivist system could, in principle, also be secured by the use of other instruments (for instance, a sales tax or other fiscal device) without resorting to the rate of interest. This has been proved by Mackenroth, (1949, pp. 89ff.). Practical examples concerning the Soviet Union are quoted by Naville (1974, pp. 354ff.). On the other hand, the social bonus sketched above could also be considered as a kind of 'negative' tax, which could increase the price of labour power and lead, therefore, to an efficient allocation of labour power in a manner similar to the rate of interest in the case of investment goods.

In considering 'values' it must always be supposed that labour power is distributed in an optimal manner corresponding to the technical standards of the time. If the steel industry is highly capital-intensive, then this is because blast-furnaces have been invented, and if, on the other hand, a hair dresser's shop has next to no capital, this is because no robot has yet been invented which could use a pair of scissors as effectively as a good hairdresser. After all, values are determined by the degree of mechanisation which is possible for different work processes, and this mechanisation is less possible the more direct are the relationships between people that it involves.

'Values', in contrast to 'prices', indicate the distribution of the social product among individual workers. The distribution is that that would result from the hypothesis that each worker considers himself to be a member of a vast co-operative comprising the whole of society, and that the entire surplus value is distributed to co-operators not in proportion to their ownership of capital (which would no longer exist, *ex definitione*), but in proportion to their labour effort. In other words, 'values' are nothing other than the expression of a hypothetically just distribution of surplus value among all working members of society. If society chooses another criterion for the distribution of the social surplus, namely the ownership of capital, this is to be explained by the historically given social structure.

In considering the possibility of creating such a co-operative it must be understood that the distribution of the social dividend to all co-operators would take account of those members of society who are not in a position to work – namely, the old and the infirm – and certain activities making provision for collective wants, as Marx pointed out in his *Critique of the Gotha Programme*.

The sum of values can grow only when the sum of 'socially necessary labour time' grows. But this is not synonymous with the growth of real product, which shows the quantity of use values not reflected in Marx's 'values'. If 'socially necessary labour time' is saved, the sum of values will decline, even though the social product grows. This means that the value theory is unwieldly or even inappropriate for measuring the growth process.

It can thus be stated that the value theory is in fact a theory of imputation. Joan Robinson is correct in so far as she identifies value with what the price of a good would be if the labour share in the net product of this good were the same as the share of labour in the social product. In the last resort, value is not something which exists but something which ought to exist. In this sense, it can be regarded as 'conceivable' or 'thinkable', as Labriola and Croce have postulated.

The function of desirability as fulfilled by value theory has been well stated by Preiser (1953, 1961, pp. 281–2).

An administrative economy with common ownership of the means of production can distribute the 'rent', i.e. the share of the product imputed to the means of production to the working people, and it can do so by dubbing it 'the reward to labour effort'. Natural resources are given free to society, even if they exist only in limited quantities, and the same is true of man-made means of production at the disposal of society that have been inherited from earlier periods. The construction of this equipment has involved a cost. To be exact, it has required a limitation on the production of consumption goods and of consumption itself. But this is over and done with. The entire net product of the current period can, therefore, be considered as being the result of labour alone, and as an income it can be attributed to labour alone.

MICROECONOMIC COST THEORY

Another version of the labour theory of value could be based simply on short-term considerations, a fact which has been recognised by Keynes, Joan Robinson, Preiser and others. In this case, changes in labour costs in the short run are the decisive factor. It is in this sense that a '93-percent labor theory of value' has been ascribed to Ricardo. This thesis has a somewhat piquant smack, in so far as it resembles the argument, put forward by many monopolists, oligopolists and industrial organisations, that the real inflationary element in modern economic life is to be found in the claims of organised labour. In this case the cost-push argument is brought forward in a one-sided way, without considering the alternative of demand-pull. These are the things to which Joan Robinson refers when she writes (1954/60, p. 55/50),

> There would be no point in dabbling in these stagnant controversies if it were not that certain questions of great interest are still debated in terms of the theory of value. One such question is the influence of Trade Unions upon the share of labour in the proceeds of industry. . . .
> By and large, the main determinant of differences in prices, say the difference in price between a packet of pins and a motor car, is obviously differences in labour cost (including the labour cost of producing the capital equipment required for the different lines of production). Moreover the movement through time of relative prices is predominantly influenced by changes in relative labour costs. . . . Influences of this kind are in general more important than changes in relative profit margins in determining changes in relative prices. By giving up an untenable claim to complete exactness, the labour theory can establish the right to be considered broadly true and highly important.

But the partisans of an orthodox labour theory of value would probably exaggerate their claims in this respect.

THE IMPORTANCE OF MARXIAN VALUE THEORY AS A THEORY OF INCOME DISTRIBUTION

The catchphrase for the modern appreciation of Marx's value theory was probably originated by Cole, when he wrote (1934, p. 221), 'The Marxian theory of value is a theory, not of prices, but of the social distribution of the resources of production.' As a matter of fact, this view holds good for the theory of surplus value but not for the value theory as such. To measure the social product in 'values' (i.e. socially necessary labour hours) is conceptually possible even if the value added is entirely appropriated by the workers, so that there is no surplus value accruing to capitalists.

It is not a very long step from the thesis of surplus value to the theory of the distribution of income. In this context it does not really matter if Cole, at least in the opinion of Sweezy (1957, p. 990), does not do full justice to Marx in the second volume of his monumental three-volume work (1953). Sweezy argues that 'Cole can see in the first nine chapters of *Capital* . . . nothing but a gigantic exercise in metaphysics, designed to prove something that was obvious from the outset', and imputes to Cole the opinion that 'Marx would have done better to scrap the whole classical approach and adopt the new marginalist theories of Jevons and Menger'. It is doubtful whether Sweezy, in reaching this conclusion, really deals with all aspects of the Cole's work; but it is possible to accept the criticism in so far as he thinks that Cole treated 'Marx's discussion of the relation between values and prices in Volume III of *Capital* [as] a sort of shame-faced admission of the unreality of the theory of Volume I and an attempt to substitute, by the back door as it were, a cost of production theory similar to that expounded by John Stuart Mill'.

Sweezy is of the opinion that Cole's view does not differ so much from that of 'orthodox academic economists'. But he holds that 'The first nine chapters of *Capital*, it is now widely recognized, are not primarily concerned with exchange values or prices in the sense of either classical or neoclassical economics but rather with what today might be called economic sociology.'

Here his opinion is in harmony with that of the outstanding French Marxist philosopher Lefebvre, who goes so far as to assert (1951, p. 78) that Marx did not wish to concede to political economy the right to the title of an autonomous and independent science based upon the examination of economic facts, but in a total view saw it as a historical science dealing with a specific economic and social formation, capitalism, in its structure and development.

Althusser, who disassociates himself (1968, I, pp. 150ff.) from a 'humanistic and historicist' interpretation of Marx's work, has stressed (ibid., p. 113) that Marx in almost all his works 'from *The Poverty of Philosophy* to *Capital* has criticised classical economics for one particular and fundamental reason, namely, that it employs an ahistorical, and apparently eternal, fixed and abstract conception of the economic categories of capitalism'.

Another important French Marxist, Godelier, referring to certain statements in chapter 48 of the third volume of *Capital*, where Marx declares that the main service of classical economics is to trace back to surplus value and consequently to distribution the economic categories of interest and rent, has pointed out (1966, pp. 71–2) that the formation of value and surplus value is ultimately a matter of the 'true, concrete reality of the capitalist system, of the social relations of production' and, in the last resort, of distribution.

In this way, the Marxian conception reveals again the strong influence on Marx of Ricardo, who saw the principal task of economics as the examination of the problem of distribution (Schumpeter, 1947, p. 22). Antoine in his history of macroeconomic doctrines (1953) states (pp. 70ff.) that in the first place Marx dealt with the problem of the distribution of the social product among different classes. Marchal and Lecaillon in the third volume of their monumental complete analysis of the theory of distribution (1958) are also of this opinion (pp. 55–6). They admit that the 'presentation of Marx's theories frequently makes them appear somewhat ambiguous', and go on to say that 'he frequently has capitalists and workers appear in the discussion and one can ask whether, in fact, he is not constructing a theory of the firm'; but from this they proceed to affirm the macroeconomic character of Marx's analysis:

> If one reads the text carefully, one can recognise [that] both persons have simply a representative function: Marx wants to explain the relations between the group of the capitalists as a whole and the group of the labourers as a whole. . . . Böhm-Bawerk, who was completely imbued with microeconomic methodology and who could not imagine that any other was possible, seems to have been disoriented by Marx's approach, and thus committed a serious error with regard to the two themes of the labour theory of value and the theory of surplus value. Both are essentially macroeconomic theories. . . . Böhm-Bawerk, in fact, reconstructs them at the microeconomic level. . . . In the spirit of its author, the purpose of the theory of surplus value is to enumerate the factors which determine the distribution of the social product between capitalists, who pocket the surplus value, as a class, and workers as a class. . . .

THE 'MIXED INTERPRETATION' OF MARX'S VALUE THEORY

Henry Smith has pronounced himself (1962, p. 60) in favour of a 'mixed theory', which means that the creation of social surplus value, or in other words, distribution, is to be explained by value theory: 'Indeed, the theory of surplus value needs no further formulation than the expression of the view that private enjoyment of the usufruct of the non-personal factors of production is undesirable.' In this concept there are ethical elements favoured by Smith but excluded by Marx, mixed with cost elements and the theories of Graziadei.

Smith has argued that the theory of value as developed by Marx in the first volume of *Capital* cannot be a theory of price, and that, as Marx himself stressed, it ought not to be interpreted as such. He answers the question of what the nature of this labour theory of value is by citing three different major interpretations.

The first is equivalent to an orthodox interpretation linked to an attempt to translate it into reality by means of a 'dialectic' method coupled with ethical components. Smith thinks (1962, p. 61) that this interpretation cannot be adopted by economists: 'This view appears to be capable of investigation by the philosopher, psychologist or theologian rather than by the economist.'

The second interpretation is one developed by Dobb (1955, p. 19), and stems, Smith thinks (1962, pp. 59–60), from certain ideas developed by Sorel. According to this interpretation, 'the labour theory of value is a first approximation to a theory of value of the more normal type' – i.e. is an auxiliary construction that is to be considered as a preliminary step to a price theory proper. 'According to this view, the labour theory of value sets forth the distribution of income between social classes, and, moreover, introduces a measuring rod, the amount of labour. This, at a rough approximation, allows us to think in terms of quantities of value.' Smith does not think that this concept is sufficient for an explanation of prices and profits in one line of activity: 'The reason is the one which all economists who have advanced criticism of Marx have placed in the forefront: the impossibility of reconciling a general tendency for profits to become equal with a general tendency for the rate of surplus value to become equal in industries with a different organic composition of capital.' Thus Smith reaches the conclusion that this concept, which is also criticised by 'academic' economists, finally boils down to a theory of distribution.

The third interpretation is one developed by Cole and Antoine. According to this the Marxian concept of labour value does not constitute a theory of price, but is an outright theory of distribution. It is, therefore, closely related to the previous interpretation outlined.

14 The Purpose and Topical Importance of Marx's Value Theory

Marx himself contested the view that his theory of exploitation was to be understood primarily in an ethical manner. In his 'Marginal Notes' on Adorf Wagner's treatise (*Capital*, I, Annex) he denied that the capitalist, as a 'necessary functionary' of capitalist production, 'robs' the worker in any way by enforcing the production of what he claims by Law. He expressed himself similarly in his *Critique of the Gotha Programme*, which was published posthumously in 1894. If, for instance, Schumpeter's 'dynamic entrepreneur' pockets the entire profit from his competitive advantage, this ought to be the reward for the whole 'team' working in his enterprise, because it is this team that has gained the advantage. It is, however, not the profit accruing to an individual, but the existence of profit as a functional category of income within the class system, that really matters.

Marx believed that within the framework of socialisation the working class would be delivered from this category. On the other hand, he did not deny that in a socialist society the social surplus would also have to be used for net investment and suchlike. He also envisaged under the heading of 'administrative costs' the possibility of a 'political' consumption of surplus value by a class of bureaucrats, but he believed that this item could be minimised. For him the transfer of the means of production to society would mean that the decisive aspect of 'self-alienation' would be eliminated.

LABOUR AS THE SOLE FACTOR OF PRODUCTION IN 'ACADEMIC' ECONOMICS

The value theory of Marxism can be summarised in the following way: Marx begins with the assumption that there is only one factor of production. In doing so he finds himself in good company: not only in that of the classical economists, but also in that of the Keynesians. Keynes himself stated that it would be reasonable to asume that in the short term there is only one factor of production, namely labour.

Preiser reminds us (1948, p. 334) that in German 'academic' economics in the early 1930s a similar position was held by Conrad:

> The question whether there is not, in fact, only one factor of production can remain open. Everything depends upon the way the problem is posed. In considering production processes and in answering the question of the size of the share of the different factors of production in the total product, it is certainly useful to maintain the idea of the existence of several co-ordinated factors of production. For a complete theory of income distribution there can, however, only be one single factor of production, namely labour; the others are simply means of production. In this context I completely agree with O. Conrad in his work *Der Mechanismus der Verkehrswirtschaft* [The Mechanism of the Exchange Economy], Jena, 1931, and *Die Todsünde der Nationalökonomie* [The Deadly Sin of Political Economy], Leipzig and Vienna, 1934.

Joan Robinson has refined this point of view by examining the problem (1958, pp. 310–14) in the spirit of dynamic Keynesianism:

> from a long-run point of view, labour and natural resources are the factors of production in the economy as a whole, while capital goods and the time pattern of production are the means by which the factors are deployed. . . . From a short-period point of view it is more convenient to treat labour as the only factor of production, and to regard the stock of concrete capital goods as one element in the technical conditions that determine the productivity of a given quantity of labour. . . . capital (no matter who owns it) is a necessary condition for labour and natural resources to be productive. But it is not a factor of production independent of them.

The value of this single factor of production, in the sense of exchange value, is defined by the provision it makes for its reproduction within the framework of 'socially necessary labour time', considered as the requisite combination of labour and the average social endowment of the means of production.

THE EQUIPMENT AND PRODUCT OF LABOUR

The daily wage of the worker is, therefore, determined by the 'average social product' which a worker produces using an 'average' endowment of machinery. This product determines the price of labour, which, as Hicks has indicated (second edition, 1950, p. 269), may be the point around which other prices fluctuate.

Wherever labour is used with capital equipment that is below the average, its product will be less than average – the average product of the past. On the other hand, where labour is combined with capital equipment above the average, it will have a higher product – the average value of the future. But in both cases labour must receive the average wage corresponding to the average outfit of equipment. Here there operates the law of equal average rates. On the basis of Fourastié (1949, pp. 103 ff.) we may argue as follows. If a hairdresser works with practically no equipment, while a worker at the blast-furnace operates equipment worth millions, both must still receive approximately the same wage, for otherwise no one would become a hairdresser. Certain professions have already disappeared because the customers did not want, or were unable, to stick to this rule – this applies, for instance, to domestic service, although in this case special compensation for 'social de-classing' would have been necessary to reverse the trend.

In this context we may refer to the curious idea that all workers should receive the same wages on condition that they 'buy' their places of employment. This would have the consequence that the most disagreeable places would be cheapest. This is an idea that has been harboured by Dickinson and others.

The average worker with his average value, therefore, produces a product that corresponds to the average price of labour power, and workers who produce a product above or below the average must still, by virtue of the law of equal wages, receive the same wage.

Marx puts no value upon what has been invested in the past, a point of view shared by modern industrial economics. What was invested in machinery is a present from the past. In the calculation of profitability, industrial economics asks only what old installations currently cost with regard to maintenance and operating expenses; capital costs count only in the case of a new installation.

For Marx, existing capital equipment (as reflected by) constant capital, (c) represents economic value only if it has to be replaced or incurs current costs. Thus, the calculation of value means nothing to Marx but the reduction of average wages to average productivity. What remains above or below this level represents more or less value than exists from the point of view of society.

The movement of labour between branches and firms will lead to the equalisation of wages, the direction of movement being determined by whether these units are technically over- or under-capitalised. The optimal equipment will constantly return to the average; the less dynamic is the development, the less will be the difference between values and prices.

Workers employed with average equipment, therefore, determine the average wage even for activities which are worse or better equipped. The degree of equality in wages will be less the more the marginal value of equipment per head exceeds the optimum. There remains the problem of how, according to Marx, the new capital needed to raise productivity is obtained and how it can be remunerated. This can be done by means of a 'basic' or 'minimum' rate of interest, which is to be explained by the degree of exploitation within the framework of 'class monopoly' (according to Graziadei and Preiser). This means in practice that it needs to be calculated on the basis of the full-cost principle, as outlined by Lexis or Hall and Hitch. New capital can also be remunerated by an 'extra surplus value' obtained by the dynamic enterprise that introduces the new machinery. This is the 'advantage' (*Vorsprung*), as Lederer calls it.

When the efforts of a worker are combined with an inadequate quantity of the means of production, the product of that labour does not correspond to the average social product, although it has potentially the same value, for it could be combined in a better way. This is the reason why it still receives approximately the average price of labour, for otherwise the industry or firm concerned could not accommodate it.

THE WORKABILITY OF VALUE THEORY

It has been said that it does not make sense to spend great intellectual effort on a controversy over value theory, as many Marxist economists have done. This, while the more philosophically and sociologically oriented Marxists would disagree with it, is true up to a point, for the entire theoretical framework built up by Marx can be constructed without this element, which is no more than a first working hypothesis. However, it is clear that, especially from the point of view of Marxists, who have always recognised that the classical labour theory of value is inadequate for the analysis of monopolistic conditions, the Marxian value theory is badly in need of a new formulation.

The so-called labour theory of value is essentially static and, in Croce's sense, 'imaginable', i.e. arguable. It was Croce, in his Marxist period, who pointed out that 'exploitation' here signifies the divergence from the situation of the pre-capitalist artisan, who owns his own means of production.

But, for an economic system badly equipped with machinery, the problem of the rationing of the scarce means of production by the rate of interest remains particularly relevant, even if the returns accrue to society. It is therefore rather doubtful whether the labour theory of value still has a part to play in analysis of the problem of the optimum allocation of the means of production in a socialist society. Owing to this, we should not be astonished that a Marxist thinker of the status of Oscar Lange should consider the labour theory of value to be obsolete. He has written (1934–5, pp. 194–5),

Most orthodox Marxists, however, believe that their superiority in understanding the evolution of Capitalism is due to the economic concepts with which Marx worked, i.e. to his using the labour theory of value. They think that the abandonment of the classical labour theory of value in favour of the theory of marginal utility is responsible for the failure of 'bourgeois' economics to explain the fundamental phenomena of capitalist evolution. That they are wrong can be easily shown by considering the economic meaning of the labour theory of value. It is nothing but a static theory of general economic equilibrium. . . . To be exact, however, it really holds precisely only in a capitalist exchange economy of small producers each of whom owns his means of production (an exchange economy composed of small self-working artisans and peasant farmers, for instance; Marx calls it *einfache Waren-produktion* [simple reproduction]. In a capitalist economy it requires, as Marx has shown himself in the third volume of *Das Kapital*, certain modifications due to differences in the organic composition of capital (i.e. the ratio of the capital invested in capital goods to the capital invested in payment of wages) in different industries. . . . Thus the labour theory of value has no qualities which would make it, from the Marxist point of view, superior to the modern more elaborate theory of economic equilibrium. . . . Thus the labour theory of value cannot possibly be the source of the superiority of Marxian over 'bourgeois' economics in explaining the phenomena of economic *evolution*. In fact, the adherence to an antiquated form of the theory of economic equilibrium is the cause of the inferiority of Marxian economics in many fields. . . .

This is a rather crushing judgement by one of the leading exponents of Marxism, and it can be linked to the laconic statement by Schumpeter (1947, p. 25) that it is incorrect to call the labor theory of value *'wrong*. In any case it is dead and buried.' This judgement, however, would appear to be too harsh and one-sided.

THE PRACTICAL IMPORTANCE OF VALUE THEORY FOR MODERN ECONOMICS

Joan Robinson has emphasised that one should not lightheartedly renounce consideration of value terms in the sense of labour value theory, for important real-life transactions are still carried out by applying the language of value theory in its classical sense. To start with, this is true of wage increases, especially in a boom. In fact, employers, and journalists of similar outlook, curiously seem to reason in a boom almost in the spirit of Marx: from their point of view, wage increases, i.e. increases in labour value, are the decisive cost element. Furthermore, modern investigations of relative prices are more and more being conducted in labour values, although expressed in monetary terms. For instance, Fourastié (1949, pp. 108–9) establishes a hairdresser's wage or a labourer's wage as a measure of value in which all other values are expressed. The advantage of such reasoning is that one obtains a kind of basic wage, which may be variable over time but is relatively constant in representing the wage of one who works (almost) without machinery.

> Hourly wages are one of the most important cost elements within the framework of costs of the tertiary sector, for these hourly wages determine the prices of typical tertiary sectors. . . . These are *ex definitione* the sectors where technical progress has little or no influence. . . . There is, therefore, no divergence between the price in the typical tertiary sector and the price of labour per hour, for, *ex definitione*, in the tertiary sector the same labour time is always required to provide the same service. . . . The hourly wage is a tertiary price!

Thus it can be said that in practical life, in view of the increasing importance of the tertiary sector in developed economies, the labour theory of value is experiencing a joyful renaissance.

On the other hand, it must be asked whether value theory as such is really necessary in order to underpin the theory of surplus value. It can, of course, be argued that, in order to be able to establish a fixed relationship between labour effort, v (expressed in wages), and surplus value, s, Marx required a value theory that had its origin in labour alone. Otherwise, he would only have been able to establish a relationship between the total costs incurred per period – i.e., constant capital, c (capital and raw material costs) + variable capital, v (wage costs) – and surplus value. Many of his other conclusions, especially the 'tendency of the rate of profit to fall' (explained by the increasing 'organic composition of capital' – in other words, by an increasingly capital-intensive composition of costs), would thus have become untenable.

This line of argument, however, seems to be somewhat dubious. It is true that Marx's 'rate of surplus value' corresponds to the ratio between v and s and is intended to establish that 'dead labour', i.e. fixed capital and stocks of raw material, does not create surplus value, but serves only to reproduce its own value. Nevertheless, Marx implicitly assumes a certain ratio between surplus value and total or 'constant' capital as soon as he examines the consequences for the rate of profit, should an 'increasing organic composition of capital' be counteracted by a 'rising rate of surplus value'. In this context there arises the possibility of the existence of several different rates of surplus value in different activities. This is a possibility that Marx mentions only in a few passages in *Capital* (for instance, II, ch. 8, and III, ch. 3).

A reading of the third volume of *Capital* would suggest that Marx sometimes implicitly assumes that the rate of surplus value is different in different branches of production. For instance, he says in chapter 8, 'In the present chapter we assume that the intensity of labour exploitation, and therefore the rate of surplus-value and the length of the working-day, are the same in all the spheres of production.' Indeed, this could mean that elsewhere in the volume Marx considers it to be the normal case for the rate of surplus value to vary from branch to branch. If so, Joan Robinson's recommendation would have been anticipated by Marx himself.

Basically, the rate of surplus value is nothing other than the division of value added between capitalists and labourers. It is only a question of whether this division is influenced by the fact that in some firms and branches the use of capital and, therefore, the share of capital costs in total costs are larger than in others. Marx certainly wanted to consider the rate of surplus value as a macroeconomic phenomenon. However, in addition to its bearing on the problem of the share of labour in the social product, it possesses a microeconomic element.

In fact, we do not have a particular term in economics denoting the share of the individual worker in the social product, or, in other words, we are not able to represent in real values the development of the share of the individual worker in the social product, taking into consideration the share of workers as a whole in the total number of income receivers. However, a move in this direction is evident in the calculation of the 'real wage position of the worker' in the annual report of the Expert Committee for the Investigation of General Economic Development, in the Federal Republic of Germany.

It is true that Marx considers interest only as a pure 'problem of the price of money capital' and not as a general economic cost factor. Nevertheless, higher capital costs entail consequences even for him, because they bring about a tendency to increase the rate of surplus value. This, in turn, is conditioned by the fact that the increasing capital-intensity leads to redundancy of labour and, therefore, tends to exercise a downward influence on the share of labour in total value added, while at the same time increasing the share of capital in the social product only to decrease it later. The final result of all this is that capital does after all receive at least a temporary reward proportionate to the increase in what Marx calls constant capital; this is ultimately a consequence of labour redundancy and unemployment, and it is brought about in a roundabout way *via* the social distribution process.

It can therefore be said that by means of a detour we arrive at the result that the increasing 'organic composition of capital' or, in modern terms, the 'intensity of capital costs', i.e. a rising share of capital in total costs, may lead to an increase of the rate of surplus value. An interest payment will be ensured for the capitalists, and therefore the question of whether a fixed relationship can be assumed only between v and s, and possibly also between $c + v$ and s, becomes superfluous.

Interest arises through the workings of the economic forces of distribution and through weakness of the sole factor of production, labour. But recognition of this does not alter the fact that the production factor must share the value added in society with the 'power factor', capital ownership, according to a new formula as soon as the owners of capital by an ingenious use of 'dead' capital (which is, after all, an instrument of market power) exert pressure on a production factor so that it becomes less scarce. Here, unmistakably, we approach the market-power theory developed by Graziadei.

We must therefore ask, with Croce, whether the whole process will not backfire as soon as the constant capital (in other words, the equipment that has to be written off in c) loses part of its real value, either in a general crisis or because of excess capacity in certain lines of activity in individual firms. The answer is not easy. It is true that in the long run the surplus capital will lead to a relative improvement in the market position of the sole factor of production, labour power. In the short run, however, unemployed capital equipment also means unemployed labour and this need not bring about a return to the old rate of surplus value.

Joan Robinson once said (1949, pp. 15–16) that we are not obliged to assume a rigid relationship between s and v. Nor is it required for the whole economy over time or in comparing branches or firms. After all, the hypothesis of such a rigid rate of surplus value is nothing else but a supplementary construction, as Marx himself sometimes indicated (for instance, in *Capital*, III, ch. 8, cited earlier). In fact, Marx, by recognising, in the context of the tendency of the rate of profit to fall, the possibility of a change in the rate of surplus value, renounced the general applicability of this construction. In this way he assumed that the distribution of the net social product or, in other terms, the global added value or the national income, might also be changed.

The theory of 'monopolistic competition' has demonstrated that in labour-intensive sectors, such as retailing, or in trades such as construction, the preferences of customers can lead to very high rates of profit, even where all producers have similar cost curves, so that they are all to a certain extent 'marginal producers'. It can well be imagined that capital moves into such activities because there is a chance of obtaining 'advantage profits' or 'intra-marginal profits' by means of hitherto neglected opportunities for mechanisation and automation (for instance, self-service).

On the other hand, it is entirely possible that the continuing technical possibility of an even-higher degree of mechanisation in the already highly mechanised lines of activity, where the marginal producer may well no longer earn a profit, may counteract the signal of high absolute rates of surplus value or profits in the wage-intensive sector. In this case, capital remains in the already-mechanised activities or flows into them.

A certain 'equalisation of the rates of profit' through capital inflow to the service sector, and, in modern times, even into the agricultural sector, might speak in favour of the existence of the Marxian process of the equalisation of profits. However, the ubiquity of monopolistic and oligopolistic elements, as indicated by the Marxian theory of concentration, makes it doubtful how far such an equalisation is still of topical importance in modern economic life, which, after all, is characterised by a basic inequality in the rates of profit.

At any rate, we do not need the theory of labour value to carry out an analysis of all these conditions. It seems safe to conclude that many Marxists have overrated the labour-value component in its importance for the total Marxian concept of economics, and that, moreover, this total concept can be derived in a different way. The theory (also Marxian) of the profit to be gained from technical advantages ('relative' surplus value) overshadows the importance attributed to absolute surplus value by the labour theory of value. Besides, it is far from clear whether either Marx or Ricardo ever fully entertained a labour theory of value applicable to capitalism.

Part IV
Price and Cost Theory

15 'Academic' Economics and Marxian Capital and Price Theory

THE NOTION OF CAPITAL AS A FLOW: COST AND CAPITAL

The relationship between surplus value and capital is the problem that leads us to an examination of the Marxian theory of capital. The input of capital is seen by Marx essentially as a flow. This way of approaching the problem on an input basis leads us directly to price theory. Alexander Gray, who examines Marx very critically, has said (1936, pp. 314–15), 'In Marx, as indeed throughout Marxian literature, capital has a meaning to which the whole world, outside Marxian colleges, is a complete stranger. For Marx, it is not everyone who owns wealth who is a capitalist. . . . A capitalist is one who, being himself idle, lives entirely on surplus value extracted from workers in his employment.'

In this context he quotes Karl Kautsky, who in his *Economic Teachings of Karl Marx* defines capital as the 'value that produces surplus value'. Gide and Rist, however, in their classic history of economic doctrines (1921) have stressed (pp. 500–1) that only part of capital has this function:

> Taken by itself capital is, of course, sterile, for it is understood that labour is the sole source of value. But labour cannot produce unless it consumes a certain proportion of capital, and it is important that we should understand something of the combination of capital and labour.
>
> Marx distinguishes between two kinds of capital. The first serves for the upkeep of the working-class population, either in the way of wages or through direct subsistence. The older economists referred to it as the 'wages fund', and Marx calls it 'variable capital'. If this kind of capital does not directly take part in production, it is this fund, after all, when consumed by labour, that begets value and the surplus which is attached to it.
>
> That other kind of capital which directly assists the productive activity of labour by supplying it with machinery, tools, etc., Marx calls 'constant capital'. . . . It simply produces the equivalent of its value, which is the sum total of all the values absorbed during the time when it was being produced.

99

This constant capital is evidently the crystallised product of labour, and its value, like that of any other product, is determined solely by the number of hours of labour it has taken to produce. . . . The economists refer to this as depreciation, and everyone knows that depreciation implies no profits at any rate.

In this context Gide and Rist do not make it quite clear that the raw materials and other ancillary inputs, which they mention only in passing, are part of constant capital in Marxian analysis. The writing-off of inventories of raw materials and other ancillary inputs (for instance, semi-manufactured goods) is not a very far cry from the idea of depreciation of equipment.

The formula $c + v + s$ basically denotes only the addition (in 'value units') of the elements of what are called 'purchases' in our modern 'systems of value added' (value added is defined as consisting of the two elements wages, v, and surplus value or share of profits, s).

Behind this veil, however, there is the further question of how far capital as such ought to earn a remuneration in the form of interest, or whether it is a 'free good' (Marshall, 1925, p. 587).

THE RATE OF SURPLUS VALUE *VERSUS* THE RATE OF PROFIT

The first thing to be said is that surplus value arises only from variable capital. Stavenhagen states in his great history of economic doctrines (1957, p. 145) that

in a capital mix, comprised overwhelmingly of variable capital, a higher rate of profit must result than in a combination where constant capital prevails. The free play of competition will, however, distribute the volume of surplus value over the whole of co-operating capital, constant as well as variable, so that an average rate of profit is obtained. This has the further consequence that the production price of a good deviates from its original labour value. . . .

It is at this point that not only Böhm-Bawerk's criticism but a whole flood of criticism of Marx begins. The theory of the 'equalisation of the rates of profit', which leads to a deviation from labour values, was fully worked out especially in the third volume of *Capital*. Even those members of the 'academic' camp who are admirers of Marx have thought that Marx here completely compromised his basic teachings, making them appear absurd, and that his hand 'must have trembled before the inexorable act of destruction' (Loria, 1890, p. 78).

Böhm-Bawerk was of the same opinion, but expressed himself more soberly (1921, pp. 394–5):

> Nor does Marx neglect to point out with all possible emphasis the syllogism that the amount of surplus which can be produced with a capital can be in direct proportion to the variable part of the capital, but not to the total capital. . . . And it follows further, that equal capitals must produce unequal quantities of surplus value, if they differ as to their composition, with respect to relative amounts of constant and variable capital. This is what Marx calls 'their organic composition'. . . . if the degree of exploitation is equal or the rate of surplus value is equal, then capitals of varying organic composition must yield unequal 'rates of return'. Capitals which are of such composition that the variable portion predominates must bear a higher 'rate of return'. . . . But experience says that, because of the operation of the law of the levelling of returns, capitals will in the long run bear equal 'rates of return' without regard to their composition. Accordingly there is a manifest conflict between that which is, and that which, according to the Marxian doctrine, ought to be.
>
> Marx himself was not unaware of the existence of this conflict. In his first volume he had already made laconic mention of it as 'merely apparent', and referred his readers for his solution to the parts of his system which were to come later. [Volume III] . . . contains a detailed discussion of the problem, but of course no solution. He merely corroborates the irreconcilable contradiction in what proved to be an abandonment of the doctrine in his first volume – veiled, unacknowledged, glossed over, to be sure – but still an abandonment.
>
> . . . He explicitly admits that in reality, and because of competition, the rate of return of capitals, quite irrespective of their organic composition, is levelled off, and necessarily must be levelled off to a uniform average rate. . . . the law of the exchange of commodities provides that they are sold at their prices of production, and that the latter, as a matter of principle, cannot coincide with their values!

Stavenhagen (1957, p. 145) gives a definition of this production price: 'The production price of a commodity, according to the Marxian theory of prices, is then derived from the costs that actually enter into production. These costs are constant capital (c), variable capital (v) and the profit derived from this process of production (p).' Constant and variable 'capital' together comprise the 'cost price' in the Marxian system.

EQUALITY IN THE RATES OF PROFIT

The question now arises, how can there come about an 'average' rate of profit that will establish the link between the macroeconomic and the microeconomic spheres?

The rate of surplus value indicates the share of capitalists in value added or in the net social product. The macroeconomic rate of profit is equivalent to the ratio between the total sum of surplus value and the value of the social capital stock, viewed by Marx as flow magnitudes. But how is the rate of profit determined in individual activities at the microeconomic level in an overall social context?

Piettre has characterised the Marxian mechanism of the 'equalisation of the rates of profit' in the following way (1962, p. 56):

> In the first stage we should experience the rather unexpected fact that the most well equipped firms would be those where profit would be the lowest. It would follow from this in the second stage that capital would have a tendency to flow away from those firms which are most well equipped in machinery, in order to move into activities of a more artisan character [a better term would be 'wage-intensive'!] provided that their profit rate is, at least for the time being, somewhat higher. . . . But this flow of capital provokes an excess of production in the latter, and this over-production obliges them to lower their prices. . . . On the other hand, the most well equipped firms lose their capital and are, therefore, required to raise their prices in order to bring them to the average level. . . . In the third stage, therefore, the workings of competition bring about an average rate of profit. . . .

There are several problems here. First, there is the problem of the so-called 'transformation' from values into prices. We do not deal with the stock of capital, but rather with the share in costs of capital, raw materials and labour, seen as sums of income – another flow magnitude. So far we still remain within the framework of the 'static' theory of price.

Second, Piettre points to an empirical phenomenon: that capital is attracted by activities that have not yet been mechanised. The reason for such a movement cannot be that 'absolute' surplus values are higher in these activities, for, according to Marx, this would have been true only in a pre-capitalist society. On the contrary, one has to start from the hypothesis that in such non-mechanised activities there are still many possibilities for obtaining 'relative' surplus value. Advantages afforded by mechanisation create the position of 'temporary monopoly' with 'extra profits', and this is the reason why capital flows into such non-mechanised branches. We are here in the realm of 'dynamic' price theory.

Third, if the capital flow is of normal size, it can lead to a reduction in prices in the activity concerned. If the capital flow exceeds the normal dimensions, it will lead to over-production. In this way, *via* capital-movement and capital-market problems, we are led to questions of the business cycle.

16 'Static' Price and Cost Theory in Marx's Work

Marx's price theory is, properly speaking, to be found in the third volume of *Capital*. In the first and second volumes Marx considers the price structure more or less as given.

In his first and even in the second volume, Marx starts from the hypothesis that there are no differences between different industries in their 'organic composition of capital' or their capital intensity. The rift between values and prices does not yet appear. As long as the question of the 'organic composition of capital' is not debated, there is no problem of the movement of capital between different industries, and no problem of the 'equalisation of the rates of profit'.

It might even, perhaps, be supposed that the boundary between 'static' and 'dynamic' price theory is to be found in Marx's work where there are not yet capital flows. It seems that this is a sort of 'heroic simplification', which avoids discussion of dynamic circumstances for as long as the problems of the capital market, of financing and even of credit are not touched upon. Nevertheless, it must be pointed out that the hypothesis that all industries have the same 'organic composition of capital' (i.e. cost structure) does not mean that the permanent capital stock will be the same everywhere.

Joan Robinson has said (1954) that Marx's price theory as expounded in the third volume of *Capital* is really the price theory of everybody – that is, that there are no deep differences between it and other price theories current in the nineteenth century. Under certain assumptions it is even possible to formulate the idea that the theory of surplus value already contains a theory of pricing, not only in the macroeconomic but even in the microeconomic sphere.

The fixed relationship between v and s, i.e. between variable capital and surplus value, can be considered as the result of a price calculation. In this case surplus value appears as a proportional mark-up on the sum of wages by way of a 'calculation of an additional rate of profit' (*Zuschlagskalkulation*). In other words, surplus value is calculated as a margin to be allotted to wage costs per unit of output. This would also explain Marx's famous reference to the method of calculation of the small artisan. He calculates his profit with reference to his own labour effort, i.e. to the wage he would have to pay a journeyman to do the work that he himself carries out without any additional help. This theory would explain the proportionality between *v* and *s* by means of a full-cost calculation, i.e. where the margin is calculated on the sum of costs. In this way we approach the traditions of German industrial economics. There can be no doubt that Marx anticipated a number of pricing elements as developed by industrial economics.

ITEMS OF COST CALCULATION IN MARX

This is especially true for the concept of the entrepreneur's wage. The entrepreneur, according to Marx (*Theories*, III, p. 490)

> appears as *working capitalist* in contrast to himself as *capitalist*, and, further, as *worker* in contrast to himself as mere *owner*. . . . *Industrial profit* is resolved into labour, not into *unpaid* labour of other people but into *wage-labour*, into wages for the capitalist, who in this case is placed into the same category as the wage-worker and is merely a more highly paid worker, just as in general wages vary greatly.

The opinion expressed by Alexander Gray seems, therefore, somewhat one-sided.

The same is true of the rate of interest as a category for calculation. In the same context Marx distinguishes (ibid., p. 508) very sharply between

> interest [which] here is declared to be remuneration for the fact that money, etc., is employed as capital; it therefore arises from capital as such, which is remunerated for its quality *qua* capital. . . . *Interest* is only part of profit, the part which is paid to the owner of capital by the industrial, functioning capitalist. Since he can appropriate surplus labour only by means of capital (money, commodities), etc., he has to hand over a portion of it to the man who makes capital available to him. And the lender, who wants to enjoy the advantages of money as capital without letting it function as capital, can do this only by being content with a part of the profit. They are in fact co-partners, one of them being the juridical owner of the capital, and the other, while he employs it, the economic owner. . . . Capital is bought (that is, it is lent at interest) before it is paid for. Money functions here as means of payment as it does in relation to labour-power, etc. The price of capital – i.e., interest – enters therefore just as much into the advances made by the industrialist (and into the advances made to himself where a man is operating with his own capital). . . .

In this context the opportunity cost of the rate of interest on internal funds is clearly enunciated. As an economic category for the individual interest payable on internal funds it appears quite clearly in the Marxian system as the price for 'the disposition of capital', as Cassell would say. There is, undoubtedly, a certain analogy between the terminology used by Marx and that used by Cassell (see Montersano, 1971, p. 467).

The third category of item that must be calculated according to industrial economics, the risk premium, has also been clearly developed by Marx (*Grundrisse*, p. 722):

> Risk, which plays a role for the economists in the determination of profit – it can obviously play none in the surplus gain, because the creation of surplus value is not increased thereby, and it is possible that capital incurs risk in the *realisation* of this surplus value – is the danger that the capital does not pass through the different phases of circulation, or remains fixated in one of them. . . . A part of the surplus gain appears to the capitalist only as a compensation for the risk he runs so as to make more money; a risk which can lead to the loss of the presupposed value itself.

These statements reappear in various passages and clearly indicate that it is quite wrong to assume that Marx did not recognise the entrepreneur's effort as such. The contrary is true: Marx is one of the first who clearly distinguishes between the functions of capital-owner and working entrepreneur. Essential elements of price formation in the sense of modern industrial economics were clearly known to Marx.

FIXED CAPITAL AS A FLOW OR STOCK MAGNITUDE

Joan Robinson sketches (1951; 1966, p. 146) the price theory of Marx developed in the third volume of *Capital*. She stresses that the terminology is difficult to understand, because Marx starts from the idea of a 'capital flow' instead of from that of a 'capital stock'. The notion of 'variable capital' comprises the annual wage bill of the enterprise as well as the circulating capital locked in at any time to finance the wage costs of current work. 'Constant' capital, however, is defined by Marx in two ways: as meaning, first, the annual wear and tear of fixed physical capital, and, secondly, capital comprising raw materials used in manufacture and expressed as stocks. According to Joan Robinson, Marx often loses sight of the difference between these two definitions. In saying this, she overlooks the fact that Marx eliminated the difference by assuming that total fixed capital included raw materials and ancillary inputs, which he assumed turned over once in a year.

Incidentally, Marx has in various places emphasised the difference between stocks and flows. He even devoted three chapters (14–16) of the second volume of *Capital* to the problem of the turnover period. As a general rule, however, he examined only flow items. Stock items, which he calls fixed capital, and its wear and tear (depreciation), he deals with in a paragraph of volume II (ch. 20, § xi).

THE PROBLEM OF CAPITAL TURNOVER

Generally speaking, the numerical examples found in Marx's work and in that of his critics are applicable only if it is assumed that the entire capital is turned over once per time period: 'the annual rate of surplus-value coincides only in one single case with the real rate of surplus-value which expresses the degree of exploitation of labour; namely in the case when the advanced capital is turned over only once a year' (*Capital*, II, ch. 16, p. 308).

A low figure for constant capital does not necessarily mean that the activity in question is not capital-intensive. On the contrary, it can mean that capital is turned over particularly slowly in this activity, so that it is in reality quite capital-intensive. By contrast, in activities with a high figure for constant capital, it is quite possible that capital turnover proceeds very rapidly. In Marx's examples (see *Capital*, III, ch. 3, p. 68) the different sectors indicated can be considered either as industries or as firms. The rate of profit can be increased by an increase in the turnover of capital (i.e. by a more rational use of capital); by a decrease in c through a lengthening of the life cycle of installations as a consequence of technical progress; or, finally, by an increase in c through a decrease in the turnover of capital, which is equivalent to capital-deepening. In all these considerations we enter the realm of economies in the use of constant capital, as developed by Marx in the chapter 5 of the volume III of *Capital*. These questions concern the saving of capital as a consequence of technical progress, a problem which can be properly treated only within dynamic theory.

Within static theory, a rather simple pricing theory results from all these considerations. Marx assumes that the wage rate is the same in all industries. (It is true that he sometimes admits exceptions to this rule.) If prices are 'normal', there will then be a uniform rate of profit for all industries. The prices for the output of one period are, therefore, equivalent to costs for the depreciation of capital (wear and tear), i.e. depreciation caused in the course of time or through the intensity of use, plus raw materials and ancillary inputs plus wages plus a profit margin, 'in accordance with the general rate applicable to fixed and circulating capital'.

This, according to Joan Robinson, is more or less the same as Marshall's theory of the normal long-run price, or a 'production-costs theory' in the sense of Sombart, although with one peculiarity – namely, the absence of 'the complications of diminishing and increasing returns'. This explains why Samuelson classified Marx as 'Ricardo without diminishing returns', on the grounds that Marx used fixed coefficients in his calculation of the combination of factors of production. Both statements appear to be somewhat doubtful. First, in Marx's theory of production price we certainly do find a concept of increasing and diminishing returns. For instance, in his passages on differential rent (see *Capital*, III, ch. 43, pp. 680, 715–6) Marx speaks of the 'decreasing fertility of successive capital investments' and of 'equal, decreasing and increasing productivity'. Furthermore, the fact that Marx often speaks of large-scale production, which evidently means 'economies of scale', contradicts Samuelson's thesis (see *Capital*, III, ch. 5). Secondly, the Marxian theory of profit is clearly based on the hypothesis that the combination of factors can be changed, i.e. that more and more fixed capital will be used per worker, or that capital costs increase relatively to labour costs because the input mix changes.

We cannot discuss in detail the fact that in modern theory a certain sceptical attitude prevails with regard to the usual presentation of increasing or decreasing returns, as they appear in decreasing or increasing cost curves. This attitude applies to marginal analysis as such (see Kühne, 1971, p. 11), as well as to conditions that arise when the zone of increasing absolute returns is passed (see Tangrü, 1966, pp. 484ff.).

Abstracting from raw materials and other ancillary inputs and ignoring the capital locked up in v for the wage bill, the formula $c + v + s$ as a measure of turnover (in value terms) could conceal behind the same magnitude of c very different capital stocks, if the formula is applied over the period of a year.

Marx eliminates the difficulty implied in the existence of a stock of fixed capital, by assuming (*Capital*, III, ch. 13, p. 255) that 'capital turns over once a year' (here he evidently is talking about a capital stock). His rate of profit is based on a cost formula; it represents not a percentage of turnover, but a margin over and above the sum of costs, i.e. sum of profits: sum of costs, or, if total costs $= k$, and turnover $= t$, $(t - k)/k$. In other words, the period is chosen in such a way that all fixed costs, in the modern sense of the term, are turned into variable costs.

If we simplify our analysis by postulating that c only represents depreciation of fixed assets and of stocks of raw and auxiliary materials – or, in other words, turnover minus value added – and if we ignore cash held for the payment of wages, we have to admit that a lower share of c in what Marx calls the 'cost price' by no means implies that the industry is less capital-intensive in the modern sense than others, for the capital stock can be very considerable, if at the same time the annual capital turnover is very slow. On the other hand, a high share of c in the 'cost price' or in the total of $c + v$ may simply camouflage a low stock of fixed assets. To this extent the Marxian notion of 'organic composition of capital' is apt to lead modern observers astray, if the mistake is made of taking it as capital-intensity.

Any such simplification will provoke criticism, but it helps to clarify the issue. A deeper analysis would have to consider differential rates of capital turnover (or different rates of depreciation) for various fixed assets, and would regard raw and auxiliary materials not as the running-down of an inventory, but as current consumption, as would be the case with wage payments.

The confusion between Marxian and modern terminology arises principally from the fact that what Marx calls 'capital' or 'capital advanced' has been dubbed 'outlay' by modern industrial economists. Furthermore, the Marxian value calculation complicates the issue by introducing macroeconomic aspects into the business administration routine. After all, the sum of wages, v, in the Marxian sense is not the outlay on wages in the business sense, but the provision of the socially necessary labour time required to produce the wage goods necessary for workers' 'consumption'. Besides, we must not forget that this notion of 'socially necessary labour time' is subject to an upward trend. As soon as one looks at the situation from a macroeconomic viewpoint, one is justified in leaving aside the share of raw materials and so on, as was shown above.

The mixture of flows and stocks in the Marxian turnover formula, i.e. in the 'cost price' formula, has led to interminable discussions. Marx certainly recognised the importance of the fixed-cost concept. He returns to it several times in volume II of *Capital*, devotes a whole section of the book (eleven chapters) to these problems and 'simplifies' his calculations by assuming all the time that the turnover period for fixed capital is equal to one (depreciation takes one year).

Engels thought that the problem had not found a real solution in Marx's writings, and therefore added chapter 4 in his final edition of volume III of *Capital*; in so doing he put the main emphasis on the concrete calculation of the rate of profit and the rate of surplus value. Nevertheless, there still remains a gap in the reasoning.

In this context, we must stress that Marx – especially in his analysis of the circular flow and of growth, which is contained in his famous discussion of 'reproduction schemes', repeatedly refers to the problem of fixed assets and to capital as a *stock* magnitude. This does not entail the formal introduction of a capital stock into his analysis. This failure makes it extremely difficult to calculate a capital coefficient in the modern sense.

In chapter 20 of volume II, Marx speaks in section xi of the 'replacement of fixed capital'. He mentions 'such parts of fixed capital . . . whose life is longer than one year'. In the same context he cautions against the inclusion of repair costs in the permanent capital stock. We may therefore conclude that he thinks that they ought to be covered out of current receipts as part of running costs.

He is here harking back to some of his own most striking discoveries, to what is now called (in Germany) the 'Lohmann–Ruchti effect', i.e. dynamic financing of net investment out of depreciation funds. His discovery of this phenomenon is announced in some letters to Engels, and he emphasises, 'The renewal of the means of production must continually take place.'

In discussing all this, his interest always lies in monetary or cash-holding problems; he does not deal directly with the problem of depreciation. It is regrettable that his letters of 1862 and 1867 were not introduced into *Capital*.

Both Marx and Engels tried, in their treatment of the depreciation problem within the framework of their theory of capital turnover, to avoid any discussion of the notion of time as an influence on cost. Their reason was no doubt that they feared that in recognising the time dimension they would have to readmit by the back door that very rate of profit as the mystical 'remuneration of capital' that they had successfully kicked out of the front door. They did not, however, see that the rate of interest would have to be reintroduced into the calculation, under the guise of the 'average rate of profit', when it came to an analysis of industrial reality. In such an analysis, one identifies oneself with the point of view of the individual capitalist business, in which it is virtually impossible to escape from the rate of interest as a microeconomic category.

So far, all calculations of the rate of surplus value that have been carried out at plant level have suffered from the same weakness – namely, that to use at the microeconomic level a macroeconomic entity such as the rate of surplus value, which reflects the distribution of national income between capitalists and workers, seems a contradiction in terms. If this concept is to be used to denote the division of value added at plant level, one must at least take into account the possible appearance of external loan capital, which will tend to inflate the share of fixed costs in constant capital the more roundabout is the process of production, or – in Marx's language – the more slowly capital is turned over, and the higher is the average rate of profit in an economy, which in turn will determine the rate of interest, which is but a reflection of the rate of profit.

Engels, in his attempt (in his chapter 4 inserted into *Capital*, III) at simplifying the turnover problem, examined only a case where fixed capital was turned over once per year. In this context, it was perhaps pardonable to neglect the rate of interest; but Engels overlooked the fact that the rate of profit which finally resulted for an individual enterprise would depend on the average rate of profit, which has to appear as a rate of interest in the depreciation of fixed assets, with proper allowance having been made in the average rate of profit for 'windfall profits'.

MEASURING SURPLUS VALUE IN AN INDIVIDUAL FIRM

In this context, Engels applies the concept of surplus value in a manner which fortunately even the most orthodox Marxists have not followed in later specific calculations. Marx normally calculated the rate of surplus value as a phenomenon of macroeconomic distribution, i.e. as the ratio of the sum of the profits made during one year and the sum of wages paid during the same year. Engels, however, established a ratio between the sum of profits at a yearly rate and the cash held for weekly wage payments. The latter calculation results in an absurdly high rate of surplus value of 1307 9/13 per cent, as compared with a rate of profit of 33·28 per cent, which Engels himself qualified as abnormally high, admitting that it probably did not apply over a whole year. (Engels in *Capital*, III, ch. 4, p. 95.)

Now, Engels could appeal to the somewhat awkward terminology used by Marx in the second volume of *Capital*. There (ch. 16, p. 304) Marx talks about such a calculation of surplus value as a ratio of profits to the cash stock required for wage payments ('variable capital'), and used the term 'annual rate of surplus value', as opposed to the 'real rate of surplus value', which shows the division of value added over the period of one year.

Here, the misuse of the term 'capital' to denote simultaneously two different concepts – on the one hand, costs or cash flow, and, on the other, cash holding or assets – takes its toll with a vengeance.

The distinction between the 'annual' and 'real' rate of surplus value has not been maintained in modern Marxist industrial economics: on the contrary, Marxist economists have (quite reasonably) avoided confusion by retaining only the second formula. In his examples in chapter 4 of volume III, Engels deals cursorily with the problem of fixed costs. The rate of profit in his calculations remains independent of the lifetime of fixed capital:

$$p' = \frac{s}{c_f + c_z + v}$$

where c_f = depreciation of (constant) fixed capital, and c_z = current consumption of (constant) circulating capital (stocks of raw materials, auxiliary materials, and so on).

In this calculation, it does not matter whether fixed capital is amortised in a few years or over a longer period, for it is subject to straight-line depreciation without the imputation of interest.

Engels combines c and v in C and proceeds to calculate the annual rate of surplus value, in the sense of Marx's terms in chapter 16 of volume II, of *Capital*. He thus arrives at a rate of surplus value s', ascertained on the basis of situation in each turnover period, s/v, and multiplies this by n (the number of turnover periods). He then says that the annual rate of profit is $p' = s'n(v/C)$.

A Yugoslav economist, Bajt, has suggested in a recent article (1970, pp. 371–4) that has found favour with Samuelson that v be multiplied by n as well. Bajt refers to Bortkiewicz, who had shown that, in the context of the transformation problem, the influence that the various turnover periods for capital exercise on deviations of production prices from values is similar to that exercised by the organic composition of capital.

The so-called 'annual rate of surplus value' signifies nothing more than a ratio between the sum of profits (or surplus value) realised in one year and what Bajt calls 'invested variable capital': the latter corresponds more or less to cash holdings for the purpose of paying wages. This, as Engels admits is a most elusive concept, as is quite understandable; for cash is held not for just one particular purpose, but for transaction requirements generally, in the Keynesian sense.

The notion of an 'annual rate' appears reasonable only if one also multiplies v by the turnover coefficient n, but then one obtains the same result as in the case of the 'real rate'! This gives us the ratio of the sum of profits to the sum of wages on an annual basis. The only advantage in this is that seasonal fluctuations are eliminated.

Most Marxists, therefore, in their practical calculations, have used not Engel's 'annual rate', but the 'real rate of surplus value', to denote the division of value added over a year. This has been done in, for instance, studies by Hufschmid (1971, pp. 58ff.) and by the Institute for Marxist Studies and Research at Frankfurt, headed by Dieter Schmidt (1971). Hufschmid's study, however, has been attacked by Himmelmann (1974) for including taxes and the salaries of office staff in the surplus, and the same author objects to the second study cited because it includes overhead and marketing costs in surplus value.

Bajt has reported that similar difficulties have been encountered in socialist countries in attempts to derive Marxian 'production prices' and 'values'. It is true that 'surplus value' in the original sense is supposed not to exist in these countries, where the notion has been replaced by that of the 'social fund for administration, education, science, culture, health and the care of the aged'! Even if the notion of cash reserves is clarified, the problem of how to deal with depreciation and the time factor in the Marxian system is not solved, and there remains also the question of fixed costs.

CASH HOLDING AND THE PROBLEM OF INTEREST

The problem of cash holding in business has two different aspects, which Marx deals with in a number of chapters of *Capital* and in several letters. There is first of all the aspect of the cash requirements or liquidity of the whole economy, and secondly the aspect of depreciation or reinvestment at plant level. Both have to be considered in the context of growth and in microeconomic and macroeconomic terms.

With regard to cash holdings from a macroeconomic point of view, Marx analyses the financial aspect and says that within a certain time period in the course of selling the product, even before the need to replace assets becomes evident, a 'plethora' of money capital can occur, if equipment becomes more quickly obsolescent. In this context, Marx comes very near to a dynamic concept of depreciation in his global view of the economy.

In practice, all this can only mean that Marx assumes that liquid funds must become redundant in greater quantities the larger the once-for-all replacement is. (See *Capital*, II ch. 15, pp. 279–82.) He seems to imagine that cash would be set free if only renewal at the plant level would occur more rapidly – i.e. whenever the growth of the enterprise speeds up. We shall deal with this problem later. What is important here is that Marx saw the possibility that cash provisions for depreciation could become available on the capital market, and that there was a link between the time period of depreciation and the capital supply for society.

Engels was not happy with Marx's formulations in this context. His remarks (in *Capital*, II, ch. 15, p. 279) show that in principle both authors were perfectly aware of the importance of 'depreciation' for the capital market if it is not reinvested in the same firm. Any entrepreneur knows that depreciation must be met from profits earned in the market, and this fits in perfectly with the concept of surplus value, according to which interest is also part of social surplus value.

There is a curious gap in the argument presented in volume III of *Capital*, which is all the more surprising as Marx is evidently embarking on an analysis of capitalist firms and their 'production prices'. It is true that Marx had analysed quite clearly from the point of view of industrial economies the interest which has to be calculated on owner's equity. When, however, he embarks on a microeconomic analysis of the capital payback period, he does not say one word about depreciation formulas and the interest (rate of profit) to be calculated on owner's equity. For him, as for Engels, the only important thing is whether the historical cost of capital is recovered, no matter whether it has been 'locked in' for one year or for several years, and this in spite of the fact that Marx sharply delimits 'fixed' and 'circulating' capital. Interest as a factor in calculations does not exist for Marx or Engels.

As far as Marx is concerned, he may be excused on the grounds that he developed his theory of interest on loan capital in a detailed manner in his *Theories of Surplus Value*, where he explains it simply as the result of supply and demand. If Engels does not fill in the respective gaps in *Capital*, this is all the more disappointing in that one might have expected that he, as an entrepreneur, would have understood the following problem: if there were no remuneration for that 'disposition of capital' (in Cassel's sense) which is frozen in fixed assets, capitalists as a class would prefer investment in circulating capital, and this would mean that 'high capitalism', which is based on machinery and heavy industry, would never have come into being at all.

One cannot, then, be astonished to find in Marxist capital theory an idea that has also been enunciated by Seton in the course of the transformation

debate: the view that capitalism must of necessity neglect heavy industry!
Such theories have indeed been seriously advanced by a number of modern
Marxists – for instance, Bénard, who devoted a whole volume (1952) to the
notion of capital in Marxism. In it he wrote (p. 362),

> Time only [!] has an effect in the capitalist system in so far as it influences
> the rate of profit, *via* the velocity of turnover of capital; the rate of profit
> varies *ceteris paribus* in direct proportion [that is, inversely!] to this
> velocity. In this respect heavy industry, which requires large fixed
> investment . . . is at a disadvantage compared with light industry.
> Capitalists who follow the law of profits, therefore, direct their capital
> primarily to the latter. . . .

Bénard then refers to the prevalence of public investment in infrastructure;
for instance, in 'roads, bridges and railways'.

This kind of reasoning is inadmissible. First, in choosing to bring public
goods into the argument, Bénard is picking on something with which, in
any case, capitalists find it difficult to cope. Secondly, the historical
interpretation is certainly wrong: pre-capitalist forms of enterprise, such as
the artisan trades and domestic crafts, persisted in light industry in
particular. Thirdly, Bénard simply circumvents the principal problem, of
what the links are between the velocity of turnover of capital and the rate
of profit. No capitalist will allow his capital to be locked in for many years
unless he is pretty sure of earning compound interest. What role does the
rate of interest play as an instrument of economic calculus in Marxist
depreciation theory?

Marxist authors like to bypass these problems, taking refuge in
philosophical generalities. This is largely owing to the fact that Marxism,
prior to the rise of the socialist states, never developed its own industrial
economics in the proper sense of the term, in spite of the path opened by
Marx.

In capitalist society, interest accrues to the owner of (loan) capital and
in a socialist society to the nation as a whole. If Marx explains interest as
being part of surplus value, this is quite compatible with the notion that the
rate of interest is an instrument designed to ration scarce capital, so as to
distribute its use over time.

Both capitalist and socialist societies need such a measuring rod for
rationing purposes. There is only one difference between them: capitalism
uses capital predominantly in those activities which are particularly
profitable from a private point of view. It prefers projects with short
payback periods and does not provide capital for activities where a
minimum rate of profit (or interest) is not likely to be earned.

Socialism, on the contrary, sets great store by considerations of economic
efficiency (by means of, *inter alia*, cost – benefit analysis). It can still invest

in projects where profits are low, provided society's gains are considerable, and it can thus avoid production losses in recessions.

DEPRECIATION, THE PROBLEM OF TIME AND ECONOMIC CALCULUS

At this juncture, it must be emphasised that the rate of interest appears as a factor in calculations as soon as the period of depreciation exceeds a year. Marx escaped from this predicament by assuming a turnover period of one year. In this way, capital virtually lost its character as a fixed asset and became an element of variable costs in the modern sense. The turnover problem, as *Engels* deals with it, becomes a simple question of cash holding. As soon as fixed capital is introduced, interest appears as a factor in calculations.

Marx in the second volume of *Capital* gave detailed consideration to the connexion between fixed and circulating capital. He did so in an analysis that merits a modern reinterpretation from the point of view of industrial economics. We cannot go into such details here, but we must stress the difficulties arising from his failure to deal with the time dimension, which is closely linked to the choice of depreciation formulas.

Von Bortkiewicz attempted (1907a, pp. 27–30) a detailed analysis of the problem of capital turnover. He sought to escape from all the difficulties by considering only 'production prices' in the Marxian sense. He then went on to say

> In the theory of prices, just as in other regions of theory, there is nothing to prevent one from applying the principle of compound interest also to the case where the period after which interest is due, or the turnover period, is no longer expressed as an integral, but is expressed by a fractional number of years. . . . A turnover period of one year would make profit equal $\rho A \lambda$ (since ρ is the yearly rate of profit). Were the turnover period two, three, etc. years, profit would be not $2 \rho A \lambda$, $3 \rho A \lambda$, etc., but (because of compound interest)
>
> $$\{(1 + \rho)^2 - 1\} \ A\lambda, \ \ \{(1 + \rho)^3 - 1\} \ \ A\lambda, \ \text{etc.}$$

Von Bortkiewicz originally applied this formula exclusively to the case of 'variable capital' in the Marxian sense (i.e. as 'the outlay on wages caused by the production of a certain commodity . . . spread over different points of time'). He then goes on to apply the same formula to 'circulating constant capital' and to 'fixed constant capital', extending his analysis by reference to the work of the Russian mathematician Dmitrieff.

Von Bortkiewicz begins from Ricardo's theorem that all differences between commodities with regard to the greater or smaller contribution made by fixed capital in their production can be traced back to differences in the length of their periods of production. Even Bénard accepts (1952, pp. 302, 233ff.) that there is a problem regarding the distribution of investment over time. He admits that it is 'in a socialist economy in particular that the problem of how long society (and not the individual owner!) must wait is laid bare', and the problem is no longer to consider 'static alternatives, but to consider dynamic ones'.

Bénard, pointing to the inequitable distribution of income, refuses to recognise the concept of 'waiting', in the Marshallian sense, under capitalist conditions. However, though he states the problem, he does not discuss it in detail. He simply advances in arguing against Böhm-Bawerk, the principle of the unproductive character of capital as such. He later refers to Marx's criticism of certain statements made by Ricardo, who declared in a letter addressed to McCulloch (13 June 1820), 'When the times [i.e. of the turnover of capital] are unequal, . . . besides compensating for the labour, the price of the commodity must also compensate for the length of time that must elapse before it can be brought to the market.'

Bénard reminds us that Marx objected that this was not a problem of a change in relative values because of different lives of capital assets or of the passage of time until the maturity of the product. On the contrary, Marx thought it necessary to take up the hypothesis of a general rate of profit which would bring about equal production prices in spite of the existence of different values. Here we hit upon an analogy between Marx and Sraffa. Sraffa also uses the rate of profit in lieu of the rate of interest for the purpose of calculation, so that the necessity of applying the latter cannot be contested.

Marx's observations in volume II of *Capital* are extensive and contain numerous calculations, which Engels qualified as 'painful'. They suffer, in addition, from the basic defect that problems of industrial economics are discussed without reference to interest as an economic time dimension, a category which increases in importance from the point of view of the individual capitalist the longer the period of capital turnover is. On the other hand, Marx's calculations concern individual plants and are supposed to furnish the foundations for a general economic analysis.

Meek, like other authors, has pointed out (1967, pp. 176–7) that Marx's calculations closely resemble those of Sraffa. Sraffa (1960) includes interest in depreciation charges in his theory of 'dated labour' – although, as must be admitted, under the guise of an externally given rate of profit which, for all practical purposes, is identical to the rate of interest. Sraffa's treatment of depreciation even resembles the annuity method, which German industrial economics considers to be not a depreciation method but a financing formula.

Bénard, writing some years earlier, seems (1952, pp. 57–8) to be reconciled to the idea of using the 'general rate of profit' as a rate of interest for the purpose of calculation, for he writes,

It is quite evident that the use of more comprehensive or perfect means of production can increase the quantity of 'wealth' [= 'use values'] of which man may dispose. Marxists have never denied this, for they have, after all, always been keen to follow the development of the forces of production. They point out that it is simply the workers' productivity which is increased

for dead things can never be productive, from the Marxist's point of view. This would be fetishism. Unfortunately, however, certain Marxists have declared some workers to be 'unproductive' and have thus identified them with dead things, a kind of fetishism of physically tangible commodities produced by industry, and almost worthy of the 'fetishism of commodities' of capitalism!

Bénard comes nearer still to the Sraffian method of using the rate of profit as an instrument of economic calculus when he says (1952, p. 135),

> There can be no denying that the period necessary for maturity, by prolonging production periods, must be detrimental to the profitability of capital invested in these activities. [He talks, for instance, of forestry, which the German economist Eucken declares (1954, pp. 72, 106) to be the very prototype of natural interest growth; Eucken here adopts the 'forest interest principle' already ridiculed by Marx (*Theories*, III, pp. 494–5).] This only means that, within the framework of the competition of capitals seeking investment outlets, those which enter lines of production in which an additional period is required for the maturing of the product must according to the laws of competition demand and receive an average profit (presumably per investment period), and they must finally realise a profit higher than the surplus value that they could have extracted from the labour of their own labour force.

This is only a somewhat cumbersome formulation of the Marxian principle, established in the *Theories of Surplus Value*, that the rate of interest is nothing but the compensation paid because the capitalist renounces the possibility of the direct exploitation of labour in his own business; the amount of this compensation is fixed by the interplay of supply and demand, but the statement by Bénard is nonetheless the recognition by a Marxist of the rate of interest as a tool for use in economic calculations.

Perhaps it is possible to reconcile value theory and a formula for the calculation of interest, as devised above, in the following way. It is recognised that labour is the only factor of production and, simultaneously, the only 'correct' measuring rod for establishing the usefulness of economic elements in various activities, provided the labour force is correctly distributed amongst them in conformity with what is 'socially required'.

In that case, the sum of surplus values would have to be distributed over the various activities in the same ratio as the labour force. If the labour force is unequally distributed with regard to 'output', and if the possibility of mechanisation is the same in all industries, those that have already developed a high degree of mechanisation could claim a premium, i.e. an 'interest' payment for the additional use of capital – not capital already committed, but capital to be invested! This would then be equivalent to the assertion that growth industries and not weak sectors should be subsidised. This is a claim which has been advanced again and again – for instance, by the British *Economist* in the 1970s. In this case, interest would be nothing but a social premium for the efficient use of capital, although in a socialist system cost–benefit analyses would have to be carried out before deciding the uses to which capital ought to be put.

DEMAND IN MARX'S STATIC THEORY OF PRICE FORMATION

In Marxian economics, the price of production as a calculatory device, with its origin in the profit margin on top of cost price, is counterbalanced by an active demand which 'satisfies some social want'. The more macroeconomic character of this demand notion in Marx's work appears quite clearly when he says (*Capital*, III, ch. 10, p. 185),

> So long as we dealt with individual commodities only, we could assume that there was a need for a particular commodity – its quantity already implied by its price without inquiring further into the quantity required to satisfy this want. This quantity is, however, of essential importance, as soon as the product of an entire branch of production is placed on one side, and the social need for it on the other.

In this context, it becomes clear that Marx has scarcely any interest in the microeconomic examination of sales conditions for an isolated commodity of an isolated producer. He devoted much attention, however, to the microeconomics of an industry or branch, which presupposes that an 'industry' can be defined.

Incidentally, Marx does in this context mention what he calls the 'accidental monopoly . . . which a buyer or seller acquires through an accidental state of supply and demand'.

It could be supposed that Marx aimed at a static notion of oligopoly. But he deliberately eliminates this problem by supposing (ibid., p. 178) that it would be 'for no natural or artificial monopoly to enable either of the contracting sides to sell commodities above their value'. The demand determines the marginal producer: 'Should their quantity be smaller or greater, however, than the demand for them, there will be deviations of the

market-price from the market-value' (ibid., p. 181). In this context the
notion of the market value appears as a long-run regulating device or as an
average value. Marx goes on to say (ibid., p. 185) that, 'if the supply is too
small, the market-value is always regulated by the commodities produced
under the least favourable circumstances and, if the supply is too large,
always by the commodities produced under the most favourable conditions'. In other words, when there is a sellers' market, marginal
producers with unfavourable cost conditions will determine the price. On
the other hand, when there is a buyers' market, those firms with the best
cost conditions will determine the price, which will tend to sink to their cost
level, while former marginal producers will have either to sell at a loss or to
shut down.

This is the general idea of Marx's thoughts on the subject. He thinks it
may happen that 'the commodities produced under the least favourable
conditions may not even realise their cost price', where, 'if the demand is so
great that it does not contract when the price is regulated by the value of
commodities produced under the least favourable conditions, . . . these
determine the market-value'.

In this context the notion of market value evidently has nothing to do
with the value term in its original sense in Marxian economics. It only
means 'average equilibrium price', which appears in Marx's terminology
as 'market-price'. This becomes evident when Marx quotes (ibid., p. 192)
an anonymous author of 1821 who stresses, 'This proportion [between
demand and supply] must always be a proportion of equality; for it is only
when the supply is equal to the effectual demand . . . that the natural
price is in fact paid. . . .' Here, the supply side is decisive to Marx.
Demand is given with the distribution of income which is considered,
already in a very modern guise, as 'effective demand'.

It seems that demand has a less important position in Marx's works than
has supply. In fact, for him demand is more or less equivalent to the
distribution of income, as it results from the theorem of surplus value. The
reproduction schemes of the second volume of *Capital* may be regarded as a
crude macroeconomic division of the effective total demand into consumption proper and 'productive demand'.

There is . . . a demand for them on the part of producers (here
capitalists, since we have assumed that means of production have been
transformed into capital) and of consumers. Both appear at first sight to
presuppose a given quantity of social want on the side of demand,
corresponding on the other side to a definite quantity of social output in
the various lines of production. . . . The working-class must find at least
the same quantity of necessities on hand if it is to continue living in its
accustomed average way, although they may be more or less differently
distributed among the different kinds of commodities. Moreover, there
must be an additional quantity to allow for the annual increase of

population. The same, with more or less modification, applies to other classes.   (Ibid., p. 188.)

From these and similar statements we may draw some basic conclusions. First, Marx is evidently not interested in the 'distribution of the means of subsistence among the various categories of commodities' nor is he interested in (short-run) demand changes among various articles or groups of commodities. Secondly, he considers demand to be conditioned partly by certain basic needs, and partly by the growth of population and, therefore, of the national product.

Properly speaking, Marx starts from monetary demand. Capitalism in any case does not know any other but effective demand. Therefore,

> the need for commodities in the *market*, the demand, differs quanti-
> tatively from the *actual social* need, naturally very considerably for
> different commodities; what I mean is the difference between the
> demanded quantity of commodities and the quantity which would have
> been in demand at other money-prices or other money or living
> conditions of the buyers.   (Ibid., p. 189.)

Here Marx clearly refers to income elasticity. It follows that increases of income must lead to different intensities of demand for various commodities. In this context certain modern theories are already present in embryo, if not fully anticipated – namely, the theory of 'inferior goods', the problem of 'consumers' surplus', the Duesenberry 'ratchet'-effect, and other phenomena.

NORMAL PRICE AND LONG-RUN (COST-)PRICE

Marx complicates his analysis by speaking of 'value' (*Capital*, III, ch. 10, p. 178) as 'the centre of gravity around which their prices fluctuate', and of 'the assumption that the commodities of the various spheres of production are sold at their value'. This reservation means that Böhm-Bawerk was wrong in thinking that he could conclude that values to Marx were a kind of normal price. Marx's 'market value' is the price which is determined by current average production costs (always under the hypothesis of an identity of values and prices). On the other hand, his 'individual value' means the goods produced 'under the best conditions', which therefore realise an 'extra surplus value or surplus profit' – in other words, their owners enjoy differential rents because of their technical advantages.

We now reach, however, the problem of dynamic price theory. From this point Marx embarks on lengthy considerations of the various elements of 'market value', which according to him can be underpinned by the best, the worst or average conditions. Today, we should say: by the cost conditions of the leading or most efficient firms, of the marginal firms, or of the average firm in the branch or 'industry'.

In other words, the decisive factor for the modification of costs for Marx is net investment (i.e. the movement of capital from one industry to another), and, therefore, the growth of fixed capital formation. As a matter of fact, he was one of the first to recognise the importance of gross investment for the net formation of fixed assets, because gross capital formation serves as a vehicle for technical progress. The latter leads us to dynamic theory and, according to Marx, technical progress is already contained in simple replacement investment. The source of net investment is profits, and in this way static price theory leads to the theory of profits.

According to Marx, the 'real inner laws of capitalist production cannot be explained by the interaction of supply and demand (quite aside from a deeper analysis of these two social motive forces)'. Such an analysis he was not able to provide. It is, however, decisive for him that, when 'demand' does not meet 'supply', equilibrium will be restored in the following way: 'if the demand . . . fall[s], capital may be withdrawn, thus causing supply to shrink. Conversely, if the demand increases, and consequently the market-price rises above the market-value, this may lead to too much capital flowing into this line of production and production may swell'. In other words, investment is the decisive factor.

Marx's price theory is therefore evidently concentrated on the medium or long run, i.e. on a period within which capacity can be altered. In this respect it differs fundamentally from the Keynesian concept, which considers only short-run developments. Beyond that, Marx recognises that, not only does demand determine supply, but, in addition, 'supply also determines demand and production determines the market'. He quotes an example that 'the prices of means of production . . . determine the demand for these means of production'. To him, things are arranged in such a way that a 'change in the cost of production is by no means due to the proportion of demand and supply, but rather regulates this proportion'. (See ibid., pp. 189–91; also *Theories*, III, Annex: 'Revenue and its Sources'.)

This reminds us of the attitude of many modern Marxists, who pillory the manipulation of demand by advertising, consumer credits, and so on. Furthermore, we are reminded of the famous 'controversy between Storch and Ricardo with regard to ground rent . . . whether the market-value (or rather what they call market-price and price of production respectively) was regulated by the commodities produced under unfavourable conditions (Ricardo) . . . or by those produced under favourable conditions (Storch) . . . [in which] both of them have failed to consider the average case' (*Capital*, III, ch. 10, p. 183).

In this controversy one is tempted to agree with Ricardo when considering the case of atomistic competition with differential rents (a sellers' market), where the marginal producer, whose output is necessary to satisfy the market, will determine the price. On the other hand, Storch seems to have thought of a buyers' market, or even of semi-oligopolistic markets, where some producers no longer cover their costs and, therefore, suffer losses.

In static analysis the hypothesis of the existence of differential rents in an industry with various sizes of firms and different cost levels points to such an interpretation. Marx himself mentions (ibid., pp. 198–9) that 'commodities of the same kind . . . may have been produced under very different individual conditions and hence may have considerably different cost-prices'. A surplus profit, in other words a differential rent, for those who produce under the best conditions will therefore come about. Marx does not examine the reasons that lead to such cost advantages. They may consist of better location, of a more well qualified labour force, of large-scale production, and so on. There are indications to this effect in various passages in *Capital*.

On the other hand, Marx says emphatically that he is not talking of surplus profits that are the consequence of monopoly, whether artificial or natural. This would mean that quasi-monopolies in branded articles would also be excluded from this debate. Analogous statements with regard to static price theory are to be found in other parts of his work. (Ibid., ch. 27, p. 438; ch. 46, pp. 775ff.)

In modern studies, such as that of Dobias, (1970), who gives (p. 280) an algebraic formulation of the production-price model of Marx, those aspects of the real observation of economic life that, according to Leontief, are the main strengths of Marx are sometimes in danger of disappearing. On the other hand, a presentation such as that of Dobias has the advantage of showing unmistakably (ibid., p. 298) that Marx, 'by his production-price model, explained the first aspect of the distribution of profits or of the whole of surplus value produced in the economy (= total profits) to the various industries or enterprises, and, therefore, the interrelationship of long-run equilibrium prices in competitive capitalism'. The problem of transforming the rate of surplus value into the rate of profit brings us up against the so-called 'transformation problem', which, though it has given Marxist economists something of a mathematical headache, has been found of interest by a large number of authors.

17 The Transformation Problem: Values and Prices

THE TRANSFORMATION PROBLEM IN ITS NARROWER SENSE

Marx never denied that there is a discrepancy between values and prices, as becomes evident as one approaches reality and sees that the 'organic composition of capital' differs from branch to branch of the economy. When the rate of profit, as related to capital in use (in Marxian terminology = total costs), is to be the same in all activities, the hypothesis that the rate of surplus value is the same in all industries can no longer be maintained.

Correspondingly, Marx has recognised that certain goods can be sold above their value. Against this, certain other goods are sold 'below their value', because the labour costs contained in them are so high that in the final selling price there is insufficient room for normal surplus value.

According to this first variant we can state that the equalisation of the rate of profit will be effected by a differentiation in the rates of surplus value. According to the original labour theory of value, one would expect that when the share of labour cost is high the sum of surplus value would also be very high; in real life, however, things are exactly the reverse. An inverse relationship is still a relationship, as has been stressed by Lederer (1922, p. 204).

There is a second variant, which is simpler because it can be considered globally. According to Schumpeter (1947, p. 29, note 9), 'it is not absurd to look upon surplus value as a "mass" produced by the social process of production considered as a unit and to make the rest a matter of the distribution of the mass'. In other words, the Marxian analysis of surplus value relates to the relationship between the 'worker as a member of the social body' and the 'capitalist as a member of the social body'. Surplus value originates from the relationship between these two. The capitalist class, however, does not calculate its rate of profit as a share of value added in the branch or industry concerned, but as a percentage of the total sum of capital invested – which, as a general rule, means of the capital stock being used. On the other hand, it cannot be denied that in modern times the calculation of profits as a share of turnover is increasing.

If one wished to arrive at a correction of 'values' with regard to 'prices' in activities with a high share of labour cost, and attempted to do so by reducing the share of wages in the total product, this would contradict the 'law of equal remuneration for equal work', which holds implicitly in the Marxian system. The reduction of 'values' to the 'prices of production' in such industries can, therefore, be brought about only by reducing the share of surplus value.

Marx begins by postulating that the rate of surplus value should be the same in all industries. This holds for the value calculation and should lead to a smaller sum of surplus value in activities with a lower share of variable capital, and to a higher sum of surplus value in activities with a high share of variable capital. This is then corrected in the price calculation by the peculiar device of reducing the sum of surplus value in activities with high labour shares, until they reach the 'normal rate of profit' as related to the use of capital. In activities with a low share of wages, the sum of surplus value is correspondingly increased, until the 'normal rate of profit' is reached. This is the operation that underlies all attempts to 'transform' values into prices.

The Correction by von Bortkiewicz

Analysing things in this way, one is in danger of overlooking the fact that certain profits are already contained in 'constant' and in 'variable' capital, and these must be ascertained. This is a mathematical problem, which was solved by von Bortkiewicz. The Marxian presentation had remained a kind of mixed calculation, for Marx carried out a correction *via* an 'equalisation of the rates of profit' with regard to the surplus value that remained in the industry or branch in question, but he did not take into account the surplus value that had already appeared in 'constant' capital, or the 'variable' capital in earlier stages of production. Von Bortkiewicz's calculation is therefore, as it were, a correction of figures for earlier production and wage goods.

In this context it can be pointed out that Marx recognised the problem raised by von Bortkiewicz – namely, the existence of rates of profit in the figures given for constant and variable capital – even if he did not take it into account in his calculation in the correct mathematical way.

And in the same way the sum of the prices of production of all commodities produced in society – the totality of all branches of production – is equal to the sum of their values. This statement seems to conflict with the fact that under capitalist production the elements of productive capital are, as a rule, bought on the market, and that for this reason their prices include profit which has already been realised, hence, include the price of production of the respective branch of industry together with the profit contained in it, so that the profit of one branch of industry goes into the cost-price of another.

(Capital, III, ch. 9, pp. 159–60.)

Sweezy identifies the problems as follows (1966, p. xxiv) and points out that Marx had understood it perfectly well.

> The two items c and v are taken over from the value scheme and remain unchanged in the price of production scheme. In other words, input is measured in values while output is measured in prices of production. Obviously this is not right. A large part of today's output becomes tomorrow's input, and it is clear that, to be consistent, they must be measured in the same terms.

He adds,

> Böhm-Bawerk obviously did not see this problem at all. . . . Hilferding, on the other hand, seems never to have questioned the soundness of Marx's procedure. Indeed this is not surprising. Earlier Marxist writers had taken it for granted, and no hostile critic had called it in question. – It was left for Bortkiewicz . . . to take up the problem and to attempt to solve it within the framework of the Marxian theory of value and surplus value.

Sweezy refers to some passages in his *Theory of Capitalist Development* (1942; see pp. 144–15), where he shows that Marx was aware of the difficulty. It is nevertheless astonishing that Sweezy does not cite the passage from Marx quoted earlier in this section, since this demonstrates the point more clearly than any other.

Von Bortkiewicz stressed that the Marxian procedure implies a mixture of values and prices. 'It is, therefore, not possible to accept the Marxian solution to the problem, because constant and variable capital are excluded from the transformation of values into prices, though the principle of the equal rate of profit, if it is to take the place of the law of value in the Marxian sense, must take into account these elements as well.'

The Résumé of the Problem by Dobb

Of the many other contributions to the debate, those by May (1940, pp. 596–9), Winternitz (1940, pp. 276–80) and Dobb are especially deserving of note. Dobb (1955; 1965, p. 274) has given a résumé of the positions taken in this discussion:

> First, Bortkiewicz and Sweezy have argued (whereas Winternitz and

May disagree) that Marx's equilibrium-conditions of 'Simple Reproduction' (defining the relationship between the categories S, V and C, as sources of expenditure by workers or capitalists, and the outputs of the three main departments of production: capital goods, wage goods and luxury goods must form part of the conditions for a solution (if I understand them rightly) as well as a test of consistency by which to judge the validity of any solution.

Secondly, Bortkiewicz and Sweezy have emphasised (and here Winternitz concurs, although May apparently dissents) that a solution is independent of the composition of capital in Department III: in other words, that the rate of profit is determined exclusively by the situation of Departments I and II, producing capital goods and wage-goods respectively.

Contributions by Winternitz and Meek

On one point all authors agree: Marx's calculation must be corrected in the sense proposed by Von Bortkiewicz, i.e. the general rate of profit (instead of the rate of surplus value) must already appear in the calculation of constant and variable capital, if we are to get correct production prices. This idea has also been accepted by Winternitz (1940, pp. 276–80), who says that 'the rate of profit should be related to the prices of production of the elements of which capital consists'. However, Winternitz objects to von Bortkiewicz's method that it is based unilaterally on 'simple reproduction'. Winternitz submits that this solution is in itself inadequate, 'for the normal case is extended reproduction where there is some "net investment" ', and he offers an expanded formula (with its starting point in the idea of Bortkiewicz), that the rate of profit and the capital invested in the so-called 'third department' (namely, production of money or gold) would have no influence on the average rate of profit.

In this context Winternitz gives us an important hint: 'As a matter of fact, the price level goes up and down in the trade cycle at variance with the sum of values and the equation holds true only in the average over a whole cycle.' This, in fact, yields a second problem of transformation, which will be dealt with later in this chapter.

In Meek's judgement (1956) the calculation by Winternitz, which cannot here be dealt with in detail, brings an undoubted improvement and a simplification to the method of von Bortkiewicz and is particularly useful in the case of net investment. Meek, however, goes beyond the purely mathematical problem in reminding us of the 'historical' importance to Marx, of the transformation of values into prices.

According to Meek, Marxists could exclude this problem by allowing a renaissance of the 'classical' labour-value formula, a sort of 'Robinsonian fairy-tale'. It would then have to be emphasised, as by Lederer, that the labour-value formula would remain applicable even in capitalism, by making additions and subtractions. Meek himself doubts whether even in pre-capitalist society, where monopolies and low factor mobility, and so on, existed, the labour-value formula has ever been widely applicable. He then simplifies the problem by asking whether 'history did not simply bring about a transformation from one type of supply price to another'.

This would then mean that in the historical process one would have to switch over from one scheme of calculation to another. We here find a link with another parallel which modern Marxist oligopoly theory establishes, between 'full-cost theory' and the labour theory of value. This question has recently been examined in Italy by a disciple of Pesenti, de Cindio (1967).

If we follow this track, the transformation problem boils down to a question of calculation.

Summary: Seton and Samuelson

It is probably Seton (1957, pp. 149ff.) who has had the last word in this debate. After completing the mathematical presentation of the transformation theorem, he added some fundamental considerations founded upon comments by Meek. Seton is of the opinion that in the Marxist conception it is not the logical and mathematical element which prevails, but rather the historical.

> In the early stages of capitalism, when this transformation had hardly begun, the rate of profit obtainable in capital goods industries (whose 'organic composition' is held to be relatively high) will not as yet have reached equality with that of consumer goods industries. Capitalists will therefore prefer to invest their resources in the latter until the transformation has gone far enough to equalize the rate of profit everywhere. In Marxist *ideology*, therefore, the process of capitalist industrialization is bound to begin with the development of light industry (textiles, sugar etc.), and to delay the take-off of heavy industry (metals, engineering etc.) until a comparatively advanced stage has been reached . . . .

From these considerations Seton draws a bold conclusion (ibid., p. 157),: that the delay in the equalisation of the rates of profit is 'an obstacle to the realization of the fastest rate of growth attainable on technological grounds', because labour-saving methods are not fully applied, as might have been possible even in the most advanced stages of capitalism. In this way the means of production are unavoidably overpriced. Seton draws some further conclusions from these considerations:

> Thus, in the Marxist view, society is cheated of the fruits of technological advance by the capitalist requirement of equal profitability, and the claims of socialism as a speedier engine of industrialization and greater

liberator from human toil can be more plausibly advanced to the extent that it can dispense with this requirement and start the process from the opposite end of heavy industry.

It seems, however, that this argument applies only to developing countries.

Samuelson regards Seton's contribution as being particularly important, and himself deals with the transformation problem in two articles, written in 1970 and in 1971. The second article in particular contains an element of surprise, for he proves there that the correction made by von Bortkiewicz to the error in calculation committed by Marx over the non-conversion of input values into prices is not really required in one particular case. He says, in fact (1971, p. 415), that 'there is a singular case in which Marx's algorithm happens to be rigorously correct': what might be called the case of "equal internal compositions of (constant) capitals". In this case every one of the departments happens to use the various raw materials and machine services in the same proportion that society produces them *in toto*.'

In this argument, Samuelson surprisingly defends Marx's detour *via* the value formula as being logically unassailable, although he does so in an ironical manner. Simultaneously he develops an interesting graphical presentation of the exploitation theory and declares (ibid., p. 418) that 'a theory of the exploitation wage can be based solely upon the analysis of profits and prices. And some day Marxians will probably wish to formulate it in those terms.'

A SECOND TRANSFORMATION PROBLEM: VALUE, INCREASED PRODUCTIVITY AND INCREASED PRICES

There is, however, in a different context, a further problem of the transformation of values into prices. This problem, which has so far been neglected in Marxian analysis, was raised by Winternitz, as mentioned in the previous section (under the heading 'Contributions by Winternitz and Meek'). It consists in the question, what happens when the sum of the 'socially necessary labour time', i.e. the sum of values, remains constant, but the sum of prices increases – simply because, while the quantity of products increases, there is no decrease in prices proportionate to the increased productivity? This question is *a fortiori* important in times of inflationary developments. In both cases there would be an increasing gap between the sum of values and the sum of prices.

In this context a most important preliminary question remains to be answered. If the labour input, which appears in Marx's work as identical with the 'sum of values', remains constant, must this not lead to a distorted argument? The sum of values appears to be constant, while the sum of prices is inflated, if prices remain constant in the growth process.

Socially Necessary Labour Time and 'Efficiency Units'

The problem is this: if the value calculation in its strict sense is conceived as a measurement in units of labour time, there will be no increase in the sum of values if the input in labour time remains the same, quite independently of whether the sum of commodities produced increases or not. Marchal and Lecaillon tacked this question when they examined (1958, p. 126) the problem of how to measure the national income in value units:

> If the number of labour hours remains the same, can one not then say that the national income and therefore also the global sum of surplus value available to capitalists will remain unchanged, provided that we measure everything in labour hours, as Marxian theory is wont to do? Then one would maintain that there is an increase in neither national income nor in global surplus value. The process of the distribution of surplus value has no effect on the process of formation of surplus value; constant capital does not increase productivity. The argument is, nevertheless, somewhat strange, for, if the sum of national income and of surplus value remains unchanged, this is because the accounting unit which serves to measure both has changed in the meantime, for labour hours have become more productive on average.

Both authors then go on to point out that considerable difficulties might arise in applying the value concept if one considers that increasing productivity per labour hour makes it possible to produce the same national income with less labour time: in that case, one would have the same quantity of goods and services but a reduced total value of national income, expressed in 'values'!

However, this protest is not as justified as it appears to be at first sight: first, both authors overlook the fact that Marx talks not of labour hours as such, but of 'socially necessary labour time'. This will be less with increased productivity.

In this sense the 'socially necessary labour time' is to be identified with the notion of 'efficiency unit', as used in modern theory. Here we are dealing with 'labour-augmenting technical progress', as analysed by Kaldor and, especially, Solow (1970, p. 43):

> If labour is measured in natural units, man-years or man-hours, the input–output relation will shift; the same employment and stock of capital will yield more output in a later year than in an earlier year. In the later year, each man-hour of employment supplies more than 1 man-hour of labour input in efficiency units; and the efficiency-unit content of 1 man-hour rises steadily from year to year.

In Marxian terms this would be expressed the other way round: for the same social product there will be less 'socially necessary labour time'. In other words, the same quantity of labour time, if measured in time units, will produce more and more, because less labour will be necessary per unit of product. To put it yet another way, the same hour of labour time contains more and more 'efficiency units'.

We may thus characterise values as efficiency units. In this way the Marxian concept of 'socially necessary labour time' required for the production of a given quantity of commodities or services obtains a new functional importance.

We are now able to take a closer look at the version of Marchal and Lecaillon. With regard to their argument, we can say that the identity between the global sum of values and the global sum of prices, as postulated by *Marx* in various passages, can certainly be retained if we suppose that competition operates without restraint and that all productivity increases are immediately and completely passed on, in the form of lower prices, to consumers. To accept this hypothesis would be to place Marx in the company of the most orthodox neo-liberal economists.

If we adopt the interpretation given by Marchal and Lecaillon, we might be tempted to reach the following conclusion. As the sum of all values is equal to the sum of all (socially necessary) labour hours expended in the economy, the sum of values will remain the same if labour input remains the same. 'Growth' in the sum of values with equal labour inputs will not be at all possible. If this is so, 'values' can increase only if labour input grows. This would mean that there could be no growth analysis in 'values' in Marxian terminology, if this is based on an increase in productivity through investment, with labour input remaining the same. It is true that this problem does not appear at all in the reproduction scheme as contained in the second volume of *Capital*, because here the 'inputs' of capital and labour grow at the same pace. What is impossible is growth in the 'sum of values' with labour input the same; with growing productivity, 'necessary' labour input and 'values' shrink.

If the 'sum of values' grows in the reproduction scheme, while the ratio between capital and labour remains the same, this would signify an increase of production in a double sense: first, because of an increase of input, and, secondly, because of the technical progress, which would permit productivity growth even with the same input or the same sum of values. The sum of prices, however, can remain equal to the sum of values with increased productivity only if prices per unit of product are lowered.

We may therefore conclude that Marchal and Lecaillon's criticism that 'value' is a rather oscillating and variable measure and not appropriate for measurement is doubly justified. Not only may equal values signify increasing productivity, but so may shrinking values, for growing values may camouflage disproportionally growing outputs.

Value as Constant Unit of Measure

Joan Robinson's criticism of the value calculation would be less justified if a corrected system of value accounting were used, for this would no longer camouflage increases in productivity but would make them appear clearly.

Paradoxically, the system of value accounting presupposes the existence of a competitive mechanism – as recommended by the defenders of a deflationary economic policy – where all increases in productivity would immediately be embodied in lower prices. The question of the usefulness of such a value calculation leads on to the larger problem of whether, in the long run, the price level should increase slightly, remain constant or even decrease. Only in the last case could the identity between the sum of values and the sum of prices be retained in the course of time, provided that the price level decreases as quickly as productivity rises.

In any case, the goal of introducing a constant unit of measurement will not be attained: on the contrary, because of varying productivity, 'value' will constantly lose part of its contents in 'wealth' or 'riches' in the Ricardian sense, i.e. in commodities and services. The unit of measurement itself varies with the growth of the economic system. This is indeed the essential weakness of the value concept: the 'constant' value camouflages increasing quantities of commodities or services, and also the increase in prices, which runs parallel to increasing production.

The Marxian value concept in a situation of dynamic economic development, such as is typical of capitalism according to Marx, presupposes falling prices. Only in this case does the unit measure of 'value', the price of one labour hour, remain constant, but it represents, by way of counter-value, ever-increasing quantities of commodities and services. The logic of the Marxian system, therefore, leads to increasing real wages with falling prices – almost to the ideal postulated by neo-liberal economists – a further paradox!

Value and its Monetary Expression

Marchal and Lecaillon would be right in criticising the value scheme if, indeed, this had been strictly maintained by Marx right up to the analysis of the reproduction schemes, with their different time periods, and if Marx had never used the monetary unit of measurement to express the different 'value components' and with that, in practice, the efficiency units.

In this case, if the sum of values and the sum of prices are to remain the same, this would presuppose that prices per commodity-unit produced would have to decrease proportionately to the increase in output. At the same time, we have to suppose that such a development would be timeless in the sense that both movements take place spontaneously and simultaneously. In that case, Marx's world of prices would, indeed, be that of an idealistic 'perfect competition', which passes on to consumers, in decreasing prices, all increases in productivity. Only in these circumstances would the sum of values and prices be identical, provided that the number of labourers and the number of hours of work are the same.

This problem, which could be called the 'index problem', has not as yet been more clearly examined than by Marchal and Lecaillon. The problem of the value calculation through time and its collision with the price calculation, if the mechanism of competition does not lead to a constant decrease in prices, has not been examined by von Bortkiewicz, and even Sweezy does not seem to see it clearly. It must be asked whether the answer given above is entirely satisfactory. It would, indeed, be strange if the Marxian theory had to be based on the theory of competition *in extremis*.

It is true that Marx repeatedly declares that 'The value of labour-power' and 'the value of a definite quantity of the means of subsistence' are 'determined, as in the case of every other commodity, by the labour-time necessary for the production' (*Capital*, I, ch. 6, pp. 167–9). He later declares (ibid., p. 171) that 'it will, therefore, be useful, to assume provisionally, that the possessor of labour-power, on the occasion of each sale, immediately receives the price stipulated to be paid for it'.

From these and similar statements we may conclude that Marx wanted to see 'values' expressed in monetary form. Other passages seem to prove this as well: for instance, 'The value of money being assumed to be constant, an average social working-day of 12 hours always produces the same new value' (ibid., p. 303).

If we accept at face value Marx's postulate that a constant value of money must be presupposed, an assumption which would mean a constant and unchanging price level, we should, indeed, be able to conclude that he considered his 'values' to be constant prices for labour hours of average quality, i.e. as 'efficiency units'. Then there would be the implication that with the increasing productivity of such labour hours real wages would experience an increase.

Under this hypothesis, his theorem on the identity of the global mass of values and prices would apply even through the course of time. It would then be the standard of living of the workers that would change and not as Marchal and Lecaillon believed, the measurement of value. This interpretation would fully coincide with the recognised conception of Marx, according to which the level of real wages is conditioned by historical circumstances.

In that case, a number of objections raised by Robinson, Samuelson, Fellner and others, which we shall deal with in the section on distribution (Part VI), in the context of both wage and business-cycle theory, would then be inapplicable. Joan Robinson's criticism of the value system, which to her is a disturbing 'metaphysical factor', would at least be mitigated.

If it is desired to avoid terminological troubles, the calculation of 'real values' in the modern sense must be introduced into the Marxian value system, so as to permit expression of the degree of 'consumer satisfaction'.

Seen from a macroeconomic point of view, the situation can be represented as follows: the proposition that the sum of values equals the sum of prices is valid only if the sum of prices continually adapts, despite an increased volume of products, to the sum of labour efficiency units supplied. In other words, the money wages per labour efficiency unit must remain the same. If, on the other hand, we want to adopt the traditional method of equating value to labour hour, this would mean that, with the same division of value added ('identical rate of surplus value'), real wages would constantly increase, while prices would constantly fall, in line with rising productivity. This was very much what actually occurred in the so-called Kondratieff downswing of 1873 to 1896 (partly during Marx's lifetime), the ideal case of a competitive economic system as propounded by the liberal economists: i.e. the situation in which every increase in productivity immediately finds its expression in a decreasing price, a growing economy with permanent deflation of the price level. The engine to bring this about is continual 'competition'.

The interpretation of 'values' as 'efficiency units' requires a special solution to the second transformation problem which is to be preferred; but this idea has not yet been worked out. Nevertheless, the notion of 'efficiency units' must be analysed in detail, because it relates to the general problem of productivity.

18 The Concept of Productivity and Dynamic Price Theory

THE PROBLEM OF PRODUCTIVITY

In the early days of capitalism the tendency to prolong the working day in order to obtain a higher surplus value ('absolute surplus value') prevailed; in developed capitalism there is more and more a tendency to increase the productivity of the worker, either through intensification of work, or through the use of additional capital ('relative surplus value').

There is, first of all, the problem of 'productivity' in general and the problem of the 'productivity of capital' in the narrower sense. Some authors have supposed that Marx distinguished between 'productive' and 'unproductive' labour in much the same way as Adam Smith had done. In so doing, these authors overlook the fact that Marx used the notion of 'productive' from the point of view of the capitalist economy. In the capitalist system a 'productive' worker is one who produces surplus value, i.e. a dependent worker. An artisan, who is not subject to 'capital', remains an 'unproductive' worker, even if he produces exactly the same goods as the factory worker.

> An actor, for example, or even a clown, according to this definition, is a productive labourer if he works in the service of a capitalist (an entrepreneur) . . . while a jobbing tailor who comes from the capitalist's house and patches his trousers for him, producing a mere use-value for him, is an unproductive labourer. . . . Only labour which produces capital is productive labour. .... These definitions are therefore not derived from the material characteristics of labour (neither from the nature of its product nor from the particular character of the labour as concrete labour), but from the definite social form, the social relations of production. . . . The use-value of the commodity in which the labour of a productive worker is embodied may be of the most futile kind. (*Theories*, I, pp. 156–8.)

It is clear that Marx did not consider only the factory worker, who produces physically tangible goods, to be productive, for he expressly understood services to be a commodity. Indeed, he says, 'For the producer of these services the services rendered are commodities.' Marx explicitly recognises that a large part of marketing activity (for instance, packing, forwarding and transport) is part of the productive process and therefore productive in the capitalist sense. He even mentions the productive services of doctors and lawyers. (See ibid., pp. 380–8; also addenda.)

If the term 'productive' is not used for commerce, this may be because in Marx's times the 'capitalist' organisation of commerce existed only in rudimentary form. Commerce was part of the artisans' business and from the point of view of capitalism was 'unproductive'. In one passage, however, Marx enumerates among the 'productive classes' even 'middlemen', as has been emphasised by Holesovsky (1961, pp. 325ff.). One is guilty of error if one attributes to Marx an identification of productive work with commodity-producing work, for Marx explicitly says that only the first explanation given by Smith, namely the identification of productive work with work that creates surplus value is justified: 'Adam Smith's opponents have disregarded his first, pertinent definition, and instead have concentrated on the second, pointing out the unavoidable contradictions and inconsistencies. . . . It must be recognised that at the same time Adam Smith also falls back more or less into the Mercantilist conception of permanency – or, inconsommabilité' [*sic!*] (*Theories*, I, pp. 173–4). Many Marxist analysts, especially in the Soviet Union, have fallen victim to the same idea, and without knowing it are partisans of Smith or the late Mercantilists. The fact that Marx never accepted Smith's interpretation becomes quite clear from a passage in the *Grundrisse* (p. 234); in the same passage he states his own interpretation – namely, identification of 'productiveness' with 'surplus-producing activities':

> *Only labour which creates surplus value is productive* . . . that surplus value has to express itself in a material product is a crude view which still occurs in A. Smith. Actors are productive workers, not in so far as they produce a play, but in so far as they increase their employer's wealth. But what sort of labour takes place, hence in what form labour materialises itself, is absolutely irrelevant for *this relation*.

Finally, it is not correct to believe that Marx did not recognise the 'productivity of capital'. He has under this heading devoted an entire chapter in his *Theories of Surplus Value* to an attempt to prove how the capitalist form of organisation increased the productivity of labour in a wider sense. What Marx does not recognize is the definition of capital as a mysterious 'fetishistic' source of 'original interest' or profit.

Holesovsky has emphasised that Marx, in his analysis of Smith's work, unequivocally underlined that the distinction between productive and unproductive work has nothing to do with the distinction between material and non-material products. Marx speaks of the notion of 'unproductive in the most restricted sense used by Smith' (*Theories*, 1, p. 267). Unfortunately, as Holesovsky thinks, Marx does not always use the term 'productive' with sufficient clarity and has sometimes applied it to more than one set of circumstances.

For instance, he once employs the term to denote the simple production of use values: 'Every service is productive for its seller' (ibid., p. 293). He thinks, furthermore, that every activity that results in some gain can be considered as being 'productive' from the point of view of an independent worker or capitalist: '*Productive labour* is therefore – in the system of capitalist production – labour which produces *surplus-value* for its employer, or which transforms the objective conditions of labour into capital and their owner into a capitalist; that is to say, labour which produces its own product as capital' (ibid., p. 396). Marx also speaks of productivity in the sense of securing one's livelihood: 'Assume that the productivity of industry is so advanced that, whereas earlier two-thirds of the population were directly engaged in material production, now it is only one-third' (ibid., p. 218). Lastly, Labour is under certain circumstances considered to be 'relatively' productive:

> Productivity in the capitalist sense is based on relative productivity – that the worker not only replaces an old value, but creates a new one; that he materialises more labour-time in his product than is materialised in the product that keeps him in existence as a worker. It is this kind of productive wage-labour that is the basis for the existence of capital.
>
> (Ibid., p. 153)

This concept is linked to the previous notion, and it leads back to the definition of productivity quoted above: productive work is work done for the capitalist, unproductive work is work which results merely in the production of some use value. (Holesovsky, 1961, p. 329.)

Holesovsky draws the conclusion (ibid., pp. 336–7) that Marx's notion of productivity has, in any case, nothing to do with the primitive version according to which only work that is crystallised in material goods may be considered as 'productive'. Moreover, in some passages Marx mentions as 'unproductive' work certain activities which do not bring any positive contribution to 'social welfare'.

'RELATIVE' SURPLUS VALUE

Having discussed the general term 'productivity', there remains the question of the meaning of 'productivity of capital' in the narrower sense. This term is in general identified with proportionality between variable capital and surplus value in Marx. Marx, however, has introduced into the debate, in discussing 'relative' surplus value and 'extra surplus value' as a consequence of mechanisation, a term which might easily be confused with the notion of 'real rate of interest' or real productivity.

Contrary to the Keynesian explanation of interest in terms of 'liquidity preference', Marx's explanation of interest is based on the idea 'of the renunciation of the use of capital' in a social system where owning capital offers the possibility of 'exploiting' workers, who are obliged to sell their labour power on the market.

There is now the question of what guarantees the continued existence of a difference between 'cost price' and 'selling price', i.e. the existence of surplus value.

Surplus value could, first of all, be threatened by a shortage of labour and a corresponding increase in wages. Two forces counteract this tendency. The first is the permanent revolution in the process of production through the introduction of machinery, which releases labour and creates an 'industrial reserve army', under pressure of which any wage increase of a threatening dimension can be avoided, while simultaneously it imposes pressure in the direction of an increase in labour-intensity and an improvement of labour discipline. In this context Marx is in full agreement with some conservative economists, who also consider the existence of an 'industrial reserve army' as indispensable for a continuing capitalist society (Beveridge, 1945, pp. 194ff.). The second factor that serves to counteract a threatened increase in wages is technical progress in the consumption-goods industries and in agriculture, because it tends to cheapen 'wage goods'. In this sector, even in modern times, as at the time of Ricardo, a conflict of interest should appear between the protection-minded landowners and houseowners, on the one side, and the industrial capitalists, on the other.

The second threat to the existence of surplus value lies in the difficulties of 'realising' it: the capitalist has his surplus value realised only if he sells the product of labour.

Here is one starting point for criticism, for Marx's point of departure was the capitalist world of his time, which was based on the competition of a multitude of smaller producers. On the other hand, he did not overlook the rise of 'competing monopolies' (in his terms), which are the oligopolies of modern times. Finally, his theory of concentration leads directly to the 'negation of competition'. In view of the fact that he started from competition between capitalists, the moot point is whether such competition would not result in the disappearance of surplus value, looked at from the microeconomic point of view.

It is true that this question is not explicitly discussed by Marx. One may suppose, however, that the answer is implicit in other theses of his. First of all, it may be seen in his theory of accumulation, which shows the propensity to invest to be inherent in capitalism. Investment keeps creating advantages through increased productivity, which continually recreates surplus value, even if there is a tendency for it to be continually competed away.

The theory of the continuous increase in 'constant capital', i.e. of the relative growth in depreciation of fixed assets (including stocks) in relation to wage costs, points in the same direction. In this way differential profits originate which, in Marx's view, continually disappear at the very moment of their appearance, because of the depreciation of the newly installed equipment. In this case, the continued existence of surplus value would be due to dynamic factors; in other words it would be 'relative' and not 'absolute' surplus value.

A further answer is implicit in the movement towards concentration, which itself leads to a decrease in competitive pressure.

With production on an enlarged scale the advantages of mass-production or of production with large units of equipment will accrue; in other words, 'economies of scale'. This means that capitalists with large sums of surplus value will have the opportunity of installing equipment the average costs of which will be lower than those of smaller capitalists. The steady pace of accumulation is accompanied by a growing tendency to replace workers by machines. As long as 'surplus value' is determined by old production methods, the individual capitalist can obtain an 'extra surplus value' by economising on labour. This means that there is a permanent tendency to set workers free, which exercises a downward pressure on the general wage level.

MACRO- AND MICROECONOMIC ASPECTS OF VALUE THEORY

Basically the macroeconomic aspects of the theory of surplus value mean only this: with a given division of work within society (in hours = 'values'), surplus value results from the sum of labour hours after deduction of what is necessary for the production of commodities and services consumed by workers and of what is needed to replace machinery and stocks of raw materials and other ancillary inputs. What then remains corresponds to gross profits. Net profits correspond in a static view to labour used in producing the goods and services consumed by capitalists; in a dynamic setting to capitalist consumption plus 'accumulation' (= net investment). In this way, Marx anticipated the theorems developed by Keynes and Kalecki according to which the sum of profits corresponds to the sum of goods and services consumed by capitalists plus net investment (provided that workers do not save!).

In its practical aspects, Marxian value analysis boils down to the statement that the division of value added in individual firms or industries must correspond, in principle, to the average division of the net social product between workers and capitalists. If the sum of wages per firm or industry is given, this would mean that, compared with reality, value added and, therefore, prices appear 'inflated' in labour-intensive firms and artificially deflated in capital-intensive firms. All this is set on a higher plane, in a dialectic sense, through the dynamisation of Marx's theory of price.

This 'dynamisation' of price theory appears in three different aspects. First, Marx directly explains the reasons for an alteration of capacity in one activity by pointing at the microeconomic level to the effects of innovations, i.e. innovations which have been carried out by a 'pioneer entrepreneur' and which are imitated by others. He says (*Capital*, 1, ch. 12, p. 300),

> Now let some one capitalist contrive to double the productiveness of labour. . . . The value of the means of production remaining the same, the value of each article will fall. . . . Despite the doubled productiveness of labour, the day's labour creates, as before, a new value of six shillings . . . which, however, is now spread over twice as many articles. . . .

With this Marx wants to imply that labour time or labour costs remain the same in total, while decreasing per unit of commodity produced.

Secondly, Marx presupposes that the market price will initially remain approximately at the same level, in spite of the increased production of one of the competing firms: 'If, therefore, the capitalist who applies the new method sells his commodity at its social value of one shilling [i.e at the current market price; strictly speaking, Marx abstracts from the difference between values and prices!], he sells it for three-pence above its individual value [because there is less labour embodied in the individual product than before], and thus realises an extra surplus-value' (ibid., p. 300).

Thirdly, the industry as such is initially not affected. It is solely a matter of the existence of differential rents within a supply curve, which is constructed within the framework of the model of perfect competition. Marx implicitly recognises that cost advantages are competitive advantages which undermine the model from within. To him the problem of dynamic changes in market shares is paramount. For the capitalist who increases his productivity and the capacity of his firm,

> the demand must be double what it was, i.e., the market must become twice as extensive. Other things being equal, his commodities can command a more extended market only by a diminution of their prices. He will therefore sell them above their individual but under their social value. . . . By this means he still squeezes an extra surplus-value . . . out of each.   (Ibid., p. 307.)

Marx argues in a similar manner in the third volume of *Capital* (ch. 10,

p. 194): 'one begins to dispose of his goods at a cheaper rate and the others must follow . . . if one produces more cheaply and can sell more goods, thus possessing himself of a greater place in the market . . . he will do so, and will thereby begin a movement which gradually compels the others to introduce the cheaper mode of production'.

GROWTH OF THE FIRM AND GROWTH OF THE INDUSTRY

The 'temporary monopoly' of a firm which enjoys a certain technical advantage is by no means permanent:

> However, the *privileged position* of our capitalist is not of long duration; other competing capitalists introduce the same machines, the same division of labour, introduce them on the same or on a larger scale. [The latter remark should be sufficient proof that Marx recognised the existence of economics of scale.] The capitalists find themselves, therefore, in the same position relative to one another as *before* the introduction of the new means of production, and if they are able to supply by these means double the production at the same price, they are *now* forced to supply the double product *below* the old price. On the basis, of this new cost of production, the same game begins again. More division of labour, more machinery, enlarged scale of exploitation of machinery and division of labour. . . . We see how in this way the mode of production and the means of production are continually transformed, revolutionised, *how the division of labour is necessarily followed by greater division of labour, the application of machinery by still greater application of machinery, work on a large scale by work on a still larger scale.* . . . That is the law which again and again throws bourgeois production out of its old course and which compels capital to intensify the productive forces of labour, *because* it has intensified them, it, the law which gives capital no rest and continually whispers in its ear: 'Go on', 'Go on'.
> (*Wage Labour and Capital*, in *Marx–Engels, Selected Works*, 1968, p. 90.)

The economies of scale, i.e. acquisition of plant of greater capacity, which with optimum use has lower costs than the older equipment, arise partly through expansion of the industry (external economies) and partly through the growth of the individual firm (internal economices). According to Marx the economies in the conditions which characterise large-scale production originate in certain costs of fixed equipment, which grow less than proportionately to the growth of the firm. Thus,

> the cost of these motors does not increase in the same ratio as their horse-power. . . . The cost of the transmission equipment does not grow in the same ratio as the total number of working machines which it sets in

motion. The frame of a machine does not become dearer in the same ratio as the mounting number of tools. . . . Furthermore, the concentration of means of production yields a saving on buildings of various kinds. . . . The same applies to expenditures for fuel, lighting, etc.

(*Capital*, III, ch. 5, p. 79)

Marx further mentions additional receipts which are obtained by 'the reconversion of the excretions of production, the so-called waste'.

Thus it can be seen that it is completely erroneous to assume, as Samuelson does, that Marx worked with fixed coefficients of production. On the contrary, capital-saving on a large scale is to Marx one of the features of large-scale production. He explicitly mentions (ibid., p. 83) 'economies in constant capital' and the 'capitalist's fanatical insistence on economy in means of production', which leads to an increase in the rate of profits; he considers shifts in the one and the same production function (as we should say today) to be possible; and he sees capital-saving as part of the process of growth to a larger dimension of business activity.

He is, on the other hand, fully aware of the existence of external economies, for he says,

the development of the productive power of labour in any *one* line of production . . . may again be partly connected with progress in the field of intellectual production [research!] . . . and consequently of the cost of means of production in *other* lines of industry . . . the rise in the rate of profit in *one* line of industry depends on the development of the productive power of labour in *another*.   (Ibid., p. 81)

The revolution in the structure of prices is, therefore, largely conditioned by long-run supply developments. The development of long-run demand is considered by Marx as dictated by the social structure, in so far as it concerns final demand.

Marx directly explains the capacity changes in individual firms and whole industries as being brought about by an initiative to lower costs. Such an initiative includes the tendency 'to reduce the direct employment of living labour' (ibid., p. 87). Which of these two tendencies, economy in capital or in labour, will have the upper hand, is not stated by Marx within the framework of his production and price theory.

With regard to the individual enterprise there is the question of whether the leadership position in technical progress changes, one firm after another taking a turn, or whether the pioneer firms are always the same. In so far as the latter tendency prevails, we must envisage the possibility that such firms as retain a particular advantage will take over other firms, because Marxian price-cutting competition seems to be directly aimed at other firms. '. . . every weapon that he [the capitalist] forges against his rivals recoils against himself' (*Wage Labour and Capital*, in *Marx – Engels*,

Selected Works, 1968, p. 91). Incidentally, in the *Grundrisse* Marx spoke extensively of the rôle of science in the creation of external economies; his analysis finds its climax in his anticipation of automation.

In Marx's view, the 'social demand . . . is essentially subject to the mutual relationship of the different classes and their respective economic position, notably therefore to, firstly, the ratio of total surplus-value to wages, and, secondly, to the relation of the various parts into which surplus-value is split up (profit, interest, ground rent, taxes, etc.)' (*Capital*, III, ch. 10, p. 181). Thus, total demand and its composition is a function of distribution.

Furthermore, the growth of enterprises, which finds its expression in the increase of constant capital, touches upon the problem of the concentration of capital. This would then explain why the capitalist takes an interest in carrying out mechanisation, for, if the turnover of the enterprise is enlarged because of an increase in constant capital, while profits decrease, there is a possibility that weak firms will go bankrupt.

Before discussing this problem, it is useful to consider what happens when constant capital is increased. For Marx, it is only the cost that will be affected, for c increases but not value added $(v + s)$. This must appear paradoxical, and it is here that criticism by many economists, even Marxists, begins.

The contradiction is to be explained by the fact that Marx, as so often, anticipates certain outcomes but does not always represent the intermediate positions. He assumes that total value-added does not grow, because all capitalists in the same industry do the same thing in turn — namely, increase their outfit of machines as denoted in c. Value added will grow in firms only for as long as they are in a position to withdraw sales from others by means of slight reductions in price. What is awkward in Marx's presentation is that, in the figures he quotes, he presents the total output of the firm at a time when the phase of 'advantage' or 'temporary monopoly' is already over.

One must assume an intermediate stage, for if growth occurs in constant capital, determined essentially by mechanisation or an increase in fixed assets, this must raise the productivity of the individual undertaking in the first stage and thereby increase also its particular value added, i.e. $v + s$. Marx ought really to distinguish between different stages.

It is now assumed that the industry concerned suffers a crisis, or there is a general recession or depression. Prices have fallen; if wages are 'sticky', this would lead to higher real wages, although during the recession short-time working and unemployment would not allow an improvement in real income per household.

At the same time there remains as a permanent result the shift in the rate of surplus value in favour of capital. This, mostly of benefit to large-scale entrepreneurs, promotes reinvestment, which gives rise to a further extension of their capital equipment (c).

This dynamic development results in a twofold concentration of capital. First, large capitals grow faster than small ones (this is Marx's process of concentration), and, therefore, increase their market shares. Secondly, smaller firms are ruined or are forced to merge with larger ones or be absorbed by them (this is Marx's process of centralisation). The more that such large-scale enterprises predominate, the more smaller capitalists will be expropriated and forced back into the proletariat.

At the same time, with the decrease in the number of capitalists, an increase will take place in the volume of surplus value available for accumulation. There will, therefore, be, absolutely and relatively, larger sums for further investment. Simultaneously the tendency towards competition between large-scale enterprises will become even sharper. The fight for extra surplus value through mechanisation will increase. This means that there will be a faster substitution of labour by machinery and a quicker dismissal of workers, feeding continually the industrial reserve army, which exercises pressure on wages and labour conditions. With this pressure, 'the volume of misery' at the margin of the working class will increase.

This continuous tendency towards investment and mechanisation has the further consequence that the organic composition of capital, or rather the current capital cost as related to labour cost, will change. In other words, the share of depreciation in total costs will increase. If now the ratio between the sum of wages and the sum of profits remains the same, this must inevitably mean that the share of profits in total costs plus profits, namely in turnover, will decrease, and that there will be a tendency for the rate of profits to decrease.

On the other hand, there are counteracting tendencies: the rate of surplus value, i.e. the ratio between total profits and total wages, may rise, and this may partly counteract the tendency towards a falling rate of profit, or at least mitigate it. At the same time, the production of machinery may be cheapened, so that depreciation does not grow so rapidly.

THE RATE OF SURPLUS VALUE AND TECHNOLOGY

The rate of surplus value may be raised considerably by a cheapening of the necessary means of subsistence; this would mean that technical progress takes place chiefly in the consumption-goods industries. This would permit the possibility of a decrease in wages, or at least that capitalists would be able to keep wages at a low level.

This leads us to the weak link in the analysis: 'academic' economics has emphasised the contradiction that is to be found in the principle of the equalisation of the rates of profit. This contradiction is based upon the hypothesis that capital will move into industries where firms have a high share of variable capital and, therefore, high value added.

This may be meaningful in so far as there is the possibility in this high value added and in this high absolute sum of surplus value of obtaining even higher relative sums of surplus value, i.e. the industries or firms are capable of further mechanisation. It may even be the case that an industry that has already been mechanised to a high degree and, therefore, has a high organic composition offers possibilities for further mechanisation, even more so than industry that is still relatively labour-intensive.

The question arises of which is the stronger attraction: a high absolute surplus value in activities that have not yet been mechanised but have the potential; or a high relative surplus value in activities that, by already being mechanised to a high degree, have proved that their capacity for mechanisation is high? If the attraction towards the latter activities is stronger, there will be an equalisation of the rates of profit in the inverse sense, i.e. by high differential rents and high relative (but not absolute) surplus value. It is then quite conceivable for two different groups of industries to coexist: first, a group of industries with a high absolute surplus value, which exists even for marginal producers and which, because of the existence of monopolistic competition, cannot be competed away, though, on the other hand, it does not attract potential capital; and, secondly, a group of industries which have already been mechanised to a high degree and had or still have a high profit income, but which, nevertheless, contain further possibilities for even stronger mechanisation, still stronger technical progress of a different kind, and still higher 'relative surplus value'.

In such a way Marx has introduced the possibility of a modification of the rate of surplus value, and expressly within the context of (and as a counterbalance to) the 'law of the tendency of the profit rate to fall'. If such a modification takes place, the static proportionality of v to s no longer holds, because we enter the realm of dynamics.

To that extent proportionality between v and s is actually an additional hypothesis for the labour theory of value in its proper sense. If then a particular activity requires a certain amount of labour or labour time in order to produce certain goods, this does not necessarily mean that the labour time actually used in this industry is at the same time 'socially necessary'. It may be the case as a consequence of the structure of an industry (small firms with difficulties of finance, cartels with a premium on backward methods of production, oligopolies that put a brake on technical progress, and so on) that the industry is not able to reach the highest degree of mechanisation that is technically possible.

In such a case, as Marx explicitly stresses, the 'socially necessary labour time' is below the actual labour time (v) expended. In so far as surplus value remains proportional to the latter, it is then artificially inflated.

The inflated surplus value would lead in turn to inflated prices, under the value scheme. For Marx, this would be corrected by the influx of capital attracted by the higher surplus values and rates of profit: capital moves from capital-intensive to wage-intensive industries and firms, so decreasing production and increasing prices in capital-intensive sectors, and increasing production and reducing prices in labour-intensive sectors. This is in line with the strict logic of the theory of 'socially necessary labour time'. Marx explicitly says that it is not actual labour time expended as such, but only labour time that is absolutely indispensable because it cannot be replaced by machinery, that is actually 'socially necessary'.

The question must, therefore, be asked of whether the labour and labour time concentrated in wage-intensive industries and enterprises are really 'socially necessary'. The element of 'social necessity' was emphasised by Labriola at an early state. More recently, it has been stressed by Henry Smith (1962, pp. 62, 67). In both cases, it boils down to the consideration that behind this notion there is, on the one side, an anticipation of actual needs, which coincides with the notion of demand, and, on the other, a valuation of what is 'socially useful'. In those industries in which individual firms have demonstrated the possibility of mechanisation, the labour time expended by the more backward firms (in so far as their activities are as capable of mechanisation as others) would not correspond to 'socially necessary labour time'. The same follows with regard to certain industries as compared with others. It would not be justified simply to compare a given 'value' of labour as expressed in the sum of wages in these activities, in accordance with the postulate of an equal division of value added in all industries, with an amount of surplus value generated by the average social rate of surplus value.

The sum of surplus value in such industries would have to be reduced to make it coincide with the theoretically correct 'value' of variable capital (v). In a large part of labour-intensive industry with possibilities for mechanisation, the sum of surplus value would, without 'equalisation of rates of profit' and an appropriate inflow of capital, have to be reduced. These values would have to be corrected within the framework of a mere system of recalculation, for the initial 'increase' of value added in these industries would appear as a triple mistake, namely as an error in logic with regard to the 'strict' labour theory of value, which does not recognise labour time actually expended, but only such labour time as is 'socially necessary'.

How, in practice, is this 'correction' to be made? Even if we start from the hypothesis, propounded by capitalists themselves, of an 'equal distribution of value added over all activities', the following aspects will have to be considered. If a firm modernises its productive equipment, it thereby lowers the 'socially necessary labour time' for the same quantity of product and realises an extra profit or 'relative surplus value', because the original price level of the industry still applies, at least in the beginning. In this case the relative wage bill will be reduced in this firm as a part of the total sum of values. But if the firm sticks to the rule that value added should be divided in the same way as before, high absolute wage increases will ensue for the firm's remaining workers. At the same time the firm will exercise pressure on the price level of the industry, and it will be recognised that the old sums of value added no longer correspond to the effective values as they prevail in the mechanised enterprise. The result is that the industry's prices and values are lowered to an adequate level even without a further influx of capital, for this result is brought about simply by accumulation on the part of the pioneer enterprise. What is decisive in this case is relative surplus value.

Only if there are no special circumstances and no one by the introduction of machinery proves the possibility of mechanising the industry in question can the original values and prices be maintained. This would be the case where all firms in the industry are 'marginal producers'. If monopolistic competition prevails, they may all realise abnormal profits (= absolute surplus value) for some time. In this case, which Marx thought might have been overlooked by Ricardo and Storch in their controversy, the 'average conditions' of medium-size enterprises determine the price.

The Marxian 'equalisation of the rate of profit' is applicable here, for capital may move in from industries that are already mechanised, because some firms scent new profits. Capital will be enticed into the industry by the high 'absolute surplus value' (for instance, high margins in retailing); but in reality the new capital will make most of its profits not by sharing in former monopolistic excess profits, but by undermining them by means of further mechanisation. In this case we again end up with 'relative surplus value'. This 'relative' or 'extra surplus value' takes on new aspects as soon as we examine hypotheses other than that of the 'strict' labour theory of value. In practice, the labour theory of value is applicable only in one particular case: namely, where capital-intensity and surplus value are the same in all activities or firms in the whole economy and where dynamic excess profits are absent.

A UNIFORM RATE OF SURPLUS VALUE?

Joan Robinson (1949, pp. 15–17) and others have attacked the hypothesis of a uniform rate of surplus value. That, properly speaking, is not the problem. What is decisive is that the question of whether one recognises one or more factors of production and whether one accepts the labour theory of value is in no way unconditionally relevant for this supposition of proportionality in the division of value added.

Marx himself offered some examples. He refers to the case in which a progressive method of production is introduced into a particular industry; in this case the labour time expended in backward firms in this particular industry is no longer 'socially necessary', and the number of hours of labour time actually expended in such backward enterprises no longer represents the equivalent number of hours of 'socially necessary labour time'.

(*Theories*, II, ch. 8, pp. 38–4, see also *Theories*, I, ch. 4, p. 232).

If, however, the rate of surplus value is always proportional to v, even if v is no longer 'socially necessary', this would no longer correspond to the strict rule of labour value. In such cases, a lower rate of surplus value will be necessary on labour actually expended, in order to take into account the loss of productivity in such backward industries. In this way one would arrive at several different rates of surplus value, and this because of the strict application of the labour theory of value rather than from a failure to apply it. Joan Robinson arrived at this conclusion after a different train of reasoning. On the other hand, we should in this way renounce our point of departure, i.e. the hypothesis of a uniform proportional relation between v and s in all industries, but this would by no means be disastrous for further Marxian reasoning – for instance, with regard to the theory of the tendency of the rate of profit to fall.

To arrive at such a tendency, a further hypothesis, which need not necessarily be derived from the strict labour theory of value, will suffice. Such a hypothesis is that value added and the rate of surplus value may be different in each industry, but the division of value added should remain the same over time in each industry. This may, for instance, be the case if a powerful trade-union movement lays claim to its share as soon as profits rise, or if there is a proper scheme of profit-sharing for the workers or if a shortage of labour arises because of the increasing accumulation of capital, particularly of specialised labour, for this would lead to a corresponding increase in wages.

If labour-saving innovations prevail and capital-deepening takes place, the tendency towards a falling rate of profit can take place either within the business cycle or in the long run, especially under the influence of growing trade-union power, which prevents compensation through a rising rate of surplus value.

From this it can be deduced that, if one assumes that the increase in productivity consequent on an increase in constant capital, c, does not bring about an increase in value added, and if c does not experience any depreciation, the rate of profit is bound to fall, provided that the working class can prevent an increase in the rate of surplus value.

The essential problem is not whether there exists a uniform relation between v and s in the whole economic system. The fall in the rate of profit may occur even when the rates of surplus value are different in different industries, provided that in each industry the particular rate of surplus value (= division of value added) remains constant over time.

For this intermediate stage, Marx supposes that the additional value added that would arise if the normal price in the industry concerned were only slightly lowered would lead to an increase in surplus value alone. He assumes that there will be a change in the rate of surplus value in favour of capital. Hence he subsumes 'extra surplus value' under the category of 'relative surplus value'.

If we allow this hypothesis of a constant division of value added even during the intermediate stage, it is true that there will be an 'extra surplus value' accruing to the surplus value of the pioneer firm, but it can no longer be called 'relative', at least not according to the Marxian definition, for it is rather an increase of the 'absolute' surplus value. At the same time, however, labour value v (or the value of the work done by labour force) is also increasing: value added grows without any increase in the hours of work in the case of the pioneer firm, and therefore surplus value, the sum of wages and the wage per worker increase too, for the firm's sales are enlarged and the price at which the additional units are sold is in the beginning almost the same, only costs, including profit per unit produced, are much lower.

Nevertheless, we must not forget what our hypothesis really means: whereas in the final stage the amount of capital added to c will not receive any additional remuneration, in the intermediate stage worker and capitalist share in the profits. Whether this actually happens will remain a moot point. Was Joan Robinson right, then, when she dismissed the labour theory of value as a mere 'magic spell', or was Oscar Lange, who wanted to drop it altogether?

As long as price in the industry does not go down to the level of the new 'values', and Marx himself says that the 'progressive' entrepreneurs are not immediately willing to go down to the new price, would not the backward, as well as the progressive, entrepreneurs obtain an 'extra surplus value' in the industry? This would mean that the fixed-value relationship between the shrinking sum of wages in backward enterprises and the sum of surplus values obtained by them would break down. In other words, there is no rigid relationship between labour value and 'absolute' surplus value, but a relationship that varies, for surplus value becomes 'relative'. The ratio between the sum of wages and the sum of surplus value within value added depends on the market price or the rapidity with which the market price adapts to the change in 'real values'.

There is still another question to be solved: how does the distribution of the labour force among industries and enterprises take place? The postulate of a rigid ratio between labour value as a whole and surplus value must start from the hypothesis that the labour force is 'correctly' distributed among different industries, i.e. in such proportions as are 'socially necessary'. This also presupposes that various industries can be mechanised to different degrees, for otherwise a uniform 'organic composition of capital' would prevail, and the discrepancy between values and prices, which is one of the chief worries of Marx, and the chief reason for his quarrel with Böhm-Bawerk, would not even appear. This, of course, presupposes that 'values' are expressed not on the hypothesis of constantly falling prices, but in constant prices per unit of product.

THE PROBLEM OF 'MECHANISATION TO AN EQUAL DEGREE' AND 'SPURIOUS' VALUES

First it may be assumed that mechanisation is equally possible in all industries, but does not come about – for instance, because of a shortage of capital. In that case the labour force would not be distributed according to what is 'socially necessary', and its value expression would have to be corrected in each of the industries concerned if even only one enterprise in the industry had demonstrated the possibility of mechanisation or if only· the mere possibility exists at the technological level.

As a result of the correction, and even if we suppose that there is a fixed ratio between surplus value and value added, a discrepancy between value and prices would no longer exist, for industries with a low capital-intensity would no longer obtain higher 'values' than mechanised industries and an 'equalisation of the rates of profit' need not occur. The labour-intensive industries would have 'spurious' values, as it were.

The distribution of the labour force would simply not correspond to 'social necessity', for too many workers would be engaged in labour-intensive industries. An equalisation would then have to take place by means of a decrease in value added and in wages in such industries. Capital and labour would not move out of activities that are already mechanised, but out of branches that are not mechanised. This process would seem to be more realistic than the contrary process harshly criticised by Piettre (1962, pp. 56, 59).

Is it possible to postulate that 'mechanisation to an equal degree' can be brought about in all industries?

For undertakings within the same industry one must presuppose the same potential for mechanisation, because the idea of an industry assumes a more or less uniform product and production method. Within each industry, therefore, there would have to be a migration of capital and labour away from backward enterprises of a high labour-intensity – a process that would be the inverse of the 'equalisation of profits'.

It seems that Marx presupposed that, owing to differences in the technology available, industries would differ from each other with regard to their potential for mechanisation. This leads us to the problem of technical progress. The question arises of whether in given industries a technological constraint or a lack of capital is more important. The factors, among others, that determine this are the structure of the undertaking and the degree of competition.

If the mechanising potential of firms or even of industries does not vary greatly, one thing seems to be certain: the ratio, within value added, in enterprises, in industries and in the economy as a whole, between the value of labour power or the sum of wages, on one side, and surplus value, on the other, can no longer be clarified in an unequivocal way by the labour theory of value. This theory in itself would no longer lead to a uniform ratio, because one would again and again have to distinguish between the 'genuine' socially necessary use of labour and a 'spurious' use of labour. The time actually expended in labour ceases to be a useful measure. We shall therefore have to ask whether Graziadei and Oscar Lange were right, and whether we really need the labour theory of value, even as a theory of distribution.

There is a second possibility. It may be presumed, in principle, it is not possible for all industries to have the same potential for mechanisation. There are many arguments in favour of such a theory, especially with regard to the service sector. We must not, however take this latter notion as coinciding with the tertiary sector as defined by Colin Clark and Fourastié, for this covers the transport sector, which is quite capital-intensive. If we stick to the second possibility, it would be possible to develop a concept of 'values' as a formula for a division of the social product according to the co-operative principle – namely, of distributing it to all workers, for in many industries the actual amount of labour time expended would more or less approximate to the 'socially necessary' level.

Finally, a 'reconciliation' of the labour theory of value with modern price theory is possible through the following formula. At the very moment that a 'capitalist' introduces improvements or machinery, which on account of increased productivity reduce the 'socially necessary labour time' per unit of product, there arises not only 'relative surplus value' for the individual capitalist, but the 'value' of the product is lowered in parallel to the decrease in price. This means that 'value' is reduced not when the new method becomes the average method in the industry, but rather it adjusts to the optimum of 'cost prices' in the Marxian sense, for it is not determined by the average.

At the same time, the 'equalisation of the rates of profit' takes place through the flow of capital into industries that have hitherto been labour-intensive. It takes place not because variable capital is high in these industries, but because they offer a good opportunity to obtain high differential profits (= relative surplus value) through mechanisation.

DYNAMIC PRICE THEORY IN MARX'S WORK

If Joan Robinson did not discover much that was new in the 'static' price theory of Marx, it is on the other hand possible to say that his dynamic price theory, as contained in the theory of 'relative surplus value' and 'extra surplus value', certainly presents new concepts that go far beyond his time and which must be considered as anticipating oligopolistic conditions.

There are quite a number of authors, the prototype of whom can be considered to be Scitovsky, who thought that the theory of marginal utility as developed by Walras, Menger and Jevons shortly after the publication of the first volume of *Capital* represented a reaction to the Marxian concept, for the Marxian theory with its long-run cost price characteristics seemed to push demand into the background, although the long-run social demand element is inherently contained in the notion of 'socially necessary labour'.

In modern times, there have been many voices denying that the marginal-utility theories represented a sort of reaction to Marxism. For instance, Bronfenbrenner in his paper to the American Economic Association on the occasion of the centenary of the first volume of *Capital* said (1967, pp. 626–7),

> I should like to help lay an extraordinarily durable ghost. This ghost is the perverse influence some people suspect that Marx exercised on the subsequent development of theoretical economics. It is the belief that the subjective, marginal or utility revolution in value and price theory was prompted ideologically, to escape from the consequence of the labor theory of value as developed particularly by Marx. This thesis is not proven; in fact, the weight of evidence seems to be against it. . . . *Das Kapital* itself succeeded so slowly, except in primitive, precapitalist Russia. . . . By the time the first volume became reasonably well known, in the 1880's, the utility revolution was independently in full swing, and marginal productivity was peering marginally over the marginal horizon. As for the German anticlassical revolution, it was well under way by 1867. . . .

Bronfenbrenner recognises, however, that one has to consider the marginal-utility theory as a reaction, if not to Marx, at least to the revolutionary consequences that could be drawn from Ricardo's value theory. The fact that Böhm-Bawerk was at the same time one of the earliest exponents of marginal-utility theory and one of the first adversaries of Marx may be indicative of some connexion. On the other hand, we must not forget that Lloyd, Gossen, Dupuit and Cournot in the 1830s and 1840s and Jevons in 1862 developed the foundations of the marginal-utility principle, and this again speaks in favour of Bronfenbrenner's opinion.

In this context it may be interesting to quote Samuelson (1971, p. 423) on the attitude of one of the forerunners of the marginal-utility school, John Bates Clark:

> Some twenty years ago at a conference at American University, I touched a filial nerve in John Maurice Clark when I cast some doubts about his father's belief that he, John Bates Clark, had irrefutably proved in the last decade of the last century the ethical justness of the marginal productivity mode of distribution. In his reply . . . J. M. Clark said that his father had been deeply conscious of the challenge offered by Marx's notion of exploitation ('under whose theory any share

capital gets is outright robbery') and felt under a necessity to defend the competitive system from those charges, which if true would have admittedly constituted a grave indictment. – Marx had to be refuted by orthodox economists – if only because he was there!

This statement by a trustworthy witness and adversary of the rank of Samuelson should properly decide the issue against Bronfenbrenner. Also against Bronfenbrenner is the fact that 'Marginal utility theory spread very slowly and did not effectively replace the labor theory of value until the last decade of the [nineteenth] century' (Blaug, 1968, p. 298). One might, perhaps, say that it was less the *discovery* of the marginal-utility principle than its *breakthrough*, especially after Marshall, that owed something to the reaction against Marxism.

However this may be, in retrospect it seems fairly certain that the marginal-utility school gained a victory in the static element of price theory. It is certainly true that the main emphasis has been on the refinement of the analysis of price on the basis of given demand functions. As taste undergoes only slow changes and as analysis of the connexion between the structure of demand and income changes – for instance, over the business cycle – is quite a late development, a consideration from the supply side, such as in the cost-of-production theory and especially in that of Marx, would *a priori* have appeared the more 'dynamic' approach.

In Marxist analysis, the dynamic elements are decisive, for in the last resort the social structure and with it also the structure of demand are seen as the product of productive forces. The final quintessence of this concept is the conclusion of modern oligopoly theory, according to which demand curves can be manipulated by suppliers.

As a matter of fact, the price theory of the marginal-utility theorists is a consequence of anonymous and more static forces in the market. Whereas the demand curve reflects the (given) wants of consumers, the supply curve reflects the (given) production data. The point of intersection of the two curves indicates the market price: this price is determined for the individual entrepreneur in a relatively passive way through the intersection of his (marginal) cost curve with the anonymously-formed market price, which appears as a horizontal curve.

This more 'static' price theory is a thoroughly passive doctrine, for it considers the individual entrepreneur as an atomistic and powerless market-unit, who does not make price but has to accept it – the creation of anonymous market forces. Marx, by contrast, introduces a dynamic entrepreneur who revolutionises his productive forces. Marx destroys the myth of anonymity and furnishes an analysis which explains the creation of the market price through identifiable forces.

Part V
Rent and Profit

19 Land Rent and Marginalism

The link between the theory of surplus value and the modern theory of profit is to be found in the Marxian variation of the Ricardian theory of rent.

The problem of monopoly leads us to the phenomenon of 'scarcity rents' as it was developed by the classical authors in their analysis of the rent of land. Ricardo identified the income from landed property as residual income. With a given demand and a given price, agricultural land will be exploited to the extent that is necessary to meet demand. When demand and price increase, new land is brought into use until all the areas that are economically useful are cultivated. The surplus of price over the costs of cultivation has, according to Ricardo, the character of a rent or residual income, because it is determined only by the level of the price and plays no part in the determination of price.

Marx's point of departure was likewise the idea that the value of land increases with increasing demand, and that the 'power of landed property' is able to appropriate 'an increasing portion of these values, which were created without its assistance'. An increasing price for agricultural products or the forces of nature (Marx quotes as an example water-power) leads to an increasing rent: 'it is evident that this rent is always a differential rent, for it does not enter as a determining factor into the general production price of commodities, but rather is based on it'. (*Capital*, III, ch. 37, pp. 639, 646.)

RICARDO'S THEOREM

Ricardo saw in the general scarcity of land a danger that could drive up wages to meet the higher prices of the means of subsistence and thereby cause the profits of capitalists to fall. Marx considered that this danger could be met by the cultivation of overseas lands, but, even so, he supplemented Ricardo's argument by introducing the idea of an 'absolute land rent'. According to the interpretation of Benedikt Kautsky (1957, p. 713), this 'absolute land rent' originates when the 'organic composition of agricultural capital remains below the average composition, but the monopoly of landed property prevents an equalisation of values with the price of production (which is lower than its value, because of the higher share of variable capital)'. In other words, with regard to agricultural as well as urban landed property, Marx presupposed the existence of a monopoly position, resulting in a monopolistic rent. Besides, he foresaw that there would be a tendency towards an increase in the price of land for building purposes.

THE OBJECTION OF LEXIS

Lexis (1913, p. 89) has raised a fundamental objection against Ricardo, on the basis of whose ideas Marx has developed his own thinking. He contests that there is, in principle, a difference between landed property and industrial property:

> If one would adopt such reasoning [i.e. following Ricardo, that rent does not determine price, but, rather, is determined by price], one could also defend the theory that the entire profit of capital of any enterprise does not constitute a part of the price of its total product, because . . . this profit is determined only by the difference between the price realised on the market and the cost of production, which in the same way as land rent must be different for various firms.

It is true that Marx in his analysis of 'relative surplus value' came quite close to characterising profits as rent, in the sense of intramarginal rent. Since he recognised the increase in the fertility of land through agricultural investment or the increase of receipts through the construction of houses as intensity rent, the idea that rent originates without 'any intervention' on the part of landowners has, in fact, to be dropped.

Lexis was by no means wrong when he said (ibid.), 'It is not possible to make a distinction between the receipts of landed property and other forms of capital either in agricultural enterprises or in any others (railways, for instance) where land is of overwhelming importance.'

MODERN INTERPRETATIONS

The theory of rent has been seized upon by modern Marxists. Mandel, for instance, says (1962, 1, p. 337),

> In industry, abnormal profits result when the productivity of an enterprise is higher than average productivity. Even if this higher productivity makes it possible to sell goods above their production price [in other words, costs], this leads to a decrease in average market price. In agricultural enterprises . . . the extra profit does not coincide with a

reduction, but with an increase, in market price. As soon as the demand for agricultural products exceeds the supply, because of an increase in population and because of lagging productivity in agriculture, the price is determined by the value of agricultural goods, which are produced under the worst conditions of profitability.

Nevertheless, the objection of Lexis remains valid. In industry as well, less productive enterprises, plants, installations and labour will be mobilised in response to increasing demand. In other words, the extra profit of intramarginal firms coincides with an increase in price! Mandel also senses the danger that it may be possible to develop an entirely new concept from Marx's theory of rent, for he objects to a 'transformation of this theory of rent into a general value theory'. In so doing he refers to 'the peculiarities of, and the different institutional conditions of, landed property'. He is here referring to the remnants of the feudal system. Disregarding the fact that there are numerous other economic sectors – transport, electricity, coal – which experience such peculiarities and could, therefore, lay valid claim to a special theory of price, one cannot justify the allusion to institutional peculiarities if one assumes that agriculture is carried out in a purely capitalist manner. Lexis (1913, p. 89) has already said, 'When a tenant buys land – a case of which Ricardo, with his English background, could not conceive – he pays interest instead of rent, and the property is now part of his capital and forms the basis of his profits on capital in the same way as other elements.' Mandel stresses (1962, p. 367) that

> the theory of rent, as developed by Ricardo and completed by Marx, was the point of departure for the marginal theory of value, which called into question the labour theory of value in the second half of the nineteenth century. According to Marx's theory of rent, it is, in fact, the demand for agricultural products that in the final analysis determines the price of these products. This price is based upon the value of the unit of output, produced on land with the worst productivity conditions (marginal price) for which there is still a buyer.

TRANSITION TO MARGINALISM?

The labour theory of value brought about its own competitors. We shall see what further affinities exist between Marx and the marginalists as soon as we begin to examine his dynamic theory more closely.

There remains the problem of whether the distinction between 'rent' and other kinds of income at the level of the entrepreneur or individual enterprise is really justified. What is characteristic of 'rent' is, after all, the fact that the relevant surplus is 'residual' and not created in a conscious way. As any improvement in land or in a productive unit in an industry means that 'advantages' are created, the entire complex of quasi-rents, as developed by Marshall, will, according to this definition, have to be eliminated from the notion of rent.

In that case, only 'pure' ground rent, including rent on primary products or riches in the soil, remains. On the other hand, extraordinary qualities in a man (for instance, managerial abilities) can also be considered as a 'source of rent'. There is, however, still the further objection that such a 'rent' would enter into the price of the relevant means of production – for instance, the waterfall, as quoted by Marx, would be sold by its first owner (or the person who appropriated it). This was the objection that Lexis raised against Ricardo's theory of rent. In this way, rent as a category would disappear, or would reappear as an 'intra-marginal rent' or 'quasi-rent', as long as the fiction of an average price level for the products of a particular industry could be maintained.

If we want to explain 'absolute surplus value' in a manner analogous to 'absolute rent', as the terms are used by Marx, we must postulate that the 'marginal workers' have to produce more than they receive in wages, while the market situation will not permit the hiring of additional workers.

It then remains to explain which forces, in an explanation of exploitation which is not based on the labour theory of value, are decisive in determining the relative power positions of workers and capitalists.

20 Competition and Equalisation of the Rates of Profit

The problem of the equalisation of the rates of profit can first of all be considered, in abstract terms, as a 'transition from values to prices'. An economic system in which prices are determined by values would, even according to Marx and Engels, be of a pre-capitalist character, in historical development reaching far into the past, and thus of little interest for the present.

There is, however, a form of 'equalisation of the rates of profit' that is of topical importance for the capitalist economy: namely, the relation between absolute or normal surplus value, on one side, and relative or extra surplus value, on the other.

'SLEEPY' *VERSUS* 'DYNAMIC' INDUSTRIES

In industries in which relative or extra surplus value is obtained in a considerable number of firms, there is by definition a great difference in cost from one firm to another. Individual entrepreneurs compete to undercut each other by continually introducing refinements. This is a fundamentally oligopolistic situation. These industries are dynamic, for dynamic enterprises dominate them. In such industries intramarginal profits (in Marxian terms, relative or extra surplus value) are decisive. Absolute or minimum surplus value appears in the course of time only in marginal firms, which become fewer and fewer, because they are outcompeted by firms with cost advantages. In this way, in the formation of total surplus value, relative surplus value finally prevails. This presupposes that differences in cost will be substantial, which implies that new firms appear that obtain 'advantages' in costs and in this way realise intramarginal profits (surplus profits). Here we encounter the difficult problem of whether, and how, it is possible to construct a supply curve under oligopolistic conditions (Aubert, 1949).

In so-called static or, more accurately, stationary industries, the entrepreneurs rest, as a rule, on their laurels. They are quite content to earn absolute or minimum surplus value. The existence of such minimum

159

surplus value may be explained by the prevalence of elements of monopolistic competition as described by Chamberlin.

In modern theory, in so far as the notion of the supply curve of an industry has been retained, Shove (1933, pp. 119–21) and Joan Robinson (1934) have introduced the notion of two different levels of profit. The 'normal level' in a stationary industry is the profit level necessary to prevent existing firms from leaving the industry, while the higher 'minimum profit level' is the level at which new firms will be attracted into the industry. These two levels may be compared in broad terms with the Marxian notions of absolute and relative (or extra) surplus value.

If we accept this representation, then surplus value will be measured differently in a dynamic industry from in a stationary one. If we assume that in both industries the same number of workers are employed, this means, according to Marx, that the sum of value will be the same in both, if we can suppose that in both cases not more than the 'socially necessary labour time' is being worked. If, now, different amounts of surplus value arise, while the share of labour value is the same, it follows that the rates of surplus value differ: the same number of workers produce different quantities of surplus value. In the industry with innovations we have a higher sum of surplus value and a higher rate of surplus value, because extra surplus value accrues to the different firms of this industry. If the capital input into both industries is the same, this means higher rates of profit for the industry with innovations.

We must now suppose that the continuing innovations in the dynamic industry signify a currently higher use of real capital. If this is the case, we may assume in the limiting case that both industries have the same rate of profit, with the higher rate of surplus value in the innovating industry being spread over a larger capital stock and meeting a higher rate of depreciation and the higher costs of raw materials, so that the rate of profit would be the same in the innovating industry as in the technically backward industry.

THE MARXIAN 'EQUALISATION OF PROFITS' – A SPECIAL CASE?

The result just obtained would appear to agree with the Marxian idea of the 'equalisation of the rates of profit'. However, it is an exception that can be entertained for only as long as production undergoes a limited expansion. As a general rule it must be postulated that the output of the dynamic industry would grow to such a degree that prices would decrease and the mass of surplus value as well as the rate of surplus value would shrink. On the other hand, one might assume that capital invested in 'dynamic' industries would lose its value more rapidly. If the two tendencies counterbalance, we should again have an 'equalisation of the rates of profit'.

What is decisive is, of course, the question of whether capital will tend to leave the 'sleepy' industry for the 'dynamic' industry. If it does not, oligopolistic barriers to entry must exist in the dynamic industry.

In Marx's view, the crux of the matter lies in the notion of 'socially necessary labour time'. In general, Marx interprets this notion as an average: the methods of production of the 'representative firm' in the sense of Marshall would find their expression in this term. On the other hand, if we were to assume that this notion would always embody the most progressive conditions, even if they were not yet fully operative, the result would be rather paradoxical. In an industry with 'steep' supply or cost curves and, therefore, with a high degree of dynamism, more of the firms would have to be considered as working with lower than average labour-intensity than would be the case in 'sleepy' industries. Here we encounter the question of whether the notion of 'socially necessary labour time' is not more appropriately a global measurement for the entire economy than a measurement for each industry, whereby 'stagnant' sectors erroneously appear as progressive when average values are used. Industries with very steep supply curves, indicating large differences in productivity between firms, are those in which 'those who produce at the worst extreme' encounter 'those producing at the best extreme' (*Capital*, III, ch. 10, p. 184.)

Marx started from the prevailing market structure of his time, i.e. more or less free competition. This can be deduced from various passages in his main work, but also from the general framework of his theory. He did not stop at this point, as we shall go on to show.

If the labour theory of value is in the first place a theory of distribution which measures the macroeconomic shares of workers and capitalists in the social product, Marx relies on competition to explain the division of the capitalists' share among themselves. If in an industry high average rates of surplus value or profits are realised, capital will flow into it. In this way competition between the different firms in this industry will be intensified, and at the same time the demand for labour will increase. The sum of variable capital can, therefore, again increase at the expense of the rate of surplus value.

A capitalist will try to counteract this tendency by applying a higher degree of mechanisation, which will lead to the redundancy of workers. The capital inflow will then predominate and lead to an increase in fixed capital, c. According to the law of the tendency of the rate of profit to fall, this must again lead to the disappearance of above-average profits, which in the first place will be threatened by the tendency for wages to increase. 'The competitive struggle among capitalists . . . is accompanied by a temporary rise in wages and a resultant further temporary fall of the rate of profit' (ibid., ch. 15, p. 256). Now, the same instrument as has been used to prevent an increase in wages will be used in the same direction: 'As a result of the increase in wages, the unpaid portion of total labour would be different and thereby the surplus-value too . . . the reduced surplus-value would express itself in a still more reduced rate of gross profit . . .' (ibid., ch. 50, p. 855).

PROBLEMS OF FINANCE AND 'EQUALISATION BETWEEN DIFFERENT SPHERES OF ACTIVITY'

In essence we are concerned here with a problem of finance. 'The incessant equilibration of constant divergences is accomplished so much more quickly . . . the more mobile the capital, i.e., the more easily it can be shifted from one sphere and from one place to another . . . (*Capital*, III, ch. 10, pp. 195–6). Unfortunately, Marx in this passage as well as in others mixes up a financing process and transfer of capital with the problem of the transformation of values into prices; according to his own interpretation the latter is a historical process, which he describes in the same chapter. This had led to much confusion among his supporters.

Piettre and Brenner have tried to explain the equalisation of prices and profits among different industries as follows. There is a 'flight of capital from the industries with a high organic composition of capital' (Brenner, 1966, p. 96) in order to 'move into more artisan-like enterprises' (Piettre, 1962, pp. 55–6). We can well understand why Piettre should say that it is 'totally unexpected' that 'the best-equipped enterprises are those with the lowest rate of profit'. His mistake is to be found in the fact that he has misinterpreted Marx, who uses the term 'spheres' to mean industries and not firms or enterprises.

If we suppose that in labour-intensive industries, where 'small capital' concentrates, higher profit rates exist than in capital-intensive industries, this may remind us of the 'thinking in profit margins' and of fixed mark-ups in small business, especially retailing, in our time. There are three possible explanations for the coexistence of high rates of profit in labour-intensive industries with lower rates of profit in mechanised industries.

First, small enterprises with high rates of profit may predominate in labour-intensive industries if there are monopolistic competition and strong consumer preferences, while in a large mechanised industry 'unstable' oligopolistic competition may prevail. In this way we come to the problem of large enterprises and their origin through 'concentration'. Secondly, the situation may arise in large enterprises that 'absolute surplus value' and the rate of profit of marginal producers are lower than in labour-intensive sectors where small enterprises predominate, although the chances of obtaining more 'advantages' by even greater mechanisation and decreases in cost (in Marxian terms, an increase in 'relative surplus value') are higher in large enterprises. Thirdly, high surplus value and high rates of profit in labour-intensive firms need not signify that capitalists fare better in these sectors, if they have to pay high rates of interest for their capital. The scarcity of capital may well explain why mechanisation has not been introduced into these sectors.

Where is it that capital exists in abundance, from where it can move into 'badly nourished' industries? One is tempted to refer to the modern debate on the investment problems of giant monopolistic enterprises. If, as Baran and Sweezy affirm, these firms practise a restrictive investment policy in their original activities, it is clear that they can use their liquid assets in sectors that have not yet been monopolised. This can be done through participation, the takeover of firms or the foundation of subsidiaries. In this case, fixed capital will be formed in the industries concerned, permitting mechanisation to proceed there.

If one industry after another becomes more mechanised, prices will decrease, as will the rates of profit and finally the average profit of the economy as a whole. This may go on to the point where the capital is written off because profits are low, in consequence of a 'crisis', and this will then lead again to an increase in the rate of profit.

The lower rates of profit in relatively capital-intensive, as compared with labour-intensive, industries can be explained by the Marxian hypothesis that there are identical rates of surplus value in both. Only in a few passages does Marx mention the possibility that the rates of surplus value might vary, and admit the possibility that value added might be differently divided in different industries (*Capital*, III, ch. 3, p. 57, and ch. 18, p. 150, and *Grundrisse*, p. 395, note 4).

If we continue to follow the Marxian argument, keeping strictly to Marx's own logic, we may in fact reach the conclusion that higher rates of profit and higher rates of surplus value may be expected in dynamic industries, and that the 'temporary monopoly' held by a firm that enjoys certain advantages should alter the distribution of value added within that industry. If a number of such 'temporary monopolies' coexist, there must be an increase not only in the volume of profits but also in the quantity of surplus value, the rate of profit and the rate of surplus value, in the short run at least. In such a case we are confronted not only with the problem of the equalisation of the rates of profit, but also with the problem of the equalisation of the rates of surplus value, between industries.

The boundary between industries with higher and those with lower rates of surplus value ought to coincide with that between strictly oligopolistic industries and others. Following this, industries with fewer 'temporary monopolies' and fewer technical innovations are 'undermechanised'. They may be favoured by possible differences in wages. If such industries are less unionised, it may happen, as Jung writes (1964, p. 103), that they obtain 'traditionally labour at wages that are below general rates, and are able to avoid an increase in capital intensity for a longer time'.

THE TRANSITION TO THE PROCESS OF CONCENTRATION

As a rule, Marx explains the uniformity in his rate of surplus value (for instance $v:s = 1:1$) by 'competition among labourers', which brings about an 'equalisation through their continual migration from one sphere of production to another'. This, he admits, is a 'theoretical simplification'.

In the third volume of *Capital* Marx says (ch. 10, p. 178) that it would only be 'natural' that 'value' should be 'the centre of gravity around which . . . prices fluctuate', and that 'there is also the *market-value* . . . to be distinguished from the individual value of particular commodities'. This individual value lies in socially necessary labour time: in branches of production with a low organic composition of capital the price is very high and in this case exceeds individual value; for goods which are produced with a higher organic composition of capital, the market-price lies below the individual value of marginal producers.

How is this equalisation effected in an 'imperfect' market, where the equalisation will occur first to prices and then to the rates of profit?

One firm after another becomes mechanised, constant capital grows in proportion to value added, and in the end the rate of profit lies at or below the average level. The point may be reached where firms can no longer finance their mechanisation from their own capital growth, i.e. 'accumulation', but have to fall back loans from banks or from the capital market. To an increasing extent, interest on loans will have to be paid and other obligations settled, and this will reduce the already diminished rate of profit even further.

The decisive point is, therefore, finance, with self-finance the crux. Large-scale enterprises prefer to obtain their funds on the capital market, a process which permits the transfer of capital from industries where the rate of profit is low.

In this context, Marxian analysis is no longer compatible with the principles of free competition. Competition in the Marxian sense is in this way no longer identical with perfect competition in the neoclassical or neo-liberal sense. This is already apparent in the formula, 'One capitalist always kills many.' 'Centralisation' means the 'transformation of many small into few large capitals', and that 'larger capitals beat the smaller'. (*Capital*, 1, ch. 32, pp. 714; ch. 25, pp. 586–7.) Competition in the Marxian sense is, therefore, a dynamic concept – a market structure which constantly becomes narrower and, for this reason, becomes imperfect.

Piettre's reference to the movement of capital from sectors in which big business prevails should not be understood only in the sense that there is less investment in such industries. This would contradict the Marxian theory of 'accumulation', which finds its decisive realisation in just those industries in which relatively few capitalists have at their disposal relatively large volumes of profit and can, therefore, consume only a small percentage. It is just here that the famous dictum 'Accumulate, accumulate! That is Moses and the prophets!' (*Capital*, i, ch. 24, p. 558) finds its application.

While it is true that Marx speaks of the 'ruin of many small capitalists' and says that 'larger capitals beat the smaller', it would be utterly wrong to believe that he saw in this ruin a development that would proceed straightforwardly. On the contrary, he says in the same passage, 'The smaller capitals, therefore, crowd into spheres of production which Modern Industry has only sporadically or incompletely got hold of' (ibid., ch. 25, pp. 586–7).

Besides bringing ruin to some capitalists, the process of concentration brings about a shift in the position of capitalists generally. In the joint-stock companies, in the hands of individual or associated capitalists, financial resources that had been dispersed in greater or smaller quantities are combined (ibid., iii, ch. 27). Marx also speaks of the result of activities on the stock exchange, 'where the little fish are swallowed by the sharks and the lambs by the stock-exchange wolves'. He mentions that some small capitalist firms are forced into industries where labour-intensity prevails, and that this occurs not because the relatively greater amount of variable capital there promises a greater sum of surplus value and a higher rate of profit, but simply because the 'increase in the minimum amount of individual capital' gives the smaller capitalists no alternative (ibid., i ch. 25, p. 587). In other words, the 'threshold value which capital must attain to be effective' increases continually. 'Economies of scale' are effective within the framework of the 'law of mass production'. The 'minimum of capital required with the increase in productivity for the successful operation of an independent industrial establishment' rises (ibid., iii, ch. 15, p. 262).

This threshold value, according to Marx, is one of the main forces making for concentration. 'Originally a certain minimum size of individual capital appeared necessary . . . to make a capitalist out of a small master and to establish formally the capital relation. It appears now as a material condition for the transformation of many dispersed and individual work processes to a combined social work process.' Marxian competition is, therefore, a dynamic process in which the mechanised sectors constantly experience 'advantages' through an increase in capital. This leads to an extra profit, 'relative surplus value' in Marxian terminology, gained by the so-called 'pioneer enterprises', but at the same time this process periodically lowers the average profit per unit of capital in the industries concerned.

ELEMENTS OF 'IMPERFECT' COMPETITION IN MARX

Here we start from the analysis of 'relative surplus value' developed by Marx in the first volume of *Capital*. According to this, mechanisation, or in

other words the intensified use of constant capital, can, in Marx's words
(*Capital*, 1, ch. 10, pp. 300–1) have the following effect: 'let some one
capitalist contrive to double the productiveness of labour . . . the market
must [then] become twice as extensive. Other things being equal, his
commodities can command a more extensive market only by the
diminution of their prices'.

It follows (ibid., iii, ch. 15, pp. 264–5) that a capitalist who has gained a
certain advantage in production and slightly undercuts his competitors
attains an 'extra surplus value'. 'He pockets the difference between their
costs of production and the market-prices of the same commodities
produced at higher costs of production.' This undercutting is, a typical
process of oligopolistic competition, for it shows that the enterprise in
question has the potential to manipulate the parameter 'price'.

But then competition sets in, and now 'the capitalists working with the
old methods of production must sell their product below its full price of
production'. Competition, therefore, leads to the following results.
Whereas the volume of profits and the profit rate in the 'pioneer' enterprise
increase, all other entrepreneurs in that particular industry earn lower
profits. In addition, the 'organic composition of capital' (or capital–
output ratio) is increased over the entire industry with the consequence
that the (decreased) volume of profits must be related to a higher volume
of capital, which means that the rate of profit in the industry as a whole
sinks.

Joan Robinson has pointed out that in perfect competition each
enterprise has to work at full or optimum capacity. A firm that does not use
its full capacity will not be able to cover fixed costs and will soon go
bankrupt. This is to be explained by the fact that in perfect competition
price coincides with the optimum cost point of the mass of 'representative'
firms. Inefficient firms will be eliminated. This is the process which Marx
had in mind, but he did not analyse it in marginalist terms.

The objection has been raised by Weddingen (1934, p. 35) that the
tendency towards the elimination of firms, as foreseen by Marx, does not
necessarily lead to a preponderance of large-scale enterprises, for there is
such a thing as an 'optimum size of firm', placing a limit on the growth of
the individual enterprise. Those who argue in this way overlook the fact
that in many industries this optimum has not yet been reached, that in
Marx's times it certainly had not been reached at all, and that this
optimum is variable and itself tends to grow.

Now, Joan Robinson is of the opinion (1949, pp. 74, 77) that in real life
'full capacity working is a rarity' even in conditions of prosperity. For this
reason, imperfect competition must be the rule. Elsewhere it is pointed out
that there are certain analogies between the Marxian theory of surplus
value and the modern theory of imperfect competition. On the other hand,
as Joan Robinson recognizes (ibid., p. 77), there are essential formal
differences between Marx's theory and modern analysis: 'the modern

theory exposes many relatively minor defects in capitalism which Marx, concentrating on major issues, was content to ignore.'

It is true that even Marx speaks occasionally of 'the amount the merchant advances in its purchase price, i.e., for a certain quantity of it' (*Capital*, III, ch. 18, pp. 306–7). In another passage he says, 'a merchant may reduce his selling price (which is never more than a reduction of the usual profit that he adds to the price)'. This could be interpreted in line with the following formulation by Joan Robinson (1949, p. 79):

> The gross profit margin, or rake-off on prime cost, therefore, probably depends very much upon historical accident or upon conventional views among business men as to what is reasonable. . . . So long as all adhere to the same set of conventions each can enjoy his share of the market . . . though in fact the group as a whole, by unconscious collusion, is imposing a mild degree of monopoly upon the market.

In reasoning thus, Joan Robinson has perhaps found a special formulation for Marx's theory of surplus value, such that it offers an answer to the question, raised by Lederer, Gestrich and even Graziadei, of why surplus value is not competed away. She states in the same context that in essence modern economics 'has not yet solved its first problem – what determines the price of a commodity?' As to the question of 'normal profits', 'academic economics fails to provide any theory which is relevant to the real world'.

It is significant that Joan Robinson herself, in her theory of imperfect competition, includes a 'normal profit' in her cost curves. This notion of normal profit appears in various passages in Marx's work in the form of 'social average profit' – for instance, in his analysis of 'commercial capital', which, according to him, does not create any surplus value.

In the same context Marx wanted explicitly to exclude 'the cases in which the merchant is a monopolist and simultaneously monopolises production'. For the other cases he declared that 'nothing can be more ridiculous than the current idea that it depends on the merchant whether he sells many commodities at a small profit or few commodities at a large profit on each individual piece of the commodities' (*Capital*, III, ch. 18, p. 306).

This sounds as if Marx were refuting the thesis of imperfect competition, but one ought not to be mistaken about this. Even in the theories of Chamberlin and Robinson a given firm is not in the position to fix its output at will. On the contrary, the cost and demand conditions are given, and output as well as price is determined.

Marx always takes demand as given, but he meets Joan Robinson's idea of normal profit by naming 'two limits of his selling price' – namely, what he calls the 'price of production', i.e. the costs of production including normal profit, and 'the general rate of profit'. He explicitly says (ibid.) that for the merchant both items are given. In other passages he talks about 'customary profit', which shows similar connexions. Marx shows further affinities to the theory of imperfect competition when he recognises (ibid., ch. 19, p. 317) that Feller and Odermann are right in stating, 'Surely the fact that one and the same commodity may be had from different sellers at considerably different prices is frequently due to mistakes of calculation.' This observation is interesting, in so far as Marx calls it 'naïve but at the same time correct'. In so saying he implicitly recognises that price need not be given, but can vary, and that it is the seller himself who fixes it, even if by means of a 'wrong calculation'!

The idea of 'normal profit' even in competition is already implicit in the theory of surplus value itself. It first of all appears in the fact, as Lederer has emphasised, that surplus value is not competed away. Secondly, it is contained in Marx's hypothesis that as a general rule a certain proportion of value added is always retained for surplus value. This hypothesis appears to be strangely confirmed by the so-called 'mystery of constant shares in the social product', as Joan Robinson has christened it.

SURPLUS VALUE AND THE PROBLEM OF THE BUSINESS CYCLE IN MARX'S WORK

The existence of profit will prompt capitalists to enlarge their production. In this way every capitalist will increase his demand for labour power, assuming that the increase in production cannot be brought about simply by an increase in machinery, which would mean an increase in constant capital. The increased demand for labour will next lead to an increase in wages, which in turn may bring about a decrease in the rate of surplus value and also in the rate of profit. As capitalists consider a 'minimum rate of surplus value' and, *a fortiori*, a 'minimum profit rate' or a 'natural (minimum) rate of interest' as indispensable, they will finally launch a 'capital strike' or at least an 'investment strike', if they do not obtain it. This means that there will be a recession.

In such a recession, all those calamities will occur that Marx depicts in his theory of the falling rate of profit: the capital value will be annihilated. This will then lead to a relative increase in the rate of profit, but at the same time workers will be dismissed. This 'reserve army' will bring about a decrease in wages, or will at least prevent further wage increases. Thus investment will be revived, and recovery will begin anew.

Here we have the transition to the dynamic system. The competitive process and the equalisation process of 'classical' competitive capitalism is eventually interrupted in our era of big business. If large-scale enterprises are at least temporarily satisfied with a lower rate of profit, they possibly will not engage in an 'investment strike' at the time when a medium-size enterprise would do so. This would then mean that a recession would begin somewhat later than in normal competitive capitalism, but would also signify that it might last longer, because the destruction of capital and the setting free of labour would occur more slowly. This could also mean that in the long run the average level of profits would decrease. In that case, the 'law of the falling rate of profit' as a cyclical phenomenon would recede more and more and, as in Ricardo and the classics, become almost exclusively a long-run phenomenon *via* increased oligopolistic practices. This theory, which would mean that 'socially conscious' oligopolies would seek only moderate profits, and which would vindicate the Marxian theory of the long-run decrease in the rate of profit, may be seen as the exact counterpart of the neo-Marxist theory developed by Baran and Sweezy (examined later). (See Chapters 33 and 36).

In the short run, if the profit rate falls below the 'normal level', the consequence could be a decrease in investment and an increase in unemployment. On the other hand, if, generally speaking, the productivity of labour grows more slowly in the course of such developments, this must signify that in the long run national income will increase more slowly. This again favours consumption and the increase of the wage share in the social product.

From this we may conclude that a certain degree of 'monopolistic competition' could be considered useful from the point of view of the economy as a whole, in so far as it could prevent the rates of surplus value from being depressed. Conversely, the higher the degree of monopoly, the greater the possibility that wage increases will not be as large as they might have been under conditions of free competition. However, a decrease in the rate of profit, and paralysis of the propensity to invest, could lead to periods of stagnation.

In this way the discussion of competitive conditions leads us to the analysis of monopoly and oligopoly problems. It is true that Marx mentioned these problems only sporadically, but, nevertheless, it cannot be denied that he developed them in essence. According to Marx (*Capital*, 1, ch. 15, p. 383), the advantageous position that a capitalist actually attains and that leads to the formation of 'relative surplus value' by means of reinforcing 'machinery' 'is a sort of monopoly' and 'the profits are therefore exceptional' in 'the sunny times of this his first love'.

Marxian analysis leads finally to the conclusion that there must be different rates of profit in individual industries ('production spheres', as Marx calls them).

21 Microeconomic Analogies with Marxian Profit Analysis

The similarities between the theories of Marx and Schumpeter are very strong. After all, in Schumpeter's static system (1926, pp. 241–2) there is no rate of interest, but only entrepreneurs' wages and a risk premium, if any. It must be stressed that the same theory was developed a quarter of a century before Schumpeter by Walras (1874; 1952, p. 42), not for the rate of interest, but for entrepreneurs' profits. In this line of reasoning, 'surplus value' as conceived by Marx would be a continuously re-created product of a dynamic development: either as an 'advantage' enjoyed over less economic combinations of the means of production ('relative surplus value'), or as 'absolute surplus value', the profits of 'socially necessary' marginal producers in an industry.

Marx did not want his theory of surplus value to refer to a single industry and even less to a single business firm: he thought of it rather as applying to the entire social product. According to Schumpeter (1947, p. 29), 'it is not absurd to look upon surplus value as a "mass" produced by the social forces of production as a unit and to make the rest a matter of the distribution of that mass'.

Quite a number of attempts have been made to interpret the theory of surplus value and the idea of exploitation linked to it in such a way that they appear compatible with the further development of modern economics, especially within the area of the theory of profits. Some of these attempts must be understood as being implicitly analogous to Marxian theory.

THE MARK-UP THEORY OF LEXIS

The first attempt of this kind was made by Lexis. In an early discussion of Marx's *Capital*, he devised some formulations which were received positively by Engels himself. According to Lexis, surplus value originates not in production but in circulation. Entrepreneurs calculate their prices according to the principle of full cost: in other words they add a minimum margin to the costs of commodities produced by them. This implicitly presupposes that they limit their production as soon as the market no longer affords them these 'minimum profits'.

The only commodity-owner who cannot add on a margin and who is constrained in the sale of his commodity, because as a service it vanishes at the moment of its non-use, is the supplier of labour power – the worker. In availing himself of his opportunities, he is further hindered by the existence of the reserve army of labour. Engels accepted the theory developed by Lexis as an equivalent to the Marxian theory of surplus value and he discussed it in detail. According to Engels, Lexis said that 'the profits on capital could, indeed, be explained in the Marxian way, but one should not be obliged to accept such reasoning'. Engels (Preface to *Capital*, III, 1894 edition, pp. 9ff.) quoted Lexis as follows:

> The capitalist sellers . . . all make a gain on their transactions by selling at a price higher than the purchase price, thus adding a certain percentage to the price they themselves pay for the commodity. The worker alone is unable to obtain a similar additional value for his commodity; he is compelled by reason of his unfavourable condition *vis-a-vis* the capitalist to sell his labour at the price it costs him, that is to say, for the essential means of his subsistence. . . . Thus, these additions to prices retain their full impact with regard to the buying worker, and cause the transfer of a part of the value of the total product to the capitalist class. . . .

Continuing from this Engels states,

> One need not strain one's thinking powers to see that this explanation for the profits of capital, as advanced by 'vulgar economy', amounts in practice to the same thing as the Marxian theory of surplus-value. . . . In reality, however, this theory is merely a paraphrase of the Marxian. For if it is a common property of all commodities to be sold at a price higher than their cost of production, with labour being the sole exception since it is always sold at the cost of production, then labour is simply sold below the price that rules in this world of vulgar economy. Hence the resultant extra profit accruing to the capitalist, or capitalist class, arises, and can only arise, in the last analysis, from the fact that the worker, after reproducing the equivalent for the price of his labour-power, must produce an additional product for which he is not paid – i.e. a surplus-product, a product of unpaid labour, or surplus value. . . . It is plain as day that we are dealing . . . with a Marxist disguised as a vulgar economist.

In his main work (1913), Lexis repeated his argument in its essentials (pp. 143–4):

How does distribution . . . come about? If we consider the economy as a whole, this will undoubtedly come about through the fact that the entrepreneurs, first of all, hand over only part of the receipts of production in the form of wages; of the remainder, they retain part and distribute the rest to the owners of the capital tied up in the firm. The entrepreneurs are the owners of the means of production, without, which the workers cannot make their labour power productive . . . nevertheless, the wages paid to workers do not constitute an advance, but are the price of labour, which is finally bought on his own account by the entrepreneur in a process which involves some degree of speculation. . . . In this way, workers probably fare better than if they were to pay, in the manner implied, rent and interest themselves, so as to sell the product at their own risk. . . .

Joan Robinson has provided an analogous formulation (1949, p. 76):

the main influence upon the share of labour in the total product is the degree of imperfection of competition in selling commodities and in buying labour. At each stage of production, from the raw-material industry to the retail shop, the seller takes a rake-off on prime cost, governed by the elasticity of demand in that market, and the rake-off at one stage enters into prime cost at the next. – In the market for consumers' goods, a relatively small number of sellers face a large number of buyers, so that the imperfection of competition tells in favour of the sellers. In the labour market the position is reversed. Thus the share of labour in total output is ground between the upper and the nether millstones of monopoly and monopsony.

In this way the 'mark-up theory' of Lexis is integrated with the theory of imperfect competition.

THE THEORY OF PROPERTY POWER – GRAZIADEI AND OPPENHEIMER

Graziadei's analysis resembles the theory developed by Lexis. The Italian author practically renounces the microeconomic theory of surplus value; for his surplus value is simply the macroeconomic 'share in the social product' attained by the dominating class. In one of his early works (1897), Graziadei tried to prove that the labour theory of value as such was a *reductio ad absurdum*.

Graziadei emphasised (1925, pp. 251–2) that the entrepreneur pays the worker without having sold the commodity, or, in Marxian terms, without having 'realised' his product.

The wage paid to the worker, seen *in toto*, is nothing but an advance of part of future production. . . . This advance is necessary because . . . the worker has neither the means of existence to allow him to wait, nor the technical means to begin production on his own account. . . . It is the case that the capitalist entrepreneur, and he alone, controls the capital, which gives him a decisive superiority from the very beginning in his contract with the workers. . . . The excess price (or surplus value) is nothing but a 'just' premium for the stronger.

Graziadei does not examine in detail the 'historic reasons which explain, why the worker has to endure such circumstances'. In his opinion, such an analysis must 'go beyond a simple analysis of commodities'.

It is necessary to supplement Graziadei's analysis, and this has actually been done by Oppenheimer. He explains the inherent weakness of the worker in the labour market not only through the existence of an industrial reserve army but also by the fact that, when the industrialisation began, access to land was blocked, largely under feudal conditions. The fact that it was no longer possible to obtain free land within Europe forced the masses to join the industrial reserve army. (The origins of this theory are to be found in the works of Sismondi, who saw elements of appropriation in land- and capital-owning interests. He thought that capitalists and landowners used their rights of domination to force the propertyless worker to provide labour services.) The theory developed by Graziadei, has been accepted by a number of Marxists – for instance, by Lucien Laurat (1934). This French Marxist said concerning Graziadei's book *Le Capital et la Valeur*, (1940, p. 20),

There can be no doubt that value theory, as handed down to us by Marx and as developed by a number of his supporters, suffers from certain deficiencies. . . . We may only point in this context to certain aspects of the labour theory of value that need a detailed elaboration. A serious objective criticism, even if it is not considered to be well founded as a whole can, nevertheless, help us to enlarge our vision and to bring about a general clarification of our ideas. – It seems to us that such criticism has been provided by Graziadei in his recently published book *Le Capital et la Valeur*. . . . A theory shows its real value in its ability to explain concrete phenomena. . . .

LEDERER'S THEORY OF 'ADVANTAGE'

Lederer's interpretation of the theory of labour and surplus value starts from a rebuttal of the criticism offered by Böhm-Bawerk. Böhm-Bawerk's criticism is based on the idea that Marx, when recognising, in the third volume of *Capital*, price formation in competition, renounced the principle of value. Lederer (1922, p. 104) states Böhm-Bawerk's position as follows: 'After all, one could maintain that the exchange ratio between commodities was determined by weight. If some commodities are sold at a higher price than corresponds to their weight, others are sold at a lesser one. . . .' Lederer takes exception to this argument:

> This would be true if the labour theory of value were only to say that commodities are sometimes sold above and sometimes below their value without giving an exact measure of these deviations. Such an exact measure exists, however, in the organic composition of capital in the enterprise. In a sale above or below value, a deviation or distortion is indicated the extent of which can be theoretically determined. Hence this formula of production prices offers a solution and not, as Böhm-Bawerk thought, a spurious solution. . . .

In the rest of his argument, Lederer puts the main stress on the 'theory of differential rent', which is based on the principle of a permanent dynamic development of capitalism. He says that 'the labour theory of value is valid only on the further assumption that free competition prevails everywhere'; and he adds, 'By free competition we not only understand that producers compete with each other, and that each tries to obtain the greatest advantage, but indirectly we also want to say that commodities . . . can be produced in any quantity at the same cost.'

Lederer declares shortly afterwards (ibid., p. 107) that this, his own, definition is not valid: it would mean that average and marginal cost curves of individual firms were identical. He admits that in agriculture, and even 'within industry' (for instance, in coal-mining), one must reckon on the existence of 'decreasing returns or increasing costs'. In such cases, 'the exchange conditions for the total quantity produced will be determined as if it had been produced at the highest cost' and 'for producers, who work under more favourable circumstances than marginal producers, a differential rent will accrue that is a consequence of, and not the cause of the higher price'.

In this way Lederer extends the application of the principle of rent from land to all combinations of capital goods. He then asks (ibid., p. 159) the decisive questions which lead to a modification of the labour theory of value:

> Why or when does the entrepreneur not compete over the worker to the point where he produces without profits? Why are wages and the prices of the means of production not increased so much that finally only costs will be covered in selling the product? Why are not all kinds of production without profit in the long run, or, under what conditions are not all forms of production profitless in the long run?

In answering these questions, Lederer refers to Schumpeter's 'theory of economic development', according to which the stationary economy would be without interest and, therefore, without any profit. According to Schumpeter, profits and interest arise continuously within the framework of new combinations, in the form of advantages, and partly also through economies of scale. Lederer goes on to say (ibid., pp. 162–3) that

> if we assume that an industry consists of a hierarchy of firms, interest would not be part of the price but a consequence of the price attained in 'marginal firms'. It is easy to understand that all prices could then be conceived as if they were determined by labour cost, because, after all, even rent is a differential rent. All prices would then be determined by marginal utility, but this would correspond to the costs in marginal firms. . . . Under free competition, a surplus and with it interest would continuously disappear and continuously reappear. . . .

With this 'advantage theory' based on Schumpeter, Lederer has effected the most significant synthesis between the labour theory of value and the theory of marginal utility. It is now labour cost (including the entrepreneur's wage!) in the marginal firm which determines price. In the short run, this marginal firm need not even earn enough money to pay interest on its own capital – interest disappears as a category, even at the microeconomic level! The marginal firm performs work that is just necessary from the point of view of society. Lederer attempts to bring about such a synthesis because he sees (ibid., p. 115) that 'the entire modern [subjective!] value theory is nothing more than an attempt to understand the problem of exchange and of continuous production from the demand side – as the labour theory of value tries to tackle the same problem from the supply side'.

Lederer is fully aware of the difference between his theory and that of Schumpeter when he says (ibid., p. 161),

> The element of the advantage in production is able to explain more than it would appear at first sight, and even more than Schumpeter himself explains by recourse to that theory. In particular it transpires that large profits can always be realised in economic life without requiring a really path-breaking innovation. If Schumpeter emphasises the rôle of the economic leader and his heroic achievement, he sees only part of the story.

In this way Lederer anticipates some of the most modern formulations of the theory of large-scale enterprise, among others the rôle of the firm as an organisational unit in Penrose's works, where the firm is able to change even the purpose of its activities at will. He anticipates also Galbraith's theory of the 'technostructure'.

Schumpeter's work still contains a justification of the capitalist, because he identifies him with the path-breaking, innovating entrepreneur, to the pioneering function of whom he attributes differential profit as a reward. For Galbraith, however, the shareholder is no longer of interest, nor even the 'revolutionary manager' as extolled by Burnham. On the contrary, for him the decisive element is the new combination, and, therefore, the cost advantage, which is the achievement of a 'team', of the 'technostructure'. The latter term embraces a vast range of workers, from the leading managers down to the skilled workers. 'Profits' are to be imputed 'collectively' to this technostructure. In the final analysis one would then have to accept the idea not only of participation in profits, but also of the sharing-out of profits.

Lederer's most important contribution perhaps lies in his synthesis of the labour theory of value and the theory of marginal utility. He himself, however, was not content. He wanted to do more – to explain why 'marginal firms' could still obtain profits: 'After all, it is not the normal condition of an industry for a group of 'marginal firms' to obtain no profit at all; on the contrary, the problem is why a surplus is obtained in all firms, even normal ones, and this is the solution we must seek' (Lederer, 1922, p. 170).

In this context, Lederer thought of industries in which quite a few or even the majority of the firms were 'marginal'; and after due consideration he returned (ibid., p. 177) to the solution offered by Marx, who explains the permanence of an absolute profit by the existence of an industrial reserve army.

> With a growing population the competition among workers for the means of subsistence and jobs is necessarily greater than that among capitalists, this latter competition tending to eliminate profits. For, if profits were completely competed away (*via* a cheapening of products), it would be true that the means of subsistence at the disposal of the masses would first grow, but then would remain unchanged; and, if the population continued to increase, real wages would necessarily sink. At the very moment when pressure was exercised on wages, profits would originate, the entrepreneurs would gain additional purchasing power, and the means of production would be produced. The forces that lead to the creation of surplus in value in capitalist production are always active. . . .

Lederer has offered probably the most important modern reinterpretation of the labour theory of value. It is true, however, that one further decisive element was not recognised in his analysis, for he thought (ibid., p. 119) that 'monopoly price . . . cannot be explained by the principle of labour value'.

PERFECT COMPETITION AND THE THEORY OF SURPLUS VALUE

According to the theory of perfect competition in the ideal case there should not be any 'profits' except those contained in what is called in German *kalkulatorische Posten* (standard depreciation, risk premium, entrepreneur's salary and interest). This is possible if one accepts the basic conditions of perfect competition, as, for instance, developed by Jöhr (1946), retaining at least the most important elements of his more complicated reasoning: all firms (or a large number of firms) have the same cost curves, price appears to all of them as given, and their cost curves remain unchanged (in other words there is no dynamic development).

Under these circumstances output will always correspond to the optimum point of each cost curve, at which average and marginal cost curves intersect each other. The question is, what is hidden in these cost curves? 'Orthodox' theory presupposes that all three standard items, namely entrepreneur's salary, risk premium and interest (including standard depreciation), are contained in costs. Under modern conditions, we can eliminate the entrepreneur's salary in the case where there is a hired manager administering a large firm. Risk premium and interest, however, will have to appear as costs even under perfect competition.

There is no controversy about that in industrial economics. The economic reasoning of 'orthodox' theory runs as follows. If the risk premium and a minimum rate of interest cannot be guaranteed, there is no stimulus to capitalists to supply capital. What else, however, can they do with their capital? What is the alternative?

From the point of view of the economy as a whole it is basically a paradox if capitalism in its totality has to be compensated for risks, which it engenders itself through competition and business cycles, conditions which are part of its very nature. Their risk premium can at the most be considered only as part of the minimum interest which capitalism needs in order to function. Why, however, does capitalism need this? What is the alternative to the productive use of capital?

Marshall said that interest is the reward for 'waiting'. In the first edition of his principal work (1890), in a passage which, significantly enough, he was later to remove, he defines this concept quite clearly (p. 614):

> that surplus benefit which a person gets in the long run by postponing enjoyment, and which is measured by the rate of interest (subject as we have seen to certain conditions), is the reward of waiting. . . . But if, having the power to consume that property in immediate gratifications, he chooses to put it in such a form as to afford him deferred gratifications, then any superiority there may be in these deferred gratifications over those immediate ones is the reward of his waiting.

In a note Marshall adds, 'but on the whole it is perhaps best to say that there are three factors of production, land, labour, and the sacrifice involved in waiting'.

In later editions, which proved to be less colourful, Marshall deleted these passages, probably because the notion of 'sacrifice' brought him in dangerous proximity to Senior's theory of abstinence', which had been successfully ridiculed by Marx and Lassalle. Striking a balance, it can be said that Marshall's argument coincides with Böhm-Bawerk's theory of the higher valuation of goods (or enjoyments) in the present.

First of all, it must be emphasised that this idyllic image of the individual capitalist hovering between enjoyment and investment hardly corresponds to our times. The mass of investment is nowadays carried out by large-scale enterprises within the framework of self-finance; the decision on the declaration of a dividend is, generally, imposed on shareholders. In so far as these shareholders are of an institutional character (banks, insurance companies, the state, etc.), one cannot speak of a choice between enjoyment and investment. Marx's words 'Accumulate, accumulate! That is Moses and the prophets!' therefore incorporate effectively the reality of modern capitalism. Galbraith, indeed, sees the virtue of capitalism as lying in the automatic 'saving' out of profits. Here we may quote Joan Robinson (1949, p. 21):

> Marshall's use of the term *waiting* provides an example of verbal suggestion. He is concerned to show that it is necessary for the owners of wealth to receive interest, in order to overcome the temptation to dissipate their capital in present consumption. It would be natural to draw the moral that if capitalists have to be bribed to keep their capital intact, they ought rather to be expropriated and their capital put into safe keeping for the benefit of society.

In other words, if it comes to the point that saving is largely of an automatic character, having been institutionalised in mammoth enterprises and in enterprises belonging to the state (including social insurance, 'para-state' enterprises, and so on), we must ask whether it is then still justified to consider interest as one of the 'necessary costs' in the economy as a whole. On the other hand, it cannot be denied that interest retains an allocative function in basic calculation, even if it is bereft of all its mystical aspects.

It is true that Marx himself said that the stimulating effects of profit would be dulled and accumulation would be restricted if the rate of profit were to sink: 'the rate of self-expansion of the total capital, or the rate of profit, being the goad of capitalist production (just as self-expansion of capital is its only purpose), its fall checks the formation of new independent capitals and thus appears as a threat to the development of the capitalist production process' (*Capital*, III, ch. 15, p. 242). One can ask whether his entire theory of the tendency of the rate of profit to fall does not implicitly recognise the importance of the stimulus of profit. This, however, need not be so, for the variation in investment, according to Marx, is to be explained by changes in the volume of profits.

In Marx's view, it is characteristic of capitalists that their main drive is towards accumulation and that they thus abstain from consumption. If this is so, one may presuppose that in the cost curves of 'perfect competition' there is no longer a 'minimum profit' (including risk premium), but that competition has allowed this last difference between 'cost' in the proper sense and 'price' to disappear without bringing about capital consumption. All firms, which by definition have the same cost curves, would finally be in the situation of marginal producers, who earn just enough to meet the depreciation of their capital and to pay the entrepreneurs' salaries but no longer enough to pay interest.

This would be an 'equilibrium without profits', which would correspond to the static situation described by Schumpeter. Nobody could move into another industry – not even in the long run through liquidation of capital, because the same conditions would, by definition, prevail everywhere. 'Surplus value' would have disappeared, but at the same time a proof would have been given that in essence it had no economic justification.

At this juncture Marx would protest. With the disappearance of surplus value the essence of capitalism itself would have disappeared! As a matter of fact, such a world of small producers without any 'profit-making' would resemble pre-capitalist conditions, where each artisan worked only for his 'nourishment'. Only those capitalists working in their own firms would earn an entrepreneur's salary.

But to Marx dynamics and capitalism are more or less synonymous, and therefore surplus value is for him inherent in capitalism. This leads us to the conclusion that the existence of surplus value can no longer be explained in a static sense, but has to be explained dynamically, in the sense of the 'advantage' realised by a particular firm, as outlined by Lederer, according to whose theory all producers except marginal ones realise profits. Indeed, according to Lederer's thoughts on 'absolute' profit, the marginal producer himself can realise a profit, provided it is not so great that new marginal producers with higher cost curves appear in the particular industry. In the latter case a threshold profit would be possible for marginal producers and this would turn into a profit based on cost advantage only when a new marginal producer appeared.

MONOPOLISTIC COMPETITION ACCORDING TO ROBINSON AND CHAMBERLIN

The modern theory of monopolistic competition has created a new point of departure for the theory of surplus value. From a microeconomic point of view this occurred in theories of imperfect competition developed by

Sraffa, Chamberlain and Joan Robinson. (It is one of the ironies of the history of economic doctrines that Joan Robinson in her studies on Marx did not fully see the analogies between her own theory of competition and the Marxian theory of surplus value). At the macroeconomic level the theory can be identified with the 'degree of monopoly', a concept developed by Lerner and Kalecki. The theory can best be described in Chamberlin's own words (1946, p. 213):

> the typical outcome of free enterprise is not pure competition, but monopolistic competition. Commodities are differentiated partly by their very nature (without regard to demand) and partly in response to differences in buyers' tastes, preferences, locations etc. . . . Heterogeneity from these causes is vastly increased by businessmen under 'free enterprise', in their efforts further to distinguish their commodity from others and to manipulate the demand for it through advertising. In other words, an essential part of free enterprise is the attempt of every businessman to build up his own monopoly. . . . There is no tendency for these monopolies to be competed out of the picture. . . .

This would mean that monopoly profits, which approximate to 'absolute surplus value' as understood by Marx, can no longer be competed away! Chamberlin says, 'In many cases it would be quite impossible to establish [pure competition], even supposing it to be desirable. . . .'

It is possible to simplify this theory as follows. If we suppose that cost curves represent wages only, 'surplus value' originates because the entrepreneur does not carry his production to the point where, though lowering price to sell the additional product, average wage and average price per unit produced coincide. He can, however, try to manipulate the parameter 'price' by resorting to resale-price maintenance. The difference between marginal cost and average price in this case is surplus value.

Now, we may object that this theory is, in fact, a reproduction of 'miniature monopoly'. Marx himself, however, explicitly excluded monopolies from his analysis, limiting it to 'competition', and, therefore, one might conclude that the analogy is not relevant.

To argue in this way would mean that one had overlooked the real problem. It is true that Chamberlin (1946, pp. vii, 56ff.) sees in 'monopolistic competition' an extended market form, but he does not see it as identical with 'monopolisation' in the sense of a monopoly of the whole industry through trusts or cartels. On the other hand, Joan Robinson in her *Economics of Imperfect Competition* sees it as the normal case for the whole economy: each producer has a 'relative' monopoly for his article. Further still, Joan Robinson (1933, p. 307) sees the monopoly profit of the individual firm as the result of the 'exploitation of factors of production' in the Pigovian sense.

A French writer on oligopoly, Chamley, has found a very expressive formula (1944, p. 5): 'Formerly monopoly was considered an absolute. . . . This could no longer be so when it was recognised that monopoly, far from being an exceptional régime in a pure, competitive system, itself supplied the competitive régime.'

This is precisely Joan Robinson's idea. The criterion of perfect competition implies that each seller is unable to influence the market price. 'The point is, at least, that he believes he cannot do so. . . .' It is of decisive significance that Marx, in talking about free competition, never understood it in this way. On the contrary, the passages (for instance, *Capital*, I, ch. 10, p. 332, III, ch. 10, p. 220, and ch. 13, p. 253) where he presupposes that sellers vary price and are able to use it as a parameter within the framework of his theory of 'relative surplus value' are quite explicit. Therefore, Joan Robinson is right in stating (1949, p. 4), 'The modern theory of imperfect competition, though formally quite different from Marx's theory of exploitation, has a close affinity with it.' Even if Joan Robinson has some doubts about this in the formal sense, it cannot be denied that Marx was in this sense actually 'Robinsonian'!

This conception of a strong affinity between the theory of Joan Robinson and that of Marx is corroborated by Jean Marchal, who says (1950, p. 137) that 'one of the results from the work of modern economists is that in the market economy workers do not receive what in strict justice they might claim, as soon as imperfect competition exists'. After all, imperfect competition is the rule, according to Joan Robinson!

A new formulation of the Marxian theory of surplus value in the sense of the theory of imperfect competition can be formulated as soon as we take into account macroeconomic ideas such as the concept of the industrial reserve army. If one presupposes identical cost curves in all firms in the economy, each of which is faced by a sloping demand curve, one has to envisage a situation of 'monopolistic competition' or a 'world of monopolies', in the sense of Joan Robinson. Oligopolistic reactions are already reflected in such sloping demand curves, so that these firms employ labour power only up to the point of equilibrium explained by Cournot. This means that there will be a considerable reserve army left, at least if we suppose that sufficient labour power would have been available to reach a perfectly competitive optimum. The existence of such a reserve army makes it possible to avoid a sharp increase in marginal-cost curves.

Such a 'world of monopolies' would never make full use of its capacity. This would have to be considered as a serious kind of cancer in capitalism. At the same time, this 'world of monopolies' would never attain full employment. Provided Chamberlin's 'tangency situation' (in which the average cost just touches the demand curve, which has been moved to the left) does not exist in all firms, certain profit margins can persist.

If one now combines such a situation with the 'full-cost theory' of Hall and Hitch, according to which firms calculate their profits as margins on wage bills, one reaches an intermediate situation between the 'tangency solution' of Chamberlin and the 'mark-up theory' of Lexis, in its refined version. Such a mark-up calculation would be quite plausible, particularly with marginal and average cost in the sense of Kalecki (i.e. they are horizontal over the relevant ranges). Such an analogy goes beyond the concept of Joan Robinson, for she thought that by devolving economic life into individual monopolies we should obtain a 'world full of monopolies'.

Beyond that Marx saw the possibility that a number of or all producers in a market might co-operate. He thus anticipated the Chamberlin 'small group', which was neglected by Joan Robinson. This 'small group', under the new term of 'oligopoly', was destined to become the basic problem of cartel analysis and of the theory of monopolistic competition in the widest sense.

Marx approaches the Robinsonian theory of the ubiquity of monopoly when he says (*Capital*, I, ch. 15, p. 383) that a firm using machinery which then obtains an 'advantage' in Schumpeter's sense can already be considered in a transitional period to be 'a kind of monopoly'. In this respect Marx is more progressive than other economists of his time: the latter still considered monopoly to be a clearly definable and exceptional fact.

In the other passages where Marx mentions 'monopolies', the term should be understood in the sense generally accepted at his time. That he knew of the need to distinguish between the general use of the term and his own, wider interpretation is shown by, for instance, his reference to traditional 'monopolies' as 'monopolies in the usual sense' (*Capital*, III, ch. 10, p. 198).

Later monopoly theory took its point of departure from declining costs: Marx himself already talked of economies of scale: 'The cheapness of commodities depends *ceteris paribus*, on the productiveness of labour, and this again on the scale of production. Therefore, the larger capitals beat the smaller' (ibid., I, ch. 25, p. 586).

In modern terms this means that the cost curve of an enterprise with a larger output is to be found on the envelope curve of average long-run total costs at a lower position than the cost curve of a smaller enterprise. Marx therefore recognises (ibid., III, ch. 15, p. 262) that the long-run average cost curve is not horizontal but falling. It may also be legitimate to assume that he understood the decline in costs inside a growing firm, as well as the rise in the curve after optimum capacity had been passed. At any rate, he recognised that too small a scale of production would not be competitive, for he mentioned the 'increasing minimum' or the 'minimum dimension' that is necessary for the 'successful operation of an independent industrial establishment . . . under normal conditions'.

THE PIGOU–BLOOM THEORY: THE 'MARGINALIST' NOTION OF EXPLOITATION

In 1920, Pigou formulated a new concept of exploitation in his *Economics of Welfare*. According to this theory, 'exploitation' exists when workers do not receive the marginal net product of their work:

> Provided that the wages paid to workpeople in all places and occupations were equal to the values of the marginal net product of their work – and provided that the distribution of all grades of workpeople among different places and occupations were such as to maximise the national dividend in the wide sense [remember that this is part of our definition of 'values'!] there would be established between different people's wages a certain relation. This relation I define as fair. . . . It is of the utmost importance to distinguish between two principal sorts of unfair wage. . . . Wages may be unfair in some place or occupation, because the marginal net product of the labour . . . there is not equal to the wage of labour . . . elsewhere. . . . On the other hand, wages may be unfair because workpeople . . . are paid less than the value which their marginal net product has to the firms employing them.
>
> (Fourth edition, 1938, p. 549.)

It has been said with justice of this formulation that exploitation in this sense exists within the framework of monopolistic competition for all factors of production. Bloom, in pointing out this fact, said moreover (1940–1, pp. 413ff; 1946, p. 247), 'If we adopt the Pigovian definition, the only possibility of removing exploitation is by restoring conditions of perfect competition'. Even in this context, it is clear that the definition given by Pigou is nothing but another form of the theorising of Joan Robinson and Chamberlin.

In his important work on distribution problems (1971), Bronfenbrenner has said (p. 195) that Pigou's definition has apologetic undertones, just because there can be no exploitation in this sense in perfect competition; he thinks it stands a good chance of being recognised as 'orthodox'.

A vast literature has been built up on these formulations. It begins with Hicks, who thought (1966, pp. 82, 332) that 'monopsonistic exploitation' was unimportant, especially where wage-rates had been equalised by trade-union activity. This was a thesis to which Shove (1933b) took violent exception. Shortly after the Second World War, there was the great controversy about the principle of the applicability of marginalist formulas to the labour market; Lester contested (1947, pp. 135ff.) that it was possible to apply the marginal principle to wage determination. For him, the decisive reason why additional labour was hired did not consist in its marginal product, but in the increase of turnover or orders experienced by the firms. More recently, Machlup, who in those days defended the marginalist principle along with Stigler, has admitted (1967, p. 2) that one could perhaps say with hindsight that 'Machlup won the battle, but Lester won the war'.

Be that as it may, the Pigovian theory is of interest as an analogy with that of Marx only if we adopt it in the version of Bloom (1940–1; 1946). The latter eliminated the problem of imperfect competition by postulating (1946, p. 246) as a criterion for exploitation that the worker should be paid less than the net marginal product. He then mentions a special case (ibid., p. 268) in which there occurs the 'payment of the same wage to men of different efficiency', for in this case 'the least efficient man . . . is not exploited, although all men of higher efficiency are'.

The salient point is this: how can one explain the curve of decreasing productivity from the first to the last worker? Can it be explained by differences in individual qualifications, by shortcomings of management in the face of increasing turnover or by the overloading of capacity in factories? It is only in the first case that one can speak of 'genuine' exploitation.

Bloom assumes that the wage of the last worker required, namely the 'marginal price' of 'labour power', represents the wage for all employed. According to this version, the last worker would receive exactly what he brings in; contrary to Marx's theory, he would 'not be exploited at all'. All the others, however, would be effectively 'exploited'.

This version of 'exploitation' is at the same time unavoidable and 'justified', in so far as it may not be possible to pay individual workers on the basis of the average product they produce. If one wanted to do so, this would mean that workers would have to be paid differentiated rewards, corresponding to the form the productivity curve takes. With increasing marginal returns, which imply decreasing costs, those workers who were last into employment would get the highest wages; if returns decrease and marginal costs rise, they would receive the lowest wages. In so far as examples of the former occur in economic life, they are generally the result of what has been called 'wage-drift', i.e. of attempts to attract workers – for instance, where there is a scarcity of secretaries.

In this case it is doubtful whether the reasoning is still of a marginalist character. At any rate, such a solution seems to be even more unjust than any other solution, for the last person hired cannot be responsible for the fact that the optimum point on the cost curve or in capacity utilisation has been exceeded; nor can the original team of workers. On the other hand, this fact is responsible for the 'marginal productivity' of that worker. Moreover, the uniformity of the labour market and the structure of wages fixed through collective bargaining prevents such a 'differentiated system of wages', except perhaps in the piecework system.

The whole idea of 'exploitation' in this sense would appear rather unsatisfactory in principle. Nevertheless, it is quite near to practical life. In practice, it is not rare for those who have been hired first to receive lower wages and salaries, because the enterprise holds a sort of 'monopsony position' with regard to them. These workers are too old or too specialised to be able to change jobs. Newcomers, by contrast, have to be paid a premium to persuade them to join the firm, and a further 'premium' to retain them, to avoid too high a turnover of younger workers. This is the situation which occurs at times of full employment, when the 'industrial reserve army' no longer functions, but it can also result from the fact that this reserve army consists chiefly of an unemployable class of old workers and employees.

It was Adam Smith himself who recognised the tendency for employers to favour monopsony, when he wrote (1835, p. 65) of the tacit combination of 'masters . . . not to raise the wages of labour above their actual rate'. Marx (*Capital*, III, ch. 10, p. 198) spoke of 'a veritable freemason society *vis-a-vis* the whole working-class'. Joan Robinson (1949, p. 88) sees the primary task of trade unions, when they are introduced into fields where there previously were none, as being able to raise the real wage through squeezing monopsony profits. This result she sees as being dependent upon the introduction of a 'general rule', and she refers in this context to her theory advanced in *The Economics of Imperfect Competition*, where she deals in detail with the notion of exploitation, especially as defined by Pigou.

PIETRANERA'S 'ANTI-AGIO-THEORY'

A modern Marxist, Pietranera, has treated Bohm-Bawerk's teachings in the same way as Marx dealt with Hegel, i.e. by turning the author upside down. By carrying the analysis of time preference to the limit, Pietranera came to the conclusion that, in the majority of cases where the 'marginal pair' of borrower and lender confront each other, there must, in the case of capital-owners, be a preference for future enjoyment, and in that case interest must be negative, not positive, if it is considered that interest exists because there is a difference in valuation with regard to goods that are available, in the present or in the future.

Pietranera starts from the hypothesis that objections to the labour theory of value would have to be dropped if one could prove that capital could be provided without interest, if certain goods were more highly valued than others in the future. This point of view has certainly been examined by a number of important economists. For instance, there are similar considerations in Schumpeter's early works (1926, pp. 46, 286, 241, 253):

> A lower subjective valuation of future needs must exact a toll from each economic being. . . . Most economic agents do not have a choice between the present and the future. . . . It is self-evident that anybody who expects an inheritance . . . would value present money more highly . . . and . . . in the same way . . . somebody who contemplates

a reduction of his income from work in later life would do the reverse. . . . The rate of interest would certainly not be an essential element of economic life.

Even Fisher has declared (1933, p. 192), in all frankness, that the nature of men or things provides no compelling grounds which require that the rate of interest should be positive rather than negative. Schumpeter reproached Fisher with the statement (1926, pp. 48–9) that his treatment of abstinence 'is vitiated by his considering time discount as a primary factor the existence of which is almost self-evident'. This criticism is unjust, for Fisher gave a number of examples (for instance, his famous 'biscuit' example) to show that, so long as the goods not required at present could be kept intact for the future, the real rate of interest could not possibly sink below zero. Fisher considered a negative real rate of interest possible only where the goods in question are highly perishable (for example, figs, strawberries and such like agricultural products).

It seems, therefore, that the argument of Pietranera is of a rather abstract and special character, unless we consider money in our epoch of permanent inflationary conditions as a highly perishable good, if kept in liquid form. In this case, there would be an exact counterpart to Keynesian liquidity preference, with an aversion to liquidity and a seeking for refuge in real values, such as shares. We should then encounter the paradoxical case that the demand for securities would increase as the consequence of a tendency to 'negative' rates of interest on more liquid investments. The 'negative' rate of interest on liquid assets would then make shares, as a less liquid form of investment, appear more attractive, at the same time raising share prices, which, if dividends remain unchanged, would in turn bring about a reduction in effective earnings and, therefore, restore the 'original interest', in Wicksell's sense. The question remains of how great a pressure this flight into real assets would bring to bear on the exchange value of fixed-interest securities. If the pressure is strong, there will be a rise in the rate of interest, which would cause the 'negative rate' to disappear.

In quoting Keynes (1949, p. 221) one must at the same time note that the Keynesian theories of the 'euthanasia' of the rentier and of the tendency towards a decreasing rate of interest or of a movement in the marginal productivity of capital towards zero approximate to the theories of Marx and Pietranera. It is true that Keynes envisaged this development as occurring in the near future, when real capital assets would be abundantly available. In this case, the labour theory of value would gain importance in the near future. However, there is a diametrically opposed view, for a number of important authors (for instance, Sweezy, 1942, p. 52; Dunayevskaya, 1944, 1945; and perhaps even Mandel, 1970, p. 95) consider that Marx thought the labour theory of value valid only for pre-capitalist conditions, and thus did not seek to apply it to future society.

22 Macroeconomic Theories of Profit and the Marxian System in Sraffa's Renaissance Version

Right from the outset Marx distinguishes himself from the majority of modern profit theories: these start in most cases from what can be called the 'natural rate of interest' (Wicksell) or from an 'agio', from the justification of a sort of 'original interest', in the manner of Böhm-Bawerk's theory, or from Keynes's 'liquidity theory'. Marx, by contrast, derived interest from the existence of profits. His theory of surplus value is narrowly linked to the idea of constantly returning dynamic 'cost advantages'. From here the link which identifies profits in general with dynamics and development, and which denies the existence of profit and interest on capital in a static society (for instance, in Schumpeter's works) is an easy step.

Marx would therefore appear to belong in the rather narrow group of theorists who establish a connexion between profits and interest and the dynamic character of capitalism. One cannot raise the objection against this group that the rate of interest used to be quite high in past, quasi-stationary societies. This historical phenomenon may be explained by the element of risk premium and by the fact that the capital was used in a rather unproductive way in those days.

There are at least four different older types of profit and interest theory – namely, the abstinence or 'waiting' theory, the use theory, the agio theory and the liquidity-preference theory. Newer groups exist which explain the rate of interest, and other, more recent theories explain profit as such. The latter group of theories have to do with variants of risk theory, of the theory of marginal productivity, and, finally, of the dynamic cost-advantage theory. The former group of theories give a reason for the existence of interest in the narrower sense, and do not directly explain the further residual element of 'windfall profits', as described by Keynes in his *Treatise on Money* (1930, 1).

Modern industrial economics has carefully separated elements that enter into the price calculation from profits in the proper sense, distinguishing in this way entrepreneurs' salaries, risk premium (according to the risks typical for the industry in question), and interest on own capital, this last as a residual item. It can be said with full authority that Marx made decisive contributions on all three elements, although he considered the last as being part of profits *par excellence*, and not a sort of minimum profit. The founders of modern marginalism and of equilibrium-price analysis clearly understood these distinctions. Walras wrote as follows in 1874 (1952, p. 421): 'A mistake which obscures the entire theory of interest lies in the confusion over the functions of capitalists and of entrepreneurs, respectively. Under the pretext that it is difficult to be an entrepreneur without being a capitalist at the same time, these economists do not sufficiently distinguish between these two functions.'

THE REFORMULATION OF 'CLASSICAL THEORY' BY VON NEUMANN AND SRAFFA

The version of the 'mark-up theory' developed by Lexis and recognised by Engels reappears in certain theories of distribution, such as that of Preiser, which gives priority to the 'deduction theory' based on labour value. Besides this, the degree of monopoly (in the sense of Kalecki or Lerner) can be used.

According to Pigou and Joan Robinson, the sum of social surplus value results from the excess productivity of all workers in relation to their wages, with the exception of those workers who have been hired 'at the margin' and who just 'earn' their wage. In this context, the concept of general economic equilibrium as developed by von Neumann perhaps goes farther than any other theory; for his 'factors of production' (including labour power, which is to be considered as being produced by consumption) are all goods produced in the preceding period. Thus one could easily arrive at the position that there are no longer original factors of production. Since von Neumann sees the economic system as undergoing positive expansion, from one equilibrium to another, there is a surplus in his system. This has led Napoleoni, among other observers, to say (1963; 1968, p. 91), 'Von Neumann reminds us of the classical Marxist notion of surplus value.'

Von Neumann's theory contains a concept of profit which does not represent the remuneration of a particular factor of production, but is a residual. It is, however, quite possible that the 'residual' mentioned by von Neumann need not appear simply in the form of profit, for part of this social surplus may accrue to workers as well. According to Sraffa, 'two components of wages have to be distinguished. One refers to the means of subsistence and should be subtracted from the value of production to obtain the surplus, while the other represents the share of the worker in the division of the surplus produced by the system' (Napoleoni, 1968, p. 136). As Napoleoni emphasises (ibid., pp. 137–9), Sraffa

> follows the classical tradition, which assumes wages are determined by factors outside the economic system (on the basis of the historically determined level of subsistence and of the ability of workers to share in the appropriation of the surplus), so that the rate of profit becomes a function of the wage rate. . . . His concept of wage rate . . . has no connexion whatever with the marginal productivity of labour, and is determined by social and historical mechanisms.

Napoleoni, having studied the works of Sraffa closely, doubts 'whether one can say of the prices used by Sraffa that they represent market prices or accounting prices' – the latter, in Sraffa's view, might offer an analogy to 'values' in classical theory. The 'neo-Ricardian' work of Sraffa, which is very concisely written, has not yet led to a general renaissance of the 'surplus' concept, but has stimulated a number of attempts to interpret it.

One of the most interesting modern attempts of this kind is that by Kregel. He points out (1971, p. 119) that Marx and von Neumann have offered nothing more than an expansion of the earlier works of Ricardo. In one particular case at least, the analysis by Sraffa leads to the conclusion that 'Marxian values rule unquestionably' (ibid., p. 20).

The analysis by von Neumann is to be distinguished from that of Sraffa by the fact that von Neumann grants workers as well as capitalists (!) a kind of 'subsistence income': 'the real wage is unalterably fixed in subsistence. . . . workers do not (indeed cannot) save, and profit-earners do not consume (except in production of themselves). . . . all income in excess of subsistence is reinvested. . . .' This in a way is the frugal world of Stalin, in which investment is deified. On the other hand, Sraffa seeks 'to free labour from its role as a physical factor of production with a technologically determined wage, and allow any portion of the net surplus to be paid as wages'. (Ibid., pp. 13, 37.)

At this point we cannot discuss the growth aspects of the two theories. What is significant in both systems is that there is no question of 'marginal product' or 'marginal utility'. The notion of 'capital' does not even occur in Sraffa's work and 'nowhere is the marginal product of capital necessary to determine the rate of profit on capital or the relative prices' (ibid., p. 39).

Sraffa avoids the discussion of the 'transformation problem' by choosing as a unit of measurement a commodity which has an average relation between the use of labour and the use of other means of production. As such a commodity does not exist in physical terms, he construes a 'composite commodity' with this property. In this way, he creates a 'standard system' with a 'standard net product'. This leads to a kind of 'labour measure' or 'labour value', which is 'the quantity of labour that can be purchased by the standard net product'. He then reduces indirect labour in the productive process to direct labour values, which he calls 'dated labour', a concept which is similar to the roundabout methods of production of Böhm-Bawerk and Wicksell. The value of the means of production is then expressed through the addition of these labour values. He then attains fixed capital values by an additional differentiation of capital goods according to their age, and by anticipating depreciation according to the age structure. Finally, he comes to the kernel of his criticism of the dominant economic theory by comparing various techniques of production. He challenges the neoclassical thesis according to which labour-intensive production techniques are chosen as soon as the rate of interest rises, and capital-intensive techniques are chosen when the rate of interest falls. In his opinion, this relation need not exist, either in a qualitative or in a quantitative sense. What are decisive are technical differences and the exogenously determined rate of profit. (Ibid., pp. 22–9, 31–8.)

Samuelson recognised that 'the Sraffa system threatened the very foundations of the neoclassical marginal analysis' (ibid., p. 40). His attempt to establish similarities between the two rests on the validity of a 'special sub-class of realistic cases' (Samuelson, 1962). Napoleoni, on the other hand, sees (1968, pp. 140–1) in Sraffa's work an example of the fact that 'modern economic thinking needs once more to deal with the question of the surplus and the subject of exploitation'.

Marx started from the hypothesis that the distribution of the social product or the sum of value added was best measured by the wage level, which is historically given and which is regulated by the industrial reserve army. This wage level would then determine profit as a residual, in the same way as Sraffa did in his work.

It is true that the reasons which determine the level of the rate of surplus value are not fully discussed by Marx. They are to be found in the general complex of the 'class-struggle', which, as it were, finds its institutionalisation in the trade-union movement. Only the changes in the rate of surplus value are motivated, especially, within the framework of the theory of the tendency of the rate of profit to fall. Even in this theory, as in his work as a whole, Marx starts from the hypothesis that capital can be quantified as a flow and even (as soon as the velocity of turnover is taken into account) as a stock item. In other words, he does not share the preoccupations of the modern 'Cambridge School', which doubts the quantifiability of capital and thus tries to undermine the starting point of its adversary, the neoclassical school.

In this context Sraffa's work is of decisive importance, for, as Kregel says (1971, p. 31), Sraffa reduced the value of fixed capital to dated labour and 'has demonstrated that the valuation of capital is impossible without reference to the distribution implied in the rate of profits'. Other interpreters of Sraffa, such as Macchioro (1961; 1970, p. 760) have reached the same conclusion.

We come, therefore, to the question of how the rate of surplus value is to be determined. This is related to the problem of distribution or of the division of the social product, which is discussed in the next section.

Part VI
The Analysis of Distribution

23 Earlier Interpretations of Marxian Wage Theory

Typical of the older interpretation of the Marxian wage theory is Haller's *Is There a Wage Theory?*, which was published in the mid 1930s. Haller starts from the hypothesis of Marx and Ricardo that 'man is a machine of production, which must be reproduced like any other machine'.

In this way Haller anticipates the modern version put forward by von Neumann, who, indeed, considers the normal subsistence requirement as a sort of input. At the same time he overlooks the differences there are between Ricardo's analysis and that of Marx. In the case of Ricardo it is true that input is clearly defined as the subsistence wage. In the case of Marx, however, the standard of living is by no means identical with the minimum subsistence level; on the contrary, it is historically determined and embodies an increase in living requirements, which are of a changing character, though the change is always in the direction of a higher standard of living.

Haller dubs the Marxian theory a 'monopolistic wage theory'. He does not recognise that entrepreneurs as a class hold a monopolistic position, and he thinks that such a monopoly can exist only 'if one postulates from the very beginning that capital does not increase'. According to him, only a developed economic system is realistic, and this cannot recognise a monopoly of the kind in question, because 'anybody [!] can have access to this system by special effort' – that is, 'through saving or technical innovation'.

Haller considers the significant contribution of Marx to lie in the thesis of a relative increase in constant capital in proportion to variable capital; this is the cause of a decreasing demand for labour power, which brings about the existence of an industrial reserve army. Haller quotes Marx to show that he thought that demand for labour would fall with the decreasing share of 'variable capital'.

This movement in the relation has in modern times been contested by Krelle, among others. He pointed out that what is really decisive is not the ratio of capital to the level of employment, but the sum of depreciation and the cost of raw and other ancillary materials in proportion to the sum of wage costs. It is true that the ratio between constant capital and the level of employment increases, but not the ratio between constant capital and the sum of wages (c: we, i.e. hourly wages multiplied by the level of employment), for wages increase with productivity. Krelle draws the conclusion (1962, p. 36) that the Marxian law according to which the sum of values embodied in constant capital should increase in proportion to the sum of values in variable capital (both expressed in money) is not in accord with what we know from the statistics.

This resort to empirical work and statistics is by no means a decisive argument against the theorem, which according to Marxian dialectics may be concealed by contrary tendencies.

From the point of view of criticism of Marx, it would be more to the point to seek an explanation for why the sum of wages should increase so rapidly that it compensates for the increase in constant capital. If constant capital grows, with the level of employment remaining more or less constant or decreasing in the long run, the factor of production which is more abundant, namely real capital, may lose in value proportionately to others, and this would explain why real wages have a tendency to increase.

It is here that the dynamics of the Marxian system, which comprise also the theory of business cycles, really begin.

The presentation of Marxian wage theory given by 'academic' economics stresses the situation of the working class. For instance, Stavenhagen in his history of doctrines (1957) writes (pp. 152–3),

> The concentration of capital is the cause of a further sociological process: the development of relative over-population or an industrial reserve army and the growing poverty of the working class. The accumulation and concentration of capital bring about the relative decrease of variable capital and increasing technical progress and the mechanisation of the entire productive process. Both elements lead to increasing redundancy among workers. . . . The existence of an industrial reserve army exercises pressure on the wages of the active labour force and leads to a decrease in the value of labour power. . . . The pressure of the industrial reserve army creates a tendency towards growing poverty and pauperism in the working class as a whole, a fact which becomes evident in the decrease of real wages and of the living standards of better-paid working groups. . . .

This is the stereotype version retailed by 'academic' economics, and Stavenhagen, who in general is quite critical, presents it without any reservation. He even goes so far as to ascribe to Marx the Lassallian version of the 'iron law of wages': 'For capital a mass of latent manpower exists whose standard of living can never go beyond the minimum subsistence level, because of existing sharp competition between workers.'

This interpretation has been transposed onto the sociological and political level and persists right up to the present. For instance, Lindauer draws the conclusion (1968, p. 230) that according to Marx 'the ever more miserable workers finally assume control of the economy's production from the ever smaller number of capitalists'. This is the rather mechanistic and primitive interpretation which certain 'academic' economists give to the Marxian theory.

Piettre (1962, p. 65) offers a similar theory in rather more moderate terms:

> A considerable *part* of the working class is condemned to become redundant and unemployed as a result of its own activity. . . . In this way relative overpopulation, permanent unemployment and an 'industrial reserve army' come into being, sometimes floating, sometimes latent and sometimes stagnating, but incessantly a deadweight on the working class. The situation of the working class under capitalism is, therefore, radically without hope. . . . This categorical assertion, however, has not prevented Marx from recognising that the situation of the working class has improved as a result of wage increases, the result of trade-union action or 'factory laws' . . . . Marx has left it to his interpreters to eliminate this apparent contradiction. . . .

This moderate version, it must be stressed, is by no means typical of 'academic' theory.

Even such a generous judge as Schumpeter thought (1947, p. 34) he had to maintain the so-called 'theory of growing poverty', which, in fact, was first ascribed to Marx by certain revisionists:

> Marx undoubtedly held that in the course of capitalist evolution real wage rates and the standard of life of the masses would fall in the better-paid, and fail to improve in the worst-paid, strata, and that this would come about not through any accidental or environmental circumstances but by virtue of the very logic of the capitalist process. As a prediction, this was of course singularly infelicitous. . . .

In this area, two different categories of 'orthodox' economists clash. First, there is the group of 'academic' teachers who believe that Marx committed a fundamental error, and they base their case on the statistical facts. Second, there are some representatives of Marxist orthodoxy who either do not want to see the indisputable statistical facts or, in a curiously devious manner, try to explain them away. In reality, the misinterpretation is absolutely staggering in both cases. It will be analysed later.

In this context it can, however, be stated that there were at least some representatives of 'academic' economics who tackled the problem more prudently. It is after all surprising that the word *Verelendung* (progressive deteriorioration, growing poverty) never occurs in Marx's works, nor does it occur in the classic history of doctrines published by Gide and Rist (1921), who remark laconically (p. 508), 'Marx describes the development of pauperism, which is a product of crisis and unemployment'. This 'pauperism', as Marx's work makes clear, concerns only a group of submerged elements on the fringe of the proletariat, a group by no means typical of the working class in general. We have now to ask: what actually is the wage theory contained in the Marxian system?

The clearest presentation of it is to be found in Marchal. (In general, it can be said that French 'academic' economists treated Marx in a more prudent fashion and with greater exactitude and sympathy than did professional economists in other countries.) With regard to the minimum subsistence level Marchal writes (1955, pp. 108–9),

> This law of the reduction of wages to the minimum subsistence level has often been misunderstood. First of all, it must be remembered that it has to be understood in the macroeconomic sense and in the long run, like all Marxian laws. . . . The minimum we are discussing here is undoubtedly a psychological or sociological minimum and not a physiological minimum. . . . This minimum consists of the wages that correspond to the means of subsistence that are necessary for the worker to live in this style. These wages depend on the physical peculiarities of the country concerned and on the level of civilisation the population has reached. . . . On this point Marx is quite precise and formal. . . . Must one not then ask whether the law of the decline of wages to the minimum standard of living does not lose much of its serious character from the social point of view and, therefore, of its efficiency from the revolutionary point of view? One might be tempted to conclude from Marx's exposition that it would suffice to raise the accepted standards of the working class to a higher level in order to make income follow. Can one not conclude that the situation of the working class is not necessarily wretched, that it is relatively easy to improve it, and that even the exploitation of the working class may one day stop?

It has been said quite correctly that the Marxian idea of the minimum wage is something different from the classical theory of normal wages. Another Frenchman, Ansiaux, has given (1926, p. 506) a precise statement of the position: 'The wage required to meet the necessities of life is certainly something more human than the "normal wage" of the classicals, and it is more concrete than the "just wage" of the scholastic authors. Nevertheless, this notion is still prone to a rather pronounced inexactitude. . . .'

Finally, critics have taken up what can be called the 'harbinger theory' in Marx's work. According to this theory, wage increases only indicate a turning point in the business-cycle situation. The Italian author Papi has sketched the transition to the problem of business cycles in a few words (1959, p. 5):

> in a certain way, even Marx recurs to the idea of the wages fund. If accumulation can raise employment and the wage in the long run, the

rise in wages has the consequence that the entrepreneur is driven to the use of machines to eliminate human labour power from the business and to enlarge the reserve army of labour and correspondingly to bring pressure on the wage rate. Marx is led by this argument to consider crises as an unavoidable component of the capitalist system. . . .

24 Marx's Wage Theory

The wage theory of Marx may be summed up as follows. Wages are the basis of the specific capitalist exploitation relationship. They are conditioned by the standard of living, the growth of which is seen as a sociological and historical phenomenon. This standard of living follows the long-run trend of productivity, but always leaves a minimum profit structure intact. It periodically undergoes pressure from the unemployed lower strata of the population. On the other hand, it can be raised at the expense of the profit level by collective action.

Marx starts from the hypothesis that there is only one factor of production. In so doing, he is in good company, not only in that of the classical economists but also in that of the Keynesians. Indeed, Keynes himself stated (1949, pp. 213–14),

> If capital becomes less scarce, the excess yield will diminish, without its having become less productive. . . . I sympathise, therefore, with the pre-classical doctrine that everything is *produced by labour* aided by what used to be called art and is now called technique, by natural resources which are free or cost a rent according to their scarcity or abundance, and by the results of past labour, embodied in assets, which also command a price according to their scarcity or abundance. It is preferable to regard labour, including, of course, the personal services of the entrepreneur and his assistants, as the sole factor of production, operating in a given environment of technique, natural resources, capital equipment and effective demand. This partly explains why we have been able to take the unit of labour as the sole physical unit which we require in our economic system, apart from units of money and of time.

Here, Keynes, rather like Molière's M. Jourdain, who talked prose all his life without knowing it, is speaking Marxian language, even though he declared *Capital* to be 'an obsolete economic textbook' (ibid., p. 3, note 1). On the other hand, he used in his main work the term 'classical', which, as he says himself, he found in Marx's work. Joan Robinson has further developed, from the viewpoint of dynamic Keynesianism, the position outlined by Keynes.

The wage of the worker is, for Marx, determined by the average social output of the worker, using the average endowment of machinery and equipment. This output is reflected in the price of labour, which, in Hicks's sense (1950, p. 269), is the pivot around which prices fluctuate: 'The upward instability of the price-system can be checked by movements of the rate of interest, but instability downward cannot necessarily be checked in that way. The only reliable check within the system is the rigidity of wage-rates. . . .'

THE 'LABOUR VALUE' OF THE FUTURE

Where labour power is used with a lower than average endowment of equipment, it will realise less than the average result, because it represents, as it were, the average value of the past. In cases where labour power is combined with more than the average amount of machinery, it will obtain above-average results; this is the average value of the future. In both cases, however, the labourer will receive as high a remuneration as in the average case. Here, a law of the 'equalisation of wage-rates' operates.

Marx does not give a penny for what has once been invested, and modern economics fully agrees with him on this point. What there exists in the way of machinery is a present from the past. Industrial economists examine the maintenance and current costs of an old installation only with regard to its profitability; capital cost is relevant only for new equipment which has not yet been installed.

For Marx, in an analogous manner, existing fixed capital (contained in *c*) has a value only in so far as it must be replaced or incurs current costs. The entire value calculation in Marxian theory represents nothing but an imputation of average wages to average productivity. What remains above and below this figure represents less or more 'value' than is 'socially given'. The inward or outward movement of workers leads only to an equalisation of the rates of wages in different industries and firms, according to their level of technology. The 'composition of values' changes in proportion to the realisation of innovations in a particular industry or in the whole economy. Optimal equipment continually becomes average equipment. The less dynamic is the process of development, the smaller will be the gap between values and prices. Workers with average equipment, therefore, determine the average wage even for industries that are worse or better equipped. The scale of wage inequality from industry to industry is narrower the more the minimum-value of equipment per head approaches the optimum.

There remains the problem, according to Marx, of how new capital is to be obtained in order to raise productivity. How should it be remunerated?

In the first place, it will be remunerated by the original or minimum rate of interest, which is to be explained (in the manner of Graziadei and Preiser) by exploitation within the framework of class monopoly, and, in practice, by calculation according to the full-cost principle (as developed by Lexis or later by Preiser). In addition, capital will be rewarded with an 'extra surplus value', which is obtained by a dynamic firm through the introduction of new machinery. This is the 'advantage' of which Lederer speaks, or the Marxian 'temporary monopoly'.

Even if a worker is less well endowed than average with means of production, his labour power has potentially the average value, because it could, after all, be better endowed, and it obtains, therefore, approximately the average price, thereby enabling it to remain in the job where it is. This labour, however, represents a performance which no longer corresponds to the average social value. In the last resort, the significance of the labour theory of value is that, independently of the possibility of imputing a particular output to certain real factors, only labour has a claim to a share in the distribution of the social product.

The average level of equipment in capitalism changes continuously. Indeed, it is the chief characteristic of capitalism that it brings about a continuous transformation of productive conditions and an increasing mechanisation: 'this growth in the mass of means of production' characterises, according to Marx, the 'law of the progressive increase in constant capital'. This increasing importance of constant capital is to be seen in the increasing relative share of capacity or fixed capital cost – including depreciation and raw and ancillary material costs – in total costs. This will entail a reduction in the share of wages in total costs, at least at the microeconomic level.

From a macroeconomic point of view, raw materials, ancillary inputs and semi-manufactured products that firms procure dissolve, according to modern theory, as capital and wage costs. Thus gross social product comprises depreciation (or replacement investment), labour costs and the sum of profits. This has been proved by Burchardt (1932, pp. 147, 151):

> The original materials of a technical and real character have been won from nature, which means that economically speaking they have been acquired from nowhere in the stage of production that is farthest from consumption. The 'costs' of producing those raw materials simply consist in the using-up of capital goods and consumption goods in the process. For two reasons these intermediate products must, for a period, not appear in the circular-flow calculation: (1) because the size of their value depends on the number of productive stages, which can be determined arbitrarily; (2) because their inclusion would mean 'double counting', and their annual production is included in p (profit) and v (wage bill). . . .

If we speak here of the theory of wages, we must take into account that the share of wages in the individual firm must first be seen at the microeconomic level, where it loses in relative importance as compared with the weight of wage goods in gross social product. This is because, at the microeconomic level, raw materials, ancillary inputs and intermediate products have to be taken into consideration.

The problem of the distribution of the social product as a whole will be discussed later.

THE MOVEMENT AND SHARE OF WAGES IN THE BUSINESS CYCLE

In the theory of wages in the proper sense of the word, we shall have to analyse first the development of wages in the business cycle and later their long-run trend. For Marx this long-run trend is no longer determined by demographic development, as it was with the classical economists, especially Malthus, and with some of their socialist epigones, such as Lassalle. Marx criticises (*Capital*, I, ch. 25, p. 597),

> the dogma of the economists. According to them, wages rise in consequence of accumulation of capital. The higher wages stimulate the working population to more rapid multiplication, and this goes on until the labour-market becomes too full. . . . Wages fall, and now we have the reverse of the medal. The working population is little by little decimated as the result of the fall in wages. . . .

The so-called 'iron law of wages' of Lassalle is a chimera, according to Marx. 'A beautiful mode of motion this for developed capitalist production! Before, in consequence of the rise of wages, any positive increase of the population really fit for work could occur, the time would have been passed again and again, during which the industrial campaign must have been carried through, the battle fought and won.'

On the other hand, it is true that mechanisation creates a 'relative overpopulation': 'By means of machinery, chemical processes and other methods, [modern industry] is continually causing changes not only in the technical basis of production, but also in the functions of the labourer, and in the social combinations of the labour-process' (*Capital*, I, ch. 15, p. 457).

For Marx it is the dynamics of capitalism itself, namely the continual technical progress, which determines the development of wages. Marx starts from the hypothesis that 'machinery is . . . introduced into spheres of production in which the capitalist mode of production already exists' (*Theories*, II, p. 556).

Here the origin of the theory of the 'industrial reserve army' is to be found, a force which keeps the labour market under permanent pressure, and which subjects it to stronger pressure after each wave of mechanisation. At the same time, we find here an answer to the problem of how profits can arise. The permanently existing or continually replenishing reserve army sees to it that wages, even where they are rising sharply, cannot menace profits.

In connection with his rejection of the under-consumption thesis, Marx pointed out that an explanation of crisis in this manner would be erroneous because 'crises are always prepared by precisely a period in which wages rise generally and the working-class actually gets a larger share of that part of the annual product which is intended for consumption' (*Capital*, II, ch. 20, p. 415).

Amongst modern authors, Steindl has taken great exception to this formulation. He concluded that Marx was suggesting that the share of labour in the social product would rise during a boom and sink during a depression. Steindl referred (1952, p. 237) to global statistical data for the phases of boom and recession in the complete cycle: 'The share of wages . . . depends indeed on the cycle, but in a way quite contrary to Marx: it falls in the upswing and increases in the downswing.'

In arguing in this way, Steindl has overlooked the fact that Marx did not speak of an increased share in the social product – only of an increased share in the amount of consumption. He also overlooks the fact that Marx did not refer to the entire period of the boom, but only to the peak phase of the boom shortly before its downturn.

Furthermore, there are modern statistical studies – among others, those of the Federal German Expert Council of 1970 and 1971 – which explain quite clearly that the movements in the wage share are by no means inversely related to the course of the business cycle. Steindl, in arguing the contrary, did so in the beginning of the 1950s, when there were not yet any exact statistical surveys covering several cycles. The wage share decreased neither in the boom of 1963–6 nor in that of 1968–71; but, on the contrary increased very sharply towards the peak of the boom (1965–6 and 1970–1) and most sharply of all immediately before the onset of the recession. This brilliantly justifies Marx's intuition! We must add that the same tendency still prevails, although in a reduced way, when the relative increase in the number of dependent workers in the total active population is eliminated – in other words, when we refer to the share of the individual worker in the total product.

THE SECULAR INCREASE IN REAL WAGES AND THE PROPENSITY TO INVEST

In fact Marx did in no way deny in principle the possibility that wages would rise under capitalism, although he said (*Capital*, I, ch. 25, p. 575; I, ch. 20, p. 415);

Under the condition of accumulation supposed thus far, which conditions are those most favourable to the labourers, their relation of dependence upon capital takes on a form endurable or . . . 'easy and liberal'. . . . A larger part of their own surplus-product . . . comes back to them in the shape of means of payment, so that they can extend the circle of their enjoyments; can make some additions to their consumption-fund of clothes, furniture, &c., and can lay by small reserve-funds of money. (ibid., 1, ch. 25, p. 579)

This is a very important statement, for it shows that, contrary to the usual assumptions wrongly dubbed the Marxian hypothesis', Marx did indeed contemplate, within the framework of his theory, the possibility that workers would save.

To him, such an increase in real wages means 'that the length and weight of the golden chain the wage-worker has already forged for himself allow of a relaxation of the tension of it'. He even thought it possible that wages could rise over a longer period without any interruption in the prosperity of capitalism: '. . . the price of labour keeps on rising, because its rise does not interfere with the progress of accumulation. In this there is nothing wonderful . . .' (ibid., pp. 579–80).

It is therefore not quite correct of modern analysts to say, as does Güsten (1960, p. 103), that Marx 'left no doubt that the propensity to invest would collapse, if wages rose'. But Marx did indeed believe that the minimum-profit necessary for the smooth functioning of the capitalist machine might be threatened at a certain point if wages rose within the business cycle: 'accumulation slackens in consequence of the rise in the price of labour, because the stimulus of gain is blunted. The rate of accumulation lessens . . .' (*Capital*, 1, ch. 25, p. 580).

Güsten was right to note (1960, p. 104) that the slowing down of the boom as a result of increasing wages should not be seen as a 'fully automatic' brake: 'On the contrary, such a braking effect is exercised by technical progress, which is chiefly labour-saving or capital-using. The boom, in fact, is stopped by the behaviour of capitalists.' As soon as minimum profit is in danger, capitalists will go on an accumulation or investment strike. There is the crisis.

As a result of the crisis, Marx says (*Capital*, 1, ch. 25, p. 581), 'the price of labour falls again to a level corresponding with the needs of the self-expansion of capital, whether the level be below, the same as, or above the one which was normal before the rise of wages took place'.

We see that Marx considers the possibility that money wages may remain during and after the crisis, at a higher level than before the rise. But he also says ('Wage, Price and Profit', in *Marx–Engels Selected Works*, 1968, p. 227), 'With the development of the productive powers of labour the accumulation of capital will be accelerated, even despite a relatively high rate of wages.'

Such an increase is especially possible in times of a boom, when the reserve army decreases or disappears completely. 'In times of prosperity, intense expansion, acceleration and vigour of the reproduction process, labourers are fully employed. Generally, there is also a rise in wages . . .' (*Capital*, III, ch. 28, p. 446). At least 'a portion of the reserve army of labourers, which kept wages down, is absorbed. A general rise in wages ensues, even in the hitherto well employed sections of the labour-market' (ibid., II, ch. 16, p. 320).

As a general rule, the industrial reserve army will not quite disappear even in times of high prosperity, and certainly not during periods of middling prosperity. The reserve army, 'during the periods of . . . average prosperity, weighs down the active labour-army; during the periods of overproduction and paroxysm, it holds its pretensions in check' (ibid., I, ch. 25, p. 598). It is the bottom stratum of the unemployed, which remains in permanent existence or is periodically refilled, and which ensures (in the long run; in the short run it can easily be otherwise) that 'the law of capitalistic accumulation . . . excludes . . . every rise in the price of labour which could seriously imperil the continual reproduction, on an ever-enlarging scale, of the capitalistic relation' (ibid., p. 582).

Within the framework of wage theory we have encountered a number of business-cycle elements that cannot be dealt with extensively until later. In the present context we can only state the following.

Marx does, indeed, envisage (ibid., p. 581) a compatibility between wage increases and the process of accumulation: when there arises 'the excess of capital that makes exploitable labour-power insufficient'. Labour can even become scarcer. Because 'the scale of accumulation may be suddenly extended . . . the requirements of accumulating capital may exceed the increase of labour-power . . . and, therefore, wages may rise. This must, indeed, ultimately be the case if the conditions supposed above continue' (ibid., p. 575). Such was the case during the long periods of prosperity in the nineteenth century and in the first half of the twentieth, and it can therefore be said that Marx actually considered such secular possibilities in the long run.

Such a phenomenon must, of course, lead to a decrease in the share of profits, because of the pressure that rising wages exercise. In this case, 'the long run fall in the rate of profit is not because of a rising composition of value [i.e. technical progress with excess capital consumption = an increase in fixed capital (discussed later)], but rather the profit rate falls because the composition of value has not increased and the demand for labour exceeds the supply'. On the other hand, 'the fall in the rate of profit, which accompanies accumulation, introduces a competitive struggle'. (Ibid., III, ch. 15, p. 256.) We encounter another explanation, which has to be distinguished from the classical Marxian one, of the fall in the rate of profit. It is that the rate of profit falls because labour becomes scarcer in proportion to real capital. This would be easier to accept in marginalist reasoning. Curiously enough, Marx, in his 'harbinger theory', accepted it, in a further version, for the peak of the business cycle. According to him, wage increases signal the downturn of the business cycle. This presupposes that at least at the climax of the business cycle the 'industrial reserve army' must be considerably reduced, if it does not disappear altogether; in this way the pressure that it exercises on the wage level will stop for a short time.

THE THEORY OF REDUNDANCY

Marx, however, did not accept this explanation as valid for the medium term. Here he joined Ricardo in presupposing, as Haller has pointed out (1936, p. 96), that

> workers who have been displaced by technical progress are not absorbed again, and there will be no compensation. This presumption is purely arbitrary and has been disproved by experience. Marx assumes that capital does not increase so rapidly, that there will be at the same time an enlargement and an intensification of the capital base, so that the whole growing population will always be employed at the old wage level.

Haller's hypothesis does not apply to the core of the Marxian argument. Today, it is recognised that the 'theory of redundancy' developed by Ricardo and Marx starts, *ceteris paribus*, from the hypothesis that the capital invested remains the same. If so, it cannot be attacked. This has been clearly shown by Sylos-Labini (1970, p. 26) in particular:

> Marx, like Ricardo, does not deny that if, subsequently, additional (variable) capital appears, the labourers can be absorbed. He recognises that machinery . . . can bring about an increase in production in other sectors (especially in those which supply the means of production for the industries in which the machinery will be used, and in this way increases production in general). In the same way as Ricardo, he admits that the formation of additional capital can be stimulated through a reduction in the prices of goods produced with the help of such machinery, because the price reduction enables part of the income of 'capitalists' to be available for use in other sectors. But he points out that this is quite a different question from that developed by the protagonists of the compensation theory.

Marx, indeed, explicitly recognises (*Theories*, II, pp. 571–2) that it is

> partially correct . . . that because of the spur given to accumulation, on the new basis requiring less living labour in proportion to past labour, the workers who were dismissed and pauperised, or at least that part of the population increase which replaces them, are either absorbed in the

expanding engineering-works themselves, or in branches of production which machinery has made necessary and brought into being, or in new fields of employment opened by the new capital, and satisfying new wants.

It is true that he remarks ironically that it would really be 'a beautiful prospect' if the working class had to suffer redundancy and redeployment, and wage labour 'were reproduced on an ever increasing scale'. Nevertheless, from these and other passages, it is clear that he never denied, as Sylos-Labini has emphasised, that the use of new capital could lead to the employment of workers who have been displaced.

Just as Ricardo did, he denied that the dismissal of workers would be automatically compensated, *ceteris paribus*, within the framework of the former conditions of accumulation. Further remarks of his show that he did not think that the surplus population which is continually being created by the introduction of machinery must exist at all times, and that he believed that it could disappear at least at the peak of prosperity: 'The constant artificial production of a surplus population, which disappears only in times of feverish prosperity, is one of the necessary conditions of production of modern industry' (*Theories*, II, p. 560).

On the other hand, this peak will also be the turning point, because of the lack of pressure on the wage level by the industrial reserve army. In his 'harbinger theory' Marx pointed out that a rapidly increasing wage rate can lead to a reduction of profits and to a downswing in the cycle. Steindl committed a mistake in identifying the 'harbinger theory' with the thesis of the decreasing share of wages in the social product. This would be quite wrong, for the latter theory must be ascribed to Rodbertus.

PRODUCTIVITY AND INCREASE IN REAL WAGES

As a matter of fact, Marx in quite a number of cases maintains the hypothesis of a 'constant rate of surplus value' or a 'constant degree of exploitation of labour by capital', in spite of a 'gradual fall in the general rate of profit'. On the other hand, he always stresses that this is nothing more than a hypothesis. It is certainly not completely clear what Marx considers to be the regular case. This is a question of fact which can be considered only in a dialectic manner.

Increasing productivity, however, necessarily leads to an increase in the rate of surplus value if real wages remain the same. Even if Marx ought to be correct in his assumption that increasing capital costs, absolutely and relatively, lead to a falling rate of profit *via* the inflation of capital values (seen as a stock, though Marx always measured the rate of profit in flow terms: for instance, as a percentage of turnover) the question as to how far an increasing rate of surplus value is forthcoming depends in the first instance on whether the wage bill or wages remain constant.

Here we have to point out that Marx certainly considered the possibility of an increase in wages in the wake of increasing productivity:

> To say that the interests of capital and those of the workers are one and the same is only to say that capital and wage labour are two sides of one and the same relation. The one conditions the other, just as usurer and squanderer condition each other. As long as the wage-worker is a wage-worker his lot depends upon capital. That is the much-vaunted community of interests between worker and capitalist. . . . Let us assume the most favourable case: when productive capital grows, the demand for labour grows; consequently, the price of labour, wages, goes up. . . . A noticeable increase in wages presupposes a rapid growth of productive capital.
>
> (*Wage Labour and Capital*, in *Marx–Engels, Selected Works*, 1968, p. 84.)

Here and elsewhere in the speeches he gave in Brussels in 1847 and which appeared as articles in the *Neue Rheinische Zeitung* in 1849, Marx recognised these possibilities. Similar passages can be found in a study, 'Wages', which was written at the end of 1847 but not published until 1927. There he says that, if wages did not vary, the worker would have no share in the development of civilisation, and he would then remain in a stationary situation.

The possibility of a 'perceptible increase in wages' is stressed in the *Neue Rheinische Zeitung* and even in *Capital*. However, Marx clearly pronounced himself against the theory of Rodbertus, as Engels has underlined in a footnote (*Capital*, II, ch. 20, p. 415, note 46). Rodbertus thought that a decrease in the share of labour in the social product was responsible for the business cycle.

THE SHARE OF WAGE-EARNERS IN WEALTH

The question of whether the share of surplus value in the social product or in value added increases in the long run, so as to bring about a decrease in the share of labour, will have to be discussed within the framework of the theory 'of the tendency of the rate of profit to fall', which we shall examine later (see Vol. II of this work). Here it suffices to stress that Marx would never have been able to maintain his favourite theory if he had not implicitly assumed that the movement in the shares of labour and capital is possible only in a limited form, for otherwise the growing rate of surplus value would always destroy the theory. This problem too we shall examine later. In this context it is interesting to note that the tendency towards an increase in the rate of surplus value can, indeed, be offset to a certain extent by an increase in the sum of wages because of increasing real wages. This phenomenon may explain Joan Robinson's 'mystery of constant shares'.

What happens when increasing wages simultaneously imply an increasing share of value added in the total mass of products? The most important instrument for impeding the shift in relative shares to the detriment of the working class is for Marx the trade unions. It is true that he recognises only limited possibilities of success for them, for he considers that there are strong forces working to the contrary – namely, mechanisation, substitution, tendencies towards the displacement of labour, and the pressure of the world market; nevertheless, it must be remembered that Marx at least considered the possibility.

While it is not certain whether one can attribute to Marx the thesis of a decreasing share of labour in the social product, it cannot be denied that there are certain passages in Marx which emphasise an increase in property in the hands of big business, i.e. an increasing inequality in the distribution of wealth, which inequality serves as an explanation for social tensions. This is exemplified in the famous comparison between the house of the worker and the villa of the capitalist:

> A house may be large or small; as long as the surrounding houses are equally small it satisfies all social demands for a dwelling. But let a palace arise beside the little house, and it shrinks from a little house to a hut. The little house shows now that its owner has only very slight or no demands to make; and however high it may shoot up in the course of civilisation, if the neighbouring palace grows to an equal or even greater extent, the occupant of the relatively small house will feel more and more uncomfortable, dissatisfied and cramped within its four walls. . . . Thus, although the enjoyments of the worker have risen, the social satisfaction that they give has fallen in comparison with the increased enjoyments of the capitalist, which are inaccessible to the worker, in comparison with the state of development of society in general. Our desires and pleasures spring from society; we measure them, therefore, by society and not by the objects which serve for their satisfaction. Because they are of a social nature, they are of a relative nature. . . . The division of social wealth between capital and labour has become still more unequal. . . . Thus if the income of the worker increases with the rapid growth of capital, the social gulf that separates the worker from the capitalist increases at the same time.
>
> (*Wage Labour*, in *Marx–Engels, Selected Works*, 1968, pp. 84, 86, 88.)

We might be inclined to say that this statement can be related to a shift in the distribution of income. But this is not absolutely necessary: for instance, if increasing concentration were to lead to a shrinking number of capitalists sharing the rate of surplus value among themselves with this rate remaining the same, the 'social gulf' as seen by Marx would increase without any shift in relative shares.

At any rate, it is possible to imagine that Marx wanted to discuss shifts in the distribution of wealth. It is true that as a rule he assumes that workers do not save, but in certain passages he considers saving to be possible by workers during certain favourable periods of the business cycle. It is on this hypothesis that the increase in the inequality of wealth, even among capitalists of the 'middle classes', assumes increasing importance. In a similar vein Marx mentions in his *Theories of Surplus Value* the possibility of a relative change for the worse in the position of workers, through an increase in the 'relative wealth' of capitalists and their co-partners.

DISCONTENT AND THE FUNCTION OF TRADE UNIONS

It is not very probable that a decrease in the share of the workers in the social product would on its own lead to unrest, especially as workers would hardly perceive such a development where the social product keeps growing as a whole. Unrest would be likely here only if wage increases are clearly disproportionately smaller than the increase in profits. In this case, we have to reckon with the possibility of explosions of spontaneous character, as, for instance, happened in the Federal Republic of Germany in 1969–70. In that case it was not the absolute growth of the social product, but the relative growth of shares, that was decisive. Even more striking is the unequal development of wealth.

How far are the problems of distribution crucial in the desire for change? We may dare to offer a hypothesis: it is not the fact that absolute differences in the distribution of income or wealth exist, nor is it injustice in distribution in general or its gradual accentuation, that is decisive. It is that at certain times changes may become obvious, and, practically speaking, such sudden changes may be brought about only within the course of the business cycle. A history of the correlation between revolutionary movements and sudden, clearly distinguishable changes in real income, or obvious decreases in the accustomed rate of income growth, or even of decreases in real income, has still to be written.

The concept of distribution in Marx's work is by no means fully elaborated and the same is true of his theory of classes and the class struggle. This is no mere accident, for there is a close relationship between the two. The essential problem does not lie in the static concept, but must be seen within the context of dynamic developments in the social structure, not only in the material foundations but also in the sphere of consciousness, which is formed more or less by conditions reigning in distribution.

Marx quotes the complaints of capitalists that trade unions by either their demands or their actions in some degree 'lay taxes on the advance of industry' (*Capital*, 1, ch. 21, p. 523).* In another passage (ibid., ch. 25, p. 599) he reminds us of the defensive function of trade unions: 'by Trades'

---

* Chapter 21 in the English edition corresponds to Chapter 20 in the German edition of 1953.

unions, & c., they try to organise a regular co-operation between employed
and unemployed in order to destroy or to weaken the ruinous effects of this
natural law of capitalistic production on their class'.

In his early works he was rather sceptical of the possibility of effective
action by trade unions, and shared the prevalent ideas of the era of the
wages-fund theory, for he admitted that the objections of economists to
workers' associations were justified; that the costs they imposed on workers
were mostly greater than the gains that could be attained through them,
that they could not resist the laws of competition in the long run, that they
would call forth more and more new machinery and increased division of
labour, including transfers from one location of production to another, and
that all this would lead to a decrease in wages.

In 'Wages', Marx not only considered what is nowadays called the
'Ricardo effect' of mechanisation on wage increases, but went on to
envisage that an industry might change location in order to escape local
wage pressures. He saw this factor as potentially affecting whole countries,
not just regions, and perceived foreign trade as a factor limiting trade-
union power. Where wage claims are exaggerated, there may be a
stagnation of investment as far as home trade is concerned. Marx stresses
that, if trade unions are able to maintain the price of labour at a very high
level in one country, bringing about a considerable decrease in profits as
compared to average profits in other countries, or slowing down capital
growth, this will lead to stagnation or recession in industry, and the
workers will be ruined along with their masters.

In this context the debate on wages leads on to the problems of foreign
trade. Again, in 'Wages' he says that, when people speak of an increase in
wages, one must always consider the situation of the world market and the
fact that such an increase can be obtained only by throwing workers in
other countries out of work. This reminds us of the theory later developed
by Rosa Luxemburg according to which the world market permits a high
standard of living in the leading countries at the expense of less developed
countries. There are also other aspects of Marx's work that are touched
upon in 'Wages', although in a rather incomplete form. This is true of the
theory of money and also of the theory of monopoly.

In the second volume of *Capital*, Marx, in treating of the wage theory,
mentions monopoly in a rather superficial way (p. 344)

it is said: If wages rise, the capitalists raise the price of their
commodities. . . . If it were in the power of the capitalist producers to
raise the prices of their commodities at will, they could and would do so
without a rise in wages. Wages would never rise if commodity prices fell.
[The possibility of rising real wages is therefore envisaged by Marx –
doubtless because of the possibility of growth to greater industrial
dimensions, with a more favourable cost curve corresponding to such a
growth.] The capitalist class would never resist the trades' unions, if it

could always and under all circumstances do what it is now doing by way of exception, under definite, special, so to say local, circumstances, to wit, avail itself of every rise in wages in order to raise prices of commodities much higher yet and thus pocket greater profits.

25 Later Interpretations of the Marxian Wage Theory

Marx's theory has received a great variety of interpretations. In its static approach it is closely linked with the theory of surplus value, and to that extent is part of the debate on value theory.

There is also a dynamic approach in Marx's wage theory, and this leads to Marx's general view of economic development. Divergences in interpretation apply especially to this dynamic approach. Here we may distinguish at least four different versions: Steindl's; Samuelson's; that of Dobb and Rothschild; and that of Marchal and Tiano.

STEINDL'S INTERPRETATION

Steindl (1952, p. 231) has raised the question of what, specifically, Marx's wage theory is. He refers especially to chapter 25 of the first volume of *Capital*. It is there that Marx himself asks the relevant questions: is an increase in real wages possible, and what would be the consequences of such an increase?

According to Steindl, Marx's answer is clearly positive: an increase in real wages is possible provided that the increase does not disturb the process of accumulation. If, however, the accumulation process is disturbed by increases in real wages, investment has at least temporarily to be curtailed, so causing unemployment. This will exercise pressure on real wages until a kind of equilibrium is reached. According to Steindl, Marx starts from the hypothesis that the long-run rate of accumulation is given – a hypothesis that Steindl considers to be admissible.

By what mechanism, however, may the long-run level of real wages be adapted to the requirements of this investment trend?

'The mechanism, then, works as follows: when real wages rise above the 'equilibrium' level, the rate of accumulation is slowed down. This leads to an increase in the degree of unemployment. The greater unemployment depresses the level of real wages; their fall leads to an increase in capital accumulation, which now rises above its trend level' (ibid., p. 232). Now,

Steindl believes that there is a contradiction between the short- and long-run analysis of Marx: 'Without disentangling the two it is impossible to get a clear understanding of Marx.' In Marx's view the percentage of unemployed is decisive: 'The real wage is a function of the degree of unemployment.'

It is here that a comparison with the modern 'Phillips curve' seems unavoidable, for its discoverer develops his thesis in a similar way: 'The rate of change of money wage rates can be explained by the level of unemployment and the rate of change of unemployment . . . except in or immediately after those years in which there is a sufficiently rapid rise in import prices . . . ' (Phillips, 1958, p. 299).

Steindl tries to expand Marx's remarks on trade unions by forming the hypothesis that growing trade-union power could mean higher real wages at a given level of unemployment. According to Steindl, technical progress must logically lead to an ever-increasing level of real wages, for the reserve army must necessarily shrink with steadily increasing technical progress. Marx, however, started from just the opposite hypothesis, of increasing unemployment because of technical progress, and for him technical progress was not to be determined by the level of real wages. '. . . if we assume a given trend rate of growth of capital, the rate of growth of employment must fall short of it' (Steindl, 1952, p. 234).

Additional labour power is provided by two means: first, technical progress currently releases labour, and, secondly, pre-capitalist artisans etc. are proletarianised. The process of accumulation creates its own labour force, its own reserve army and, therefore, its own level of real wages. In the last resort, as Steindl emphasises, the process of accumulation is the decisive factor, and the development of real wages is the dependent variable – a result clearly compatible with Marx's unequivocal statement, 'To put it mathematically: the rate of accumulation is the independent . . . the rate of wages, the dependent . . . (*Capital*, 1, ch. 25, p. 581). Steindl then proceeds to discuss the thesis of the declining share of wages in the social product, which he attributes to Marx in the same way as Kaldor (1957, p. 621) and Samuelson (1957, p. 912). He adds, however, that Marx at least thought that an increased share of wages would be possible during the upswing. We have already pointed out above that this interpretation is too simple-minded and does not do justice to Marx, who was referring only to development at the peak of the boom. To this extent the basic hypotheses from which Kaldor and Samuelson start are refuted.

On balance Steindl reaches the conclusion (1952, p. 237) that the short-run analysis of wages in Marx's work contains many elements that are not acceptable, but this does not mean that his long-run analysis is without value. On the contrary, this analysis finds a firmer foundation in Marx's distribution theory, as already outlined in his 'Wage Labour and Capital'. Distribution is determined automatically by the competition between capitalists, the mutual undercutting, the higher profit margins in 'pioneer-enterprises' and the unused capacity that intensifies competition. These problems belong, however, to the general area of distribution theory.

SAMUELSON'S INTERPRETATION

Samuelson devoted an extensive article (1957) to the Marxian wage system. He begins by stating (p. 884) that one should take seriously Marx's belief that he was 'baring the inner workings of competitive capitalism'. In his presentation Samuelson pays much attention to the theory of wages. Unfortunately, he starts his discussion on the theoretical problems of wages with a wrong premise: 'First though, we should note a contradiction in Marx's thinking that analysts have pointed out. Along with the "law of the falling rate of profit", Marxian economists often speak of the "law of the falling (or constant) real wage of labor"' (ibid., 892).

In this context Samuelson alludes (ibid., p. 893) to a phrase by Joan Robinson, who was the victim of a similar misconception: 'Marx can only demonstrate a falling tendency in profits by abandoning his argument that real wages tend to be constant.' Such a statement is not to be found in Marx's works. What Marx actually assumes is only that with the increasing use of real capital the sum of wages in relation to the sum of real capital does not grow proportionately. Incidentally, Marx believed, contrary to Joan Robinson, that it is possible to measure real capital in money terms, as a flow magnitude (for instance, in the form of depreciation). Marx sets out from a kind of mark-up calculation, at the same time presupposing that the sum of profits can grow only at the same rate as the sum of wages. This explains his 'fall in the rate of profit'.

In his argument Marx has by no means excluded the possibility that the sum of wages and the wage per head of employed workers may increase. Even if there were to be a shift within value added in favour of the share of profit, this does not signify that the sum of wages, or the real wage or the nominal wage per head, must remain constant or have to fall.

It may be stressed that the Marxian value calculation, which Joan Robinson repeatedly and not without justice dubbed a source of confusion, conceals the problem in itself. Fundamentally, Joan Robinson starts from the hypothesis that the sum of constant and variable capital plus surplus value (i.e. turnover) must increase if the productivity of labour increases. In a value calculation, however, increasing productivity does not lead to an increase in the sum of values, for greater quantities of product will be produced by the same or a smaller quantity of 'socially necessary labour'. In this case there is no pressure in the direction of an increase in wage payments, unless an inflationary rise in prices takes place.

At the centre of Samuelson's considerations stands the problem of technical progress. Samuelson declares, as has been particularly stressed by his critic Gottheil (1960, p. 717), that a rational capitalist will not use a technique that will lead to the lowering of the rate of profit. Indeed, Samuelson says (1957, p. 894), 'A technical improvement must be an improvement or it will not be introduced in a perfect-competition market economy.' His real concern is to show that wages and the rate of profit cannot decrease simultaneously.

In this context we cannot deal with the theory of the 'tendency of the rate of profit to fall' nor with the general thesis of Samuelson's article, which basically concerns the problem of growth. His references to wage theory are concerned partly with empirical facts and partly with the relation between the reserve army, technical progress and real wages.

As far as empirical problems are concerned he states (ibid., p. 907), 'this wage-floor is advancing dynamically from year to year, decade to decade, at a rate that doubles perhaps about every 30 years'. With regard to this he criticises Marx without reserve and reproaches him for a lack of foresight:

> Indeed, writing in 1860 . . . an economist . . . should have expected the odds to favour a strong increase in real wages, the only exception arising from an extreme 'bias' of inventions toward the extreme labour-saving type. . . . To have been judged lucky by economic historians, Marx should have phrased a theory to explain the approximate constancy of wage's relative share of the national product, not the secular decline of this relative share.   (Ibid., p. 912)

This criticism is unjust. First, we can by no means attribute such a theory of a decreasing relative share of wages to Marx, because this was the theory of Rodbertus. To Marx, such a decreasing share in the social product is simply a factor that may help compensate for falling rates of profit, as long as the other effective 'counter-tendency' (i.e. technical progress in the capital-goods industry) does not come into play.

Incidentally, Schumpeter is diametrically opposed to the hypothesis from which Samuelson starts. Even Samuelson himself harboured some doubts (ibid.): 'His [Marx's] actual models . . . were perhaps better. . . . they contain in them no tendency for real wages to fall or to lag particularly behind the growth of output. . . .' As has already been emphasised, Marx generally started from the hypothesis of 'constancy in the relative share of labour'; his theory of the tendency of the rate of profit to fall is based precisely on this hypothesis. In view of this, Samuelson ought to have praised Marx as 'a lucky man'.

Basically, Samuelson believes that the penetration of technical progress in a competitive system must finally lead to an increase in real wages. He, therefore proposes that it would be better to leave 'the law of the declining (or constant) real wage for the junk pile'. (ibid., pp. 894–5.)

At the same time, he mentions the possibility, in referring to Schumpeter and Fisher, that 'technological change may raise sagging interest rates, just as plucking a violin string restores its dissipating energies'. In the case of an increasing supply of labour, he concludes there is such a thing as a 'law of the rising profit rate'. He reaches this conclusion by equating secular rates of interest and rates of profit. On the whole he is of the opinion that 'interest rates have historically oscillated in such a way as to lead many economists to the view that there is a fundamental law of constancy of the interest rate' (ibid p. 898).

One might think that Samuelson here comes quite near to Marx's notion of the 'industrial reserve army'. This, however, he calls (ibid., p. 905) a 'red herring' or at least a mere slogan, for he thinks that reference to it camouflages the proper relation betweeen demand and supply. He later devotes a whole passage to the notion of the reserve army. He is chiefly interested in the question of whether pressure by the reserve army could lead to a decrease in real wages.

In discussing these problems, he excludes (ibid., p. 908) quite a number of aspects: namely, 'monetary assumptions . . . institutional assumptions with respect to unionism, labour mobility, interpersonal differentials in skills and zealousness . . . the mix of demand'. He then turns to the analysis of the 'reserve army', basing his arguments on the theories of Keynes and Kalecki, and reaches the conclusion that even the sharpest competition between employed and unemployed would not lower real wages to the minimum subsistence level.

In his argument Samuelson abstracts (ibid., pp. 908–9) from conditions of monopsony and monopoly,

> in order to see where cruel competition leads us to. . . . If men out of work do offer to work for less, the money wage cannot remain stationary in a perfectly competitive labour market. The money wage will fall and continue to fall until no more excluded men bid it down. . . . falling money wages need not mean falling real wages. . . . We can construct models of hyperdeflation . . . with unemployment never disappearing and real wages not necessarily changing . . . in which money wages push down prices indefinitely. Had Marx used a reserve army of the unemployed as a reason for falling *money* wages, one could better understand the logic of his system. . . .

Samuelson's lengthy exercise proves to be rather misdirected in the field of wage theory, for he is tilting at windmills. After all, Marx's argument did not refer to real wages, for he reasoned in 'values', in which, by definition, the counter-value of goods for use or consumers' goods (Ricardo's 'riches') does not appear. As has been pointed out above, there can be no question of Marx thinking that real wages could be kept near the minimum of existence, and he cannot be lumbered with Rodbertus's theory of a tendency for the share of wages in the total product to decrease, Samuelson abstracts in an unjustified manner from the elements of monopolistic and oligopolistic competition which do appear in Marx's work, and starts from a completely unrealistic hypothesis, for he takes it (ibid., pp. 884–6) that Marx, in the same way as Ricardo, worked with fixed factor proportions and constant returns (in fact, he later – ibid., p. 907 – drops this assumption). Gottheil, in his reply (1960), particularly emphasised (pp. 717–19) that the last two assumptions do not apply to Marx's model. Samuelson's remaining argument concerns, essentially, the relation between capital, labour and growth conditions within the context of technical progress. It need not concern us in the present context.

THE DOBB–ROTHSCHILD INTERPRETATION: THE 'RIVIERA THEOREM'

In a discussion of Marx one can as little abstract from 'institutional' factors as one can from sociological and monopolistic ones.

On the side of the worker the 'positive' factors are, according to Marx, the (historically given) minimum of existence, trade unions and the increasing scarcity of labour power during periods of prosperity (within the framework of his 'harbinger theory').

On the side of the capitalist, the positive forces at work in his favour are, according to Marx, the process of mechanisation with its constant renewal of the 'industrial reserve army' underpinned by the propensity to accumulate, the monopolistic tendencies towards concentration and, within business-cycle theory and the theory of the long-run 'tendency of the rate of profit to fall', the threat of 'investment strikes'. It may be possible to add further factors, such as the resistance of capitalists in the face of a 'minimum subsistence standard', which is historically given and which brings us to the 'Riviera theorem', as it has been christened by the present author (Kühne, 1955b).

The 'Riviera theorem' takes up an idea expressed by Maurice Dobb (1929; 1965, pp. 28–31), according to whom the propensity of entrepreneurs to save out of their profits and to invest, i.e. to create new places of employment or to maintain existing ones, depends on their idea of a 'proper conventional standard of living'. This standard, in turn, is the result of wage negotiations in the past: real wages 'today' could be increased even more if workers had been in a stronger position 'yesterday' and ensured that the entrepreneurs stuck to a more frugal way of life, made fewer claims on consumption goods, saved and, therefore, invested more. We may add that this argument does not absolutely contradict the conventional wisdom, according to which the profits of entrepreneurs correspond macroeconomically to their own consumption plus net investment, seen *ex post*.

Robertson, the doyen of British economics, has never been outdone in his impressive writing style. He took up this argument, which sounded suspect in the mouth of a **Marxist economist** even of the rank of Dobb, and imbued it with respectability (1931; 1946, pp. 233–4): 'Hence if the bargains had been more advantageous to the wage-earners, the capitalists might never have thought of going to the Riviera [hence the term "Riviera theorem"], and might have saved more instead: thus wages would have been higher today.'

Dobb started from the premise that Marx, in 1865, had been one of the first to refute the theory of the wage fund. Marx had indeed argued that any scarcity in the wage goods consumed by workers could exist only for a short period, while production or investment in wage good industries could not be increased. Wage increases and increases in the wage bill for the economy must necessarily lead to an increase in turnover, and, therefore, in the rate of profits in the wage-goods sectors, that would attract the capital required for the expansion of those sectors. In the same way, any objections to the Marxian formula which argue that his idea of variable capital resembles the wage-fund theory are not relevant. Authors who argue in this way claim that variable capital is based on the value of wage goods, i.e. on the share of labour input society devotes to the production of wage goods. But Marx does not talk in simple 'monetary terms' about sums that are destined for wage payments, for this in the end would be a problem of liquidity or of cash accounting; neither does he bother about 'inventories of finished consumption goods', as Samuelson characterises the theory of wage funds (1957, p. 904). The Marxian formula resembles more the 'resurrection . . . [of] the wage-fund doctrine . . . [of] Taussig' [1896] of which Samuelson says that the idea 'merely becomes a reminder that production does take time and that men do not consume unfinished goods, with the implication of a certain short-run inexpansibility in the consumption goods'. To Marx such a 'fund' is nothing more than a revolving labour input which can be increased or reduced in the short run.

The proportions in which labour input is used for wage goods, i.e. consumption goods or investment goods, are largely determined by technical progress and its potential. If innovations are introduced which lead to a cheapening or improvement of machinery, investment in machines will be relatively more profitable and there will be relatively more capital invested in machinery. These are the considerations upon which Dobb's wage theory is based. Dobb says, for instance (1948, p. 125), 'It was this reason which Marx adduced to show that the demand for labour did not increase proportionately with the accumulation of capital, but that as capital accumulated the demand for labour tended to fall relatively: it will still increase, but increase in a constantly diminishing ratio as compared with the increase of capital'.

This line of argument may suggest that Marx was 'nothing other than a follower of the marginal productivity theory and of the Cobb–Douglas theorem', i.e. of a comparison between relative growth rates of capital and labour, however insoluble the problem of measuring both in monetary terms may be. Dobb (1959) is of the opinion that, from the Marxian presentation of the law of the tendency of the rate of profit to fall, it could hardly be concluded that it was intended as a historical prognosis independent of the struggle between capital and labour and of the resulting division of the total product. Dobb stresses the central position of the class struggle in Marx's theory.

He also points to the 'Ricardo–Hayek effect'. It was traditionally supposed that such substitution effects would be produced by wage increases. But there is an obvious objection: machines are also products of labour and must be influenced by changes in wage costs. Quite recently, Leontief has reached the conclusion that there need not be any substitution effect in this respect. The validity of such objections depends, according to Dobb, on movements in the rate of interest (which is an essential part of the construction costs of machines); but at the very least it is a matter of controversy whether or not the rate of interest will fall because of an increase in wages.

Dobb seems inclined to think that the rate of interest will not fall. He also supposes that innovations are mostly of a labour-saving character. This would then lead to a tendency for the share of labour in the social product to decrease. However, we have still to consider the fact that 'at least . . . some two-thirds of working-class expenditure in the past has been on the products of the building trades and of agriculture', where the effects of technological improvements are smaller (Dobb, 1948, pp. 127–8).

In his earlier study already cited, Dobb concentrated more on the relationship between the class struggle and the movements in the workers' share: 'A rise of wages may develop new standards and habits which increase his [the worker's] wants and increase the utility of income to him; while a fall in wages, by contracting his standards and habits, may decrease his wants and lower the intensity of his desire for income . . .' (1929; 1966, pp. 26–7). In the latter case, Dobb assumes that there will be a decrease in the utility of income, but he admits that this can be overcome by a readiness to compensate absolute losses in income through an intensification of labour effort.

He then proceeds to analyse (ibid., p. 28) the effect of wage increases on capitalists:

> But the case of the capitalists presents an opposite situation. Any change in the bargain between themselves and their labourers . . . will affect their willingness to accumulate and invest capital, not in the same, but in the opposite direction. . . . In the case of the capitalist, this relation between income and habit is likely to be of much greater importance . . . for the reason that the desire for luxuries is much more influenced by habit, custom and conventional standards than is the desire for necessaries. . . . When the national income is expanding . . . it may well be that if a diminished share accrues to the

owners of property, the effect may appear, not in a slackened rate of saving, but merely in privileged standards of consumption, precluded from rapid advancement, remaining on a more modest scale. . . .

It is true that in introducing the notion of 'privileged standards of consumption' Dobb would, if such a correction of consumption standards is to have any quantitative importance compared with investment or with the consumption of the working class, have to define the privileged as a rather large class, consisting of independent workers, entrepreneurs, owners of capital and leading elements in various enterprises. However, if the conditions are satisfied we should then have the 'Riviera theorem'.

Robertson has expressed this theorem very neatly (1931, p. 233): 'The alleged demand curve for labour, [Dobb] says, is itself not an "independent" factor in the problem, since its height depends upon the willingness of the capitalists to save, this again upon their conventional standard of comfort, and this again upon the outcome of the bargains they have made with wage-earners in the past'. With his 'Riviera theorem' Dobb has furnished a basis for the modern trade-union thesis, which descends from Marx, that a change in the share of the social product would not necessarily lead to a decrease in investment activities.

The Austrian economist Rothschild has done his best to underpin Dobb's argument by pointing out the importance which Marx attributes to the negotiating power of trade unions in what might be called the organised class struggle. He is of the opinion that Marx's argument remains much more realistic, because he takes sociological factors into account, than are the theories of those economists who limit themselves to mathematically measurable concepts. Marx did his best to correct the subsistence theory of the classics. According to him, it is not the pressure of population as such which regulates wage developments. In the controversy with Lassalle, he stresses that 'the battle' would be 'fought and won' long before wage increases brought any change in the numbers of the working population (*Capital*, 1, 25, p. 597).

For Marx, the regulation of wages occurs not through the influence of demographic factors, but through technical progress and increasing mechanisation, which constantly re-create technological unemployment and exercise periodic pressure on wages, according to the rhythm of the business cycle.

Rothschild has declared (1957, p. 215) that Marx was one of the first to point out that an increase in nominal wages may stimulate the production of investment goods. Above all, as Marx says, the negotiating power of entrepreneurs is decisively strengthened by their ability to launch an investment strike at any time (ibid., p. 15). Whereas Dobb believed that one could avoid an investment strike by a self-imposed cut in the consumption quota of the upper classes, provided that this took the form of a slow transition by eliminating the peaks of growth, Rothschild placed greater emphasis on wage movements in the medium-term business-cycle.

For the record, it is interesting to note that the 'Riviera theorem', which Dobb and Robertson drew from Marxian logic, was anticipated in the 1920s by one of the most intransigent adversaries of the Marxian system. Muhs advanced this thesis in response to Marx's opinion that accumulation could be jeopardised by sharp increases in wages. This means that it was an anti-Marxist who thought that 'investment strikes' could be avoided.

Muhs, arguing that capitalists could compensate for increases in wages either by refraining from consumption or by other measures, thinks it entirely possible for the growth in surplus value to be, in the end, completely exhausted by wage increases while accumulation (or net investment) is maintained. If capitalists were to cease to accumulate, the eventual result would the destruction of the basis of their existence and the end of the possibility of building up a fortune.

> Stronger still than the goad of profit is the goad of the existence and security of property. The reduction in funds for accumulation because of wage increases will be compensated for by provisions from the consumption funds of capitalists and by measures to rationalise the management of the firm, so as to make good the losses by reducing costs. For this reason wage increases have often proved to be an agent contributing to an improvement in production. (Muhs, 1927, p. 435.)

This last sentence is reminiscent of the so-called trade-union 'torture theory', which was formulated by Marschak and Tarnow during the 1920s. According to this theory, wage increases could force entire economic sectors to rationalise, as a part of which some inefficient marginal firms would have to shut down.

Here we have a very curious confrontation: the Marxist Dobb and the anti-Marxist Muhs attest that capitalism can absorb wage increases largely without cutting its investment quota and, therefore, without impairing technical progress. Marx, on the other hand, is more sceptical and sees in wage increases beyond certain limits his famous 'harbinger effect', leading to a cut in investment. Such a cut would play a decisive rôle in the course of the business cycle and be influential in disrupting the capitalist system, either at the economic level by bringing about a crisis, or in the sociological sphere by exacerbating the class struggle.

All participants to the debate, including the partisans of the 'torture theory', agree in stressing the importance of the stimulus to rationalisation and mechanisation that is exercised by wage increases. The institutionalised class struggle carried out by trade unions in this way becomes the driving power in the process of concentration, in which, according to the Marxian vision, mammoth enterprises and giant trusts bring about a degree of socialisation of the spheres of production.

In this way the problem of wages leads us on to the theory of business cycles, as well as to the problems of concentration and oligopoly.

THE MARCHAL – TIANO INTERPRETATION

Sociological and institutional factors have received particularly close attention from the French school, which sets out from the 'domination effects' developed by Perroux and refined by Marchal and his disciples Lecaillon and Tiano.

According to Marchal and Tiano Marxian wage theory starts from, on the one side, the division of the social product as historically given (i.e. in Marxian terminology, the 'rate of surplus value'), and, on the other side, from a historically given 'sociological' minimum real wage. 'The notion of wages is [in Marx] sociologically conceived. The most frequently attained minimum wage is not the wage which would permit the worker not to starve, but that which would permit him to live as a worker.' Tiano here (1957, p. 180) alludes to, on the one hand, Marx, and, on the other, Marchal, who stressed (1955, pp. 229ff.) that an increase in effective wages in the Marxian system would allow the 'sociological minimum wage' to be modified upwards, and that this minimum wage tends to rise to the level of the effective wage.

According to Marchal (ibid., p. 227) one must in wage analysis direct oneself 'more to a historical and moral element; in other words, one must deepen the idea of a psychological minimum'. This psychological minimum will rise, under the influence of an increasing level of effective wages, until it coincides with the average wage level of 'yesterday' or 'today'. 'One may presume – even if Marx did not explicitly say so – that the number of ostensibly natural needs increases proportionately to the increase in the national income.'

This thesis of Marchal and Lecaillon (1958, III, p. 95) needs to be modified to a certain extent, especially with regard to the experience of the Great Depression and of the recessions since the Second World War. It is actually possible for the effective wage to 'give' during a recession.

On the other hand, the level of wage rates, especially hourly rates, fixed through collective bargaining is considered to be relatively rigid and 'sticky'. The 'sociological minimum' as understood by Marchal and Tiano would tend to coincide with the level of standard wage rates, which in itself also tends to rise in the long run. If this is so, the 'value of labour', which is based on the 'cost of reproduction' in the Marxian system, will itself be variable: it increases with rising productivity, rising national income and rising 'sociological minimum'. 'Value . . ., namely the unit used in measurement, varies in itself, the more productive an hour of labour becomes' (ibid., III, p. 126).

What is essential in this context is the link between the wage, conceived as 'value', the 'sociological and psychological minimum' and the increase in productivity. In this interpretation Marxian wage theory boils down to a (sociological) productivity theory, in which the floor or the lower limit to wages tends to become 'rigid' and constitutes a lower limit for wage decreases in the historical process. At the same time this lower limit also secures a minimum of consumption, which the capitalist system needs if it is to recover from its excesses.

In such an interpretation it has to be asked whether the obstinate rise in the lower limit will not in the long run also lead to an increase in the share of wages in the social product, with the implication that the rate and volume of surplus value, as traditionally handed down, will be menaced. We must further ask whether such a compression of the total volume of surplus value will not lead to a permanent decrease in the propensity to invest and to stagnation. Here wage theory runs into general distribution theory and growth theory.

26 Pauperisation and the Error of 'Growing Poverty'

The so-called 'theory of growing poverty' has been a red herring in the interpretation of Marx's work. A large number of analysts, even some of those whom we have to treat seriously, have (often *bona fide*) taken this theory for granted. This at least suggests that they have read Marx rather carelessly, including Schumpeter, who speaks of 'immiserisation'.

Those analysts who claim that such a theory exists refer in the first place to the following famous passage in the *Communist Manifesto*: 'The modern labourer, instead of rising with the progress of industry, sinks deeper and deeper below the conditions of existence of his own class. He becomes a pauper, and pauperism develops more rapidly than population and wealth'.

This passage is by no means easy to interpret: the fact that the worker sinks below the conditions of his own class need not signify that the whole class sinks below its own conditions. After all, how could this be possible? The sense is, rather, that these 'conditions' constitute the normal level of the class, and that part of the class sinks below this normal level.

The second passage generally quoted in this context occurs in the first volume of *Capital*, in the famous twenty-fifth chapter (chapter 23 in the German), in which Marx develops the theory of the 'industrial reserve army'. In section iv he speaks of the 'different forms of existence of relative overpopulation' and develops a 'general law of capitalist accumulation':

> The fact that the means of production, and the productiveness of labour, increase more rapidly than the productive population, expresses itself, therefore, capitalistically in the inverse form that the labouring population always increases more rapidly than the conditions under which capital can employ this increase for its own self-expansion.
>
> (*Capital*, I, ch. 25, pp. 603–4.)

THE 'PAUPERISATION' OF FRINGE GROUPS

The second group of the pauperised consists of the 'industrial reserve army' in its proper sense: 'The greater the social wealth, the functioning capital, the extent and energy of its growth, and, therefore, also the absolute mass of the proletariat and the productiveness of its labour, the greater is the industrial reserve army.' Of this Marx says 'that the quantity of paupers increases with every crisis, and diminishes with every revival of trade'. (*Capital*, I, ch. 25, p. 596.) The long-run average rate of the unemployed as a percentage of the working class will rise.

> But the greater this reserve army in proportion to the active labour-army, the greater is the mass of a consolidated surplus-population, whose misery is in inverse ratio to its torment of labour. The more extensive, finally, the lazarus-layers of the working-class, and the industrial reserve army, the greater is official pauperism. *This is the general law of capitalist accumulation.* (Ibid., pp. 603–4.)

Here it should be quite clear that the notion of 'misery' refers only to the 'over-population', i.e. to the army of unemployed. Pauperism is then identical to the 'lazarus-layer' of the working class. This can be seen very clearly from the general context of this chapter.

A few pages earlier, Marx stated (ibid., p. 595) that the 'condemnation of one part of the working-class to enforced idleness' is confronted by 'the over-work of the other part. . . . The over-work of the employed part of the working-class swells the ranks of the reserve, whilst conversely the greater pressure that the latter by its competition exerts on the former forces these to submit to over-work and to subjugation under the dictates of capital. . . .' This is the modern 'Phillips curve', which shows wage developments as a function of the movement in the rate of unemployment. Here we clearly see that Marx anticipated modern economics. To him, overtime working 'accelerates at the same time the production of the industrial reserve army on a scale corresponding with the advance of social accumulation'.

By the term 'pauperisation' Marx denotes one of the contradictions between, on the one side, the development of productive forces, and logically also the average real income of employed workers, and, on the other, the situation of those who are not part of the productive process or are excluded from it. The reasons for such exclusion are to be found either in the labour-saving tendency of technical progress or in the intensifying fluctuations of the business cycle, which may result in a tendency towards stagnation. The whole outcome is that an increasing part of the population is excluded from normal employment opportunities.

Marx himself never spoke of *Verelendung*–progressive deterioration, or growing poverty – but only of 'pauperisation', which is used in a quite different sense. Those authors who misinterpret Marx should have noted this long ago, for the relevant passages show quite clearly that Marx actually took for granted an increase in real wages in the course of capitalist development. Is it possible to imagine an increase in the poverty of the working class as accompanying an increase in real wages? No. Some degree

of 'pauperisation', however, surely is possible, as may be seen by
considering the meaning of the terms in question.

Marx understands by 'a deterioration in the situation of the worker',
which he sometimes mentions, something other than a deterioration in
wages, for he expressly says that it does not matter whether the 'payment is
high or low'. What he intends to cover here is the inner psychological
impoverishment of the man who is dominated by machinery instead of
being its master, and thus becomes an 'appendage to the machine'; a
manual worker whose 'intellectual power' and creative force are lost
because he performs only partial processes, which by themselves seem
senseless. This is part of the alienation of man that Marx, with such
uncanny foresight, depicted in his early writings 'The Holy Family',
'Economic and Philosophical Manuscripts' and 'The Critique of Hegel's
Philosophy of Law'. We can now recognise this inner impoverishment not
only in the worker doing assembly-line work on piece-rates, but also in the
worker tied to the soulless routine work of office life. 'Automation', in
which man contents himself with pressing buttons, does not mean the
disappearance of this alienation but its highest triumph. Man no longer
sees what he has created; the machine takes it away from him.

This is only one part of Marx's argument, and it has been misinterpreted
as a materialist 'theory of growing poverty'. It is the other part of the
argument that contains the essence of the economic theory of
'pauperisation'.

This 'pauperisation' does not at all concern the whole of the working
class, but only part of it. What Marx really wants to say here is that on the
one hand the increasing intensity of work leads to an increase in the number
of workers who are invalided at an early age, and on the other hand the
cylical development in the rhythm of the business cycle leads in the long
run to an increase in the percentage unemployed, i.e. in the 'industrial
reserve army'.

From the fertile discussion on social reform the first fact should be
familiar to us. We know that the majority of invalids living on pensions
retired from work long before the age-limit of sixty or sixty-five years. As
Marx says (*Capital*, 1, ch. 25, p. 603.) they are

> chiefly people who succumb to their incapacity for adaptation, due to
> the division of labour; people who have passed the normal age of the
> labourer; the victims of industry, whose number increases with the
> increase of dangerous machinery, of mines, chemical works, &c., the
> mutilated, the sickly, the widows, &c. Pauperism is the hospital of the
> active labour-army and the dead weight of the industrial reserve army.

A 'TRANSLATION MISTAKE' OF REVISIONISM?

Here one thing is quite clear: the word 'pauperism' must never be equated with 'growing poverty', and it is even more erroneous to apply the latter term to the working-class in its entirety, as even some leading socialists have for some time been prone to do. This is one of the gravest misinterpretations of Marx.

It is really a matter of an error in translation. The word 'pauperisation', which means that a class of underprivileged appears, has been confounded with the idea of a deterioration of the living standards of the working class as a whole. The error was pointed out by the present author in his presentation of Marxian theory in 1955. There he said (Kühne, 1955a, p. 64) that 'it appears clearly from those passages of *Capital* that Marx did not mean an increase in the misery of the entire working-class, but only the relative decline of large parts of this class into another layer below this, the "paupers" in the proper sense, the so-called "lazarus-layers of the working-class" '. Bernstein was seen as possibly the originator of the error. He has said again and again that a development of productive forces concurrent with a decline in the level of the proletariat is unimaginable, and in saying this he starts from the hypothesis that Marx never believed that such a negative correlation could exist. He writes (1919, p. 772), 'the phrase of the "hopelessness" of the worker's position was coined more than fifty years ago. It permeates the entire radical socialist literature of the 1830s and 1840s and it seems that many well-established facts justify it'. Bernstein refers to the *Communist Manifesto* and to certain statements made by Marx in *The Poverty of Philosophy* and in 'The Class Struggles in France: 1848 to 1850', which have a rather pessimistic ring. But he is not able to quote from the works of the older Marx a single passage that might confirm his thesis.

On the other hand, Bernstein's opinion that Marx held such a theory, seemed to be corroborated by the fact that some representatives of 'orthodox' Marxism, such as Karl Kautsky and Plekhanov, protested just because Bernstein did not believe that such 'hopelessness' could exist. It was this that led the latter to the completely unfounded opinion that the 'hopelessness of the position of the worker . . . is an irrefutable axiom of "scientific Socialism" ' (ibid., p. 172).

THE CORRECTION OF THE NOTION OF 'PAUPERISM' IN MODERN MARXISM

In modern socialist literature truth is gradually beginning to get the upper hand, and modern economists depart more and more from the thesis of fatalistic hopelessness, which is in fact in fundamental contradiction to the theory of the movable 'sociological minimum', as developed quite early by Marx.

Almost at the same time as the present author published his own denial of the 'theory of growing poverty', Rosdolsky was writing his *magnum opus* (1968), in which he too flatly denied (1, pp. 352–8) that such a theory featured in Marx's work. Rosdolsky furnished a number of well-judged arguments. To make it possible to speak of Marx as holding such a theory, he would have had to have believed in the existence of a minimum subsistence level, but he specifically argued otherwise, especially in his criticism of the Lassallian 'iron law of wages'.

> What matters is not the question of how at this or that point in time Marx and Engels judged the concrete development of wages in England and on the Continent, but only the question of whether there can be derived from the economic system of Marxism, from the laws of development of the capitalist production as established by Marx, the necessity of an increasing absolute deterioration in the situation of the working class . . . . It has to be determined whether, according to Marx, as for instance is affirmed by Sternberg, the concentration and accumulation of capital will not lead to an increase in real wages, but to a decrease in them. This assertion must be most emphatically denied, because Marx was an obstinate adversary of the concept of a minimum subsistence level.

Rosdolsky, it is true, thinks that 'even great intellects can sometimes be rather illogical'; he admits that 'even Marx (and Engels) often overrated the pressure of the factors bearing down on the situation of the proletariat'. But he declares the theory as developed by certain modern socialists (for instance, the notion developed by Sternberg and even by Strachey) to be 'incredible'. According to Rosdolsky, 'these ideas have to be relegated to the realm of scientific misunderstandings'. He declares them to be 'clearly contradictory to the spirit and the contents of [Marx's] wage theory'.

Somewhat later Mandel stated in his main work (1962, 1, p. 179), 'The theory of the absolute pauperisation of the proletariat is not to be found in the work of Marx. It has been imputed to him by political adversaries, especially by the so-called "revisionist" movement in the German Social-Democratic Party. . . .'

Hofmann was probably wrong in criticising Mandel on the grounds that this rather categorical statement neglected the early publications by Marx. Even Hofmann has to admit that there are only a 'few clues' in these early writings, particularly as regards the theory of a 'relative' growth of poverty. On the basis of his own hypothesis, which has something of a psychological character, he comes to the conclusion that the entire Marxian concept must be understood in an intellectual and psychological sense. He says that Marx, with such expressions as 'the stunting of the individual worker', 'his intellectual desolation', and 'his transformation into the self-conscious appurtenance of a part machine', took up again, from his youth, the concept of alienation, though not in connexion with real income. Hofmann further says that Marx spoke of a general increase in human misery in the sense of a 'deformation of the worker in his totality as a person', of a 'psychic, mental and spiritual impoverishment'. Hofmann recognises that the economic term, 'pauperisation' is to be understood as a 'sliding down of an increasing part of the working class . . . into the lazarus-layer of pauperism', and in so doing he refers to the early works of the present author (Hofmann, 1967, pp. 27, 42, 56ff.).

It is possible to reproach Mandel for another reason. It is not only the opponents of Marxism and the revisionists, but also many orthodox Marxists, including some Bolshevists, who did Marx the injustice of attributing such a thesis to him. It is only recently, in such publications as the 1961 compilation by Kuusinen, published in Moscow, that the Communist Party of the Soviet Union has finally contradicted the 'orthodox dogmatism', as Varga dubbed it, by recognising (pp. 234ff.) that 'social development . . . in its totality . . . follows a rising line'.

OVERCOMING THE MISINTERPRETATIONS IN 'ACADEMIC' ECONOMICS

In the meantime, even 'academic' economists have become convinced that Marx never held a 'theory of growing poverty'. They have had, therefore, to drop a rather cherished prejudice, based on received opinions.

Proof of such a change in attitude is an article published in 1960 by Sowell, who in it puts right some statements made by Samuelson and others. Sowell stresses (1960, pp. 111–12, 115–17) that in no way did Marx ever make the assumption that there was such a thing as a minimum subsistence level of wages. After all, Hofmann had already pointed out that an 'absolute deterioration' from a level that represented a physiological minimum could not be imagined.

Sowell points out that the 'sociological minimum' in Marx's works was not only a movable criterion, but also something even workers were able to see from a relative point of view. Sowell goes on to emphasise that 'pauperisation' relates to the army of unemployed, while ' "official pauperism" covers those no longer in the labor force', who vegetate 'upon public alms'.

THE MISCONCEPTION OF 'RELATIVE INCREASE IN POVERTY'

Sowell does, however, pronounce himself in favour of the theory of a 'relative increase in poverty' – the thesis according to which 'real wages in Ricardo's terminology', i.e. 'the value of wages, that is the amount of labor contained in the commodities which the workers received', tend to decrease. This would then mean that Marx advanced the thesis of a relative decrease in the share of workers in the social product.

The thesis of a relative increase in poverty has led to a number of controversies, especially between the wars – for instance, the controversy between Nathalie Moszkowska and Braunthal. Nathalie Moszkowska thought (1932, II, pp. 233ff.) that a relative increase in poverty would occur even in periods of prosperity, and that in periods when the business cycle took a turn for the worse there would be an absolute increase. Braunthal, on the other hand, believed (1932, II, pp. 245, 249) that an absolute increase (i.e. a reduction in the standard of living of the working class) could occur in a depression, but that there would be no relative increase, because the share of workers in the social product would often rise during priods of depression. Braunthal emphasised that many 'paradoxes show how unfortunate the term "relative increase in poverty" is'.

Sowell referred to some statements in *The Poverty of Philosophy* (1847), that are liable to give a wrong idea of the Marxian attitude. Engels, in a note to this work (1884), stated that such statements could be seen as a link with the theory of subsistence wages, which Marx perhaps still accepted around 1848. The remark made by Sowell is formally right.

But if we examine the statements in their context, we find that Marx says only that 'the natural wage-price is nothing other than the minimum-wage'. He does not, however, say anything about how this 'minimum' is made up. It is true that Engels assumed that Marx accepted the subsistence theory of wages in this context, but he did not offer any proof for this interpretation. Finally, he says in his note that Lassalle made the theory his own, and that he was wrong in doing so, because the theory is itself based on a 'false' assumption, as Marx emphasised in his polemics against Lassalle in *Capital*.

Lichtheim writes (1966, p. 146),

> The Marxian argument that capitalism accumulates wealth and poverty respectively at the two opposite poles of society is not contradicted by the observation (which Marx did not challenge) that, with growing productivity, real wages have a tendency to rise. Pauperisation relates to the 'reserve army', not to the working class as a whole, and it is an ascertainable fact that, where the market economy has remained 'free', it has invariably produced an immense bottom layer of paupers.

We may therefore conclude that attributing a theory of growing poverty to Marx is to fall an easy prey to an interpretation which Bernstein and the revisionists developed, even if it cannot be said that they were the only source of it. A large number of 'vulgar critics' of Marxism took up the thesis, and some 'academic' economists accepted it rather uncritically.

On the other hand, it has to be admitted that 'orthodox' Marxist analysts have been largely responsible for keeping the misunderstanding alive. Until very recently it was possible to find, especially in France, authors of Marxist persuasion, such as Mossé (1956, p. 176), who flirted with the thesis of an absolute increase in poverty. In the Soviet Union, the 'dogmatists', as Varga dubbed them, for a longtime refused to acknowledge the reality of increases in real wages under capitalism. Only recently has more impartial judgement prevailed in this area.

Even the use of the slogan 'relative increase in poverty' to denote Rodbertus's thesis of the workers sinking share in the social product was a terminological mistake, because it gave the appearance of a retreat from a starting position that had been relinquished, a starting position had had never, in fact, existed.

Marx did not deny the possibility of an increase in real wages. He even emphasised the likelihood, although the trend was not so obvious at the time he wrote as it is now. For instance, he speaks of the possibility of 'more luxuries than before [being] consumed by labourers', and says that in periods of prosperity wages are bound to rise, and that 'real wage rises . . . with the productivity of labour', although not in the correct proportion. To Marx, who expressly emphasised the growth in the 'volume of products' with the productivity of labour, and who was one of the first to point out the immense increase that capitalism had brought about in the flow of goods, it would have been impossible to suppose that the workers should not receive a certain share of this ever-increasing flow. After all, Marx also clearly pointed out the possibility of increased real wages through trade-union activity.

Blaug was right to declare (1968, p. 262) that the 'theory of growing poverty' belongs to the realm of fable: 'Marx never denied that real wages might rise under capitalism. . . . The notion that he propounded a theory of the growing poverty of the working class is just folklore Marxism. . . .'

Hofmann's interpretation, which stresses the human alienation in capitalism, has found its counterpart in the English-speaking world in the revival of the discussion of the thesis of 'alienation'. West has defended the view that the notion of the loss of human dignity and self-fulfilment that enters the scene with the division of labour and industrialisation was familiar to Adam Smith and his contemporaries. Smith, however, wished to bring human costs into the reckoning, and Marx inveighed against the process of commercialisation of man. For this reason, Marx could not simply accept a juster distribution, for he 'was not so interested in the production of material things' as

the extra 'service' of enjoyment of life, of self-realization, and of humanity. The totality of these 'joint products' was more important than the vast output of one conventional 'commodity'. In other words, Marx would claim that his society would be very much less 'affluent' in the ordinary statistically measured sense of the G.N.P. but more affluent in his (human) sense. . . .   (West, 1969, pp. 13, 18.)

Here Marx would find himself in accord with the tendencies in modern socialism, which refuse to pay homage to growth and which put the stress on human values.

The thesis developed by West has been attacked by Catephores, who thinks (1972, pp. 125, 134) that the notion of alienation hardly appears in *Capital* and that Marx did not seek for an improvement in the quality of life. Other authors, such as Roberts and Stephenson (1970, pp. 439, 441ff.), have advanced the theory that the alienation caused by the soulless market process can be overcome only by the conscious application of the human will through planning, which, it is envisaged, could make possible the solution of the problems of scarcity and unjust distribution.

27 Leading Theories of Distribution

It is today no longer a matter for controversy that Marxian theory provides one of the great basic concepts of income distribution.

Kaldor distinguished (1955–6, p. 83; 1968, p. 349) 'four main strands of thought, some of which contain important sub-groups': the 'classical' theory of Ricardo, the Marxian theory, the neoclassical or marginalist theory, and, finally, the Keynesian theory as developed by Kaldor himself. Under neoclassical thinking he deals with two groups of theories: namely, the 'marginal productivity theory' in the narrower sense, and the 'theory of the degree of monopoly', the chief representative of which is Kalecki. In the latter case one may have reasonable doubts whether the label 'neoclassical' is really applicable.

THE 'NEOCLASSICAL' MARGINAL PRODUCTIVITY THEORY

Kaldor recognises (1955–6; 1968, pp. 359–60) that the heading 'neoclassical or marginalist' is applied to 'a whole army of distinguished authors, and schools of thought, between Ricardo and Keynes (Marx aside)' and that, in view of the fact that such 'non-marginalists' as the followers of Walras, along with the protagonists of the theories of 'imperfect competition', are included in this group, the grouping is difficult to justify. He nevertheless believes that there are certain aspects that all the authors covered have in common.

The basic idea of the group, Kaldor states, is to be found in the 'principle of substitution', or, rather, the 'principle of limited substitutability', which Ricardo applied only in the case of the use of labour on the land:

> in neo-classical theory this doctrine was formalised and generalised, and assumed to hold true of any factor, in relation to each other . . . any factor variable in supply will obtain a remuneration which, under competitive conditions, must correspond to its marginal product. Thus if the total supply of *all* factors (and not only land) is being taken as given, independently of price, and all are assumed to be limited substitutes to one another, the share-out of the whole produce can be

regarded as being determined by the marginal rates of substitution between them.

The whole theory depends, first of all, on the assumption that various factors can be varied and combined as one likes. Robertson (1959, II, p. 188) found a witty formulation: 'that in each industry the demand for the factors of production is joint not in the strictest, but in the looser sense . . . analogous not to the demand for cups and saucers . . . but to the demand for whisky and soda-water'.

The continuous possibility of exchange or substitutability of the factors of production is interrupted if (a) an absolute scarcity in one of the factors of production occurs, or (b) a minimum wage must be paid for a factor of production and its remuneration cannot sink below this.

Ricardo made the former assumption where land was concerned, and the latter for the minimum subsistence level of labour. As regards land, the nineteenth century brought a relatively great increase in overseas territories. If land scarcity sets in locally, especially in congested urban areas, it can be overcome to a certain extent by more intensive use (skyscrapers) and by the development of surfaces above and below ground (for instance, through elevated roads and underground railways). A degree of absolute scarcity will remain, which should not be confounded with a particular sort of 'ground rent', but should be analysed as a peculiar case of the monopolistic use of scarce resources.

The problem of a minimum remuneration for a factor is of a more complex character. Evidently, the Clark–Pigou theorem of the continuous and limitless variability of factor combinations cannot apply when the price of one factor remains rigid. If this factor is labour, part of the labour force must, by definition, be unemployed, to the extent that the minimum price of labour remains above its minimum marginal productivity in the next-best factor combination. Here we find even in the reasoning of marginal-productivity analysis a basic point in favour of Marx's 'reserve army'! But the approximation goes further.

Indeed, the Marxian theory of wages starts from the assumption that the 'accustomed' wage-level developed through history is more or less 'frozen' at any time. Wages are, therefore, 'sticky', i.e. they do not yield in a downward direction. For this reason the minimum wage paid for the factor labour is much above Ricardo and Malthus's minimum subsistence level. Unemployment must occur much earlier than in their systems.

Kaldor says that Marshall, as the chief representative of the 'neoclassical' theory, avoided the formulation of a distribution theory. At best, he developed a very short-term analysis 'which regards profits as the "quasi-rents" earned on the use of the capital goods of various kinds, the supply of which can be treated as given for the time being, as a heritage of the past' (Kaldor, 1955–6; 1968, p. 362). Kaldor particularly points to Marshall's assertion (1930, p. 617) that 'a more or less definite rate of profits on the turnover is . . . regarded as a "fair" or normal rate'.

Looking more closely, one finds surprising correspondences between the views of Marshall and those of Marx – not only formally, for even Marx connects his profit rate with turnover, but also in content, because Marshall's theory approximates to the labour theory of value in the short term. This can be seen from Kaldor's (1955–6; 1968, p. 362) presentation:

> The doctrine of the 'quasi-rent' assimilates capital as a factor of production to Ricardian land. . . . Here the problem of the measurement of capital as a factor of production does not arise. . . . Prices are equal to, or determined by, marginal prime costs; profits are determined by the difference between marginal and average prime costs; prime costs, for the system as a whole, are labour costs (since raw-material costs, for the closed economy at any rate, disappear if all branches of industry are taken together). . . .

This tradition of the 'Cambridge School', as continued by Keynes and Joan Robinson, is distinguished by the fact that in the short run only one factor of production is considered. This means, more or less, that the labour theory of value is practically being accepted, and becomes acceptable even to 'marginalist' reasoning. Paradoxically, the attitude of industrialists (who in the short run consider labour cost as the decisive factor), coupled with a mentality characterised by the full-cost principle, also approaches a labour theory of value.

It is true that Marshall thought, as far as the distribution theory itself is concerned, that 'distributive shares in the short period are determined by long-period forces'. Kaldor holds very strong views with regard to this opinion, concerning which he says (ibid., p. 363),

> this short period approach . . . does not really get us anywhere: for the extent to which diminishing returns operate for labour in conjunction with the capital equipment available to-day is itself a function of the price-relationships which have ruled in the past because these have determined the quantities of each of the kinds of equipment available. The theory does not therefore really amount to more than saying that the prices of to-day are derived from the prices of yesterday. . . .

An attempt by Wicksell to introduce a 'time dimension' and to treat capital as a two-dimensional quantity, as 'the product of time and labour', came to grief, according to Kaldor, (ibid.)

> owing to the impossibility of measuring that period in terms of an 'average' of some kind . . . since owing to compound interest, the weights to be used in the calculation of the average will themselves be dependent on the rate of interest . . . and owing to the impossibility of

combining the investment periods of different 'original' factors in a single measure.

Wicksell realised this towards the end of his life.

Kaldor (ibid., p. 364), like Joan Robinson (1953–4, p. 81), passes a very hard judgement on marginal productivity theory:

> Its inadequacy becomes evident as soon as it is realised that the 'marginal rate of substitution' between Capital and Labour . . . can only be determined once the rate of profit and the rate of wages are already known . . . the theory focuses attention on a relatively unimportant feature of a growing economy. For accumulation does not take the form of 'deepening' the structure of capital (at a given state of knowledge) but rather in keeping pace with technical progress and the growth in the labour force. It is difficult to swallow a theory which says, in effect, that wages and profits are what they are for otherwise there would be too much deepening or too little deepening (the capital/output ratio would be either too large or too small) to be consistent with simultaneous equilibrium in the savings-investment market and in the labour market.

In this way one of the most important competitors to the Marxian system, namely the marginal productivity theory in its continuation, is eliminated by adversaries, the Keynesians, who are antagonistic to this predecessor though to some extent they developed from the same foundations.

THE KEYNES–KALDOR ANALYSIS OF DISTRIBUTION

Kaldor seems to have made the distribution theory that results from Keynesian analysis his own. He expresses two important reservations. At the outset he admits (1955–6; 1968, p. 368) that 'Keynes . . . was never interested in the problem of distribution as such'. He goes on to say (ibid., p. 375) that the whole of Keynesian and post-Keynesian analysis has tried to avoid the problem of measuring capital properly speaking.

Kaldor himself, in another article (1957), tried to solve the latter problem in a most drastic manner, for he wished (p. 599) to 'measure the stock of real capital . . . in terms of the total weight of steel embodied in the capital equipment'. As an alternative to such a simplification he could see only measurement in terms of horsepower, which seemed to him even more arbitrary.

Kaldor refers to the simile of the 'inexhaustible widow's cruse', which Keynes mentions in his *Treatise on Money* (1930, 1, p. 139). The more one drinks from it, the more it contains. In the same way, the pockets of entrepreneurs, in a macroeconomic view, are filled with greater profits, the more they spend on investment or on consumption.

In this context the period analysis developed by Robertson is particularly useful. The money that entrepreneurs spend on their own consumption and on net investment in period one appears as profits in period two. In the framework of such a period analysis a financing problem arises, which does not occur in the Keynesian world of timeless simultaneity. 'This model . . . in a sense is the precise opposite of the Ricardian (or Marxian) one – here wages (not profits) are a residue, profits being governed by the propensity to invest and the capitalists' propensity to consume, which represent a kind of "prior charge" on the national output'. (Kaldor, 1955–6; 1968, p. 372).

The conclusion suggests itself that the dynamic initiative is held by capitalists only because of their key position. The share accruing to them must be the larger, the greater the growth process launched by them. This, however, might contradict the 'mystery of constant shares', as Joan Robinson has dubbed it. Such a conclusion would bring the Keynes–Kaldor theory into precarious proximity with the theory of Rodbertus, which is wrongly attributed to Marx, and which offers an explanation of the sinking share of the working class in the social product. This was the theory that in the last resort gave rise to the thesis of a relative increase in poverty.

Kaldor, indeed, in his later work, reached such a conclusion for a whole epoch of capitalism (1957, p. 619):

> In the early stage of capitalist development the growth in productivity was not attended by a rise in the standard of living of the working classes. The stationary trend in real wages in Britain despite considerable improvements in production per head during the first half of the nineteenth century was the feature of capitalist evolution which so strongly impressed Marx and forms one of the main themes of Volume I of *Das Kapital*. The same has been true of other capitalist countries: in the case of Japan, for instance, real wages increased very little between 1878 and 1917, despite a one-and-a-half-fold increase in real income per head over the period. This suggests that in the first stage of capitalist evolution, productivity, though rising, is not large enough to allow for a surplus over the subsistence wage which permits the rate of investment to attain the level indicated. . . .

At the same time, paradoxically, Kaldor, by recognising that during this period the 'organic composition' of capital increases, confirms the existence, at this early stage of capitalism, of the precondition for the Marxian thesis of the tendency of the rate of profit to fall: 'In this first stage of capitalism therefore the capital/output ratio . . . will show a steady increase, in accordance with both the Marxian and the neo-classical models.'

Kaldor agrees with the statistical calculations made by Gillman, though it is true that they are applicable only to the period before the turn of the century in the United States, when Kaldorian 'early capitalism' was long past there. Kaldor thinks he can invoke the Marxian 'counter-tendency' of an increasing rate of surplus value when he says (ibid., pp. 619–20), 'Since, however, the share of profit in income will also increase continuously, the rise in the capital/output ratio will not necessarily imply a falling rate of profit on capital. . . .'

Up to this point there exists a curious coincidence between Marxian theories and Kaldor's world, for Marx himself did not exclude the aforementioned counter-tendency to the fall in the rate of profit. If we look closely at the matter, however, it emerges that the apparent similarity to Marx, in so far as Kaldor assumes the share of wages to have fallen during the early nineteenth century, is again rather a pattern taken from Rodbertus.

Kaldor then takes the decisive step (ibid., p. 620):

> This first stage of capitalism, however, must sooner or later be brought to an end when the capital stock attains the level of 'desired capital'. . . . Profits are no longer determined in the Marxian manner, as the surplus of production over subsistence wages; on the contrary, the share of wages becomes a residual, equalling the difference between production and the share of profits as determined in a 'Keynesian' manner, by the propensities to invest and to save. From then onward . . . real wages will rise automatically at the same rate as the productivity of labour, so that distributive shares remain constant through time.

Explicitly denying the thesis of modern Marxian authors – here he thinks of Sweezy and Baran – that increasing concentration leads to a weakening of competition, which then leads to an increase in the share of profits in the social product, which in turn leads to 'under-consumption', he appeals (ibid.) to the facts:

> At any rate, this has not happened. Though the growing concentration of production in the hands of giant firms proceeded in much the same way as Marx predicted, this was not attended by a corresponding growth in the share of profits . . . empirical investigations . . . do not lend any support to the hypothesis that differences in profit margins are to be explained by differences in the degree of concentration of production. Typically monopolistic industries, where output is largely controlled by a few firms, have in many cases lower profit margins than industries where the degree of concentration is small.

In this way, Kaldor has anticipated the later thesis of Galbraith. Yet he deals with it rather cursorily. He does not examine the relation between capital values, over-capacity and profit margins, which form the scheme examined by Steindl, and he simply identifies the variations in the share of profits in the social product with variations in the profit margins.

THE RICARDIAN THEORY OF DISTRIBUTION

Kaldor (1955–6; 1968, pp. 352–4) takes his departure from the Ricardian theory of distribution, and justifies this not only in historical terms, but also methodologically. He sees Ricardo's theory as based on two different principles, which have to be clearly distinguished: the principle of 'surplus' or 'surplus value', and the 'marginal' principle. The latter is of primary importance, for the share of the rent in the social product is determined by it. When landowners receive their share, there remains a residual, and for the distribution of this residual between wages and profits the principle of 'surplus value' has to be introduced.

How is the share of wages determined? Ricardo starts from the hypothesis that real wages coincide with the minimum required for subsistence. This is not quite right, for Kaldor shows that Ricardo presupposes constant real wages (in 'corn'), but speaks at the same time of 'an infinitely elastic supply curve of labour at a given supply price. The demand for labour is determined . . . by the accumulation of capital . . .'. Accumulation forms a wage-fund, which, according to Kaldor can be increased only by additional accumulation. An increase in the share of wages does not occur in Kaldor's interpretation of Ricardo. ' . . . profits are thus a residue, arising from the difference between the marginal product of labour and the rate of wages'.

We must ask ourselves whether Kaldor really interprets Ricardo in the correct way. The latter, in a famous letter to Malthus, dated 9 October 1820, wrote that what he was interested in was not the problem of 'wealth', in which Malthus had a lively interest. For Ricardo political economy was the science which should investigate 'the laws which determine the division of the produce of industry among the classes who concur in its formation'.

In view of this, it is astonishing that Ricardo was content to establish the 'residual' after deducting rent and that he refrained from the analysis of the distribution of the residual between profits and wages. Kaldor however, thinks that Ricardo's theory can be justified on the grounds that he thought only of continuous growth over a longer period, and that he supposed that the increase in population would adapt to the constant rate of social progress.

According to Kaldor's interpretation of Ricardo, the share of wages cannot be increased, or accumulation and the rate of growth will suffer. Here we must raise a question, for according to Kaldor's own argument an increase in the share of wages would produce a decrease in the number of employed workers. In this way Ricardo would have thrown into the debate a Keynesian employment problem! With a falling rate of profit the system could escape the 'state of gloom' only through technical progress. But Kaldor refers to Malthus and Sraffa to support his belief that a work of Ricardo's that would have completed the picture has been lost.

We must, therefore, be satisfied with the dismal picture as drawn in the *Principles of Political Economy* (1817; ed. by Sraffa, p. 422, London, 1951): 'Profits are so low as not to afford [the capitalists] more than an adequate compensation for their trouble and the risk which they must necessarily encounter in employing their capital productively'.

28 The Position of the Marxian Distribution Analysis

THE MARXIAN ANALYSIS OF DISTRIBUTION ACCORDING TO KALDOR

Kaldor's presentation of the Marxian theory of distribution suffers from some serious defects. First, he reproaches Marx for not observing the 'law of decreasing returns' – a reproach also made by Samuelson. Both say that Marx did not distinguish between rent and profit in the proper sense, and that he regarded real wages as constant. For him, therefore, the share of profits in the social product would be a residual, for it is the 'surplus of the product per unit of labour over the supply price (or cost) of labour' (Kaldor, 1955–6; 1968, p. 356).

In spite of the apparently plausible approximation to the surplus-value concept, this criticism is not justified. First, the Ricardian differential rent was perfectly familiar to Marx; after all, he explicitly contrasted it with 'absolute' monopoly rent and sharply distinguished the latter from profits in the proper sense. Secondly, Marx explicitly considered the possibility of rising real wages and of a rising minimum wage level; the latter is quite unknown to Kaldor. Thirdly, Marx works in many passages with the notion of 'an increased scale of production', which means that he is effectively taking into consideration increasing returns and variable returns. Marx did not explicitly state that he was making the hypothesis of declining returns, in spite of the fact that his theory of 'the tendency of the rate of profit to fall' comes quite near to a theory of a decreasing marginal return on capital.

Kaldor in his argument sets out also from other false points of departure. For instance, he accepts quite uncritically the usual interpretation of the 'theory of growing poverty' and thinks that according to Marx the share of wages in the social product must fall. Here there is at least a partial confusion with Rodbertus.

From these false premises Kaldor arrives at his conclusions. Nevertheless, he correctly analyses the relationship between the 'industrial reserve army' and distribution in the Marxian system. The 'unemployed fringe of the population', which is constantly replenished by pre-capitalist elements and 'redundant' workers, exercises pressure on wages; nevertheless, at the height of the boom there can be a scarcity of labour. Technical progress, however, soon refills the reserve army, partly by setting labour free, partly by eliminating formerly independent workers, who, in view of the cost advantages of larger enterprises, go bankrupt.

Capitalists are subject to the continual drive to accumulate, which leads chiefly through self-finance to a continual increase in the dimensions of enterprises, to concentration, and finally to oligopoly and monopoly.

Kaldor reaches the conclusion that in principle the share of wages in the social product must sink in the Marxian system. He admits, however, that Marx did calculate the possibility that the trade-union organisation of the working class could act as a counterpoise. Kaldor's conclusion on the share of wages results from the assumption that the rate of surplus value must increase continually through technical progress. On the thesis of the countervailing power of trade unions he writes (ibid., p. 359), 'This hypothesis, however, will only yield a constant share of wages on the extremely far-fetched assumption that the rate of increase in the bargaining strength of labour, due to the growth of collective organisation, precisely keeps pace with the rate of increase in output per head.'

CRITICISM OF KALDOR'S INTERPRETATION

It is not easy to understand why this assumption must be considered far-fetched. If, through monopsony tendencies or the overbearing negotiating power of entrepreneurs, wages in the labour market are prevented from rising while on the other side workers as consumers fall easy prey to monopolistic tendencies in the markets for goods and services, a decreasing share of wages and salaries in the social product would appear to be more plausible.

Modern critics emphasise that the Kaldor's formula itself suffers from certain defects. Bombach, for instance, has stressed (1959) that Kaldor does not distinguish the undistributed profits of large-scale enterprises from the profits of small businessmen; the latters' profits are mainly consumed by themselves. On the other hand, one could raise the objection that the salaries of directors employed in large firms appear under 'wages and salaries'. It must be admitted, however, that the latter distortion does not counterbalance the former.

Ferguson has pointed out (1964, p. 341) that the Kaldor model is indeterminate in two respects. He stresses that in Kaldor's theory investment is a completely exogenous variable, the behaviour of which is not determined by the model. He also argues that the model determines only the share of profits which is compatible with full employment, in so far as the exogenous level of investment and the different propensities to save are given. This, he claims, is very different from a genuine theory of distribution.

Sen has made the criticism (1963, pp. 53ff.) that in the neo-Keynesian model a constant propensity to save is linked to the propensity to invest without reference to price movements, while, in the case where the expectations of entrepreneurs are not fulfilled, no kind of feedback mechanism is available.

In the view of Rothschild (1965, pp. 650ff.), the foremost objection to Kaldor is that he does not consider the 'influence and the effects of group action [i.e. Marx's class struggle] on the distribution problem'.

Rothschild himself attempted (ibid., pp. 656–61) to reconcile Kaldor's formula with Marx's. 'The "sociological" fact we want to introduce into the Kaldor system is the reluctance of workers and trade unions to accept a deterioration of their acquired incomes in the face of rising investment.' The resistance of trade unions

> will stop investment at a certain limit. . . . The higher wages will either destroy the entrepreneurs' desire to go on with their investment plans or, more likely under our full employment assumptions, the ensuing wage–price spiral will prevent the growing investment expenditure from leading to a further increase in real investment and investment shares.

This means that trade unions as an institutional factor (in a sense, 'the institutionalised class-struggle') have a rôle to play. 'Kaldor's distributional mechanism finds, therefore, also a fairly narrow downward limit.' In this sense, Marx would appear in the end to be right. Investment and therefore profits again become 'residuals' in so far as they are the result of organised wage pressure.

In a wider sense and in the longer run sociological and economic influences will have an impact upon the propensities to save and consume, according to Rothschild:

> In particular, we believe that the longer-run development of saving and consumption standards among entrepreneurs will not be independent of the conditions they meet in the labour market. If wages can always be set at a low level, this will probably encourage waste and carefree consumption among capitalists. This is not untypical of many underdeveloped countries. Constant wage pressure, on the other hand, will make entrepreneurs more concerned about their position in the business world and will encourage higher saving appropriations out of income.

Even in this case, one could advance the thesis that such an effort to protect one's business position would be synonymous with an intensification of competition and of oligopolistic struggles. These would then lead to a decline in the share of profits in national income, and the claims of workers for higher wages would finally be reinforced by tendencies toward the lowering of prices, which might even lead to autonomous increases in real wages and, therefore, to an increase in the share of wages in national income.

The paradox, outlined by Rothschild, that wage claims would tend to increase the share of investment in surplus value, which practically would amount to a renunciation of consumption by capitalists, reminds us first of all of the trade-union 'torture theory', developed by Marschak and Tarnow in the 1920s. This envisaged trade unions as prodding firms into rationalisation by means of wage claims, which would also lead to the closing down of inefficient firms. Secondly, we are reminded of the 'Riviera theorem', originated by Dobb. This has been examined in chapter 25 above. Rothschild also sees the other side of the coin: 'If wage demands are continuously very high, a counter-effect may set in: saving and investment may be discouraged in some cases in face of such high odds' (ibid., p. 661). The decisive point for Rothschild is that 'in the short run investment activities will influence distribution within narrow limits, while . . . in the longer run saving propensities will be influenced by wage policy and by social imitation' (ibid., p. 667).

These considerations lead us right into the problem of the business cycle. Rothschild, in arguing this way, only wants to demonstrate (ibid., p. 665) that

> in the longer run the saving propensity of profit-earners is a function of wages. . . . The income distribution is still influenced by the investment share; but wage policy (through its long-run effect on saving propensities) has also a say in the final result. . . . Whatever the investment share may be, there will be a certain wage policy which will yield a minimum long-run equilibrium value. . . . That is to say, aiming at high wages and wage shares trade unions should raise wages beyond the minimum as long as the wage increases stimulate greater saving attitudes among the entrepreneurs. . . . When wages are raised beyond the maximum . . . point, the reduced saving of the entrepreneurs will mean that . . . prices begin to rise faster than wages so that their real level and their share in income declines.

It would not be inadmissible to suppose that in the latter case entrepreneurs would envisage an investment strike. In that case, there would no longer be a single employment equilibrium corresponding to a given volume of investment. One could say that in the short run Kaldor was right, but that in the longer run that Marx was, especially in the versions of Rothschild and Dobb.

THE THEORY OF THE DECREASING SHARE OF WAGES IN THE SOCIAL PRODUCT

There are quite a number of authors who advance the proposition that Marx considered that the share of wages in the social product must decrease. In the older Marxist literature, all authors holding the thesis of a 'relative increase in poverty' may be considered as holding this view. Among present-day authors there are Marxists, such as Pesenti (1959), who are of the view that numerous passages show that Marx implicitly postulated an increasing rate of exploitation. Pesenti quotes just one passage: that where Marx says, 'The tendency of the rate of profit to fall is bound up with a tendency for the rate of surplus-value to rise, hence with a tendency for the rate of labour exploitation to rise' (*Capital*, III, ch. 14, p. 240).

Here we may harbour some doubts. It is true that many authors thought that Marx hypothesised that a long-run tendency for the rate of profit to fall would prevail, but these authors can hardly suppose that this tendency would be completely balanced by an increased rate of surplus value. It is true that Marx unequivocally expressed the opinion (ibid., ch. 15, p. 247) that 'the degree of exploitation [and thus the rate of surplus value], has certain insurmountable limits. It may, for this reason, well check the fall in the rate of profit, but cannot prevent it altogether.' One must admit that Marx in some degree supposed that there might be shifts, to the disadvantage of the workers, in the shares of the social product. In another passage, however (ibid., ch. 14, p. 239), he emphasises that there exist 'counter-effects, which hamper, retard, and partly paralyse' such falls, and it is clear that a temporarily increasing rate of surplus value, which would correspond to an increase in the share of profits in the net social product, is entirely compatible with a general fall in the rate of profit.

Meek, a disciple of Dobb, supports the theory that Marx hypothesised an 'increasing rate of exploitation', i.e. a growing share of profits in the social product, as normal. Meek (1960) quotes quite a number of passages in which Marx speaks of an 'increasing degree of exploitation' (*Capital*, III, ch. 13, p. 254 (Meek quotes pp. 224–36); ch. 14, pp. 26off.; ch. 15, pp. 269, 276). Blaug advances the same theory (1968, p. 281): 'Marx did believe, however, that labor's share would fall'. In the same context Marx speaks of an 'increasing rate of surplus-value' (ibid., I, ch. 22, p. 635).

The thesis of shifts, to the detriment of workers, in shares in the net social product appears to be well founded. We cannot be astonished if, following from this, similar conclusions are drawn with regard to a theory of revolution. This has in fact happened in a number of instances, and one thoroughly conservative author, the American economist Hildreth has written (1966, p. 63),

However, there are certain limits to the possible distribution. At some point, if too high a proportion of the income is received by too small a proportion of the people, that society is not stable and revolution is likely to occur. . . . (It is recognized that income distribution is not the sole cause of revolutions.) This limit changes over time and cultures. . . .

Unfortunately, such a simplified 'theory of revolution out of distribution' exists nowhere in Marx's work. Even the thesis of the relative decrease in workers' share in the national income cannot be ascribed to Marx with certainty. Against such an attribution we may quote the judgement of Schumpeter (1947, p. 35): 'Though some passages in Marx will in fact bear interpretation in this sense, this clearly violates the meaning of most. . . .' In his later work Schumpeter goes so far as to advance a theory diametrically opposed to the thesis so far developed. According to this later theory, Marx saw 'a tendency of longer span, for the degree of exploitation to fall through reduction in daily hours brought about by trade-union action, legislation, and so on' (Schumpeter, 1959, p. 650).

The question of whether or not the relative share of workers declines in the long run cannot be discussed in this context, and the empirical facts are not of real importance for the basic problem, of whether Marx supported such a hypothesis. Schumpeter was actually of the opinion (1947, p. 35) that, judging from statistics, 'the relative share of wages and salaries in total income varies but little from year to year and is remarkably constant over time – it certainly does not reveal any tendency to fall'.

In arguing in this way Schumpeter accepts the theory of certain authors of a Marxist bias, such as Kalecki, and espouses Joan Robinson's thesis of the 'mystery of the fixed shares'. Much can be said in favour of this thesis, for large parts of the argument in *Capital* are built upon the hypothesis of unvarying shares in the national income, and the expression 'with an equal degree of exploitation' turns up again and again.

According to John Maurice Clark (1931, pp. 167ff; 1946, p. 64), and contrary to Kaldor's hypothesis, the Marxian distribution theory 'is an implacable carrying out of Ricardo's theory of value and distribution'. Does this mean that it stands in fundamental opposition to the Keynes–Kaldor theory? Steindl believes that this is possible in the matter of macroeconomic profits. Steindl, whose attitude towards Marx is in general positive, reproaches Marx with bitter words in connexion with the Keynesian distribution theory. According to him (1952, p. 237), Marx

has run counter to the best established truth of Keynesian economics: namely, that a given amount of profits can only materialise (assuming capitalists alone to be net savers) if there is a corresponding amount of net investment and capitalists' consumption. . . . these 'other factors' are incomes, which rise or fall so as to provide just enough saving to finance the investment.

Steindl here does Marx an injustice, as we shall see later. He starts from the premise that, according to Marx's 'harbinger theory',

> the upward pressure of wages in the boom reduces the rate of profit and therefore discourages accumulation; and . . . the lowering of wages in the depression raises the profit rate and therefore gives a stimulus to accumulation. This is, of course, straightforward 'classical economics', a faulty reasoning from which Marx did not manage to detach himself completely, and which most other economists got rid of only in the comparatively recent past.

Marx said no such thing. In his 'harbinger theory' he most explicitly speaks not of the upswing as a whole, but of the *end* of the upswing, of the 'upper turning point', when profits are already on the decline and wage rates are still increasing. Furthermore, Marx in this context does not speak of the share of wages in the social product, but only of their rate of increase as compared with the former level of hourly or effective wages. If one takes into account the premium paid to workers recruited from other firms, such a phenomenon during periods of boom is undeniable.

Steindl's interpretation is, therefore, erroneous. Marx is far from arguing against what Steindl considers to be the 'best established truth of Keynesian economics'. After all, Marx established this truth himself! First of all, he anticipated (*Capital*, II, ch. 17, p. 338) the 'inexhaustible widow's cruse', i.e. the idea that capitalists create their own profits by investing and consuming:

> The capitalist class remains consequently the sole point of departure of the circulation of money. . . . The capitalist class as a whole cannot draw out of circulation what was not previously thrown into it. . . . Indeed, paradoxical as it may appear at first sight, it is the capitalist class itself that throws the money into circulation which serves for the realisation of the surplus-value incorporated in the commodities. But, *nota bene*, it does not throw it into circulation as advanced money, hence not as capital. It spends it as a means of purchase for its individual consumption.

This is, after all, exactly the Keynesian concept! If investment remains the same, capitalists can increase their profits only if their consumption is increased. In this case, investment really does remain the same, being only investment for replacement purposes, for these passages are to be found in the chapter on 'simple reproduction', which in Marxian terminology denotes the condition in which there is no net investment and, therefore, no clearly defined growth process.

In his *Theories of Surplus Value* Marx examines the reverse case, the one, according to Keynes (1930, I, p. 139), when 'entrepreneurs are making losses, and seek to recoup these losses by curtailing their normal expenditure on consumption, i.e. by saving more, the cruse becomes a Danaid jar which can never be filled up; for the effect of this reduced expenditure is to inflict on the producers of consumption-goods a loss of an equal amount.'

In his discussion of the Malthusian theories (*Theories*, III, ch. 19, p. 49) Marx formulated the same idea with perhaps even greater clarity than Keynes, and this seventy-five years earlier, anticipating, moreover, the notion of 'effective demand'.

> In connection with this increased cost of luxuries, it occurs just in time to Malthus that accumulation and not expenditure is the immediate object of capitalist production. . . . the capitalists of class A . . . are compelled to moderate their demand for luxuries. But if they do so, and increase their accumulation, then effective demand falls, the market for the necessaries they produce shrinks, and this market cannot expand to its full extent on the basis of the demand on the part of the workers and the producers of constant capital. This leads to a fall in the price of necessaries, but it is only through a rise of these prices, through the nominal surcharge of them – and in proportion to this surcharge – that the capitalists of class A are able to extract surplus product from the workers. If the price were to fall from 120 to 110, then their surplus product (and their surplus-value) would fall from $2/12$ to $1/11$, and consequently the market, the demand for the commodities offered by the producers of luxuries, would decline as well, and by a still greater proportion.

We see that Marx and Keynes correspond to each other in every respect, as Kaldor has fully recognised. Does this mean that Marx anticipated the Keynesian distribution theory?

Steindl is right in stating (1952, p. 237) that there is an essential difference between the two, though it is true that Marx's 'basic idea shows a remarkable family resemblance to the type of thought which Keynesians apply to the short run: capital accumulation (investment) is here the primary motive force. Other factors are adjusted so as to make the given rate of capital accumulation possible.' This means that the other factors are the incomes of the other classes, incomes which according to the Keynesian theory represent a residual. But Marx has a long-run analysis, in which 'the adjustment concerns the distribution of income between workers and capitalists . . . ; this . . . in the long run is adjusted in such a way as to provide just the necessary saving to finance the given trend of accumulation' (ibid., p. 238), i.e. in the case of capitalists.

The question arises, upon what does Marx base his analysis of long-run forces in the economy?

According to Steindl, he bases it principally on the industrial reserve army and partly on competition between workers, 'which does all the tricks'. This is in line with the argument of Samuelson, according to whom conditions of perfect competition are supposed to prevail.

Marchal and Lecaillon in their analysis of the Marxian distribution theory (1958) object (III, p. 227) that Marx 'never used the general hypothesis of perfect competition, which would have extended to the labour market'. What is it then that distinguishes the Marxian analysis from others? According to Marchal and Lecaillon (ibid., p. 228), the distinction is to be seen in the fact that 'Marx never had the intention of analysing in the long or even the very long run an economic system which remained perfectly competitive from beginning to end.' The degree of competition will be reduced through concentration, which increases the degree of monopoly. In this way the Marxian analysis, as is already the case with the theory of surplus value, approaches that of Kalecki. This is not in itself surprising, because Kalecki took his starting point from Marx. What, however, is it that distinguishes the Marxian theory from that of Kalecki?

One of the distinguishing factors is to be found in dynamics. Wage increases threaten the rate of surplus value at the top of the boom. This spurs on mechanisation and rationalisation in the downswing and in times of depression. The rising reserve army of the unemployed stops the growth in the wage rate. In this way the degree of monopoly is lowered in the downswing. Now, there is a connexion pointed out by Kalecki (1956, pp. 30ff.) and stressed by Preiser (1964, pp. 36ff.), between the theory of distribution and the theory of growth. This connexion is reinforced by the theory of concentration.

According to Kalecki the increase in the degree of monopoly serves as a brake to the growth process. This statement is true at least with regard to the long-run equilibrium. In so far as the degree of monopoly is strengthened by an increase in concentration, the increasing concentration will also harm the rate of growth. This thesis is supported by Marxist authors and others influenced by Marx (for instance, Lederer and Steindl).

The 'industrial reserve army' serves as an instrument for ensuring that the limit of a permanent investment-strike is never reached. An 'external proletariat' in the sense of Toynbee, which we find in modern Europe in the shape of millions of foreign workers, now fulfils the function of the reserve army and serves as a safety valve.

It was Marx's opinion that 'cheating' among themselves by capitalists could not change the overall total of surplus value. This is true only under the hypothesis of the existence of competition. As soon as monopoly profits are attained along with 'normal profits' at their normal level, the volume of surplus value is bound to grow.

The quota of surplus value for the whole economy depends not only on the distribution of power between workers and employers, but also on the power relationship between workers themselves, a condition that finds its expression in the 'degree of monopoly' at different stages, in industries or even individual firms. It should not be forgotten that Marx anticipated in his concentration thesis the notion of the 'degree of monopoly' and the different forms of monopoly, oligopoly and monopsony, even though he generally based his own analysis on 'competition', albeit one with the possibility of price parameters.

29 The 'Ideal System of Distribution' in the Conception of Marx

Any consideration of the Marxian analysis of distribution has to start from the hypothesis that the entire Marxian system of value and surplus value is concerned in the last resort with the problem of distribution as posed by Ricardo. The character of the Marxian theory of surplus value as distribution analysis becomes quite evident when we consider that the Marxian system relies heavily on Ricardo. Kaldor emphasises this in a somewhat exaggerated manner when he writes (1955–6; 1968, p. 351), 'but then the Marxian theory is really only a simplified version of Ricardo, clothed in a different garb'.

In his posthumously published critique of the German Social Democratic Party's Gotha Programme, Marx got down to the notion of the distribution problem. In this critique he juxtaposes 'what ought to be' with the reality of society. In the process, it becomes clear that the labour theory of value is to be considered as a theory of the desirable 'just' distribution, against which Marx sets the reality of the present-day distribution. Marx demonstrates that a 'just' distribution in the higher sense will be possible only in the socialist state of the future, and that the present-day distribution 'on the basis of the present-day mode of production' cannot be different from what it actually is, and is even 'just' in a narrower, historically-bound sense. Accordingly, the communist society can only be considered 'not as it has developed on its own foundations, but, on the contrary, just as it emerges from capitalist society'. In such a society, where

> the instruments of labour are common property and the total labour is co-operatively regulated . . . the individual labour time of the individual producer is the part of the social working-day contributed by him, his share in it. He receives a certificate from society that he has furnished such and such an amount of labour (after deducting his labour for the common funds), and with this certificate he draws from the social stock of means of consumption as much as costs the same amount of labour.

The worker has, of course, to render a certain part of his labour to the community; from the 'co-operative proceeds of labour' which 'comprise the total social product' (i.e. gross social product) there must be deducted

First: cover for replacement of the means of production used up.
Secondly: an additional portion for the expansion of production.
[This is Preobrazhensky's 'socialist accumulation'.]
Thirdly: reserve or insurance funds to provide against accidents, dislocations caused by natural calamities, etc.

Up to this point Marx deals with 'deductions' which, in the interests of the maintenance or expansion of the apparatus of the means of production, have to be handled in the same way as in the capitalist system of distribution, even if in the capitalist system deductions are generally effected through the income which accrues to the capitalists.

What remains is the use of social labour for purposes of consumption. Here Marx thinks that a transfer can take place from individual consumption by capitalists and their administrative functionaries (in the widest sense) to collective consumption, for he emphasises that, before the other part of the total product, intended to serve as means of consumption . . . is divided among the individuals, there has to be deducted from it

First: the general costs of administration not belonging to production. This part will, from the outset, be very considerably restricted in comparison with present-day society and it diminishes in proportion as the new society develops.

Here the question arises of the size and development of administrative costs in a socialist state. In this the tendency towards bureaucracy within the framework of a planning system has to be set against the present over-valuation of management, as seen, for example, in expense-account living.

Secondly: [there must be deducted] that which is intended for the common satisfaction of needs, such as schools, health services, etc. From the outset this part grows considerably in comparison with present-day society and it grows in proportion as the new society develops.

Here Marx anticipates Galbraith's thesis of the necessity for enlarging collective consumption.

Thirdly: [there must be deducted] funds for those unable to work, etc., in short, for what is included under so-called poor relief today. Only now do we come to the 'distribution' which the programme, under Lassallean influence, has in view in its narrow fashion; i.e. to that part of the means of consumption which is divided among the individual producers.

The critique from which this is extracted contains most of the little that Marx has to say with regard to the future socialist society. It also contains a clear analysis of the 'functional' elements of distribution in the Marxian sense.

Two further statements with regard to the Marxian analysis may be of interest. First, Marx supposed that in the socialist system of distribution we should return to what in his opinion had existed in the epoch of 'simple reproduction'; i.e. to an exchange on the basis of labour values. Secondly, Marx declares himself in opposition to Ricardo's opinion that the problem of distribution is the proper theme of economics. Marx thought it

a mistake to make a fuss about so-called distribution and put the principal stress on it. Any distribution whatever of the means of consumption is only a consequence of the distribution of the conditions of production themselves. The capitalist mode of production, for example, rests on the fact that the material conditions of production are in the hands of non-workers in the form of property in capital and land.

The decisive factor in distribution according to Marx is the 'monopoly of the capitalist class' over the means of production. 'In present-day society the instruments of production are the monopoly of the landowners; the monopoly of property in land is even the basis of the monopoly of capital and the capitalists. . . .'

This statement seems to confirm the relationship with the theory of 'class monopoly' advanced by Preiser, while the indication that 'the monopoly of property in land is . . . the basis of the monopoly of capital' reminds us of the fact that Oppenheimer is a direct follower of Marx. Furthermore, the primacy accorded to production has the consequence that the link with the Ricardian school is weakened, so that the Marxian theory of value as a theory of distribution appears in a new light. The Keynesian theory also starts primarily from production. If one assumes that the propensities to consume of capitalists and of workers remain constant, the propensity to invest of capitalists is the dynamic factor which determines variations in the share of profits in the national income and, therefore, the share of the workers, which is a residual. In volume II of this work we shall show that the relationship to Keynesian theory is even closer, for Marx emphasises that it is the capitalist class itself which mobilises the funds necessary for the realisation of profits through its own consumption and investment.

In this way the problem undergoes a shift. There are two urgent questions. Is it possible to understand such a development by recourse to Robertsonian period analysis, and what are the conditions for the finance of such activities in the monetary sphere?

30 The Theory of Class Monopoly and the Problem of Distribution in Capitalism

Preiser took over the notion of 'class monopoly' from Marx; occasionally, he calls it a 'quasi-monopoly theory'. This theory is based on the interpretation by Lexis of the Marxian theory of surplus value and has, furthermore, been supported by Schumpeter, who identified perfect competition, the 'stationary' economy and absence of profit with it. According to Preiser (1959, pp. 620 ff.; 1961, p. 299) this theory starts from the hypothesis that 'if competition is completely free there can exist only income from work; all income from property, whether profit or rent, must, therefore, be derived from limitations of competition'.

Preiser, who in this case follows his teacher Oppenheimer, argues that completely free competition means that land is free and that all the other means of production

> can always be procured in any required quantity. If these conditions are not fulfilled, i.e. if means of production are 'specifically scarce', competition is limited to those who possess the required stocks. To that extent, even if 'capitalists' compete with each other, there exists a monopoly among property-owners as compared with persons who are not owners, and it is this fact that allows the realisation of property income . . .

It seems that the situation of monopoly, which rests on ownership of the means of production, cannot exist in the long run, because they can, after all, be acquired.

Conrad reasons, in truly 'classical' fashion, that the increase in capital depends on the ability to save, which in turn limits the 'speed of growth', 'so that at any given time "capital" is available only in a limited quantity'. At the same time, the means of production are unequally distributed. This, according to Preiser (ibid., p. 300), is the decisive condition for the existence of profits and interest.

If distribution were absolutely equal, income from interest would be impossible, because in the normal case there would be no demand for the use of means of production belonging to third parties and because a mark-up on the price of products, when using one's own resources, would leave everybody's income in the same relative position as would be the case without the mark-up. It is, therefore, only the unequal distribution of wealth which makes the means of production a source of rent.

This is the 'theory of class monopoly', which in the final analysis is nothing but a reformulation of the Marxian theory of surplus value. It was Marx himself who offered the term 'class monopoly', and this provides the link with the Marxian distribution theory. It is not a proper theory of distribution, for it 'basically only answers the question as to why income from property exists' and 'it only explains static profit, not the dynamic'. Above all, 'it is not able . . . to explain the relative size of wage and property incomes'.

Here a transition towards dynamic distribution theory is necessary. Such a dynamic theory can be brought about by a synthesis of the works of Kalecki, Marchal and Preiser, and it would appear to be the proper completion of the Marxian analysis.

Kalecki (1956, pp. 11ff.) starts from a point of view other than that offered by the theory of 'monopolistic competition', for he considers the degree of monopoly not at the microeconomic but at the macroeconomic level. Kalecki builds his theory on the results of the theory of 'monopolistic competition', results which had a microeconomic orientation, but he arrives at a theory founded on macroeconomics. Average prime costs, i.e. average variable costs of the individual firm or industry constitute the basis for the calculation of price. Kalecki simplifies the picture by assuming that the curve in the relevant area is a horizontal line. In this way variable and marginal costs coincide. Everything above this, i.e. the sum of fixed costs and of profits, is to be maximised. Instead of postulating the maximisation of profits, Kalecki operates with the maximisation of this aggregate. The 'degree of monopoly' is the ratio between price and 'prime costs' at the degree of capacity use at which such a maximisation occurs. From the macroeconomic point of view, the 'degree of monopoly', according to Kalecki, is determined by a number of factors: the degree of concentration in industry (oligopoly or formal cartels), the share of advertising costs, trade-union bargaining power, and so on. The readiness to form narrower quasi-cartels or to raise prices with the same prime costs can increase after very intensive advertising campaigns, which also lift overhead costs in proportion to profits. Along with prime costs, wages are influenced by the costs of raw materials, especially the prices of imported materials.

As Preiser has emphasised, this is the decisive component in Kalecki's conception of distribution theory. Kalecki anticipates (1956, p. 46) the

Keynes–Kaldor theory of the determination of the share of the capitalist class in the social product through investment decisions, for he says, 'their investment and consumption decisions determine profits, and not *vice versa*'.

However, he further supplements his theory by taking into account all the 'distribution factors' which are reflected in the modifications of the degree of monopoly, and by quoting external elements such as the development of raw material prices. Preiser is right in saying (1959; 1961, p. 307) that Kalecki's 'degree of monopoly' corresponds to the Marxian rate of surplus value, but that, through 'the all-embracing conditions which determine the monopoly relationship of classes', the distribution factors, it has a more comprehensive form.

It is in the modification of these distribution factors that Kalecki's truly dynamic contribution to the theory of distribution lies. If the degree of monopoly rises and the capital – output ratio remains constant, a steady rate of growth of the economic system can no longer be assured. Even where investment increases while consumption remains constant, or, *a fortiori*, shrinks, a recession will take place in the development of the economy. Preiser formulated it as follows (ibid., pp. 308): 'Since, according to Kalecki's hypothesis, profit is a function of past investment and is therefore fixed in its absolute level, an increase in the share of profits can come about only through a decrease in national income.' According to this theory, 'an increase in the degree of monopoly [in Marxian terms, an increase in the rate of surplus value] entails that . . . demand grows more slowly than supply, with the result that in practice growth will be retarded' (ibid., p. 311).

Here three remarks are in order. First, Kalecki modifies the Marxian analysis in so far as he directly postulates a modification of the rate of surplus value. Marx, by contrast, worked with a constant rate of surplus value.

Secondly, Kalecki in dynamising the rate of surplus value, ensures a more realistic approach in the short run, and he emphasises that the basic Marxian hypothesis of constancy in the share of surplus value or wages in the national income is completely justified in the long run. At the same time, he indirectly touches upon a version of the under-consumption theory within the general framework of business-cycle theory. In particular, there may be a tendency for the share of profits in the national income to increase in periods of boom, and this contains the seeds of a breakdown of the growth process. One difficulty is that Marx did not have such a version of the under-consumption theory.

In other words, and this is the third point, the increase in the degree of monopoly or in the rate of surplus value stimulates additional investment activity, but this only allows for potential growth of the social product. In reality, stagnant consumption (with some sort of accelerator effect) leads to a decline of the actual social product.

At the same time the problem of the remuneration of capital appears in a new light. If, in 'academic' analysis, one starts from the hypothesis that an increase in the degree of monopoly is justified, in view of the scarcity of the production factor 'capital', one would have to go on to consider the fact that an increase in the rate of surplus value could have a paralysing influence on the economy as a whole. Induced investment decreases, and this leads to a simultaneous decrease in income and savings, so that we finally arrive at the paradoxical result that an increase in intended capital remuneration, thought necessary to compensate for the scarcity of capital, may in reality lead to an even greater scarcity of savings and, thereby, of the production factor 'disposable capital', in Cassel's sense. The 'productivity' of capital is here of a negative character. In this context we may point to the effect of increased equipment and the danger of over-capacity, as has been stressed especially by Domar.

This whole argument is stated in Keynesian terms. The argument from the other side would run as follows. A decrease in the degree of monopoly/ rate of surplus value leads simultaneously to a decrease in capital remuneration, but at the same time increases investment activity and the national income, and the gross national product, and thus in the last resort even savings!

An increase in the degree of monopoly must, according to the Marxian analysis, already be in train within the framework of the concentration process, which Kalecki mentions as one of the decisive factors. Modern analysis of the subject of concentration has pointed out a possible connection between, on the one side, the increase in concentration and the degree of monopoly, and, on the other, the possible phenomenon of stagnation. Suggestions of this are to be found in Marxist authors, in other authors influenced by Marx (for instance, Lederer and Steindl), and also in the works of non-Marxist authors such as Berle and Means , and Blair and Houghton to whom Schumpeter stands in sharp opposition.

At this stage we reach a controversy in business-cycle and growth theory, which leads us far beyond the framework of purely distributive considerations. On the other hand, there is also a transition to wage and social policy. According to Marx there arises in the course of this development a bottom stratum of the almost permanently unemployed – those who, as Robertson indicates, do not find work under any conditions. The ghost of technological unemployment appears as a symptom of the era of automation. This possibility has been investigated by Fellner in particular.

Kalecki's theory boils down to the idea that the degree of monopoly in the modern economy is growing steadily. Properly speaking, the share of entrepreneurs in the social product should have risen. On the other hand, raw materials and foodstuffs continually fall in price, partly because of higher productivity in overseas countries, and partly because the terms of trade deteriorate for overseas suppliers. All this constitutes the exploitation of developing countries. (Kalecki, 1933, p. 33.) This latter idea reveals an important element in Rosa Luxemburg's theory of the life-prolonging function of the 'third person' (or 'third world') for capitalism.

There may be yet another realistic element in Marx's theory, according to which it can be anticipated 'that the development of trade-union power has been just sufficiently rapid to prevent the rate of exploitation from rising with the productivity of labour'. Joan Robinson, who makes this statement (1949, p. 81), may not be quite right when she says that both' explanations given by Marx and Kalecki are 'somewhat lame' and that the 'mystery of the constant relative shares' remains unsolved. Marx's very starting hypothesis of a constant rate of surplus value, based on counter-vailing tendencies, offers a foundation for this 'mystery', and Marx's realistic estimate of growing trade-union power appears in many passages of his work (for instance, *Capital*, I, ch. 25, p. 599; see also ch. 8 and 19; II, ch. 17, p. 344).

The theory of class monopoly leads us on to examine monopolistic and oligopolistic connections. On the other hand, there is a direct link from distribution analysis to growth theory and to dynamic problems in a wider sense.

Part VII
Concentration and
Monopolistion

31 Monopoly Elements and Concentration in the Judgement of Marx's Critics

The number of critics who have contested Marx's primacy in anticipating the wave of concentration in the modern economy is rather limited. Some of these critics start out from assumptions that are too narrow, as, for instance, did Heller, who in the 1930s spoke (1931, p. 16) of a theory of 'plant-concentration' in Marx's work. Even Weddigen (1934) assumes that Marx maintains that 'the size of the plant grows constantly', which means that he 'overlooks the decreasing part of the revenue curve'. Weddigen is one of the few critics who speak of a 'refutation of the Marxian theory of concentration'.

On the other hand, Gide and Rist, for instance, in their classic history of economic doctrines (1921), (p. 506) admit that the concentration is

in reality . . . only partially accomplished even in the more capital-istic countries, but . . . there is a general movement in that direction . . . [through] the growth of production on a large scale, resulting in the employment of machinery and in the rise of new forms of organisation such as trusts and cartels, new systems that were unknown in Marx's day, but which have helped to confirm his suspicions.

The two authors state, however (ibid., p. 521), that the theory of concentration has been somewhat shaken by objections on the part of the revisionists.

Yet even Muhs, a clear opponent of Marx, found himself constrained to admit (1927, p. 439) that the concentration thesis is correct: 'In principle, Marx has recognised the process of accumulation and concentration quite correctly.' This judgement has been repeated by many non-Marxists; for instance, Haberlandt affirms (1970, p. 22) that 'the thesis of increasing concentration has never been refuted, but has only been modified'.

The dynamic aspect of Marxian monopoly analysis, the 'temporary monopoly' of the innovating entrepreneur with all its consequences, has been developed in particular by Schumpeter. The same aspect has been very clearly sketched by the Italian theoretician Papi (1959, III, p. 4)

> According to Marx the capitalist economy is characterised by the constant necessity to innovate. If capitalism is to survive, technical progress must be intense. While the classical economists expected the capitalist system to develop from a progressive into a stationary economy, a 'stationary' economy was inconceivable for Marx.

The financial advantages enjoyed by big industrial concerns, especially those which dominate the market, should play a considerable role in the further discussion and explanation of the concentration process. The modern analysis of the process of concentration sees in Marx's presentation, even though he constantly uses the term 'competition', an early stage in the representation of the monopolistic development of our times. Gunzert, for instance, says (1961, p. 59), 'Here we must remind the reader that Karl Marx considered concentration to be the cause and the preliminary stage of monopolisation'.

It has many times been said that Marx was primarily concerned with the more sociological phenomenon of the concentration of wealth in the hands of a few. To this Lenel says (1962, pp. 1–2),

> For Marx concentration was essentially a concentration of wealth. He was of the opinion that ownership of the means of production would gradually be concentrated in the hands of an ever-smaller circle of private persons. The concentration of wealth as he saw it need not be the characteristic element of the concentration process which has taken place since Marx's book was published. The concentration of the property of persons (in the judicial sense) in the means of production was of lesser importance than the concentration of the power of control over the means of production which goes on independently of the distribution of property and assets.

This opinion is directly contrary to Gunzert's statement (1960, p. 34) that

> The present discussion of the problem of economic concentration depends to a very large degree on Karl Marx. . . . His thesis that concentration in a competitive economic system, i.e. in a market economy, is inexorable and inevitable, is strangely shared by politicians of all shades of opinion in a more or less modified form, even if they take explicitly anti-Marxist stances. . . .

Gunzert also (and again in contrast to Lenel) states (ibid., pp. 32–3) that Marx by no means limited his considerations to the single aspect of the concentration of assets, but held at least five different notions of concentration.

Marx defines concentration as follows:

(1) as a progressive growth of enterprises as a consequence of the piling up of profits,
(2) as a combination of hitherto independent enterprises through manipulations in the financial sphere (= centralisation of capital). . . .

Whereas to begin with centralisation may take place 'by force through annexation', through the 'expropriation of many capitalists by a few', it later is effected by the 'smoother procedure of forming joint-stock companies' (*Capital*, 1, ch. 25, p. 586) predominantly with the assistance of the credit-system, i.e. above all of banks. . . . For the sake of completeness we have to mention that Marx also used the term 'concentration' with reference to:

(a) 'concentration of production', in the sense of exploiting local preferences or preferences for a product,
(b) 'concentration of the means of production' (and of labour power) as the constituent principle of industrialisation . . ., and
(c) the increasing 'concentration of money-capital' in banks.

Bartoli (1950, p. 173) sees in Marx's work a 'capitalism of large business units'. According to him, 'the Marxian theory does not at all oppose the modern theories of oligopoly and imperfect competition, but helps in their elaboration. It is a theory of points of departure, and by no means a theory which is complete in itself.'

Furthermore, the process of concentration does not proceed undisturbed. On this point Bigo, a French Jesuit, states (1953, p. 116), 'Marx is much less apodictic with regard to the tendency of capital to concentrate in fewer hands than most of his critics are prone to believe. This tendency runs counter to an inverse tendency to dispersion: large capitals are split up, and new capitals appear.'

It may finally be said that Marx had in mind not only the concentration of enterprises but also plant concentration, all the more so as he anticipated the 'law of mass-production' in the sense of increasing returns to scale. This has been underlined by a historian of economic thought, Whittaker, who refers (1947, p. 430) to a passage in the third volume: 'Marx was not unfamiliar with the 'laws of returns' or 'principle of proportionality. . . . [He] states the principle of increasing returns on capital as production expands. . . .'

Stavenhagen (1957, p. 152) confirms this opinion, according to which the Marxian thesis of concentration is relevant to the analysis of plants and to the analysis of business firms. He explains this as follows:

Only a concentration of capital is able to finance economic undertakings of the magnitude of constructing a railway. The process of concentration of capital calls forth far-reaching technical transformations of the production process, and is visible in the triumphant advance of big business, in the increasing mechanisation of the production process and in the gigantic industrial estates.

Here is the link with the increasing 'organic composition of capital' through technical progress within the framework of concentration, which according to Marx leads to the tendency of the profit rate to fall. On this, Papi says (1959, III, p. 5), 'With the passage of time investment in fixed capital becomes ever greater. If the sum of profits remains the same, the rate of profit must decrease.'

From the fact that each individual entrepreneur strives for 'extra profits', a fact that leads to intra-marginal profits being made on 'innovations',

> the outcome is that enterprises in their totality continuously undergo a more rapid growth of constant capital (machinery) than of variable capital (costs of personnel). From this it follows that the average rate of profit is bound continually to sink. Consequently, as Marx affirms, the development of machinery leads the capitalist system to be undermined from within, because its inner spring, the rate of profit, is gradually weakened.   (Piere, 1962, p. 57.)

In this statement by Piettre, we may see a certain contradiction. If 'relative surplus value' and monopolisation lead to an increase in the share of capital in the social product and apparently to a general increase in the rate of profit as well, the rate of profit ought, according to Marx, (periodically) to fall, because of the more than proportionate rise in capital values.

32 Concentration, Monopoly and Oligopoly in Marx's Work

The notion of dynamic competition, as contained in Marx's work, leads directly to the theory of concentration and of the centralisation of capital. It should be noted that Marx's use of the term 'concentration' differs from modern usage in that it does not extend to the phenomena that are in the foreground of present-day interest: namely, those relating to the formation of mammoth enterprises by way of amalgamation or merger. This process he calls (*Capital*, I, ch. 25, p. 586) 'centralisation of capitals . . . expropriation of capitalist by capitalist . . . centralisation proper as distinct from accumulation and concentration'.

For Marx, 'concentration' arises out of the growth of an enterprise from its own resources, i.e. through self-finance. According to Marx, this is the 'kind of concentration which grows directly out of, or rather is identical with, accumulation'. Growth with the help of capital from outside, i.e. by means of equity capital, he summarises under the heading of 'centralisation', which in another passage (ibid., p. 658) he nevertheless calls the 'concentration of capitals already formed'.

It is of interest to note that Marx remained faithful to his dialectic method in his theory of concentration. In concentration he by no means saw a constant or unidirectional process, but rather a process with many counteracting tendencies:

> the increase of each functioning capital is thwarted by the formation of new and the sub-division of old capitals. Accumulation, therefore, presents itself on the one hand as increasing concentration of the means of production, and of the command over labour; on the other, as repulsion of many individual capitals one from another.

He anticipated the objections of the revisionists in a majestic manner (ibid., p. 586):

> At the same time portions of the original capitals disengage themselves and function as new independent capitals. Besides other causes, the

division of property, within capitalist families, plays a great part in this. With the accumulation of capital, therefore, the number of capitalists grows to a greater or less extent.

THE CONCEPTS OF CONCENTRATION IN MARX'S WORK

It is true that the notion of concentration appears in a variety of forms within Marx's work. First, there is the 'concentration of production' in the sense of a conglomeration function, i.e. as a favoured position based on local factors or on the character of a particular product. Easily perishable articles of a limited 'time of circulation' (Marx instances beer and milk) can be objects of large-scale industry only in 'thickly populated districts' or 'to the extent that improved transportation facilities eliminate distance' (*Capital*, II, ch. 5, p. 131). It is interesting that Marx writes that 'the concentration of production . . . can also provide a relatively large market for such articles'. He thereby comes very close to the notion of local domination of the market for mass consumption articles. In another passage he mentions 'the accumulation and co-operation of labourers', i.e. the demographic increase in certain areas in connection with the 'concentration of means of production'. (ibid., III, ch. 5, p. 79)

Finally, he speaks (ibid., ch. 22, p. 362) of a growing 'concentration of money-capital' in banks: 'The development of the credit system and the attendant ever-growing control of industrialists and merchants over the money savings of all classes of society . . . and the progressive concentration of these savings' offer to banks a point of departure for the indirect domination of economic life.

The theory of concentration contains at least four different elements.

(1) The sociological aspect. The shrinking number of capitalists is equivalent to the idea of the disappearance of small businesses and the workshops of artisans, who are pushed into 'spheres of production which Modern Industry has only sporadically or incompletely got hold of' (ibid., I, ch. 25, p. 587).

(2) This argument leads to a consideration of plant-growth determined by technology. This throws up the question of how to minimise or optimise capacity with regard to costs.

(3) Marx's perspective ignores optima of this kind and extends to the accumulation of profit, seen as the decisive motive power responsible for the growth of the individual enterprise (the proper meaning of 'concentration' in Marx's work).

(4) Finally, Marx understands by 'centralisation' the merger of hitherto independent enterprises or, in other terms, the 'swallowing' of smaller firms by larger ones (ibid., p. 586).

The reasons for concentration, mentioned in (1), (3) and (4), are largely conditioned by technical factors. There is, however, a possibility that (1) is brought about by (3) or (4), and (3) and (4) can exist independently of pure cost optima in the sphere of production, for they may arise from financial and sales advantages.

The objection has been raised against the Marxian theory of concentration that, contrary to what Marx assumed, the middle classes are, in real life, by no means condemned to disappear, but may in many respects experience a kind of renaissance.

Such a consideration raises the question of precisely what the 'middle class' is. If one includes in it a large part of the top-ranking employees, one simply bypasses the problem. After all, Marx's prediction concerned the disappearance of a large stratum of independent 'capitalists', and extends to the idea that the functions of ownership and control would be separated within the joint-stock company; in other words, Marx's theory (ibid., III, ch. 13, p. 219) actually presupposes the transformation of independent entrepreneurs into dependent 'leading' managers.

There is a further objection: revisionists have insisted upon the widespread dispersal of securities in modern society. This argument, which was promoted by the experiments in 'popular shareholding', is contradicted by the fact that there are complaints in almost all European countries about the weakness of the capital market and the reticence of savers with regard to equities and even government stock.

Marx, however, saw in the course of dynamic development with its accompanying process of concentration a possibility that 'a mounting concentration of capitals' would be 'accompanied, though on a smaller scale, by an increase in the number of capitalists'. In the same passage (ibid., p. 219) he speaks as well of 'a progressive expropriation of the more or less direct producers', a tendency which to him is preponderant. And in another passage (ibid., p. 219) he speaks of 'the expropriation and impoverishment of the great mass of producers'.

The sociological problem of the shrinking number of independent capitalists will be balanced, in the view of some economists who are not absolutely opposed to Marxism, by certain economic advantages for the community. Lexis, for instance, states (1910, p. 232),

> It cannot be considered a disadvantage from the social point of view if the number of independent units is reduced, for their independence could only be guaranteed at the expense of the mass of the working population, which had to pay higher prices than would have been necessary if the relevant business forms had been thoroughly rationalised. . . .

In arguing in this way, Lexis refers to his theory of profit mark-ups, a feature which Engels had accepted. On the other hand, Lexis, who thought that the notion of the middle class was determined by social considerations such as relative income and not according to the size of business units, believed that a new middle class was being created from top-level employees.

What, however, is decisive is not the sociological question of the structure of the population or its income. The Marxian thesis of concentration refers exclusively to structural transformations within the business sector, especially industry. Here the trend towards big business has become more and more spectacular in modern times, and has finally found its apotheosis in a wave of mergers at international level.

THE TECHNOLOGICAL ELEMENT

A second view, which finds its origins in technological growth, was developed by, in particular, Bücher (1910, pp. 429–44), who spoke of 'the law of mass production'. Here we have to do with an expression that Marx had already employed (*Capital*, III, ch. 13, p. 219). Marx saw 'the development of the social productiveness of labour' in 'the mass [volume] of the conditions of production' and in the 'relative smallness of the portion of total capital laid out in wages, i.e., in the relatively small quantity of living labour required . . . for mass production'. And he adds, 'It encompasses this along with the concentration of capital.'

Marx went even further than Bücher, because he considered the concentration of enterprises as a precondition for dimensions appropriate to the use of high-level technology. Many Marxists follow Bücher in accentuating the technological cost component in the movement towards concentration. In this context note should be taken of Lenin's work, the political and empirical importance of which has been stressed by Gunzert (1960, p. 82) and others.

GROWTH OF THE INDIVIDUAL FIRM AND THE CONCENTRATION OF ASSETS

The third way of looking at the matter in Marx – concentration through growth of the individual firm by means of self-finance – is characterised by modern authors – for instance, Lenel (1962, p. 2) – as especially narrow. It is, nevertheless, the real point of departure for the analysis of the phenomenon of market-power, because it considers the disproportionate growth of mammoth firms in certain sectors. Other recent authors find in Marx, a 'mechanistic' approach, in contrast to the 'biological' approach, in so far as the technical conditions of the productive process lead to a forced growth in the size of enterprises (Haberlandt, 1970, p. 20).

The ruling opinion is that Marx considered such individual firms as resting in the hands of a capitalist. Lenel, for instance, says (1962, p. 1); 'For Marx, concentration is essentially a concentration of assets'. He goes on to quote Keiser, who advanced this notion of asset concentration in the 1930s (1931, p.11).

This leads us back to the sociological notion. Here we have to object that Marx in the passage to which Lenel refers (*Capital*, I, ch. 25, p. 586) points to countervailing tendencies: 'At the same time portions of the original capitals disengage themselves and function as new independent capitals'. Here we are not concerned with the concentration of personal assets.

Keiser and Lenel's interpretation of the concentration of assets seems to point in the direction of the fourth component of the theory of concentration: concentration through merger, or, in Marxian terms, 'centralisation' – 'destruction of their individual independence . . . expropriation of capitalist by capitalist, transformation of many small into few large capitals' (ibid.).

With regard to Lenel's view, it can be admitted that the organisational element – i.e. the extremely large growth of certain enterprises as compared with others and the swallowing of smaller firms by bigger ones – has come more to the fore, thus supplanting the notion of asset concentration developed by Keiser. Yet in the same context Lenel says (1962, p. 2), 'Marx did not clearly see that it is possible to exercise control without owning property. Still less did he suspect the extent to which juridical persons, independently of natural persons who hold shares, may and did acquire property.' In this Lenel is wrong.

Against the one-sided view that Lenel attributes to Marx, we may quote, for instance, Gunzert, who says (1961, p. 59), 'Here we must remind the reader, that Karl Marx considered concentration to be the cause and the preliminary stage of monopolisation.' Gunzert also remarks, with regret (ibid., p. 34), 'that the discussion about concentration among journalists and entrepreneurs depends to an astonishingly large degree on Karl Marx'. This statement is all the more remarkable as Gunzert thinks that Marx does not really offer a good basis for a solution of the practical side of the problems of concentration. He believes (1960, pp. 50–1) that such a basis is to be found in Sombart (1922, III, pp. 816ff.), who thought that concentration arose less from the swallowing-up of small and medium-sized business firms, and that big business generally conquers new territory in economic life.

MONOPOLY AND OLIGOPOLY IN MARX

It can be argued that the Marxian analysis of a competitive capitalist system, which was treated under aspects of value theory, has its foundations in supply, especially that of labour. As to monopoly capitalism, Marx saw it (*Capital*, III, ch. 46, p. 775) as based primarily upon demand components and argued that thinking in values is in this case out of court: 'When we refer to a monopoly price, we mean in general a price determined only by the purchasers' eagerness to buy and ability to pay, independent of the price determined by the general price of production. . . .' He then proceeds to mention the case of 'a vineyard producing wine of very extraordinary quality'. In the last resort this is an example of an oligopoly position based on the preferences of customers.

At the same time Marx appears to assume that the demand function based on 'social needs' offers a certain stability. He carefully distinguishes between final demand, which can be regarded as relatively constant as long as income conditions remain constant, and intermediate demand: 'It would seem, then, that there is on the side of demand a certain magnitude of definite social wants. . . .' Side by side with this we find the more volatile demand for 'productive consumption', i.e. the demand which derives from producers; in this case, 'the prices of means of production . . . determine the demand for these means of production' (ibid., ch. 10, p. 190).

In this context it could be presumed that Marx hypothesises the existence of monopolistic and oligopolistic factors even in static analysis, particularly in the production of investment goods. Normally, the 'temporary monopoly' or oligopoly appears in Marx's work only within the framework of dynamic price theory, in which technical progress leads to a revolution in cost and production conditions.

It is true that Marx did not examine in detail the problem of oligopoly in the proper sense and the cartel problem linked to it. Nevertheless, he referred to the oligopoly problem in quite a number of passages in his work. One of the first references is to be found in *The Poverty of Philosophy* (1847; 1920, p. 138):

> In practical life we find not only competition, monopoly, and their antagonism, but also their synthesis, which is not a formula but a movement. Monopoly produces competition, competition produces monopoly. The monopolists are made by competition, the competitors become monopolists. . . . The synthesis is such that monopoly can only maintain itself by continually passing through the struggle of competition.

These rival monopolies are obviously nothing other than an early version of oligopolistic interaction. In this context it should be emphasized that Marx quotes quite a number of passages from Thomas More's *Utopia* in its Latin version (1518), where the notion of oligopoly turns up for the first time. In the relevant passage (p. 54), More speaks of sheep-farmers who evict thousands from the land and then give employment to a single shepherd.

But, however much the number of sheep increases, their price does not decrease a farthing, because, though you cannot brand that a monopoly which is a sale by more than one person, yet their sale is certainly an oligopoly, for all sheep have come into the hands of a few men, and those already rich, who are not obliged to sell before they wish and who do not wish until they get the price they ask.

Marx certainly knew of this concept of oligopoly in More, but he did not use it in his own work. It nevertheless seems, as Röper has pointed out (1949, p. 591), that he translated the passage in question.

The term 'oligopoly' was reintroduced into economics by Schlesinger (1914, pp. 17, 57) shortly before the First World War, but the concept received its definitive treatment at the hands of Chamberlin (1933), who introduced it into the professional jargon.

Marx cites (*Capital*, I, ch. 31, p. 705) Luther's fight against the 'Societies Monopolia', which were 'powerful levers for concentration of capital'. In the third volume of *Capital* Marx approaches the notion of oligopoly very closely.

In these formulations there is already contained the seed of those conditions that prevail in monopolistic competition or oligopoly. The producer does not accept the price as a datum, but uses it as a parameter of action in order to get hold of the market shares of other firms. Such shares presuppose the notion of preference. At the same time, Marx refers to the analogy with cartels: 'If the demand for this particular kind of commodity is greater than the supply, one buyer outbids another – within certain limits – and so raises the price of the commodity for all of them above the market-value, while on the other hand the sellers unite in trying to sell at a high market-price.' And he goes on to say, 'If one side has the advantage, all belonging to it gain. It is as though they exerted their common monopoly.' (Ibid., III, ch. 10, p. 120.)

This is a dynamic market analysis in the sense of modern notions of 'sellers' market' and 'buyers' market'. This presentation is, at any rate, much nearer to the truth than the anaemic analysis of the model of 'perfect competition', which appeared later. Marx's notion of competition is by no means identical with this. In another passage he explicitly speaks of monopoly price. He affirms that the total value of a commodity remains within the limits set by the newly created value of the commodity, whenever the cost elements change, or even the 'rate of rent' does. 'An exception could only take place if rent should be based on a monopoly price.' But 'this would nowise alter the law, but merely complicate the analysis. For if we consider only the product itself in this case, then only the division of surplus-value would be different'. (Ibid., ch. 50, p. 855.)

Marx formulated the argument of the third volume of *Capital* at a very early date, in a series of articles in the *Neue Rheinische Zeitung* in 1849. These later appeared under the title *Lohnarbeit und Kapital* (Wage Labour and

Capital). In this text Marx clearly depicts oligopolistic price competition directed against an adversary:

> One capitalist can drive another from the field and capture his capital only by selling more cheaply. . . . he must . . . raise the productive power of labour as much as possible. . . . Moreover, he attains the object he wishes to attain, if he puts the price of his goods only a small percentage lower than that of his competitors. He drives them from the field, he wrests from them at least a part of their sales, by underselling them. (*Marx–Engels, Selected Works*, 1968, p. 91.)

This is a clear representation of oligopolistic conditions: undercutting, the struggle for market-shares, competition directed against certain identifiable competitors. In this context it is appropriate to note that Marx in his *Poverty of Philosophy*, his polemic directed at Proudhon, outlined (1847; 1923, p. 137) a theory of modern oligopoly under the heading of monopoly:

> Everybody knows that modern monopoly is engendered by competition. . . . We all know that competition was engendered by feudal monopoly. Thus primarily competition has been the contrary of monopoly, and not monopoly the contrary of competition. Therefore modern monopoly is not a simple antithesis; it is, on the contrary, the true synthesis.

This comparison between feudal and modern monopolies finds its counterpart in the modern sociological analysis of oligopoly, which draws analogies between feudal baronies and the mammoth firms of the twentieth century. Berle, for instance, says (1955, pp. 47, 81–2) that it would not be far-fetched to make a comparison between Norman dukes and modern trust managements: 'It seems a far cry. . . . But . . . the distance is not so great. . . . the corporation has some colour of state authority. . . . It has, *de facto* at least, invaded the political sphere and has become in fact, if not in theory, a quasi-governing agency. . . .'

Berle and Means (1936, p. 350) have compared oligopolistic strategy with the strategy deployed by conquerors such as Alexander the Great, 'instead of the motives of retailers at the time of Adam Smith'. Rothschild (1947) pointed to traits that feudalism and modern oligopoly have in common, and says (p. 299) that 'if analogies have to be used . . . then they will have to be drawn from those spheres where writers deal with moves and counter-moves, with struggles for power and position – in short, from books dealing with the general aspects of politics, and military strategy and tactics'. He recommended (ibid., p. 319), that 'a short manual on the Principles of Oligopolistic War' should be written. Oligopoly seems to be of neo-feudal character.

Marx, however, sees 'modern monopoly' (say, 'oligopoly') as directly contrary to feudal conditions. He quotes Rossi, who appears to have more clearly grasped 'the synthetic character of bourgeois monopoly' than Proudhon: 'Feudal monopolies', Rossi says, 'are artificial, that is to say arbitrary: bourgeois monopolies are natural, that is to say rational'. (*Poverty of Philosophy*, 1847; 1920, p. 165.)

In *The Poverty of Philosophy*, Marx deals with cartels in connexion with competing monopolies. He writes (1847; 1920, p. 160),

> If the monopolists restrict competition among themselves by partial association [cartels], competition grows among the workers; and the more the mass of the workers grows as against the monopolists of one nation, the more keen becomes the competition between the monopolists of different nations. The synthesis is such that monopoly can only maintain itself by continually passing through the struggle of competition.

Here Marx touches upon the problem of modern industrial struggle in the world market. He takes up the monopoly problem in the proper sense when discussing monopoly rent from valuables in the soil.

The realistic Marxian theory of prices made an absurdity of the 'myth of anonymity'. By its means, any element which caused price to alter was explained, as was not the case with the Pareto conception. In Marx's work the impulse for a change in price is furnished by oligopolistic pioneering firms, which revolutionise the productive process. Price changes in individual sectors or firms Marx explains directly by the continuing compulsion to lower costs, a compulsion which stems from the pioneering firms and forces the rest to follow.

As long as the initiative always lies with the same enterprises, these gain a constantly growing 'advantage' and ever-bigger market shares. The phenomenon of oligopolistic concentration, therefore, follows directly from the dynamic price concept of Marx. Oligopolies which had been 'loose' or 'diffuse' become more well defined and 'strict'. The process of concentration turns from quantity to quality.

Some modern Marxists have wished to deny this identification of pioneering firms with mammoth enterprises. Baran and Sweezy (1968b, pp. 6off.), for instance, believe that they adduce evidence to the effect that the real initiative for innovation and inventions lies with smaller and medium-sized enterprises. Strangely enough, these two Marxist authors advance the same thesis as is advanced by liberal authors such as Jewkes: According to this theory, the big shipping companies with sailing ships would never have developed steamers, the big railway companies would never have invented the automobile, and motor-car magnates were not pioneers of air travel. The leading concerns in electric light bulbs are not important in the neon tube industry, and telephone companies had nothing to do with telegraphy. According to Jewkes (1953, p. 206) there is, nevertheless, in oligopoly a source of 'dynamics developed by fear', i.e. in the concern that others may take up the innovation first.

Considering the 'megalomania' which threatens the socialist system of society, it is all the more remarkable that Marxist authors should share in this recognition of small and medium-sized enterprises and economic decentralisation. This leads to the difficult question of whether and to what extent oligopoly may impede or further technical progress, a question which the present author has examined elsewhere (Kühne, 1958, pp. 193ff.).

The hypothesis that the rôle of introducing innovation lies with smaller business units does not absolutely contradict the Marxian initiative towards a lowering of costs. The real success in exploiting an innovation on a large scale may, none the less, lie with large-scale enterprises, after the smaller enterprise has made the breach, and possibly perished in the process.

This microeconomic view was extended by Marx by including repercussions on other activities, i.e. external economies. The transition to macroeconomic analysis is carried out within the framework, in his dynamic price theory, of his examination of the demand element.

For Marx the decisive factors from a macroeconomic point of view are movements in the capital flow. He presupposes a certain degree of mobility between the various lines of activity. In this context he approaches the problem of oligopolistic barriers to entry. He distinguishes between two areas, which Joan Robinson has described (1962, p. 42) as the 'non-specialised' and 'specialised' sectors. In the 'non-specialised' sector

> there is sufficient mobility between different lines of production to ensure that the level of wages is pretty much the same in occupations which require the same amount of training, while the mobility of investible resources is such (apart from distortions due to monopoly) as to ensure more or less the same rate of profit on capital in all lines.

Joan Robinson makes the same reservations as Marx. She abstracts from 'formal monopolies' and does not examine the problem that forms the centrepiece of her main work on monopolistic competition: i.e. whether or not we live in a 'world of monopolies' within the general framework of more or less monopolistic conditions, which in the 'non-specialised' sector would also explain the profit rate. She contrasts with this sector the 'specialised' one, the basis of which 'is some natural facility for production of a particular commodity possessed by a particular group of producers – mineral deposits, soil and climate favourable to a particular crop . . . or economies of scale'.

This is very reminiscent of the example cited by Marx to justify his idea of 'differential rent': i.e. 'the motive power of the waterfall', 'the mere application of natural forces in industry', 'relative fruitfulness of specific separate capitals invested in a certain production sphere', 'fertility', 'the location of the land' and 'the stage of agricultural development' (*Capital*, III, ch. 39, pp. 650, 658, 644, 646). The second group identified by Joan Robinson, the 'specialised sector', offers almost institutional positions of monopoly i.e. a partial monopoly of land combined with Marx's 'temporary' monopoly and 'large-scale production'.

Both Joan Robinson and Marx hold that the 'equalisation of the rates of profit' takes place by means of capital movements only within the 'non-specialised' sector. The dominant rôle in the other sector Marx sees as being played by 'rent', in the widest sense, especially the rent of land or of natural resources; even his 'extra surplus value', as the reward to special advantage, is part of this category, though Marx does not explicitly mention it. This distinction is of great importance for the formation of price: whereas in the 'non-specialised' sector we have to reckon with permanent pressure on prices, because of increased productivity through current net investment, the 'specialised', oligopolistic sector tends to rigidity in price or even to the maintenance of price at a very high level – as is clearly the case under conditions of 'large-scale production', i.e. in the case of oligopolistic–monopolistic giant enterprises.

The distinction between the 'specialised' and 'non-specialised' sectors is to be found in embryo in Marx's work, and in relation to the 'specialised' sector there naturally arises the question of rent theory. However, there is one difficulty to be considered. While Marx, in describing the pressure of innovations on productivity, thinks especially of the 'non-specialised' sector, Joan Robinson's interpretation of 'marginal producers' also takes in the 'specialised' sector. This can only be explained by the fact that in the 'non-specialised' sector there is continual change in the identity of the firms playing a pioneering rôle while in the second, where there are various restrictions to entry, the advantage is held more or less continuously by the same giant firms, to whom, because of their market power or financial position, 'innovations' accrue even if they do not come from their own laboratories.

Towards the end of the third volume of *Capital* we find indications that Marx was fully aware of the dichotomy in economic life, and that he simultaneously recognised the essential point, that the use of value analysis in monopolistic conditions is conceivable only with some difficulty. In a wider sense Marx, speaks here (ibid., ch. 36, p. 606) of 'the monopoly of social means of production by private persons', which is a precondition for the credit system (see also *Capital*, II, ch. 20, p. 425). He goes on to say (ibid., III, ch. 38, p. 642), 'These natural forces are thus quite as much monopolised by capital as the social natural forces of labour.' And that 'monopoly . . . requires state interference' (ibid., ch. 27, p. 438).

With this generalised notion of monopoly, Marx approaches Preiser's concept of 'class monopoly'. This term, however, belongs more to the realm of macroeconomic distribution theory. Marx writes (ibid., ch. 50, p. 861)

> Finally, if equalisation of surplus-value into average profit meets with obstacles in the various spheres of production in the form of artificial or natural monopolies, and particularly monopoly in landed property, so that a monopoly price becomes possible, which rises above the price of production and above the value of the commodities affected by such a monopoly, then the limits imposed by the value of the commodities would not thereby be removed. The monopoly price of certain commodities would merely transfer a portion of the profit of the other commodity-producers to the commodities having the monopoly price. A local disturbance in the distribution of the surplus-value among the various spheres of production would indirectly take place, but it would leave the limit of this surplus-value itself unaltered. Should the commodity having the monopoly price enter into the necessary consumption of the labourer, it would increase the wage and thereby reduce the surplus-value, assuming the labourer receives the value of his labour-power as before. It could depress wages below the value of labour-power, but only to the extent that the former exceed the limit of their physical minimum. In this case the monopoly price would be paid by a reduction from real wages (i.e. the quantity of use-values received by the labourer for the same quantity of labour) and from the profit of the other capitalists. The limits within which the monopoly price would affect the normal regulation of the prices of commodities would be firmly fixed and accurately calculable.

On the basis of these arguments, three different observations can be made. First , Marx recognises that monopoly price or, rather, oligopoly price contains an element of indeterminacy. Secondly, he touches on the problem of the 'transfer of surplus value' from non-monopolistic to monopolistic lines of activity, and he thus recognises that the former may 'exploit' the latter. Thirdly, he admits that the worker may be exploited as a consumer by monopolistic tendencies. This confirms the more recent judgements of Labriola and Graziadei.

Nevertheless, he still thinks that the influence exercised on market price by monopolistic forces can be calculated.

33 Monopoly and Oligopoly in Modern Marxism

At a very early date the objection was raised that Marxian theory rested unilaterally on the basic condition of free competition. It seems that this resulted from the use that was made of the labour theory of value. Lederer, for instance, says (1922, pp. 105–6), 'The labour theory of value is valid only under the further condition that free competition is everywhere effective.' More recently, Meek has expressed himself in a similar vein (1956a, pp. 285–6):

> In a world in which 'artificial and natural monopolies' have become far more widespread and powerful than they were in Marx's day . . . it does not seem to me to be reasonable to assume any longer that the *sole* source of profit is the surplus labour of the workmen employed by the capitalist. For example, there are now many cases in which a part of the excess profit received by certain monopoly capitalists should properly be regarded as something like the old 'profit upon alienation' characteristic of the Mercantilist period.

The thesis of the inapplicability of Marxian theory under monopolistic conditions has been persistently advanced. Baran and Sweezy, for instance, in their programmatic study (1968a) that has led to a new debate in Marxist circles on the problem of monopolistic and oligopolistic conditions, state that Marxist theory stagnates. This stagnation they attribute (p. 68) to the fact that 'the Marxian analysis of capitalism still rests in the final analysis on the assumption of a competitive economy'.

Non-Marxists, of course, have joined in the chorus. Heilbroner, for instance, said (1955, p. 128), 'Profits are easy to explain if we assume that there are monopolies in the system. . . . But Marx will have none of that. . . .' Schumpeter has gone even a step further. It is his opinion (1959, p. 651) that Marx would have rejected any attempt to underpin his theory of absolute surplus value by appealing to the theory of imperfect competition, by introducing frictions and institutional inhibitions.

In the same work, however Schumpeter has pointed out that it cannot be denied that Marx's analysis contained certain monopolistic elements. Yet he did not explicitly recognise that the theory of 'temporary monopoly' in Marx is clearly analogous to the theory of imperfect competition and can at least function to underpin the existence of 'relative surplus value'.

Differing opinions are beginning to stress that in any analysis of monopolistic conditions it is often better to begin directly with Marx. In this context certain remarks made in 1953 by Gurland may be of interest. In an unpublished address he specifically referred (1959, pp. 27–9) to the criticism which served as a starting point for Lederer and Graziadei and later for Baran and Sweezy:

> I believe, contrary to the criticism which is made of the Marxian system, that it represents only the schema of competitive capitalism . . ., [that] it would be more to the point to criticise the analysis . . . for trying to incorporate into the overall schema such phases as were not phases of competitive capitalism, but were rather pre-capitalist phases. . . . Marx was too strongly influenced by factors which eliminated competitive capitalism in his time.

In his criticism that too much account had been taken of pre-capitalist forms, Gurland could have referred to, in particular, the application of the labour theory of value, which, as Marx confessed, prevails in a pure form only under pre-capitalist conditions. Gurland points instead to monopolistic phenomena which result from pre-capitalist conditions, i.e. to 'the historical factors . . . the absolutist state and . . . declining feudal land-ownership'. In the first instance he thinks of Marxian rent theory; he even quotes the phrase, 'Monopoly produces competition, competition produces monopoly', but mistakenly attributes it to Lenin. If he had read *The Poverty of Philosophy*, he would have come across a justification for his thesis, for there Marx repeatedly speaks of the feudal forms of monopoly.

To our general surprise Gurland then proceeds as follows:

> In theoretical economic science the categories elaborated by Marx, i.e. the categories of absolute rent and of differential rent, permit of an analysis of modern anti-competitive factors. And the theories which, for instance, were developed in the 1920s in Germany with regard to cartel rent very often operate with the same categories as appear in Marx's work although they bear different names: what has been called 'absolute rent' in Marx at the level of agricultural production appears here as absolute cartel rent, and what Marx calls differential rent appears as monopoly profit. . . . I might also say that it is entirely possible to comprehend with the help of Marxian categories of value and surplus value certain phenomena which play a rôle in modern monopoly capitalism or semi-monopolistic capitalism . . . Indeed, that these categories are eminently suitable to describe such phenomena.

Here Gurland overlooks the fact that 'absolute rent', as defined by Marx, applies not just to agricultural conditions, but also to resources of all kinds – waterfalls, and so on. For the rest , his argument leads one on to certain ideas that were developed much later by de Cindio in Italy. Gurland, at any rate, recognised that the basic elements for the consideration of monopoly factors are already to be found in Marx's work. He says,

> One cannot expect of Marxian theory, which was developed around the middle of the last century, that it should represent all these things in a distinct manner. There are in various parts of *Capital* many incomplete representations of the theoretical conception of the development of competition of monopoly and of monopoly to competition – points which were taken up by Lenin in a simplified form. . . .

As has already been emphasised, Marx speaks of 'associated producers' and of 'associations' of enterprises in the sense of cartels. A number of attempts have, indeed, been made, by a variety of authors, to construct a theory of cartels on socialist foundations. These attempts are not directed at correcting the theoretical analysis in Marx's work by introducing the increasing degree of monopolisation or oligopolisation, but are aimed more or less at an examination of economic and political consequences of cartelisation, especially for consumers.

VALUE THEORY AND THE PROBLEM OF MONOPOLY

Marxian value theory postulates a certain proportionality between the sum of wages and the sum of profits (both expressed in 'values', i.e. 'socially necessary labour time'). Value theory also assumes an equalisation of rates of profit of different lines of activity and even within the same branch of activity. To that extent value theory seems *a priori* inapplicable in monopolistic and oligopolistic conditions. Lederer has developed in detail (1922, pp. 105–9) his judgement on the inapplicability of the labour theory of value:

> In free competition there are no boundaries as to the play of interests. Under conditions of free competition, the smallest change in the exchange ratio of commodities, which causes a sale above or below production prices, unleashes forces which eliminate such deviations. In talking of free competition, we do, indeed, refer to conditions in which every economic agent has accurate knowledge of ruling market conditions, no one operates in the dark and no one acts in an uncontrolled manner. Free competition is a state in which each participant is fully informed about the entire economic situation and takes his decisions in accordance with it.
> If this is not the case, deviations from the production prices are

greater, they last longer, and they are corrected only with difficulty. The law, however, will still apply in an approximate manner provided free competition prevails, i.e. where it is possible for capital to enter any sphere of activity without hindrance, where it is possible for workers to work where they can get the highest wage, and where buyers are possessed of acute discernment and buy where they can obtain commodities of a given quality most cheaply. An encyclopaedic view over the market by entrepreneurs, workers and consumers would bring about the pure applicability of the labour theory of value. . . .

Lederer's argument needs to be completed. It is valid only if capital-intensity (which is Marx's 'organic composition of capital', or the sum of costs) is the same in all activities; for otherwise we run up against the problem of the transformation of values into prices.

Lederer continues, 'But what happens, if [free competition] is eliminated? . . . In that case, supply will be dominated by a closed group with similar interests . . . a monopoly. It is of no importance whether the monopoly belongs to an individual or to a group provided that there is no competition within the group.' Here Lederer certainly underrates some of the special problems which arise, even in the absence of price competition, within a cartel or a strict oligopoly. He then analyses the formation of prices under monopoly and arrives at the following conclusion: 'It is clear that . . . the owners of the monopoly obtain a surplus, i.e. a surplus above average profits. It is also clear that all the other producers will similarly suffer *eo ipso* a corresponding reduction in their profits, a diminution of the wealth that enables them to buy commodities.'

As with many other Marxists, Lederer here sets out from the hypothesis that the sum of profits or the sum of surplus value in the whole economy is fixed once and for all, and that the share of profit in the social product or national income cannot be increased by the existence of monopolies. In this case monopoly positions would simply lead to a redistribution of profits within the capitalist class itself. This hypothesis is possibly the main reason why many Marxists pay very little attention to the problem of monopoly or oligopoly.

Labriola and Graziadei are an exception in this respect. Labriola gives the following judgement (1926, p. 338: 'There are technical forms of production . . . which succeed better than certain others in the sub-jugation of the labourer and of the market. . . . Marx always neglected this element in his judgement of capitalism. Capitalism entails the exploitation not only of workers, but also of consumers.'

On the other hand, Graziadei stressed (1925, p. 172) the importance of price analysis as developed by 'academic' economists:

In a certain sense it can be said that the only scientific price laws in the economic sector in the narrower sense are those that refer to variations in market prices. It is in this sector that orthodox economics has made a very important contribution and offers us a theory of relations between overall demand, overall supply and prices which at least as a first approximation one may consider as definitive. Supporters of Marx have nothing to lose if they accept the best aspects of this theory. On the contrary, in doing so they could more easily arrive at an amalgamation of the proper core of Marx's doctrine with the analysis of market prices, which since the death of the great thinker has made such spectacular progress. . . .

In this context Graziadei enters into the analysis of monopoly price as it had been formulated since the middle of the nineteenth century, though it was not until shortly before the turn of the century that it achieved its real breakthrough in 'orthodox' economics. Cournot's basic work had, indeed, appeared as early as 1836, but attracted very little attention. The development of monopoly-price theory had to wait until the first edition of Marshall's *Principles of Economics* in 1890, its chief protagonists in England being F. Y. Edgeworth and A. G. Pigou. These initiatives were taken up quite early by Italian economics. The fact that Edgeworth formulated his newly conceived theory of monopoly in the *Giornale degli Economisti* in 1897 certainly had something to do with it. In Schumpeter's judgement (1919, p. 194), 'this was the first great breach made in the *laisser-faire* system by economic theory'. Brinkmann expanded on this judgement by stating (1926; 1967, p. 119) that 'this was the first point at which classical price theory was receptive in a positive and fertile way to the decisive realities of economic organisation in high capitalism'.

When we consider the fact that socialism is the direct opposite to the *laisser-faire* system, it is astonishing that Marxists have made such little and so late a use of this argument, and that attempts to integrate modern monopolistic and oligopolistic conditions into the Marxian system were made only at a relatively late date. This fact is all the more astonishing as Marx himself in many of his statements did finally go beyond the framework of a purely competitive system. Modern Marxism has become more and more conscious of these conditions. Panzieri, for instance, who sets out from the hypothesis that a large part of Marx's work must be understood in the context of competitive capitalism, says (1964, p. 286) that it thereby loses some of its validity. Nevertheless, he adds that 'the model established in *Capital* is not in fact as completely closed as it appears to be: the incessant evolution of capital is not limited to a competitive framework'. In a similar way, Botta states (1971, p. 30),

With regard to the logical and systematic representation of this work, we find passages in Volume I of *Capital* (the chapter on 'The General Law of Capitalist Accumulation') and in Volume III of *Capital* (the chapter on 'The Rôle Of Credit In Capitalist Accumulation') that contain considerations of joint-stock capital, a stage in capitalist accumulation which goes beyond the stage of competition.

Panzieri (1964, p. 276) puts special stress on the fact that Marx in his analysis of the joint-stock company

> was aware of a deep-seated change in the capitalist mechanism, namely the transformation of profits into interest. In this way it is possible for firms to exist which do not pay more than the pure and simple rate of interest; and this is one of the reasons which retards the fall in the general rate of profit, because the constant capital of these firms exhibits an extremely high proportion in relation to variable capital, and these firms need not participate in the levelling-out of the general rate of profit.

It is no accident that the lot of working out the elements of a theory of monopoly in Marx fell to Italian Marxists. After all, it was Italian authors (above all, Pantaleoni, Amoroso, and Barone, a disciple of Pareto) who were the first seriously to take up the formulation worked out by Cournot, Marshall and Edgeworth. (Stavenhagen, 1957, p. 307).

THE HILFERDING–LENIN CONCEPTION

We must say at the outset that Hilferding and his follower Lenin contributed less to economic analysis in the strict sense than to the representation of the political and economic effects of the concentration process.

Hilferding deals in particular with the connexion between 'capitalist monopolies and banks', with the importance of cartels and trusts, and especially with the repercussions of cartels on the general rate of profit and on business fluctuations: cartels 'create a different level of profits in cartelised and uncartelised branches of production', and 'do not eliminate the effects of crisis. They modify them in so far as they transfer the impact of a crisis on to non-cartelised industries'. Fundamentally, Hilferding starts from the assumption that the rate of surplus value as a whole is not influenced by the tendency to monopoly and that it is simply a matter of a redistribution of the whole mass of surplus value or profits between branches or enterprises, all this with reference to Marx. He admits, however, that, 'the further monopolisation progresses, the more the burden of extra profits is felt by other classes'. (Hilferding, 1910; 1947, pp. 400, 405, 516.)

That Hilferding was, nevertheless, thinking essentially of a redistribution on the basis of a given rate of surplus value can be deduced from statements which are explicable in terms of the fact that he accepted in principle the theory of the tendency of the rate of profit to fall. He says,

'The increase in the rate of profit brought about by an increase in the cartel price can result only from a reduction of the rate of profit in other branches of industry.' As we have seen, Marx went even further and was struck by the possibility that workers might be exploited as consumers. It is to be noted that Hilferding played with the idea of extending cartelisation to all branches of industry and of developing a 'general cartel', as he called it, which he considered 'economically conceivable' but 'a social and political impossibility'. Today, we should see in such an idea the reflection of the theory of the 'ubiquity of oligopoly', coupled with a cartel-like fixing of prices, promoted by the state within sectors (for instance, agriculture) that cannot be 'cartelised'. (Ibid., pp. 312, 319, 403.)

Lenin, who was otherwise strongly influenced by the non-Marxist Hobson, took up the following statements by Hilferding on foreign trade:

> By capital export we understand the export of value, destined to produce surplus value abroad. . . . the condition for the export of capital is a difference in profit rate. . . . The agents of industrial capital exports today are in particular cartels and trusts . . . [because] the tendency towards an extension of production within cartelised industries is very strong, while its extension for the domestic market is thwarted by a high cartel price. . . . (Ibid., pp. 429, 431, 447.)

Lenin limited himself to a few statements on cartels and trusts, based on Hilferding: 'Instead of being a transitory phenomenon the cartels have become one of the foundations of economic life. . . . Competition becomes transformed into monopoly. . . . Monopoly! This is the last word in the "latest phase of capitalist development" ' (Lenin, 1964, pp. 201, 205 and 210).

Neither in Hilferding's work nor in Lenin's can the elements be found of a theory, such as Marx provides of 'competing monopolists' or 'monopolistic competition', though in the works of both the need for a reformulation of Marxist theory in this field begins to show through. Within the framework of such a reformulation the consequences of the process of concentration needed to be exposed, for the process of transition to oligopolistic and monopolistic market forms appeared to effect not only a quantitative but also a qualitative change in the capitalist economic structure. Lenin in his classic work *Imperialism* spoke explicitly of the 'final replacement of the ancient form of capitalism by a new one'. He thought that the decisive break took place about the turn of the century.

Nevertheless, these and later works from the pens of Marxist authors hardly touched upon the analysis of monopolistic conditions, as contained in Marx's work. On the contrary, within those circles that were most assiduously engaged in attempts to reformulate the Marxist theory, the idea was spread abroad that Marx's own analysis was based essentially on competitive capitalism.

Lenin's *Imperialism* was for the most part concerned with the problems of the world economy and the exploitation of poor countries by rich ones. Sweezy says of it (1942, p. 308) that it 'was brief and much of it was devoted to summarising supporting facts and figures'.

THE NEW FORMULATION BY GRAZIADEI

Further to what was said in the previous section, Graziadei tried to provide a deeper analysis of monopoly capitalism. This attempt has been praised by modern Marxists. Naville for instance, says (1970, II, pp. 409–10),

> Graziadei was an active Italian communist and Marxist. He tried to combine several things in one, things which Soviet reformers of today would like to make compatible with each other: namely, the Marxian theory of surplus labour and the marginalist concept of value and price, which would alter the meaning of surplus value. Graziadei's attempt . . . has been condemned. . . . Nevertheless, it seems today that his ideas are reappearing, though in a more scientific garb and under the pressure of inescapable necessity. . . . Graziadei's thesis is simple and purports to separate surplus labour from surplus value. . . . Use value and exchange value are [for him] not two sides of the same relation, but two different realities. From this results Graziadei's thesis according to which there can be and is surplus labour without the existence of surplus value even within the capitalist system. Surplus labour is a 'natural' fact and is independent of exchanged surplus values, of which it is neither cause nor source. It would therefore be possible to explain surplus values not by surplus labour but by surplus prices ['over-pricing' = *surprix*, or a price rake-off in the sense of Lexis]. Such a surplus price would result from capitalist exchange relations, especially in a system of monopoly.

Naville quotes from the condemnation of Graziadei by the orthodox communist Rudas, (1926).

We cannot here go into the reformulation of value theory (first attempted in studies dated 1894 and 1899) by Graziadei, even though it shows strange affinities with what Marx anticipated, in the *Grundrisse*, with regard to automation. Graziadei considers successively (1925, pp. 201ff.) the cases of 'total monopoly' and 'partial monopoly', including in the latter cartels. For each of these cases he considers, in the manner of Schumpeter, the possibility of a lowering of or even of an increase in costs through monopoly. In its details, his analysis strongly resembles Marshall's exposition; to justify this recourse to 'academic' economics he declares (ibid., pp. 232–3),

The results achieved by economic science [in price theory] up to the present . . . can easily be accepted by Marxists without their jeopardising anything that is really fundamental in their master's teachings. . . . It is legitimate to integrate the core of the economic thinking of Marx with the advances made by 'orthodox' economics. . . . This is a task to be completed by the most well equipped Marxists. Indeed, it will only be possible to preserve the authority of Marxism, which is in danger of being lost in the field of economics proper, if Marxism can effectively answer the 'orthodox' economists, who draw advantages from the undeniable errors in Marxism, and combat the dangerous truths of 'orthodox' economics.

Graziadei saw – in the same way as Oscar Lange did later – one of the basic weaknesses of the Marxian system as lying in the labour theory of value, because of its inapplicability to the analysis of monopoly. This view he had in common with Lederer. He says (ibid., p. 235),

the measure derived [from the labour theory of value] is of no more use when the competitive state gives way to total monopoly or cartels, in which exchange values are, in a permanent and total way, higher. The difference in the level of normal price under conditions of monopoly or cartel compared with the normal price in a competitive situation stands in contradiction to the Ricardian – Marxian theory according to which exchange value (price) must be equally high under competition or monopoly and cartels, where the labour input is the same. In this way the entire modern economic system, which is founded on cartels, would remain outside the confines of this theory.

This criticism is not entirely to the point, in that some socialist theoreticians began early on to discuss the problems resulting from cartelisation.

THE CONCEPT OF MONOPOLY CAPITALISM AS DEVELOPED BY BARAN AND SWEEZY

One of the recent attempts to reformulate Marxian theory with respect to the conditions of 'monopoly', or, rather, 'oligopoly', in modern economic life has been made by the American Marxist economists Baran and Sweezy (1968a). The fundamental concept was actually developed by Baran (1962). This attempt has led to a very acrimonious discussion, for three separate reasons: first, the authors depose the classical Marxian term 'surplus value' in favour of a new term, the 'excess' or 'surplus' seen from an all-embracing social viewpoint; secondly, they renounce the classical Marxian law of the 'tendency of the rate of profit to fall' and set in its place its opposite, the 'theory of rising surplus'; and thirdly, they espouse a version of the theory of stagnation, arguing that consumption (not only mass consumption but also capitalists' consumption) increases more slowly than the 'surplus', because even investment cannot grow rapidly enough to 'absorb the surplus'.

The argument of Baran and Sweezy starts from the microeconomic level. It cannot be said that they were able to offer significant contributions of their own to a reformulation of the Marxian concepts in this area. This is largely to be explained by the fact that the Marxian theory, despite its contribution to certain concepts in industrial economics (especially the calculation of costs) and despite its realistic observations on present conditions of economic life, did not put its main stress on microeconomic problems.

To begin with, both authors criticise older attempts to reformulate Marxian analysis. For instance, they say (1968b, pp. 18–19) that Hilferding tried to introduce monopolies into Marxian theory and did not treat monopoly (or oligopoly) 'as a qualitatively new element in the capitalist economy; rather he saw it as effecting essentially quantitative modifications of the basic Marxian laws of capitalism'.

According to Baran and Sweezy the same applies to Lenin, whose theory of imperialism was largely based on Hilferding's analysis. This is certainly true in so far as Lenin dealt with monopolistic conditions. ' . . . neither he nor his followers pursued the matter into the fundamentals of Marxian economic theory.' Indeed, Lenin, 'in analysing the domestic and international politics of the period . . . gave full weight to the predominance of monopoly in advanced capitalist countries . . . a decisive advance in Marxian theory'. However, they say that Lenin did not bring about a new formulation of this theory, in the sense of a profound analysis of monopolistic conditions. With regard to the basic analysis of the 'laws of motion of capitalism', Marx's theory as expounded in *Capital* continued to dominate without being supplemented, and 'the Marxian analysis of capitalism still rests in the final analysis on the assumption of a competitive economy'.

Here we find certain points in the premises of Baran and Sweezy that give rise to doubts. They argue that,

> If we are to follow the example set by Marx and make full use of his powerful analytical method, we cannot be content with patching up and amending the competitive model which underlies his economic theory. . . . Today, the typical economic unit in the capitalist world is . . . a large-scale enterprise producing a significant share of the output of an industry or even several industries, and able to control its prices, the volume of its production, and the types and amounts of its investments. . . .

The concept of 'monopoly' employed by the authors here is synonymous with the more current term 'oligopoly', as used in the theory of imperfect competition. In this situation it is now of importance that Baran and Sweezy do not apply the traditional notion of surplus value, but instead use their own term, 'surplus'. The difference between the two notions has, all the same, undergone considerable criticism in Marxist circles, and, while this goes beyond the framework of the monopoly and oligopoly debate proper, for it concerns a macroeconomic concept, and not any longer a microeconomic category, it is nevertheless of great importance, since the two authors underpin their notion of 'surplus' with their own version of the stagnation theory. This clearly belongs to the general framework of macroeconomic and dynamic problems and so will not be dealt with here; suffice it to quote the conclusion the authors draw (ibid., p. 113) from their comparison of the different terms:

> Twist and turn as one will, there is no way to avoid the conclusion that monopoly capitalism is a self-contradictory system. It tends to generate ever more surplus, yet it fails to provide the consumption and investment outlets required for the absorption of a rising surplus and hence for the smooth working of the system. Since surplus which cannot be absorbed will not be produced, it follows that the *normal* state of the monopoly capitalist economy is stagnation.

The authors are very explicit in stating (ibid., p. 80) that this 'law of monopoly capitalism, that the surplus tends to rise both absolutely and relatively' is in complete contradiction to the 'classical-Marxian law of the falling tendency of the rate of profit'. This Marxian law of motion can, in anticipation of a deeper analysis, be sketched as follows. Since the share of depreciation increases as a percentage of turnover while value added remains the same or decreases with a sinking share of wages, there is a tendency for a reduction in the rate of profit relative to turnover. Such a development may be counteracted by two different tendencies: either the rate of surplus value, or, in other words, the share of entrepreneurs in value added (or, seen globally, in the net social product), increases, or technical progress in capital-goods industries leads to a decrease in depreciation costs. The struggle between these various tendencies in the context of the business cycle is, for Marx, the decisive element in the capitalist economy.

In their thesis of 'increasing surplus' Baran and Sweezy put the main emphasis on the increase in the share of capitalists in value added. They deny the increase in depreciation costs and treat the problem of technical progress as of secondary importance.

With regard to the first point, one of the most sagacious Marxist critics of their work, Lebowitz, has argued (1966; 1971, p. 58) that the two authors should have conceived their thesis of increasing surplus as a theory of an increasing rate of surplus. It may, however, be possible to exculpate them, for their 'surplus' is as little related to stock magnitudes as is the Marxian rate of profit, but has to be seen as a relative share in the net social product (or national income).

What is of deeper importance is the way in which Baran and Sweezy treat the problem of technical progress. They believe that it will be pushed forward recklessly under competitive capitalism, because 'pioneers' tend to destroy the capital values of other firms. However, under monopoly capitalism, giant enterprises will introduce innovations only if the profitability of existing equipment is not endangered. According to Baran and Sweezy (1968b, pp. 99–103),

> in general there will be a slower rate of introduction of innovations. . . . the introduction of new techniques in a manner which involves adding to productive capacity . . . will normally be avoided. . . . It does not mean that there need be a slowing down of the rate of discovery of new techniques. . . . we should actually expect monopoly capitalism to speed up at a rate of discovery. . . . What the theory does imply is this: under monopoly capitalism the rate at which new techniques will supersede old techniques will be slower than traditional economic theory would lead us to suppose. . . . we should therefore except monopoly capitalism to be simultaneously character-ised by a rapid rate of technical progress and by the retention in use of a large amount of technologically obsolete equipment. . . . under mon-opoly capitalism there is no necessary correlation, as there is in a competitive system, between the rate of technological progress and the volume of investment outlets.

This is the core of the book, that on which the rest of their argument is based. An increasing surplus comes up against restrictive tendencies in the investment sector. With this statement the two authors join a debate which has not yet been fully discussed in 'academic' economics. Some twenty years ago, the present author tried to show (Kühne, 1958, pp. 193ff.) that in its quintessence this debate arrives at the result that under oligopoly capitalism restrictive tendencies prevail. Baran and Sweezy make ref-erence to the analysis of the United States oligopoly capitalism by Steindl (1952, pp. 223ff.) and to the analogous analysis by Sylos-Labini (1957, pp. 165ff.). They themselves, however, do not deal with this subject in any exhaustive or detailed way.

Here lies one of the weaknesses of their argument. It nevertheless is clear that any attempt at a new version of the Marxian analysis is going to come up against the central problem that restrictive tendencies in the investment field may lead to stagnation, not only where the 'surplus' increases, but even more so in the case of a sinking profit rate, which is the 'classical' Marxian hypothesis.

Of course, the innovation thesis of Baran and Sweezy, according to which the 'surplus' tends to grow continuously, depends on the definition chosen. If one considers 'surplus' in the way in which Baran did (1962, pp. 22ff.), difficulties arise where 'effective surplus' only is discussed. Here the notion is identified by the saving activities of society. It is by no means statistically true that saving exhibits an absolutely rising trend. Since Duesenberry (1949) analysed the relative income hypothesis, i.e. the tendency for consumption to increase in the long run with increasing income, it is not at all certain that the share of savings in richer social systems increases automatically in the course of history. If one considers Baran's 'potential surplus', comprised of upper-class consumption, advertising costs in the widest sense, armaments (and 'superfluous administration costs' to some extent) and the non-utilisation of capacity, it must be said that, historically at least, the last category might, in view of the greater tendency towards full employment since 1945 than between the wars, show a certain reduction. It is not quite clear how far the undeniable increase in other categories may counteract this tendency towards a decrease in 'surplus'. In particular, the category of what Baran and Sweezy call 'irrational organization', in the sense of 'superfluous' administrative elements, is dubious, as is the statistical situation in general.

If we consider Phillips's statistical appendix to Baran and Sweezy's *Monopoly Capital* (1968b, pp. 356ff.), the situation becomes still less clear, for Phillips employs a new notion of 'surplus', in the interests of statistical simplification. According to him, the 'surplus' consists of all 'property incomes'; profits, including 'excessive depreciation'; dividends; interest payments; rents, leases and so on; advertising costs ('waste in the business process'); and all government expenses (!). The inclusion of the last category absolutely contradicts Marx's definition of necessary community tasks as given in his *Critique of the Gotha Programme*.

In fact Phillips takes advantage of the 'Wagnerian Law of Increasing State Activity' (Wagner, 1911, p. 727), which has recently been called into question by von Recktenwald (1965, p. 159). To the extent that the law has operated, albeit with certain 'jerks', at the ends of the two World Wars, in the backlog of demand for public goods, (Kühne, 1971, pp. 141–3), the growing surplus, in Phillips's definition, reveals itself simply as the counterpart of growing state consumption. It is by no means useful to include the whole of state consumption in the category of 'surplus' if one wishes to define the 'surplus as the 'difference between what society produces and the costs of such production', i.e. the socially necessary mass consumption. After all, public goods are part of this necessary mass consumption. The cost of public goods cannot, by definition, be part of the 'surplus', but must be part of consumption, which reduces the surplus right from the outset.

Such an attempt at a renewal of Marxian theory, even if it is based on specific concepts of macroeconomics, must nevertheless be supported by microeconomic analysis. Baran and Sweezy tried to provide this in the introductory passages of their book. They do not, however, refer to modern oligopoly analysis in general, which is all the more regrettable as they would have been able to show how clearly it had been anticipated by Marx.

In fact, Baran and Sweezy discuss only one aspect of this analysis: namely, the question of whether modern oligopolistic structures still aim at the maximisation of profits, or whether the policy of 'live and let live' moderates the desire to make profits – the case of the so-called 'soulful corporation', in which, as compared with the profit motive in its pure sense, the motives of turnover, power and security of the firm obtain the upper hand. All this has been examined by authors such as Kaysen (1957) and Mason (1958).

Baran and Sweezy quote at length from Earley, who puts forward the opposite view. Funnily enough, the thesis of moderate profit aspirations would underpin the very theory, that of the 'tendency of the rate of profit to fall', that Baran and Sweezy seek to refute. It is, therefore, not without irony that they refer to the old cry of Marx, 'Accumulate, accumulate! That is Moses and the prophets!'

Here Marx serves, as it were, as witness against Marx, for Baran and Sweezy advance the thesis that the aim of profit maximisation in oligopoly capitalism still exists, since otherwise their thesis of the increasing surplus would be jeopardised. In a collective critique (Bader et al., 1969) it has been argued that the mere existence of monopolies does not increase surplus value as such; it could be drawn from non-monopolised sectors. The same critics argue that the international expansion of American capital hand in hand with low profit rates in the United States proves that monopoly capitalism need not lead to such an increase in 'surplus'. However, the strongest critique of the work of Baran and Sweezy is still that of Lebowitz (1971), according to which (pp. 47, 62–3) the general style of the work, as compared with that of Baran's main work, suffers from the attempt to write a book accessible to the general reader.

Lebowitz is right in saying that the need for a rigorous analysis treating the oligopoly problem from the Marxian point of view still exists.

THE DYNAMICS OF OLIGOPOLY, THE VALUE SCHEME AND THE 'FULL-COST PRINCIPLE' ACCORDING TO DE CINDIO

The Marxian theory of 'production price' presupposes that on the supply side a 'general rate of profit' is included in the calculation of price. This general rate of profit would be calculated not on the sum of wages (v), like surplus value, but on the total sum of costs $(c+v)$. It assumes that the rates of profit of different industries will be equalised.

We nevertheless find in Marx's work, even if only sporadically, that he also considered the possibility of the non-equalisation of the rates of profit.

If the transfer of capital from one 'sphere' to another is either difficult or not at all possible, the various sectors find themselves in the situation of different countries, which, as in the Ricardian theory of comparative costs, suffer from factor immobility. 'Yet with respect to each sphere of actual production-industry, agriculture, mining, etc.–the transfer of capital from one sphere to another offers considerable difficulties, particularly on account of the existing fixed capital' (*Capital*, III, ch. 12, p. 208). This, however, is the typical situation of modern oligopoly markets with 'barriers to entry', such as high capital requirements, know-how, advertising costs, patents, or the threat of competition.

Recent authors have underlined the fact that oligopoly prices in such markets are indeterminate. The oligopoly price contains a strong element of 'price-parameter arbitrariness'. Marginalist formulas, valid under competition and monopoly, fail, because under conditions of oligopoly there is no such thing as a determinate marginal-revenue curve. For that reason modern price theory has resort to the full-cost principle as a formula for calculation. Hall and Hitch (1951) and Andrews (1949) and a whole group of Oxford economists have noted in empirical investigations that oligopolists, particularly where there is a kink in the demand curve, apply a form of calculation that includes a margin. They calculate their profit in relation to the wage bill.

A modern Italian Marxist, de Cindio, has pointed out (1967, p. 101) that 'this analysis of the full-cost formula offers a confirmation of the applicability of the Marxian formula in an oligopolistic market'. Indeed, the value formula, considered as supply price, sets aside the proportionality between the wage bill (v) and surplus value (s), so of necessity leading to differences between industries with regard to profit rates. This is precisely the situation in oligopoly markets. De Cindio here pursues an idea that had already been suggested by Gurland.

The conclusion that de Cindio reaches here is thus the reverse of that of the many Marxists who knew the labour theory of value as applicable only under competitive capitalism. In his view it represents a scheme of calculation which can be applied in the directly opposite case of oligopoly in a manner analogous to the 'full-cost principle'. De Cindio points out that the capitalist competitive system must, according to Marx, lead to an equalisation in the rates of profit, but that a system of oligopoly is characterised by differentiation in the rates of profit, both with regard to the non-oligopolised sector and in the relationship between oligopolised sectors and individual oligopolists.

De Cindio says that in a value calculation it is necessary to renounce the hypothesis of a uniform rate of profit and of uniform wages, because there is supposed to be a 'fixed relationship between the volume of surplus value and the quantity of current labour'. He points out that according to Marx a value calculation would be possible only 'so long as the means of production involved in each branch of production can be transferred from one sphere to another only with difficulty and therefore the various spheres of production are related to one another, within certain limits, as foreign countries or communist communities' (*Capital*, iii, ch. 10, pp. 177–8). De Cindio believes that this is the case in a system of oligopoly.

He could also have referred to other passages – for instance: 'A surplus-profit may also arise if certain spheres of production are in a position to evade the conversion of the values of their commodities into prices of production, and thus the reduction of their profits to the average profit' (ibid., p. 199). All the same, de Cindio concludes (1967, p. 84) that Marx 'has here described in a schematic way the situation of an oligopolistic market, in so far as this market consists of partial markets', and that in such cases the value calculation would be applicable.

De Cindio then discusses in detail the critiques of the labour theory of value and its reformulation by Sraffa, and attempts an approach between the 'full-cost theory' and Marxian value theory. He starts from the fact (ibid., p. 100) that Marx in his value theory expresses the rate of surplus value 'as a multiple of variable capital', while Hall and Hitch in their full-cost theory calculate 'the indirect costs and profit as a percentage relationship to direct costs'. He points out (ibid., p. 96) that even the critics of Marxian value theory

> admit that their critique collapses as soon as one presupposes a uniform organic composition of capital or as soon as one considers a market situation in which the rule of a uniform profit rate does not apply. . . . The first case can be neglected as completely unreal [here we have to point out that as a first approximation it is nevertheless fully justified!] . . . [but] for the second . . . there is the concrete possibility of such markets if one renounces the hypothesis of pure compeititon.

Unfortunately, de Cindio does not examine the main problem in such a value calculation, namely the fact that it would lead to higher rates of profit in sectors that are wage-intensive, a condition that is not typical of oligopolies. He would also, if he really wanted to be realistic, have to drop the hypothesis of equal rates of surplus value. For de Cindio, the theory of surplus value becomes a scheme of calculation: surplus value is a multiple (even in the ratio 1 : 1) of the wage bill, and it is calculated with an additional margin (*Zuschlagskalkulation*). It is also conceivable that such a procedure, which is based on the most important and easily recognised part of direct costs, calculates globally the indirect costs, especially the capital costs, as a sort of gross surplus value mass, in a manner analogous to Kalecki's 'gross-profit principle'.

Quite a number of objections can be raised to de Cindio's theory. To begin with, it utterly contradicts all the traditional ideas not only in the 'academic', but also in the Marxist camp.

According to these theories and to Marx himself, the value scheme cannot be applied to monopolistic conditions. According to the thesis advanced by de Cindio, however, the value scheme is applicable *par excellence* in oligopolistic markets. De Cindio's opinion is based on the fact that oligopolistic markets are fundamentally indeterminate. He believes that he can escape this indeterminacy by allowing his oligopolists to find a resting place in the phenomenon of flight by calculating a margin based on the wage bill. We could, of course, also presuppose the calculation of a profit margin on the basis of all prime costs, including raw materials and the costs of semi-manufactured products. In Marxian terms, however, this would be to include in it part of c, thereby abolishing the proportionality between v and c, which is the core of the value calculation.

De Cindio could find a certain degree of consolation in the argument of Kalecki, who, in the framework of his conception of distribution, attributes a certain importance to raw-material costs. Furthermore, we have to consider that oligopolistic firms are in general strongly capital-intensive. Where effective barriers block entry to the sector in question, oligopolies are capable of holding out – a situation which is due to the fact that high capital requirements deter outsiders from entering the particular sector.

If such enterprises are strongly capital-intensive, it is difficult to imagine that the calculation of their profit margins would then be based on a relatively unimportant part of their total costs – namely, the wage bill. Furthermore, with uniform rates of surplus value over the whole economy and with proportionality between v and s in oligopolistic sectors, this would have the consequence for the latter of low rates of profits. *A priori* this appears to be absurd and it can be presupposed only if the thesis is based on the 'soulful' or socially conscious corporation', i.e. a corporation prepared to accept a lower level of profits than would be attainable in competitive capitalism!

On the other hand, there would of course be the possibility of applying a higher coefficient to the margin on the wage bill if rates of surplus value within the oligopolistic sectors were higher than in others. If the oligopolistic sectors were to concede generous wage increases, it could even be postulated that the quota of value added in these sectors would be higher than in the others. Consequently; over the various sectors there would be uniformity neither of rates of surplus value nor of rates of profit.

The problem of capital-intensity is now linked to the problem of the mark-up coefficient. If, under 'free competition', an entrepreneur calculates his prices according to the full-cost principle, adding a profit margin in proportion to the wage bill or to the share of wages in unit costs, it may be conceived that an oligopolist in a 'strictly co-ordinated oligopoly' would incorporate a correspondingly higher coefficient in his profit margin, because, owing to 'barriers to entry', such a high profit would not attract new competitors into the field.

The crucial argument of de Cindio is that the indeterminacy of oligopoly price makes the wage-bill mark-up calculation the preferred method of oligopolists, and that the calculation will carry over into price. In this case wages would indeed become the plumbline in the creation of value added, and the labour theory of value would experience a renaissance.

The question remains open of whether such a reduction of the problem of value to the level of a mere calculation scheme does justice to Marx's ideas.

THE IMPORTANCE OF OLIGOPOLY CAPITALISM

To sum up, we may draw the following conclusion. If we wish to conceive the Marxian analysis anew, we have to start from the hypothesis that the tendency towards monopoly and oligopoly, which is the consequence of the concentration movement depicted by Marx, has altered not only the quantitative dimensions of the problem but also its qualitative aspects. The latter concern the rôle of the profit; the 'goad of profit', to quote Marx. Besides the pure profit motive, there is built into the Marxian system a drive to accumulate. Marx emphasises again and again that, as soon as the 'goad of profit' loses its strength or becomes dulled, a slackening in investment activity will ensue, which means a crisis or a long-lasting stagnation process. Here there are certain analogies with the Keynesian system. Keynes starts from the hypothesis of 'animal spirits' with regard to investment, but he implicitly recognizes a sort of 'minimum profit' or 'minimum rate of interest', below which the famous Keynesian 'liquidity trap' sets in, and because of which effective demand fails and causes a depression. Marx would speak here of the hoarding of liquid funds.

There now arises the question of to what extent the rôle and function of profit has changed within the modern oligopoly system.

It is possible to consider perfect competition as an atmosphere in which there prevails in the short run an unbridled tendency to maximise profits and this is continually frustrated by an invisible hand. At the opposite extreme there is (in so far as competition from substitutes permits this) 'pure' monopoly, in which long-run profit maximisation is sought.

Between these two extremes there lies a whole spectrum of intermediate forms, as determined not only by the actual realisation of profits, but also by the will to make profits. The more oligopolistic forms approach perfect competition, as, for instance, in 'monopolistic competition', which could be defined as oligopolistic interdependence without consciousness of the fact, the more the tendency towards profit maximisation aims at short-run goals. The 'stricter' and more monopoly-like an oligopoly is, the more the goal of profit maximisation is shifted into the distant future; in other words, profit maximisation in the long run is being aimed at, and, in the interests of this, short-run profits may be renounced.

In this context, one still talks of 'profit maximisation'. However, there has been injected into the debate the idea that other motives and aims will push profit maximisation into the background, so that a 'soulful corporation' may even completely renounce its aspiration for profits.

By accepting a temporarily lower 'normal profit rate', big business would be in a position to reduce the average rate of profit and thus the rate of surplus value, while at the same time raising the share of workers in the social product. The question is whether, in view of the other side of the coin – namely, the monopolistic tendency inherent in big business – such results can be hypothesised.

Meek has warned us (1956a, p. 286) not to overrate the modifications that would be brought about by an introduction of monopoly analysis into the Marxian theory:

> One must be careful, however, not to exaggerate the extent to which the coming of monopoly capitalism has invalidated the traditional analyses based upon the assumption of free competition. Monopoly does not mean the end of competition, and may even at times (e.g. during periods of price war) mean an intensification of competition. And even when actual competition is slight, the fear of potential competition may in many cases induce a monopolist to keep his price at a level which affords him not much more than the 'normal' or 'average' rate of profit.

Meek then quotes Guillebaud, who in his analysis of theories of 'monopolistic competition' (1952) defends (p. 122) the idea that, 'except in those relatively few cases where there is a *high* degree of restriction of entry, and demand is very inelastic, the notion of normal value in Marshall's sense . . . has a large measure of applicability'. Meek then comes to the conclusion that monopoly-price theory should constitute a supplement, rather than an alternative, to competitive price theory. 'But naturally they do not exempt us from the obligation to work out such a theory' (ibid., p. 286).

Here we must warn the reader not to jump to rash conclusions. Even 'soulful' or 'socially conscious' corporations, whose managements might be more interested in market shares and power positions than in profit maximisation, are in a position to obtain much higher profits in 'strict' oligopolies than in oligopolies of a looser character or even in market forms that approach monopolistic or perfect competition. What can be realised, with regard to profit maximisation, in semi-competitive forms of market may lag considerably behind what would remain of profits under conditions of 'strict' oligopoly, in spite of an extensive renunciation of profit maximisation. It would be necessary to make out a whole scale of 'profit maximisations', according to the degree of intensity that prevails in each case.

34 Measuring the Degree of Concentration

How should concentration be measured?

There are three possibilities. First, we could measure the share of the particular firm in the total production of its industry or in the production of a certain product. This presupposes that an industry or a product can be clearly defined, and has the further disadvantage that it is unsuitable for multi-product firms. Secondly, use could be made of the absolute level of turnover, or of value added or of the number of employees, in relation to all other firms in the country or even in the world as a whole. This could be employed for multi-product firms. Thirdly, the degree of competitive encroachment could be used. This could possibly be ascertained, with the help of Triffin's 'cross-elasticities', by means of a price-leadership function or within the framework of the position of a particular firm inside a cartel or a more or less 'co-ordinated' oligopoly.

There is no doubt that Marx tried to measure the tendency towards concentration by applying the first possibility. He had no conception of the multi-product firm that is part of a giant trust, even though we must see in this phenomenon one of the most striking forms of the concentration process. Lenin, in his theory of imperialism, and subsequent authors on the subject of 'monopoly capitalism' (or, as we should say, 'oligopoly capitalism') see in this particularly spectacular form of mammoth enterprise both a welcome object for demonstration and an entity that can easily turn to political domination. These authors consider the cartel as an auxiliary organisation of big business, by which it is dominated.

In trying to verify the concentration movement empirically, one must be clear as to how far the notion of concentration extends. In principle one may agree with Haussmann, who (1940, pp. 71, 81) identifies the tendency towards cartels with concentration in general. Cartels presuppose that the firms involved are conscious of their interdependence, and thus the origin of cartels is almost synonymous with that of oligopoly in the widest sense. On the other hand, strict oligopolies hardly need the legal prop of a cartel in order to reach similar market results.

Haussmann's opinion was supported by Keiser at an early date (1931), and more recently by Lenel (1962, pp. 93ff.). Of opposite opinion are those who in essence consider that the cartel offers a degree of protection to small and medium-size enterprises. This opinion has been rejected particularly by Lenel.

Be that as it may, the problem of measurement loses some of its urgency, for the quantification of cartelisation presents few statistical problems. If we include cartels, the dimensions of the concentration movement are more easily demonstrable. In a statistical examination of concentration processes the reasons for concentration are not significant; they no longer show clearly in the degree of concentration. In practice, some of these methods of measurement have become standard, though they are not without inherent problems.

If cartelisation is considered as a loose form of the Marxian notion of 'concentration', i.e. as a partial 'loss of the individual autonomy' of each firm, it is hardly necessary to make a statistical effort to demonstrate the avalanche of movements towards cartels. The increase in the literature on cartels since the end of the nineteenth century is proof enough. A question that must be dealt with separately is the attitude of socialist economists to this subject. Some of them see in cartels fossilised forms of late capitalism, inevitably leading to further exploitations of consumers, while others see in them early forms of a future 'organised' society. Neo-liberals are in agreement with the former view.

What, however, is really necessary is the statistical verification of the concentration processes proper, i.e. centralisation in the Marxian sense (through takeover or merger) and concentration in the Marxian sense (by means of growth in the individual firm), in the framework of market-dominating, and mostly oligopolistic, firms.

Marxist authors, in trying to prove the concentration thesis by quoting examples, have often tended to take things too easily, for these examples may demonstrate nothing more than the growth in size of some economic giants. What really matters is the growth in market power that comes about by the decrease in the number of firms that share in market domination. At least three different stages have to be distinguished: (1) sheer growth in size, with a more or less perceptible diminution in the intensity of competition; (2) growth beyond a minimum size, which may still permit a certain degree of competition; (3) growth beyond an 'optimum' size (in a technical or cost sense) into monopoly-like dimensions. Growth in the first sense is effectively a fact of life, both in the Marxian conception and according to the dynamics inherent in modern economic life. Growth in the third sense, beyond the 'competitive optimum', presupposes that it is possible to delimit clearly such an optimum market structure.

How far has the Marxian prediction of concentration, i.e. centralisation, been confirmed? The present author has already tried to give a positive answer to this question (Kühne, 1955a).

SAMUELSON'S ATTEMPT AT DENIAL

The problem of concentration in economic life has given rise to an ever-renewing debate, which since the early 1950s has been particularly lively. The controversy has received a new stimulus in recent times from the German cartel law and from the discussion of European integration, which has to an extent made larger dimensions necessary in economic life.

In 1967, in an address to the American Economic Association, Samuelson declared (1967, p. 622) that, with regard to growing monopolisation in capitalism, Marx seemed to have been right in his prophecy for thirty years, 'even though for the next seventy years he does not seem to be borne out by the most careful of researches on industrial concentration'. In other words, Samuelson believes that the Marxian concentration theory was justified for the period 1870 to 1900, but is inapplicable to the twentieth century.

How should such a statement be judged? What are the careful studies concerned with? In this connexion it may be instructive to cast a glance at the so-called 'Adelman controversy' of the early 1950s, in which this question was treated in a most meticulous way.

Earlier discussions were largely of a theoretical character. If more concrete data were required, authors took refuge in more or less incomplete figures, which either were restricted to individual sectors of industry or concerned only isolated cases. Only in recent times, in the United States in particular, have the statistical preconditions for the measurement of concentration effects been satisfied.

THE DEBATE OVER THE TERM 'CONCENTRATION'

Before one undertakes such measurement, one must clarify the ideas involved in the notion of 'concentration'. Not only may the application of different methods of measurement produce different results, but in addition, in the course of time the various methods of measurement undergo certain modifications, which make their applicability appear somewhat doubtful. Any debate on concentration must, therefore, start with a discussion of methodology.

In our times, the discussion of the phenomenon of concentration is overshadowed by a reluctance to pay tribute to the thinker Marx, who was the one to introduce this subject of controversy into the arena of economics. Many reservations are made, of which the most important is usually that the theory of concentration is only partially right, and that Marx overrated in particular the rapidity of the concentration process with regard to capital. One of Marx's most spirited disciples, Bernstein, has introduced into the Marxian schema, following on the appearance in the tertiary sector of numerous auxiliary firms and enterprises, the thesis of the continued existence of medium-size enterprises. What he and others have overlooked, however, is that Marx, as is nearly always the case in his system, is concerned only to pinpoint 'tendencies' and that he himself underlines their contradictory nature. Thus, he speaks of a growing concentration of capitals, accompanied, though to a lesser degree, by a growing number of capitalists.

There are further misunderstandings. In this regard it must again be emphasised that the phenomenon that we know as 'concentration' – a large increase, at the expense of many, in the capital in the hands of one firm – was denominated 'centralisation' by Marx. To him 'concentration' was the 'growth of individual capital' through 'accumulation', i.e. self-finance. (*Capital*, I, ch. 25, pp. 586–7.)

The generous recognition of intellectual priority is the prerogative of the great. Schumpeter thus admits without any reserve (1947, p. 34) that 'to predict the advent of big business was, considering the conditions of Marx's day, an achievement in itself. But he did more than that. He neatly hitched concentration to the process of accumulation or rather he visualized the former as part of the latter, and not only as part of its factual pattern but also of its logic.'

This is the point at which minds divide. On the one side, we have to deal with those who consider factual developments, and on the other those who have devoted themselves to logical argument alone. The majority of Marx's disciples belong to the latter category. They complacently repeat the thesis of their master and occasionally quote a few rapidly collected data. To be just, the majority of his opponents are mostly satisfied with abstract deduction and show that things which should not occur cannot be so bad.

Much smaller is the number of those who have tried to trace out the concentration process by inductive investigations. These are economists with enough statistical and industrial sense to prefer quantification to vague and abstract duels. But quantification runs up against problems which are far more difficult than people imagined at the turn of the century, when science, owing to a lack of available data, had to rely upon 'pure deduction'. As was emphasised in 1960 in the German report on cartels, there are two problems that have to be resolved: first, that of the 'optimum size' for plant *and* enterprise (we have to distinguish sharply between the two), and, secondly, that of the 'normal' or 'representative' enterprise, i.e. the problem of the average size in industries and in the economy itself.

The alarm was sounded by Berle and Means in their epoch-making work (1933) in the wake of the Great Depression. According to them, the 200 biggest corporations in the United States, with assets amounting to $81,000 million, already possessed in the 1930s 57 per cent of the total assets of all companies, 38 per cent of all business assets and 22 per cent of all national assets. The two authors calculated that if the rate of concentration that had prevailed in the period between 1909 and 1929 were to continue, within forty years these 200 giant firms would take over all industrial production in the United States.

It can, of course, be argued that the growth of concentration would have to slow down in the long run: first, because a large part of the economy would already be concentrated, and, secondly, because resistance would increase, especially in sectors of the economy in which concentration was not appropriate. As it happens, the market shares acquired through mergers have decreased considerably since the turn of the century. Stigler argues (1950, pp. 31–2) that 'The new goal of mergers is oligopoly . . . no longer monopoly, and the Sherman Law seems to have been the fundamental cause for the shift. . . .' Kreps, for instance, has calculated (1949, p. 691) that immediately after the Second World War about two-thirds of industrial production in the United States came from sectors in which the four largest firms accounted for more than one-half of production, while one-third was from sectors in which the four biggest firms accounted for more than 75 per cent of production. According to tables compiled by Machlup (1952, pp. 478–81), between 1935 and 1947 there was an increase in the share of production of the four largest firms in twenty-one out of thirty-three comparable industries, and for the rest an increase in the share of the eight largest firms is apparent.

But here begins the real controversy! In an article published in 1951 M. A. Adelman makes a thoroughgoing attempt to disprove the thesis of increasing concentration, at least for the period 1931–3 to 1947.

He stresses that he is interested not in the development of oligopoly, but only in the measurement of concentration as such. He follows the system of industrial classification standard in the United States. After discussing the advantages and disadvantages of possible methods of measurement, he decides in favour of two methods in particular: that based on total assets and that using value added.

Adelman accepts the figures given by Berle and Means for the growth of concentration between 1924 and 1929; he has doubts, however, about the validity of the figures between 1909 and 1924, because he thinks that 'capital dilution' has done a lot to distort the statistical presentation. On the other hand, he advances the work of Berle in that he reaches the conclusion that there was a further increase in concentration between 1929 and 1933. He adds only that the figures cited for this period may be exaggerated: the share in 'durable capital goods' may be greater in the mammoth enterprises than in smaller ones. The total assets of small firms would, owing to the slump in prices and consequent decrease in the value of stocks, suffer a relatively greater reduction during years of depression, and this would lead to a statistical overemphasis of the share of big business.

At any rate, Adelman recognises that concentration did increase during the period of depression 1929–33. It is a known fact that larger companies have relatively larger profits (or smaller losses) in a period of crisis than do small businesses, and in Adelman's view the degree of concentration is bound to increase at times of depression.

His main objection to the prevailing thesis he reserves for the period 1931 to 1947. Here he points out that essential modifications took place in the structure of public-utility enterprises, which after all represent one-quarter of the '200 giant enterprises'. He therefore excludes them from his further comparisons.

Adelman in no way denies that the economy of the United States is strongly concentrated. He thinks, however, that there was a decrease in concentration between 1931 and 1947, and he draws the same conclusion for the whole period from 1901 to 1947. The latter conclusion is all the more challenging as he himself agrees that there was an increase in concentration between 1909 and 1933. It seems rather doubtful that the following fourteen years could produce an overall decrease.

The argument of Lintner and Butters (1950, pp. 46ff.) is essentially that mergers are a less important source of growth for larger than for smaller corporations. This is contradicted by Blair and Houghton (1950). They argue that Lintner and Butters compare only the assets of firms that have been taken over with those of firms active in the field of takeovers. They argue, indeed, that Lintner and Butters should, on the basis of their figures, have arrived at the contrary conclusion: if one considers only firms participating in mergers, then it is true that in 1940–7 mergers were a less important source of growth for larger than for smaller corporations; if, however, one compares the whole population of large and small enterprises and their relative growth, the reverse is the case.

Weston in turn made a counter-attack (1951, pp. 71–3) on Blair and Houghton. It could be the case that the takeover of relatively small companies by giant firms could eliminate the last outsider, thereby paralysing competition. At the same time, the merger of two small firms may only mean that competition was very sharp, and that the two combined in order to survive.

Since then, a number of fresh attempts have been made at finding better methods of measuring concentration. Well to the fore are certain methods based on the 'Lorenz' curve, establishing a ratio between the number of firms (according to size) and their cumulative percentage share in total production, total assets or total number of employees. Here the works of Rosenbluth in particular (see esp. 1955, pp. 57ff.) offer a useful survey. On the other hand, Sylos-Labini (1957, pp. 19ff.) has applied 'Gini' co-efficients to the number of employees, value added and 'assets', demonstrating increasing concentration between 1904–5 and 1938 and in part to 1947.

In this way, the 'degree of oligopolisation' (Scitovsky, 1955, p. 109ff.) in various sectors becomes measurable. On the other hand, this is only a static survey at a point in time and it does not, therefore, give an idea of the dynamic modifications occurring in the concentration process (König, 1959, p. 231). Besides, such a quantification of the notion of concentration does not offer any points of departure for qualifying considerations, which would have to include market behaviour and interrelated phenomena (Schneider, 1960, p. 631). A number of studies have appeared that include some qualifying considerations; the authors in question are not content with formal mathematical relations, but have tried to state the degree of 'intensity of economic categories' (Müller, 1959, p. 6).

Recent studies on the concentration movement within the Federal Republic of Germany are very circumspect in their judgements. This applies, for instance, to Lenel, who completely renounces the use of statistical material, and to the publication by Fürst (1960) within the framework of the large-scale inquiry on concentration by the Verein für Sozialpolitik (Society for Social Betterment).

The 1964 report of the Bundesamt für Gewerbliche Wirtschaft (Federal Office for Industrial Economy) provided useful new statistical data. From this report we learn that in the short period 1954 to 1960 there was a considerable movement towards concentration. Of the thirty sectors of industry examined, with a turnover in 1960 of some DM 250,000 million, twenty-one, with a turnover of more than DM 200,000 million showed an increase in concentration, inasmuch as the ten largest firms increased their share of turnover.

Some American studies, especially that by Rishin (1959, p. 514), point to a further increase in concentration in the United States in the 1950s. Others – for instance, a study by Collins and Preston (1961, p. 1000), – speak of a 'spurious' increase in concentration among the 100 largest industrial firms in the United States between 1948 and 1959. It must be added that Mason (1957, pp. 16ff.), similarly to Adelman, did not succeed in finding a perceptible change in the degree of concentration over the period from the Great Depression to the 1950s. Kaysen in turn found little evidence (1950, p. 88) of a significant increase in concentration up to the end of the 1950s. Gordon, who seemed ready in principle to accept these results, nevertheless stated (1960, p. vi), 'The relative position of the giants has not altered but, in an absolute sense, the area over which they wield their influence is greater'.

During the 1960s, however, an unequivocal increase in concentration was observed in the United States. As Koch and Fenili have stated in a recent study (1971, p. 1041), this may be attributed not least to the fact that 'rapid technical change may create short-run monopoly power, due to invention and innovation which may be used to increase the price–cost margins'.

In Britain, a study by Prais and Hart (1956, p. 119) and other studies by Hart (1957, and 1960, p. 127) find that a significant increase in inequality in the size of firms took place between 1885 and 1939. From 1939 till 1950 (i.e. during the war and just after) this inequality seems to have undergone a slight reduction, only to increase steadily afterwards. More recently, attempts, by the cartel authorities in the Federal Republic of Germany and at the European level, to prevent mergers seem to indicate that concentration tendencies are on the increase. In the meantime, this movement appears to have become of worldwide dimensions, especially in view of the direct investment by giant American firms in activities throughout the world and particularly in Europe.

The study by Rowthorn and Hymer (1971, pp. 25–6, 46, 75–86) investigates the 500 largest firms of the capitalist world (measured by turnover figures), amongst which there are 300 American firms. The smaller of these appear to have grown at a more rapid pace during the period 1962 to 1967 than did the largest. At first sight, this seems to speak against an increase in concentration. But, if we look at it more closely, such a development may be explained in particular by the fact that the smaller giant firms in the United States grew more rapidly than the larger giants, but that overall the giants improved their position through the fact that their international investments increased particularly rapidly. Thus the 200 largest firms over the period 1957 to 1967 grew on average 1 per cent per annum more rapidly than did the domestic economy as a whole.

In the United States, at least one-sixth of the growth experienced by giant firms as a whole for the period 1957 to 1967 is to be attributed to an increase in the share of giant firms in the economy, i.e. to concentration within the national framework, and for the rest a third of the growth in United States giant firms can be attributed to their overseas activities. From 1957 to 1967 the relative importance of domestic concentration grew; it accounted for one-quarter of the total growth of these firms, i.e. the same amount as overseas expansion. 'Towards the end of the period in 1965 and even more in 1966 the share of big firms in domestic production began to expand rapidly.' Concentration represented 29 per cent of the growth of all giant firms. Prior to 1962, United States and British firms lagged behind in growth; since then they have overtaken continental European firms, and 'this relative recovery . . . must largely be attributed to overseas expansion and to the increased concentration in their own countries', though the German recession may have played a rôle in it.

Finally, we should mention an important judgement by Scherer in 1971 with regard to the industrial structure of the United States. Scherer refers to the study by Adelman (1951) and states categorically that

Adelman's results have in the meantime been disproved. Adelman was at fault in making the comparison between the years of depression in the 1930s with the more prosperous late 1950s. In 1933 the share of the largest corporation was abnormally high. . . . The share of the 100 largest manufacturing firms in all main assets rose between 1929 and 1966 by about 12 percentage points on the assumptions of Means (e.g. from 36 per cent to 48 per cent) or by about 7 percentage points on

Adelman's assumptions. . . . Despite uncertainties one thing is clear:
the increasing domestic dominance of the 100 largest manufacturing firms since 1947 is no statistical illusion. . . . [Their share] in value
added rose from 23 per cent in 1947 to 33 per cent in 1966.

CONCLUSIONS ON CONCENTRATION

This short survey has shown the complex considerations that have to be
taken into account in the analysis of the concentration process. From a
more detailed investigation (carried out in the German edition of this
book), the following conclusions may be drawn:

(1) For the period 1900 to 1933, even Adelman accepts an increase in the
    tendency towards concentration, which has been most fully elab-
    orated by Berle and Means; there is unanimity in this finding.

(2) For the period from 1940 to 1950 it seems that concentration
    increased; this was owing to the growth of individual firms (Marx's
    'concentration through accumulation') and not so much to mergers
    (Marx's centralisation').

(3) The studies carried out for the US Federal Trade Commission and
    that of Blair and Houghton appear to show that even between 1940
    and 1950 mergers continued to contribute to concentration, and this
    during a period for which Adelman disputes any increase in con-
    centration and even goes so far as to argue a decrease.

(4) The majority of more recent studies reach the conclusion that up to
    1957–9 the concentration movement in the United States was
    relatively slow; on the other hand, it seems that concentration
    increased in Great Britain and on the continent of Europe until 1939
    and again in the 1950s.

(5) There are clear signs that in the 1960s there was an acceleration in the
    concentration movement in the United States as well as in Europe.
    This was particularly owing to giant international firms.

(6) According to Scherer, Adelman was mistaken in his conclusions on the
    period beginning with the Great Depression and ending in 1950.
    Scherer concludes that the statistics overwhelmingly show that the
    concentration movement speeded up during the 1950s and especially
    during the 1960s in the United States.

It seems to be clear beyond doubt that Samuelson did Marx an injustice
in arguing that he was wrong with regard to the development of concentration in the twentieth century. For the period from 1900 to 1933 and
from 1959 onwards an increase in the concentration movement cannot be

contested, as the most careful studies show. It is only for the period in between, which includes the Second World War, that a slackening in the tendency towards concentration can be assumed. For the last seventy years as a whole, Marx's prediction is right and Samuelson is wrong.

35 The Cartel Debate in Marxism

ARE CARTELS PROMOTERS OF SOCIALISM?

The idea, that cartels and trusts may constitute a 'social element' within the capitalist process is based on some remarks by Marx in the first volume of *Capital*, where he says (ch. 25, p. 588) that 'centralisation' leads to 'processes of production socially combined'. In the third volume he speaks of monopoly as (ch. 27, p. 438) 'the abolition of the capitalist mode of production itself . . . a self-dissolving contradiction', and as such requiring 'state interference'. (Here he anticipates modern anti-trust policy!) In the fourth edition Engels added a few remarks, in which he speaks of monopolistic trusts and cartels as constituting an unsatisfactory 'form of the socialisation of production'. Elsewhere, Engels (1891) gives the cue for a new trend of thought: 'In the trusts . . . the production without any definite plan of capitalistic society capitulates to the production upon a definite plan of the invading socialistic society. Certainly, this is so far still to the benefit and advantage of the capitalists.'

Revisionists have little use for such ideas. In stressing the evolutionary, progressive process of growth towards socialism, they nevertheless seem to indicate a more rapid approach of the 'state of the future'. Such is the case with Bernstein and Schmidt.

Karl Kautsky (1901), however, in developing some of the ideas of Engels (*Capital*, III, ch. 6, p. 142; ch. 27, p. 478), accorded to cartels the task of 'overcoming capitalist anarchy'. It was therefore more the 'orthodox' group in Marxist thought that was of the opinion, as Schönlank put it (1890), that commonweal economy had its roots in the 'associations formed by entrepreneurs on purely capitalist grounds'.

Somewhat later Heiman declared (1899, pp. 773–4) that 'anti-cartels', which were nothing more than the self-defence organisations of consumers trying to counteract the setting-up of cartels, constitute 'in their capitalist co-operative form of enterprise a further step towards the socialisation of production, and thus towards a socialist economic order'.

Cunow (1918) combined these ideas in the conception of the 'higher economic stage'. Similar opinions were expressed in declarations made on the occasion of the Congress of the Social Democratic Party at Kiel in 1927, and even in the programmes put forward by the Free Trade Unions.

A strong section of the party under Naphtali (1931, pp. 35–7) saw in the 'reorganisation of capitalism' and the 'progressive development from free competition to planned production' not a tendency towards the democratisation of the economy in itself, but – quite rightly – an even 'stronger accentuation of the autocratic position of entrepreneurs' (in other words, of leading entrepreneurs). Naphtali and his followers nevertheless believed that this trend towards an organised form of capitalism would offer at least some elements that could serve as an 'impulse in the direction of a more democratic economy'.

Here the basic idea was that it might be possible to create out of cartels a sort of parliament of employers and employees for whole sectors of industry. But this certainly was a misconception: the supporters of this idea did not see clearly enough that cartels were less an expression of 'industrial democracy' than tools in the hands of dominant giant enterprises, which used them for their own purposes.

Engels himself clearly recognise this when he says in *Capital* (III, ch. 6, p. 118, note 16 and ch. 17, pp. 429/32) that 'the trusts have no other mission but to see to it that the small fish are swallowed by the big fish still more rapidly than before'. Schönlank wrote in 1890 that the precondition for the foundation of cartels was that,

> first, a strong process of dissolution has to take place under the impact of which innumerable individual interests have to be annihilated, and the total production handed over to a few capitalists. . . . The concentration of the means of production facilitates the activities of cartels, and these for their part dissolve and absorb at an accelerated pace weak capitalist existences.

In this sense it is, of course, possible to consider the process of cartelisation as a 'further step in evolution', for, contrary to some of its apologists, it by no means acts to preserve small properties, but, rather, offers dominant large firms the best basis for the elimination of smaller capitals by control over the inner circle of the cartel, and by dictating prices and quotas and forcing outsiders out of business.

Schönlank says, 'Cartels represent associations of entrepreneurs in charge of large industrial enterprises, and they are based on the accelerated absorption of small capitals.' If small individual entrepreneurs had hardly any say in these cartels, the only form of protest available to them was to leave the cartel, and this possibility was often closed to them because of legal obstacles. How, then, could it be expected that the representatives of the workers would be given a chance to introduce a sort of 'democratic joint decision-making' into cartels, in the face of the giant firms which as a rule dominate them? The idea that cartels were a first stage towards socialism was, after all, misconceived. Its supporters thought that *any* organisational form would be identical with the notion of 'planning', for the simple reason that 'planning' presupposes organisation.

THE STATE AS AN OBJECT OF OLIGOPOLY CAPITAL

Organisations of any kind can certainly offer points of departure for superior goals. This is valid not only for cartels, though it cannot be denied that the totalitarian system of National Socialism made use of them, as it did of so many other forms of organisation, only to jettison them the moment it had its own channels for directing the economy (Ritschl, 1948, II, p. 268). It is a matter of course that any organisational form can be used under pressure from without for purposes which are completely alien to those for which it was introduced: thus a wrestling club could, if the need arose, be mobilised to reinforce an auxiliary police force. The history of many a successful putsch is full of such examples!

At bottom cartels are the expression of private initiatives in organising the branch of industry in question, and of aspirations towards particular advantages for a certain branch or group, for which reasons they cannot be identified with a central will to direct economic life. Rather than objects for use in the cause of some political–economic conception, they are active factors striving after results on quite a different plane.

One cannot deny that the modern tendency towards concentration represents a decisive stage in economic history, and that it is true that the mere fact that there is such a thing as organisational mergers in particular sectors of the economy may be seen as a starting point in the direction of a reorganisation of the whole economy. Nevertheless, it should not be forgotten that, especially with the rise of large-scale conglomerates, only the technical side of concentration gives a helping hand to co-ordination.

The shrinking number of entrepreneurs – in modern terms, the competition of the few – is the precondition for the creation of cartels: this had been recognised before the turn of the century. Today we speak of 'oligopoly'. It is stressed that the strategic manoeuvres of a small group of powerful enterprises fighting each other show a certain similarity to the strategy developed by Clausewitz. This state of the coexistence of a few large-scale enterprises, oligopoly, creates at the same time the preconditions for an encroachment upon the political sphere. If early socialists branded the state as the instrument of the bourgeoisie, the movements of modern workers would be well advised to recognise in oligopoly in its higher organisational form of the cartel a modern and more effective form of economic domination. It is the influence which large oligopolies have on the state that explains why the state is very often degraded to be the lackey of its creatures, the cartels!

The water-tight separation of the businessman's personality into that of an 'economic man', a 'political man' and probably several other men, is a legitimate simplification under atomistic competition and even for small oligopolists, where any isolated political action they may take cannot possibly have any appreciable effect on their market position. The market situation and the price of the commodity can, therefore, be quite well explained by concentrating attention on the purely economic activities of the firm. . . . But when we come to the big oligopolists, who *do* have the power to change the market situation by their own political action, then the separation of the economic from the political must necessarily result in a very incomplete picture, which will not suffice for giving us a reasonable explanation of oligopoly price.

Rothschild, of the Austrian Institute for Economic Research, whose words these are (1947, pp. 317–8), stresses that there is no sense in discussing only the vast expenses of modern giant concerns for advertising purposes and never mentioning 'the sum spent for exactly the same aims in the lobbies. For the gap that divides selling expenditure from political activities is methodologically much smaller than the one that divides the former from production costs proper.'

But as cartels are, in the last resort, nothing other than the extended arm of leading oligopolists or large concerns, they become at the same time one of the decisive factors of modern capitalism, instead of being elements to overcome capitalism, as many early socialists were prone to believe.

Cartels and concerns, the two complementary varieties of concentration, have become a kind of political fighting unit. Far from bringing about a transition towards a socialist society, they turn out to be an instrument for the ascendancy over the state of a policy to maintain capitalism; an instrument that is more direct and effective than action by the much-fragmented bourgeois middle-classes could ever have been.

CARTELS AND CONSUMERS

As early as the turn of the century, Karl Kautsky remarked (1901) that, as a consequence of cartels and their tendency to lead to high prices, workers as a class had more to lose in the political arena and at an economic and social level in their capacity as consumers than they would gain as individuals in their rôle of producers. Kautsky fully recognised that cartels solve the problem of 'scarcity in times of abundance' only by eliminating abundance. The ideology proclaiming a scarcity of commodities was even praised as a universal remedy for capitalist difficulties. To a worker capable of logical reasoning during the intense social struggles towards the end of the nineteenth century, this must have appeared as a further contradiction inherent in the system. Brentano, who engaged in social politics, found it impossible to overlook the danger that monopoly power could be used for 'the oppression of the public', but thought (1889) 'it might be enough to threaten cartels with the reduction of customs duties in order to ward off any serious abuses'.

Schönlank castigated this opinion as the 'pathetic doctrine of free-traders, who are diligent representatives of mobile capital'. The possibility of international cartel agreements was completely disregarded by Brentano, and the consumers' point of view received too little attention in the debate. Nobody dared to draw the conclusion that the consumer should tighten his belt in order to give cartels the opportunity to reach a 'higher economic stage', thus making life easier for his descendants, i.e. consumers in a future socialist society.

The negative effects of cartels affected not only the working class as final consumers, but also non-cartelised industries, which in their capacity as buyers of the products of cartelised industries suffered from their monopolistic price-dictatorship. The variety of their products and the difficulty of fixing uniform price norms for them meant that they were incapable of offering 'opposition' with a cartel of their own. Finally, the creation of 'cartel rents' in the global economic framework led to the improvement or at least to the maintenance of the 'total profits' of entrepreneurs, i.e. of the share of profits in the social product, which would then reduce the effective or at least the potential share of the working class as a whole and of all other groups as well – the famous 'third persons' of Rosa Luxemburg. From a general view this would hold good even if in individual cases a monopoly firm or a cartelised activity could try to 'bribe' its workers with relatively high wages financed from monopolistic profits.

Marx indicated the possibility (*Capital*, III, ch. 50, p. 861) that, 'should the commodity having the monopoly price enter into the necessary consumption of the labourer', pressure might be exercised on (real) wages. In her main work (1921), Rosa Luxemburg drew the conclusion (p. 434) that the pressure exercised by cartels must influence the distribution of income to the detriment of the working class.

After the Second World War the problem of monopolies and cartels was the subject of a thorough study by one of the leading authorities on social politics and economics, Lederer. He saw (1927) the danger that the monopolisation of the economy through pressure of wages combined with maintenance of prices at a high level, might cause the consumers' relative share in the social product to be reduced and that of the receivers of monopoly income to rise. Here one is reminded of Joan Robinson's dictum (1949, p. 76) that the working class 'is ground between the upper and the nether millstones of monopoly and monopsony [i.e. the monopolistic position of employers in their double capacity as sellers of goods and buyers of labour]'.

This view seems to be contradicted by the fact that the relative share of workers has remained approximately stable in most countries for the past half century. Is this conditioned by the counteracting activities of trade unions? Kalecki thinks (1930, pp. 30ff.) that the explanation may be that the increase in the degree of monopoly in economic life and the rigidity of prices facing consumers have been counterbalanced by a steep decline in the prices of overseas raw materials and foodstuffs. All these effects are bound to cease one day, and this will then lead to the consequence that any increase in monopolisation will necessarily lead to a shift in the distribution of the social product in favour of monopoly profit and to the detriment of the share of wages.

CAN CARTELS BE STABILISING IN THE BUSINESS CYCLE?

Engels and Karl Kautsky have both emphasised that the 'disproportionalities' inherent in the capitalist system, in other words the tendencies to bring about a crisis, cannot be eliminated by the existence of cartels. In the period prior to the First World War the opinion became widespread that cartels might indeed exercise a 'regulating and stabilising' effect. These arguments came from liberal advocates of cartelisation and revisionists and to some extent from circles related to trade unions. It was Brentano who influenced the latter. As early as 1889 he advanced the idea that cartels might avert not only 'overproduction, but also its consequence, namely stagnation in sales', and he believed that 'with protection against foreign and domestic competition' it might be possible to eliminate 'any excuse against granting wages that would allow workers to live'.

Brentano even went so far as to express the hope that the 'reserve army of the unemployed might disappear' and that the pressure of a crisis would be ineffective with regard to unemployment, because the 'managements of plants would no longer be obliged to dismiss workers when orders were short'. Bernstein, as leader of the 'revisionists', saw in cartels (1899, pp. 70ff.) a force that might help to diminish 'the effects of local or particular disturbances on the general business situation' in such a way that 'at least for a considerable time a "general business crisis", as it had occurred in former times, could be considered to be improbable'. Not only did he ascribe goals to monopoly associations, but he even thought they might be capable of 'reducing the danger of a crisis'. Finally, this belief took root in the one-sided opinion of Calwer, who in the *Sozialistische Monatshefte* in 1907 argued that social democracy should do all it could to further cartels, because they exercised a 'regulating and stabilising' effect.

Even in international Marxism the idea of the mitigating effect of cartels on a crisis found in Tugan-Baranowsky a representative. The French Marxist Laurat criticised him for turning away from Marxian analysis and inclining towards a 'bourgeois'-inspired thesis.

Schönlank (1890), in spite of recognising cartels as a historical development stage aimed at organising and 'increasing the continuity of business', was nevertheless aware that any hopes placed in them as aiding stabilisation had to be regarded as questionable. To be sure, the syndicated industries (he means their profits) would no longer be hit to the same extent as the atomised, but Brentano's idea that cartels might help prevent unemployment was a big mistake. 'The fight against overproduction is fought by means of a reduction in the output of commodities, i.e. numerous workers are going to lose their employment. . . . Any step forward towards cartelisation will not reduce the industrial reserve army, but add to it ever-growing contingents.' According to Schönlank, 'cartels would be the best troop of engineers' to undermine the social system; cartels were as such already a source of crisis, albeit that Brentano believed that they might insure workers against crises.

On the other hand, even Schönlank's argument is not without its contradictions. He thought that it was the 'Utopia of the petty bourgeoisie' to demand 'police action against cartelisation'; yet he himself demands, in view of cartels' superior power, effective legislation against them, in order to safeguard the social position of the workers. Even Bernstein was afraid that the working class might fall 'into a new and even stronger bondage' as a consequence of the economic power held by cartels. His thesis of the mitigating effect of cartels on crises was challenged eight years later by Rosa Luxemburg, in a series of articles that appeared in the *Leipziger Volkszeitung*. Above all she stressed that the 'beneficial effects of cartels'—i.e. the maintenance of profits in individual branches of industry—would be largely offset by their consequent dumping activities in the world market. She saw in the tendency to throttle production a factor capable of deepening a crisis.

A real understanding of the crisis-intensifying effects of cartels began with the thorough analysis by Hilferding (1909, ch. 15, ff), which supplies the decisive points of departure for modern Marxism. Hilferding argues that, if the tendency to throttle investment really is inherent in monopoly enterprises, this would have a negative influence in times of depression, when new capital investments are scarce. He clearly recognised that with the onset of a general depression and with a decline in total effective demand, cartels, in order to maintain price levels within their own sectors, cannot but cause severe slumps in prices within the non-cartelised sectors, because declining purchasing power must have its effects somewhere. 'Cartels do not diminish the effects of crises. They modify them in so far as they transfer the impact of a crisis onto non-cartelised industries.' If, finally, the cartel collapses in times of depression because of outsiders, the decline in the artificially maintained price level will be even more abrupt. Where a cartel is able to pull through a crisis, it will, by truncating tendencies towards a boom, because of excessively high prices, thus preventing replacement investment at more favourable prices, render life more difficult within the sectors producing investment goods. For example, given the importance of heavy industry for the economy as a whole, high prices for steel in times of depression would have much the same effects as the maintenance of high rates of interest by the central bank, which in this way would aggravate the difficulty of procuring capital for recovery purposes. Firms wanting to buy machinery would be deterred by high steel prices.

Hilferding (1909; 1947, pp. 403ff.) draws the conclusion that it is wrong to believe that 'it would be possible to escape from anarchy by establishing control measures on a piecemeal basis'. Only by subjecting all production to central control would it be possible to eliminate the fluctuations of the business cycle. Here there emerge curious correspondences between Marxist and neo-liberal thinking. In the latter camp we find such a renowned economist as Robbins making the following ironical statement (1935, pp. 145–7):

> But 'planning' – ah! magic word – who would not plan? We may not all be socialists now, but we are certainly [nearly] all planners. . . . The problem of planning is not to be solved by giving each industry the power of self-government. . . . This is not planning; it is syndicalism. It merely extends to whole industries the right to make plans for themselves similar to the right already enjoyed by individual entrepreneurs.

The breakdown of the economic system into a number of coexisting cartel blocs must necessarily lead to greater frictions than exist in the flexible units of an approximately competitive system. This fact becomes all the more obvious when we consider the extent to which these power blocs impede all attempts at indirect regulation, especially through monetary and credit policy, which is after all the most flexible instrument of control from the centre. Hilferding emphasises (1909; 1947, pp. 309ff.) that with cartelisation prices cease to be 'an objectively determined magnitude'. Any attempt to revive business by means of a transition from the price system to quantitative control is wrecked on the 'arithmetical problems of those who determine it by their own conscious willpower'. In other words, whereas the individual capitalist may be receptive to central direction, a cartel may have the effect of falsifying, neutralising and paralysing the regulatory influences, of central economic policy. All this may render an effective business-cycle policy impossible. 'The disturbances in the regulation of prices, which finally cause a disproportionality, will not be diminished by cartels but will be increased.' 'Cartels do not abolish the effects of a crisis. They only modify them, passing the burden on to non-cartelised industries'. (Hilferdung, 1909; 1947, p. 405).

THE TEST CASE OF ECONOMIC CRISIS

All these ideas were put to the test during the Great Depression. Dobb pointed out (1947, pp. 323–4) that during the Great Depression in

Germany 'the fall in price of cartel-controlled products was only about a third as great as that to which goods on free markets were subject'. Price decreases in producer goods were much lower than in consumption goods, which was exactly the opposite of the situation during the recession of 1907–8. On that occasion the prices of producer goods fell, as compared with those of consumer goods, by twice as much in the United States, and by three times as much in Germany. Dobb thinks that the maintenance of the price level through cartels or agreements that aim at securing the profit level is proof enough of the 'fossilisation of industrial structure'. The 'fear of productive capacity' leads to the consequence that 'the industrial reserve army will be recruited by deliberate restriction of production'. It was this that made the crisis so protracted and painful. There was, after all, only the choice between price cuts and the restriction of production, if profits were to be maintained. Cartel capitalism must in general not only exercise pressure on the share of wages, but also 'make for a deepening of slumps and a curtailment of periods of recovery' and 'aggravate the long-term problem of chronic excess-capacity and unemployment'.

Lederer (1927) had arrived at similar conclusions before the Great Depression. Through monopolisation, especially cartels, 'the tempo is increased with the result that the period of boom is shortened' and 'the period of depression lengthened'. The disturbance of the economic process as a whole is inevitable. The recognition of this was, especially in 'bourgeois' economics, of epoch-making character.

Two later Marxists who have advanced this analysis are the Frenchman Laurat and the American Sweezy. Laurat pointed out (1939) that monopolisation, 'far from reducing the capitalist contradictions, had forced it to the other extreme'. Sweezy, who is well known for his work on oligopoly, pointed (1942, pp. 277, 285) to the tendency in monopoly to intensify 'technologically conditioned' unemployment and to increase the severity of depression. Even if one does not take into account the unfavourable effects of the augmenting of profit shares in the social product on mass consumption, 'besides intensifying the old contradictions of the accumulation process, monopoly introduces new ones'.

CONSEQUENCES FOR ECONOMIC POLICY

At the height of the Great Depression, the same ideas induced Löwe (1931, pp. 57ff.), who conducted research into the business cycle, to smash the illusions of many socialists of the past, illusions which had led to 'a distorted ideology in the workers' movement' and which were nourished by popular science. 'One of the most important lessons of the World Depression should be the recognition that the dream of progressively transforming a private monopoly economy into a commonweal system through the instrument of economic democracy is, in view of the dominating political and economic opinion, a delusion.' Instead there had been a tendency for cartelisation to spread and for customs agreements to increase, 'while it became clearer than ever that the bureaucratic forms of late capitalism were in a position to paralyse the creative forces of the market, while being, on the other hand, incapable of offering any element for the creation of a socialist economic system'. Löwe stresses that any attempt to favour or tolerate the self-destructive forces of the system would by no means bring about progress towards a socialist ideal state, but would introduce the danger of chaotic conditions and of a 'regression to primitive economic structures'. He therefore demands that the working class should 'fight for a market system that is free from all monopolistic distortions in order to smooth the way to a future commonweal system'.

Similar considerations led Naphtali to formulate the ideas expressed in an annex to the Free Trade Union programme *Wirtschaftsdemokratie* (Economic Democracy), published in 1928. In this he speaks of 'the intensification of the phenomenon of crisis through the price-fixing agreements of cartels and trusts' and goes on to argue that the demand by trade unions for the 'public control of cartels and trusts and all kinds of monopolistic price-fixing agreements' should be supported anew. Neumann's demands (1930, pp. 773ff.) are of the same form. He castigates the 'complete breakdown of the cartel policy of the [German] Ministry of Economics' and, even though he does not fully recognise all the aspects of the problem, repeats the old trade-union and socialist call for an independent control office to be established. Present-day requirements and achievements represent nothing more than the clear continuation of this line of development, albeit they are described in a more precise, modern fashion.

The thesis that it would be better to allow the self-destroying forces of capitalism to exhaust themselves within the confines of a cartel cannot be acceptable to modern socialism, to the extent that it has taken over from revisionism the hope of a revolutionary transformation of society, and from Marxist orthodoxy (including the bourgeois-oriented theory of the business cycle) the sober recognition that the present system is prone to crisis. Whereas the individual planning of single entrepreneurs can disturb the economic system as a whole, the planning of individual groups combined in cartels and trusts is capable of creating much greater disturbance. Organised group egoism may lead to group anarchy and threaten the operation of policy instruments, especially in the field of money and prices.

If modern socialism wishes the economy to remain flexible and yet responsive to central directives – in the sense of 'as much freedom as possible, as much planning as necessary' – and to withstand the pressure towards nationalisation of whole sectors, it is compelled to ensure (more so than neo-liberalism, whose will to direct is limited to individual measures conforming to the system) that the sectors of the economy should not be able, through the formation and operation of cartels and combines, to obtain immunity from the influence of the state. This explains why a number of leading lights of modern socialism are opposed to cartels, which not only introduce dangerous disruptive elements into the modern economic system, but, in addition, are like sand in the driving gear of the type of economic policy that renounces brutal bureaucratic pressure as a tool of control, and that prefers to work through subtler channels, remaining sensitive to conditions, needs, and reactions to policy.

Even if the influence of cartels and trusts in the political sphere is repulsed, there remains the economic problem. If we want to introduce into economic life an element of organic planning, in conscious opposition to the totalitarian command economy, we must, first of all, see to it that the 'planning' of cartelised groups and big trusts, which could split the whole economic structure into power blocs isolated from each other, is eliminated. After all, such group planning means that there are numerous centres of resistance and retarding elements, which form obstacles to centralised management by the state and to a system of planning. Any return to the competitive conditions existing prior to 1870 is certainly impossible. But if competition continues to be eliminated – as is happening within the present economic structure even without legal sanction for the existence of cartels – this must lead to severe new obstacles to the process of bringing the economic system under responsible management. Despite widespread recognition of this, following the ideas of Marx and other leading socialist thinkers, this is a message which modern socialism must drive home.

36 Monopolisation and Instability

The problem of concentration has, therefore, to be seen in a new light. For Marx it was in essence a question of the transformation of the economic structure, an attempt to overcome the anarchic multiplicity within the capitalist system in order to bring into being large units and facilitate the self-elimination of capitalism and the rise of new structures.

In so far as concentration brought about a trend towards firms of 'optimal' size, it was possible that it would cause improvements and so anticipate a better world of the future – for it could be seen as a partial socialisation of the structure. On the other hand, there was the fact that according to strict capitalist rules this served to denature economic development. Criticism thus came both from the socialist and from the capitalist side. The argument put forward contained three main points.

First, if the notion of concentration is equated with a strengthening of the element of monopoly, if not of the degree of monopoly in the economy on the whole, the consequence must be that the element of exploitation becomes stronger and that the imbalance in distribution is greater than ever. (Lexis's argument concerning the annihilation of the middle classes posits, by contrast, a reduction in the degree of monopoly.) Secondly, the element of monopoly may increase business-cycle fluctuations. In the long run, monopolistic tendencies either bring about stagnation of investment activities or place obstacles in the way of technical progress. This is the argument advanced by Lederer. Thirdly, as Hilferding points out (1909/47, pp. 354, 402ff.) monopolistic tendencies raise the danger of inflexibility, especially in the prices sector.

All this may lead to the prolonging of depression and to greater difficulties in recovery from depression.

STEINDL'S THEORY

The Austrian economist, Steindl, who taught in Oxford cannot strictly be considered a Marxist. However, the fact that at the end of his *magnum opus*, after having set out his 'long-run theory of investment', he relates the latter to the Marxian theory of capital accumulation shows to what extent he is influenced by Marx, even though he is not at all ready to submit to this influence. He is also strongly influenced by Keynes and by Alvin Hansen's 'stagnation theory'. Hansen, as he himself emphasised, was influenced by Tugan-Baranowsky, who in turn owed a debt to Marx.

Steindl has summarised his basic ideas as follows (1952, pp. 223–5):

> In earlier parts of this book the suggestion has been made that the growth of monopoly in the economy may have an adverse influence on investment, and that it may bring about a decline in the rate of growth. For this there are two arguments. First the growth of monopoly should lead to an upward shift of the profit function. . . . As a consequence of this, utilisation should fall, and the adverse effect of this fall of utilisation on investment might bring about a decline in the rate of growth. The other argument runs as follows: if competitive conditions in an industry are superseded by 'monopolistic' conditions, which means few large units, and impracticability of gaining markets at the expense of competitors, then the fear of excess capacity in such an industry becomes greater.

Steindl admits that the first argument is not fully conclusive. It would apply only if 'the response of investment to utilisation [is] sufficiently large in comparison with . . . the reinvestment factor'. He is convinced, however, that his second argument is subject to no such limitation. 'Our second line of argument therefore does not require any quantitative condition. An increased fear of excess capacity, due to the transition to monopoly, will always reduce the limiting rate of growth.'

Steindl's argument can be combined with Marx's reasoning in the following way: oligopolistic competition leads to ever-growing concentration, until, finally, a high degree of oligopolisation is reached. This in turn means that the rate of surplus value in the respective industries must increase. In the eventuality of an oligopolistic fight, each oligopolist has, as it were, a whole arsenal of weapons to hand, in the form of productive capacity, and struggles of this type usually end up with a standstill in price competition, while technical progress goes on. All this then leads to the development of over-capacity. Up to this point Steindl's second argument fits in fully as a continuation of the Marxian theory of concentration. His first argument would be derived from the increase in the rate of surplus value, which in oligopolised branches of industry would be identical with an increase in the rate of profit. It seems to be more difficult to insert this into the Marxian scheme of ideas if one takes into consideration the theory of the 'tendency of the rate of profit to fall', which has still to be examined.

In this context we should not forget that among the 'counteracting tendencies' envisaged by Marx was a rise in the rate of surplus value because of technical progress, which he thought would be 'capital-using'. In Marx's hypothesis of increasing productive capacity, i.e. growth of c in relationship to *v*, the idea of the development of monopolistic or oligopolistic giant firms with a high capital-intensity is already present, in embryo.

Steindl, however (ibid., pp. 225, 191), combined with his first argument the idea of a cumulative process of retardation: 'a fall in the rate of growth must reduce utilisation, and this should again reduce the rate of growth and so on'. He then raises the question of whether such a cumulative process of regression would not find a lower natural limit at 'the new rate of growth at which the system settles down'. He denies that it would and thinks that 'a "long cycle", combined with a negative trend' would come into being. He further thinks that such a negative trend can be recognised in capital formation in United States since the turn of the century. The discussion of these problems leads beyond the problem of concentration and reaches into the dynamics of business cycles and growth, which we shall examine later.

BARAN AND SWEEZY ON THE TENDENCY TO CURTAIL INVESTMENT

As it happens, modern Marxists such as Baran have taken up Steindl's argument. Baran has dealt (1962, p. 64) with 'the problem of the impact of monopoly and oligopoly on the volume and the long-run effect of investment'. This concerns the restrictions that might ensue from an oligopolisation of economic life. According to Baran (ibid., p. 79), such restriction may already be seen, even if the analysis is limited to the static domain, in the fact that 'under conditions of monopoly and oligopoly there may be a strong tendency to wait with outlays on new equipment until the technological conditions have become more or less settled, or to suppress technological advance until the existing equipment is written off'.

In this context we must not forget Schumpeter's counter-argument, that giant firms of oligopolistic character are the spearhead of technical progress, and that under competitive conditions no one could ever hope to keep an advantage long enough to make research and innovation pay. Baran (ibid., pp. 72–3) objects to this thesis that

in the competitive world . . . the transition to the new, technologically improved method of production is not a matter of discretion for the competitive firm. Only at the peril of its extinction can it disregard the available possibilities of cost reduction. . . . 'The devil catches the hindmost'. . . . In this way excessive productive capacity tends to become eliminated. . . .

Under oligopoly, which frequently degenerates into price leadership and cartel-like formations, there prevails, by contrast, the principle 'of live and let live. . . . High-cost firms are not thrown out of the market. . . . Excess capacity in turn discourages new investment' (ibid., p. 82).

Baran develops some points from Sweezy's *magnum opus*. Sweezy argued (1942, pp. 275–6) that a monopolist's investment policy cannot be determined by the average rate of profit or by the rate he might get on new investment, but 'by what we may call the marginal profit rate, that is to say the rate on the additional investment after allowance has been made for the fact that the additional investment, since it will increase output and reduce price, will entail a reduction in profit on the old investment'.

In this context we must mention Sweezy's considerable contributions to oligopoly theory (1939, pp. 568ff.). He developed the concept of the 'kinked demand curve', which has been well received by 'academic' economists, before he risked his reputation by defending Marxist ideas. According to the concept of the 'kink', price under oligopoly will settle at a traditional level, which will hardly move, even under the impact of considerable cost changes. Each participant knows that others will immediately follow suit if he lowers his price, so that no market shares will be gained, while anyone trying to go it alone in increasing his prices will risk losing his entire share of the market, because others will not follow him in this game. It must not be forgotten that similar ideas were developed almost simultaneously, in the 'full-cost theory', by a group of Oxford economists.

As the present author has pointed out elsewhere (Kühne, 1958, pp. 67ff.), there are certainly many possible forms of oligopoly, but all of them seem to present, as compared with 'looser' market forms with similar cost structures, certain restrictive tendencies. Macroeconomics is interested in the question of whether the restrictive element or the progressive element prevails under oligopoly. It is not possible, however, to give a satisfactory answer to this question without reverting to microeconomic price and market analysis and also to the theory of business cycles and the theory of growth.

In their famous joint work, Baran and Sweezy (1968, p. 224ff.) shortly before the untimely death of the former, developed these ideas further. Their main conclusion was that under oligopoly, which is becoming more and more typical of our modern economy, investment activity and investment outlets are to some extent restricted. According to the two authors, a certain stagnation in investment activities made itself felt after 1907, and that this was subsequently overcome was entirely due to the 'technique of destruction' developed in two world wars, to two successive waves of motorisation and to a further wave of 'suburbanisation'.

Baran and Sweezy (ibid., pp. 22ff.) compare this tendency with their particular brand of 'surplus', which had originated with Baran. 'Surplus' goes far beyond Marxian 'surplus value', for it embraces even 'inessential' parts of production or services, including advertising and armaments, and also 'potential' production which, owing to underutilisation of capacity, to recessions and to depressions, does not materialise. Baran and Sweezy (ibid., pp. 61ff.) also advance a 'law of rising surplus', which may very well be compared with the tendency of the rate of surplus value to rise, one of the 'counteracting tendencies' in Marx's law of the tendency of the rate of profit to fall.

This problem cannot be further discussed in the present context. We must admit that Baran and Sweezy follow their own logic in assuming (ibid., p. 80) that the tendency towards increasing monopolisation and oligopolisation corresponds to an increasing surplus, which they sometimes simply identify with an increasing share of profits in the gross national product. Phillips, who produced a statistical appendix for their book (ibid., pp. 355ff.) simplified the notion still further by combining property income, 'waste' and government expenses under the same heading of 'surplus'.

Numerous Marxists have attacked Baran, Sweezy and Phillips for the curious notion of 'surplus' that they employ (Botta, 1971) – all the more so as it flatly contradicts Marx's law of the tendency of the rate of profit to fall. At any rate, the conclusion Baran and Sweezy draw depends on this antinomy: macroeconomic stagnation results from a tendency to throttle investment in the face of an overabundant supply of savings. In this respect, their theory might almost be considered a late version of under-consumptionist reasoning, although the under-consumption concerns capitalists' investment or government spending and not, any longer, private consumption.

The process of concentration is the result and manifestation of the inner dynamics of capitalism, and these Marx analyses in dealing with growth and business cycles. Technical progress, an increasing share of investment goods in total production and processes of social transformation lead to a general predisposition towards instability and towards a transition to new economic and social structures. This is the final message of Marxian economics: the laws of motion of capitalism inexorably lead to its self-destruction.

Incidentally, Marx was not the only revolutionary thinker who around the middle of the last century foresaw the coming concentration movement; as Mondolfo has pointed out (1948, pp. 191ff.), similar predictions are to be found in Mazzini's works. 'Unrestricted competition which is not tempered and bridled by association inescapably sanctions economic domination by a few rich men . . .' (cited ibid., pp. 232–3). Mazzini drew a negative conclusion. He thought that 'the exaggerated anomalous development of concentrated industry must be condemned'. He flirted with approval of cartels as a panacea.

Marx, by contrast, arrived at a positive conclusion: he argued that the future would bring 'the expropriation of the expropriators'. As an alternative to such changes in the social structure, there was, he glimpsed, the danger of 'refeudalisation', through the apotheosis of the giant corporation. Stoleru (1969, p. 402) found in the features of capitalism most strongly criticised by Marx – for instance, its tendency to put a brake on investment, to squander forces of production and to spend extravagantly, especially for advertising purposes – parallels with some of the most negative traits of feudal society. The problem of investment leads us to examine its vehicle: money.

Part VIII
Money and Credit

37 The Marxian Theory of Money in the Light of 'Academic' Criticism

The existence of money is a precondition and instrument for the dynamic development of an economic system, though in itself money can be analysed first within that framework of static theory. It was Schumpeter who advanced the view that Marx's contribution to monetary theory was slight, and inferior to that of Ricardo. Modern authors are inclined to agree. Fritsch, for instance, says (1968, p. 120), 'Because of its connexion with the particular theory of value . . . the Marxian theory of money is, seen from the standpoint of pure monetary theory . . . one of the theoretically weakest parts of the whole system.'

On the other hand, the Marxian theory of money is distinguished by its connexion with the notions of growth and development. This point has also been stressed by Fritsch, who says (ibid., p. 2) 'In Marx we have more or less to do with the derivation of money from historically given processes of development.' At an early date Block emphasised (1926, p. 68) that this association is to the advantage to the Marxian theory of money, especially as 'it is not a derivation of consecutive functions from a particular primary function, which we find in many theoreticians . . . according to whom the historical explanation of the function of money arises from difficulties which accompany direct exchange transactions at a certain stage of development'. Fritsch nevertheless recognises (1968, p. 13) that, 'in spite of certain deficiencies in the Marxian theory of money as such, it has to be said that the theory of credit developed by Marx contains many surprising and even very modern aspects'.

Lukas has stressed (1951, p. 23) that the Marxian theory of money contains quite a number of formulas which have proved effective and long-lived: 'In his well-known formula money–commodity–money Karl Marx has succinctly expressed the acquisitiveness of capitalism. This formula clearly demonstrates the organisational principle of the market economy, of which other authors, such as Johannes Plenge and von Zwiedineck-Südenhorst, have made frequent and successful use.'

Bartoli has produced (1950, pp. 101–18) a brilliant resumé of the

Marxian theory of money. He categorically rejects the view that the theory stands on weak foundations. He starts from the view that Marx was in advance of his time and of his fellow writers in so far as he took the trouble to detail the social and philosophical conclusions that can be drawn from the analysis of money. He not only portrayed the advantages of money as a technical instrument in economic life, but also painted a rather dark picture of its disadvantages. Bartoli comments,

> Here, the position taken by Marx, is exceptional. He uses the tones of the Church Fathers and thunders vehemently against money as the idol of this world, even though he knows only too well that logically speaking it is indispensable. His doctrine, red-hot with passion, is both stimulating and challenging. He is an expert in combining anathema with theory, for after magnificient pleading he knows how to return to sober analysis. . . .

Of all commentators of this subject, Bartoli comes nearest to doing justice to the Marxian theory of money. He expounded the thesis that this theory is connected with the general theory of circulation in Marx's work. This explains the movement money–commodity–money, which in the view of capitalists is the only congenial form of capitalist profit-seeking. Money as the integrating element and as the foundations on which social relationships are developed has according to Marx the task of representing the exchange values of all commodities. In this process it can be a particular commodity that serves as the point of departure. Marx thought of various types of use values capable of fulfilling the historically given functions, and seen in this context gold represents only one element in the chain. These elements, when seen in the context of the original idea of 'commodity money', must of necessity have their analogy in the theory of value. The value of such substantive money is represented by the 'socially necessary labour time' for its production. From such historically determined reasoning arises Marx's reputation as being a 'metallist'.

Marx, however, had clearly set out the basic functions of money in his *Critique of Political Economy*, in his *Theories of Surplus Value* and, unknown to Bartoli, in the *Grundrisse*. This implies that he treated the subject along time before the publication of the first volume of *Capital*.

According to Bartoli, the basic functions of money, as expounded by Marx, are the following: a measure of value or the crystallisation of exchange value, a measure of relative price, a medium of exchange, a unit of account, a store of value or value reserve, and a means of payment.

The 'unit of account function' is similar to the 'production form of capital' in Block (1926, p. 90). According to Bartoli, money as a measure of value fulfils for Marx a social function as mediator, the role of a universal equivalent against the mass of commodities, and acquires its own 'use value'. It becomes a measure of relative price to the extent that it is the monetary expression of the total of social work, which manifests itself in price. In this context there arises the idea that money is materialised labour time, which finds its expression in a certain amount of gold. However, in connexion with the 'unit of account' function, Marx maintains that the notion of money is capable of being detached from its metal substance, so that, for instance, a 'pound' becomes only a monetary unit.

In the 'metamorphosis of commodities', i.e. the conversion of money into commodities within the cycle commodity–money–commodity, money plays the role only of mediator. In the second phase, which, however, is characteristic of capitalism, the cycle money–commodity–money is of decisive importance: the capitalist has an interest in reconverting the money he advanced as capital from goods to money, for he wishes to realise his surplus value. Many cycles of exchange are involved before the commodity ends up with the final consumer. This permits many intermediate elements to exist, some of them parasitic.

Above all, two aspects are of decisive importance. In its function as a store of value or reserve, money becomes the instrument for a potential break in the cycle. The 'realisation' process then enters no further 'metamorphosis of commodities' cycle, the production process is ruptured, and questions of the business cycle enter the scene. On the other hand, there exists the possibility of speeding up or slowing down this process of circulation. Bartoli stresses the importance which Marx imputed to the velocity of circulation of money, which he thought to have a regulatory character. He did not accept the primitive quantity theory and he believed that the quantity of money depended on the development of prices and the velocity of circulation, and not *vice versa*.

This, in short, is Bartoli's interpretation and paraphrasing of Marx. His opposition to the primitive quantity theory gave Marx the reputation of being a radical opponent of the more general quantity theory. This view is advanced by Barrault (1910, p. 373) and Palyi (1925, II, pp. 477ff.), but it is a view without foundation. Bartoli says (1950, p. 119), '[only] to the extent that Marx bases himself on the hypothesis of metallic money is he determined to reject the quantity theory and to disassociate himself from Ricardo's thesis with the most outstanding arguments. When he is using the hypothesis of paper money, Marx reverts to the position of a quantity theorist'. In his *Critique of Political Economy*, Marx explicitly states that the quantity of gold in circulation does indeed depend on prices (in so far as the production of gold is stimulated during periods of falling prices), but that the inverse situation holds with paper money, the value of which depends exclusively on its quantity.

In the same context, Bartoli rejects Delpech's remark (1936, p. 258) that Marx could envisage only representative paper money. This opinion has its origin in the erroneous supposition that Marx confounds the value of money (in Knapp's sense) with its legal rate of exchange. Bartoli asks (1950, pp. 122–3), 'How could it be posssible for paper money to have only a representative character, when its value is determined by its quantity?' In the same way, he criticises Delpech's view that Marx intended to explain particular fluctuations in price by means of his price theory. This, he says, is all the more unjustified as in his theory of average profit Marx explicitly deals with specific changes in price. 'Marx explains the causes of general fluctuations in price only on the basis of the function of money.'

The question of the inner meaning of deflationary and inflationary processes has been raised in an unusual study by Deletaille. Deletaille, starting from Marxian theory, sees in inflation support for the existence of capitalism. He imputes to Marx, chiefly on the basis of the controversy with Weston, which had its outcome in 'Wages, Price and Profit', a 'law of the tendency of prices to fall'. In the face of this law, Deletaille develops his thesis that a long-term inflationary development in capitalism is the only means for securing a steady upward movement in the standard of living, a continual increase in production, and protection of the financial situation of firms. (Deletaille, 1959, pp. 28ff., 40–1, 49, 182ff.)

There can be no doubt that Marx never formulated such a 'law'. The examples he quotes with regard to the tendency of certain prices to fall, and here he thinks especially of corn on the world market, are nothing more than a reference to the increase in productivity in modern society. It is true that Kondratieff (1922) began from Marxian analysis when he formulated his theory of long waves. However, one cannot properly say that it had been anticipated by Marx. The tiny bit of truth which might possibly be found in Deletaille's interpretation is concerned with the indirect conclusion that could be drawn from the theory of value. This, as outlined in chapter 17 of the present volume, was that under certain circumstances an unrevised conception of value could lead in the long run to a declining price level. It can nevertheless be maintained that in 'academic' political economy the Marxian theory of money does not play a very great role. The fact that the above-mentioned discussion of Marxian ideas was initiated by Deletaille, an engineer interested in economics, clearly shows how little interest in this aspect of Marx's work there is in 'academic' economics.

An exception in this respect is the work of Wolfson on Marxian economics. Wolfson, however (1966, pp. 99–100), sets out from a false premise – representing a step backward as compared with the analysis of Bartoli – when he claims that Marx

is forced to reject a quantity theory of money which would adjust the value of total money demand to the volume of commodities to be transacted by adjusting their prices. This quantity theory would leave room for noninflationary flexible expansion of money capital if unemployed real productive factors were available (for example, if the reserve army of unemployed were sizable).

In place of such a quantity theory, Marx first of all developed a concept according to which money demand and the stock of value created in earlier periods should correspond to each other. He offers 'a commodity theory of gold money rigidly valued at its labor content bidding for labor and means of production which are sold as fixed values. A "ghost of gold" theory is provided for representative currency.' According to the Marxian theory, Wolfson states,

> The supply of money capital must be limited by the previously accumulated mass of value available for accumulation as capital. In plain contradiction to expansion of the money supply by the banks, Marx must have it that if demand is to be available in period two, it must first have been produced in period one, or at some still earlier time, and only now dishoarded.

This is obviously enough a wrong interpretation of Marx's hoarding theory, which leads us on to questions connected with the business cycle itself. Wolfson ignores the Marxian theory of credit, and it is wishful thinking on his part to presuppose that Marx himself thought that 'the limited supply of money capital' would lead to capital supplies rigidly fixed in the short run, and that surplus value represents a sort of rent resulting from rigid supplies on the money capital market. In a later passage (ibid., pp. 106–7) he expresses the opinion,

> It is, of course, conceivable that, given a rigid monetary system which had institutional arrangements prohibiting the development of money substitutes, a limitation on funds available for investment might become effective. Under such circumstances the rate of interest might become high enough to wipe out the net returns to enterprise. But if this is not a completely fanciful condition, it is only due to the rigidities of some nineteenth-century monetary systems and has little to do with the inherent capitalist inability to fully employ all the factors of production. Apart from short-run interest expense of liquidity preference, a firm's rate of profit can be capitalized into an acceptable money substitute.

We have still to show that Marx did not reject wholesale the quantity theory as such, for he protested only against its primitive versions. Furthermore, within the framework of his credit theory he fully approves of other forms of 'substitute money'. It is for this reason that the analysis by Wolfson completely misses the essence of the theory.

38 Marx as a Monetary Theorist

A close inspection of the early writings of Marx makes it clear that as early as 1857–8 he had described, in the *Grundrisse*, the fundamental character of money, and had done so with unsurpassable precision: 'The properties of money as (1) measure of commodity exchange; (2) medium of exchange; (3) representative of commodities . . .; (4) general commodity alongside the particular commodities, all simply follow from its character as exchange value separated from commodities themselves and objectified' (p. 146). This general analysis is expressed in nearly the same wording in his *Critique of Political Economy*, published in 1859. One might therefore, be allowed to say that Marx made his début in political economy with his monetary theory.

Let us compare the above with a more up-to-date formulation, by one of the noted adversaries of Marx, Halm (1935, pp. 1–2):

> Money serves as an instrument to facilitate exchange; it is a means of exchange that finds acceptance everywhere. . . . if we want to exchange two different commodities we must have an exact idea of what their values represent in comparison to each other. . . . Some instrument is required to facilitate their exchange. Such an aid is in the first instance of commodity in proportion to which the value of all other commodities is determined.

We can therefore say that fully developed standard formulations in monetary theory were familiar to Marx a century ago. Halm goes on to state (ibid., p. 2) that money

> makes it possible to split up exchange transactions into the acts of sale and purchase, which then become independent of each other. Thus it is no longer necessary that complete accord exist between different persons engaged in exchange, nor need there be coincidence in the particular goods in the exchange with regard to their concrete, personal and relevant characteristics and to their value, and to their temporal and locational properties.

Marx expresses this in the following way: 'With the separation of purchase and sale, with the splitting of exchange into two spatially and temporally independent acts, there further emerges another, new relation' (*Grundrisse*, p. 148).

One might begin to think that authors such as Halm copied Marx, though it is true that the *Grundrisse* was unknown to Halm. Two of its chapters, however, had been available since 1859, as part of the *Critique of Political Economy*. In these Marx describes money as a 'measuring rod for value', an 'ideal unit of measurement', an 'indicator of proportion', a 'yardstick of price', a 'unit of account', a 'means of circulation' and so on.

When Marx took up the subject a basic theory of money had already been developed. He inclined in particular to the views of Sir James Steuart, who stands between mercantilism and classical economics and can be considered to have been a beneficial influence on Marx, particularly as he was often strong where Adam Smith is unanimously agreed to have been at his weakest, i.e. in the analysis of the banking system, of the public credit system and of paper money (see Skinner, in Introduction to Steuart, 1966 edition, p. lxxxiv). All in all, we may say that Marx had a clear comprehension of the function of money. In addition, Block states (1926, pp. 66–7) that

> To distinguish between these functions and the substance of money, in addition to distinguishing between the different individual functions of money, is one of the most prominent characteristics of Marxian monetary doctrine. Other theorists discern the concept of money as residing in its characteristic of circulatory medium, or in its scale of reckoning or as a means of exchange or as a means of payment, i.e. they elevate a particular function to serve as the content of the notion of money and they then proceed somehow to derive all the other functions of money from its main function. They make the function the very substance of the notion. Marx instead sharply distinguishes between the essence of money and the services which by its very nature it is capable of offering. On the other hand, individual functions have to be isolated, though they are at the same time functions of equal significance.

We neither intend nor are able to treat here in full the subject of the Marxian general theory of money. A more detailed evaluation of this aspect of Marx is to be found in the works of Fritsch and, within the confines of neo-marxism, in works by Rosdolsky (1968) and Suzanne de Brunhoff (1967). These and the works of Block, de Cindio, Pesenti, Mandel, Altvater and others seem to show that the harsh judgement of Schumpeter, that Marx's monetary theory is the weakest part of his system, is unjustified. The same applies to Schumpeter's classification of Marx (along with Ricardo, Senior and Mill) as a 'metallist' (1959, p. 700).

THE 'GHOST OF GOLD' THEORY AND THE UNJUSTIFIED REPROACH OF METALLISM

To class Marx as a 'metallist', as Schumpeter did, is all the more unjustified as Marx in his preparatory work to *Capital*, in the *Grundrisse* and *Critique of Political Economy*, clearly demonstrates the character of money as an indicator of value. Rosdolsky is right in saying (1968, 1, p. 142), 'In the "rough copy", particularly in its first part, we find innumerable passages in which money is regarded simply as a token of value or as a "symbol" and this is true not only of paper money.' It seems that Rosdolsky considers this to be a disadvantage, for he maintains that it could be deduced from Marx 'that money must consist of a particular commodity', and that 'therefore paper money cannot express everything in the value of goods, but must act as a representative of money in the form of gold'.

In this respect, Rosdolsky advances the 'ghost of gold' theory, which Wolfson also wished to impute to Marx. Thus Marxist authors have unjustifiably added to Marx's bad reputation and have helped to stamp him as a 'metallist'. In reality the observations of Marx with regard to the function of gold concern in this context only 'universal money'.

In the *Critique of Political Economy* Marx says (p. 149),

> Gold becomes money, as distinct from coin, first by being withdrawn from circulation and hoarded, then by entering circulation as a non-means of circulation, finally however by breaking through the barriers of domestic circulation in order to function as universal equivalent in the world commodities. It thus becomes world money.

This clearly shows the pure function of gold in guaranteeing currency at the international level.

Rosdolsky's reference to the *Grundrisse* as stating that a 'particular commodity' is necessary to fulfil the function of money is based on a misunderstanding. In the *Grundrisse* Marx clearly states (p. 144);

> Thus, in order to realise the commodity as exchange value in one stroke, it is not enough to exchange it for one particular commodity. It must be exchanged against a third thing which is not in turn itself a particular commodity, but is the symbol of the commodity as commodity, of the commodity's exchange value itself; . . . say, labour time as such, say a piece of paper or of leather. . . . (Such a symbol presupposes general recognition; it can only be a social symbol; it expresses, indeed, nothing more than a social relation.)

How erroneous the idea is that Marx was a metallist is shown by his statements in connexion with monetary crises:

The entire history of modern industry shows that metal would indeed be required only for the balancing of international commerce, whenever its equilibrium is momentarily disturbed, if only domestic production were organised. That the domestic market does not need any metal even now is shown by the suspension of the cash payments of the so-called national banks, which resort to this expedient in all extreme cases as the sole relief. (*Capital*, III, ch. 32, p. 517.)

Nothing can be more remote from metallism than this remark and nothing corresponds more to the modern conception of money. We have to admit, though, that chapters 25 and 26 of volume III of *Capital* were left incomplete by Marx and had to be severely revised by Engels. For this reason Sombart, for instance, has argued (1899, p. 557) for their total omission.

Two different things brought upon Marx the reproach of being a 'metallist': first, the application which the element of gold production has found in the Marxian theory of the circular flow, and, secondly, the application of this element in the so-called 'transformation' of value into prices, as it was performed by Marx's commentators around the turn of the century.

In the latter case, there was introduced into the Marxian reproduction schemes a third department of production, as the result of a problem raised by Tugan-Baranowsky and von Bortkiewicz. This is additional to the two departments which Marx used in volume II (the means of production and consumer goods) and was assumed to be concerned with 'gold', which served as standard value for the other two departments.

In chapter 9 of the volume III of *Capital* Marx worked with up to five spheres of production, but for none of these did he, in the manner of von Bortkiewicz, introduce gold as a *deus ex machina*. The 'transformation problem' has been discussed in chapter 17 of this volume and cannot be further dealt with here. It has to be said that the introduction of gold into the reproduction schemes, a feature which even Sweezy took up, has contributed to the impression of Marx as a metallist.

The production of gold appears in the theory of the circular flow in volume II of *Capital*. Marx introduced the question of the origin of money within the framework of his scheme of 'simple reproduction' (ch. 17, pp. 334–5):

The question then is not where the surplus-value comes from but whence the money comes into which it is turned . . . But the commodity-capital must be turned into money before its reconversion into productive capital and before the surplus-value contained in it is spent. Where does the money for this purpose come from? This question seems difficult at the first glance and neither Tooke nor any one else has answered it so far. . . . [The problem has its origin in the fact that] a part of the mass of commodities thrown into circulation is a surplus-product, hence representing a value which the capitalist did not throw into circulation. . . . The commodity-capital which the capitalist throws into circulation has a greater value . . . than the productive capital which he withdrew from circulation in the form of labour-power plus means of production.

In other words, the capitalist has had to meet the 'cost price $(c + v)$, but the 'production price' then flows back from the market into his pocket, a price which in terms of volume III of *Capital* means $c + v + s$. From where, however, in a macroeconomic view, does the additional purchasing power, which represents his profits, come?

THE MONEY FLOW AND THE 'PROBLEM OF REALISATION'

In the Marxian literature the question of the origin of the money which is necessary for the process of transforming money into goods and into more money is as a rule never analysed in detail within the framework of the concept of surplus value. Fritsch, however (1968, p. 84), takes up the question in this context, because Marx himself discussed the problem in relation to the circulation of capital: 'Marx devotes more space than he does to the problem of alterations in price to the question of whence the money to realise real surplus value, i.e. the surplus product, actually comes.' Most other authors do not discuss this question in connexion with the concept of surplus value, nor do they treat it in the context of the theory of money, but only in connexion with the business cycle in the 'crisis of realisation'. The intervention of money is a question which is examined in connexion with exchange transactions. In the exchange of v_I and s_I (i.e. the value added of department I, the means-of-production department in the Marxian reproduction scheme) for c_I (the means of production delivered from department I to department II the consumer-goods department), we cannot assume that the exchange is carried out on the basis of value in kind. *Mutatis mutandis*, the same is valid for the payment of wages and capitalists' consumption in department II, and also in a number of different forms within department I. Apart from this, logically and taking into account the principle of competition, it is impossible to defend the idea of an integrated sector. Within both departments exchange transactions take place between a great number of different firms.

Here the question arises of the intervention of money in these processes of exchange between the departments and, within them, between workers (the bearers of the commodity labour power) and capitalists. In the representation of the reproduction schemes in Tsuru's work (in Sweezy, 1942, p. 369), these exchange transactions give the impression that there exists a separate flow of money besides the physical flow of goods (expressed in values), for which reason we must raise the question of whence this flow of money comes. In Tsuru's work it is assumed that credits are necessary to make such a flow of money possible. In the literature on the reproduction schemes, this problem mostly plays a secondary role, but it has been accorded greater attention in more recent years, as, for instance, from Nagels (1970, p. 128).

In simple reproduction, which has only one circular flow and no investment to expand the system, the problem of how to procure the necessary funds is solved by hypothesising that one of the means of production delivered from department I to department II is gold, which, so to speak, fulfils the monetary function as a means of production. This is assumed by Marx in Volume II of *Capital* (ch. 20, p. 474): 'The production of gold . . . belongs in class I . . .' Such an assumption would give rise to the problem that this amount would have to represent the 'value' of v_I and s_I in order to finance the exchange with c_{II}, which means that nothing would be left over for the exchange of the means of production and any further exchange within the different departments. Engels, in fact, states in a footnote ibid., p. 477, note 55) that Marx abstained from carrying out 'the study of the exchange of newly produced gold within the constant capital of department I.'

It might be more realistic to assume that this volume of gold provides a basis for central-bank credit, which would furnish the volume of money necessary for all exchange transactions. Here, of course, it must be asked whether the intervention of such credit would not mean that 'forced saving' would enter the scene, allowing enterprises to be furnished with the funds necessary for extended reproduction, which would lead us away from simple reproduction. It was Marx himself who maintained that such an image bore no likeness to capitalism. One might perhaps go further and say that the very emergence of a monetary economy presupposes the onset of capitalism.

Alternatively one could assume that a small quantity of gold, as contained in the means of production delivered to department II, i.e. c_{II} would be sufficient to create a 'monetary flow', which with the help of a banking system would correspond to the flow of physical values. In this case, the existence of an efficient banking system would be the precondition for the simple-reproduction scheme, unless it is intended to start from the hypothesis of a pure barter economy with fully integrated branches (each department = an enterprise).

A third possibility would then be for gold production to be handled independently as department 3, as has been done by Von Bortkiewicz (1907b, pp. 319ff). The production of 'luxury' goods for the capitalist class would then come within the province of this department. It is understandable that Von Bortkiewicz was driven to the conclusion that this division played no role in the analysis of the relationship of capital to labour and, in particular, did not determine the rate of profit.

Marx, however, did not treat the subject in its totality, as he saw it not as a problem of the amount of money necessary for total turnover, but, rather, as a problem of surplus value. He, therefore devotes only a short passage to the former problem (*Capital*, II, ch. 20, pp. 477–80):

> The only assumption essential here, namely, that in general there is money enough for the exchange of the various elements of the mass of the annual reproduction, is not affected in any way by the fact that a portion of the commodity-value consists of surplus-value. Supposing that the entire production belonged to the labourers themselves . . . the quantity of circulating commodity-values would be the same and, other things being equal, would require the same amount of money for their circulation. The question in either case is therefore only: Where does the money come from to make possible the exchange of this total of commodity-values? It is not at all: Where does the money come from to turn the surplus-value into money?

Marx answers this question in an offhand manner. He begins (ibid., ch. 17, p. 329) with metal coins in 'simple reproduction':

> According to the laws of the simple circulation of commodities [developed in volume I, ch. 3], the mass of the metal coin existing in a country must not only be sufficient to circulate the commodities, but must also suffice to meet the currency fluctuations, which arise partly from fluctuations in the velocity of the circulation, partly from the prices of commodities, partly from the various and varying proportions in which the money functions as a medium of payment or as a medium of circulation proper.

THE EMPHASIS ON CORPORATE CASH HOLDING OR THE VELOCITY OF CIRCULATION OF MONEY

As we can see, Marx starts from the hypothesis of corporate cash holding, which encompasses peak demand (seasonal demand conditioned by price increases, with reference to the velocity of circulation of money). In the passage just cited he still speaks of specie, and he goes so far as to assume that 'the production of gold and silver constitutes a part of the total social production within every country'. This may have contributed to the false impression that he was in favour of 'metallism'. In simple reproduction it is still possible to assume, with good reason, the existence of circulating specie, for in 'simple reproduction' we have to do with a more or less stationary circulation, which corresponds to conditions existing in medieval society.

In this connexion Marx considers the possibility that the amount of money required for circulation is 'not made good by a greater velocity of money currency, . . . i.e., by a greater mutual balancing of purchases and sales without the intervention of actual money' (*Capital*, II, ch. 17, p. 330). This means that even at this stage he assumes the existence of banking institutions, though he does not enlarge on the question.

Instead he concentrates on the problem of 'the realisation of surplus value', because in the final analysis there arises the problem of how to augment the volume of money, a problem which cannot be grasped under the assumption of a (permanent) minimum cash holding, because peak demand grows steadily even where there are improvements in arrangements for settlement in the framework of an ever-more effective banking system. Fritsch comments on this problem in the following way (1968, p. 84: 'The fact remains that, considered as a whole, the capitalist mode of production can remain effective only if its main agents, the capitalists, get more money capital back by the sale of their products on the market than they originally advanced.'

This is only one aspect of the problem. The fundamental question is how capitalists are able to advance money. In simple reproduction it is assumed by definition that there is no saving activity at all. For this reason it is impossible to presuppose 'abstinence' on the part of capitalists, or 'waiting', as Senior and other 'academic' economists have been inclined to do. Marx, who opposed such an explanation, experiences, naturally, still greater difficulties.

Fritsch is of the opinion that Marx wished to regard the problem as non-existent for surplus value. Indeed, Marx says (*Capital*, II. ch. 17, p. 337)

it changes absolutely nothing in the quantity of the money required for this circulation whether the value of the mass of commodities contains any surplus-value or not. . . . All other conditions being given, such as velocity of the currency of money etc., a definite sum of money is required. . . . So far as any problem exists here, it coincides with the general problem: Where does the money required for the circulation of the commodities of a country come from?

It seems that, by arguing in this way, Marx did his best to obstruct the way out of the difficulty, the existence of which he surely perceived, and to which he sought a tenable answer – as is suggested by the words 'other conditions being given, such as velocity of the currency of money'. His answer could otherwise easily have been that the quantity of money necessary for the realisation of surplus value arises from an increase in the velocity of circulation. That he did not argue in this way may well be because he had the feeling that the appearance of surplus value would be cancelled in the increased cash balances of capitalists. That he is dissatisfied with the 'non-existence' thesis is shown when he asks, shortly afterwards (ibid., p. 338), 'How can they continually draw £600 out of circulation, when they continually throw only £500 into it? Nothing comes from nothing.'

Here Marx has a fundamental advantage over his critic Fritsch. We are concerned here not only with the quantity of money necessary to realise surplus value, but also with the provision of money as cash balances to carry through transactions, i.e. 'liquidity' in the Keynesian sense. With Marx we can, therefore, assume (ibid.) that 'this sum of money originates in the mass of money previously accumulated in the country', which means that it has its origin in feudal or pre-capitalist wealth, or, perhaps, in money accumulated in banks. It is obvious that the sum of money necessary for such transactions depends on the degree to which the economy is integrated. If, for instance, department 1 splits up into several stages (raw materials, intermediate products, manufactured products), or if the number of stages either increases or shrinks, the demand for money will vary accordingly.

It is true that Fritsch is of the opinion (1968, p. 155) that the Marxian equations do not state the degree of integration, but Marx was fully aware of the problem, as various passages in his works show. The problem arising from the existence of different stages is recognised in, for instance, the following statements: 'some circulations of money may be entirely eliminated. . . . for instance, . . . where the industrial capitalist is himself the owner of the capital, there is no circulation of money between him and creditors' (*Capital*, II, ch. 17, pp. 345–8).

Marx mentions three cases in which cash reserves must grow: where there is an increase in the total of all prices, owing to a greater volume of production or to higher prices; in the case of 'partial, or local, rises in wages'; and in the case of a 'general rise in wages', which forces up prices in wage-intensive industries, but, according to Marx, makes them fall in capital-intensive ones.

In principle, Marx is of the opinion that 'prices in rising or falling determine the volume of money in circulation and not *vice versa*'. In his view,

> it is circulation itself [that creates] the necessary volume of the means of circulation . . . [and is] able to adopt as many money substitutes as it wishes, in which case its relative value stands in inverse relation to its volume provided the velocity of circulation remains constant. . . . For genuine paper money the quantity theory is valid, a theory which Marx sharply rejects in the case of metal and credit money[?].
>
> (Fritsch, 1968, p. 55)

At an early stage Marx recognised the quantity theory as only a tautological formula, for *ceteris paribus* implies the velocity of circulation of money to be constant. In the *Critique of Political Economy* he writes (pp. 121–2), 'Gold circulates because it has value, whereas paper has value because it circulates. If the exchange-value of commodities is given, the quantity of gold in circulation depends on its value, whereas the value of paper tokens depends on the number of tokens in circulation.'

Where, in *Capital*, Marx seems to oppose the quantity theory, he is in fact referring only to its 'primitive' versions, in which the pure quantity of money is treated as decisive. Marx, by contrast, puts the emphasis on the speed of circulation of money. Logically this results from his extensive treatment of the problem of the turnover of capital, to which he devotes large parts of chapters 5–16 of Volume II of *Capital*. Here, indeed, it is necessary to deepen the discussion of this topic, which in the present work has so far received only superficial mention.

Fritsch, one of the most careful commentators on Marxian monetary theory, gives special attention (1968, Part III, ch. 1, pp. 75ff) to the theory of capital turnover as developed by Marx. Marx did not complete his theory, for which reason Engels felt obliged to add a whole chapter on this subject to volume III of *Capital* (ch. 4); he obviously was not content with the discussion in volume II. Unfortunately, his own arguments at the microeconomic level, to which he limits himself, do not provide a conclusive outcome.

On the other hand, the problems of capital turnover and self-finance are synonymous, for the extent to which the economy resorts to credit depends on the degree of self-finance resulting from the 'accumulation' of surplus value. Even though Marx recognises that accumulation out of surplus value is of great importance, he nevertheless, thinks that capitalism must be built on the foundations of a credit system, at least to begin with.

In *Capital* Marx clearly and repeatedly demonstrates the possibility of influencing the price level through banking policy. He emphasises (III, ch. 34, p. 548) that it is not simply changes in the gold reserve of the central bank, but also the measures taken by the bank as a result, that influence the price level:

> Metallic currency has its remedy in the import and export of precious metal, which immediately enters circulation as coin and thus, by its inflow or outflow, causes commodity-prices to fall or rise. The same effect on prices must now be exerted artificially by banks through imitating the laws of metallic currency. If gold is coming in from abroad it proves that . . . bank-notes must be put into circulation in proportion to the newly imported gold. On the other hand, notes must be withdrawn from circulation in proportion to the gold exported from the country.

The rules of the game of the gold standard, the alternation of reflation and deflation, of stimulated boom and induced recession, cannot be more clearly stated.

As a follow-up to this exposition of the basic theses, we touch upon only three aspects of Marxian monetary theory: the Marxian theory of credit; the way Marx treats 'world money', within the framework of the theory of international trade; and the discussion of Say's law.

39 The Theory of Banking and Credit in Marx

In the second volume of *Capital* (ch. 17, pp. 325–6) Marx repeats his hypothesis, investigating finance that has its source in hoarded means. 'We still ignore credit-money at this point. . . . The simplest form . . . is that of a hoard.' He refers to Thompson's *Inquiry into the Principles of the Distribution of Wealth* (1824), in which it is stated, 'The mass of real accumulated wealth, in point of magnitude . . . is . . . utterly insignificant when compared with the powers of production of the same society in whatever state of civilisation, or even compared with the actual consumption for even a few years of that society . . . .

Marx's recourse to Thompson's explanation can only mean that he does not believe that self-finance by way of accumulated active funds of more or less liquid form can be sufficient, at least in the case of large-scale industry. If one takes these remarks in conjunction with those on joint-stock companies and on the credit system, one can even go a step further and interpret this passage as advancing the thesis that self-finance is inadequate for the development of large-scale industries. One could, of course, object that the discovery of the dynamic depreciation (or 'Lohmann–Ruchti') effect (see below, vol. II, ch. 14) tells us that Marx fully recognised the different dynamic forms of self-finance, by means of which provision for depreciation is immediately reinvested in the same enterprise. Further, it has to be stressed that in the Marxian theory of concentration great importance is laid upon industrial growth. Nevertheless, in the second volume of *Capital* the argument gives the impression that Marx attributes greater importance to credit creation for the specifically capitalist growth process.

Marx links the theory of the circular flow to that of credit, and modern theory recognises this fully. V. F. Wagner, for instance, says (1937, p. 106),

> Since an analysis of the functions of credit is only possible on the assumption of the actual structure of the economy, we have to find the point of departure in Marx, who in his representation of the circulation of capital offers the earliest and most penetrating examination of the morphological phenomena of the capitalist growth process.

In this context, some form of excess cash creation is needed to satisfy turnover within the reproduction schemes, in order to render possible 'the adaptation of monetary capital requirements to the economically necessary minimum' through the transfer of temporary savings (ibid., p. 117; Fritsch, 1968, p. 101).

It is no accident that, immediately after the discussion of the 'circulation of surplus value' and of the problems of self-finance, Marx proceeds to set out his reproduction schemes. In simple reproduction, liquid funds are indispensable. The pure circular flow in a stationary system does not allow for the processes of credit creation, for this would lead to a spiral.

Such a stationary economy, however, can certainly not be taken as an image of capitalism, which is what Marx had set out to investigate. For Marx, capitalism, growth and dynamics are synonymous. Here it is true that 'the expediencies developing with the credit system [increase] the productive power of social labour' (*Capital*, II, ch. 17, p. 350).

THE PROCESS OF CREDIT AND MONEY CREATION IN MARX

With an *argumentum e contrario*, Marx answers (*Capital*, II, ch. 17, pp. 350–1) the question of whether modern capitalism is at all conceivable without credit: 'This disposes also of the absurd question whether capitalist production in its present volume would be possible without the credit system . . . that is, with the circulation of metallic coin alone. . . .' Evidently, this is not the case. It would rather have encountered barriers in the volume of production of precious metals.

This concise statement ought properly to absolve Marx from the reproach of being an adherent of metallism. How would it have been possible for him to analyse capitalism if his thinking were bound to such a metal frame, which, according to his conception of capitalism, must be forcibly shattered? Marx cuts the discussion short by saying that one must not, on the other hand, form a mystical idea of the productive power of credit in making money capital available or liquid.

In volume III of *Capital* (pp. 521–2) Marx takes up the question anew. In chapter 33 he shows how 'one and the same bank-note can constitute deposits in several banks'. He speaks of 'the preponderant function of money as a means of payment for merely settling balances'. With this he indicates the money-creating function of the banking system, a function to which he refers also in other passages. This applies to the banking system as a whole. Referring to Tooke, he stresses the point that the central bank cannot force its money upon the public 'of its own volition', but that 'it has the power of reducing the amount of the notes in the hands of the public' (ibid., p. 524).

The question of additional market power is basically a question of credit creation. Fritsch is not wrong in saying (1968, p. 85) that Marx had more than one answer to this question. Just as at the macroeconomic level surplus value represents surplus labour over and above that necessary for the means of subsistence of the worker and the replacement of production goods, this surplus labour must somewhere be the counterpart to a surplus product. Gold production would be part of such a surplus product. This gold can appear as additional money or even as a luxury good, corresponding to an additional consumption of luxury goods by capitalists.

In this case, gold plays the role of a *deus ex machina*. Basically this is only an evasive manoeuvre, as it can be assumed that the gold production has already been included in the total volume of commodities. In any case, it was the mention of gold in this context that gave Marx the reputation of being an adherent of metallism, even though the latter did not solve the problem but only changed its form. A part of capitalist consumption consists of gold. Fritsch too (ibid., p. 86) sees in the manoeuvre nothing but evasion.

The real answer is given by Marx himself when he says (*Capital*, II, ch. 17, pp. 337–9),

> The capitalist . . . throws into circulation the money which constitutes originally the money-form of his constant, fixed and circulating capital; he expends it as a means of purchase or payment for instruments of labour and materials of production. . . . As for the labourer . . . he is but the secondary, while the capitalist is the primary, starting-point of the money thrown by the labourer into circulation. . . . Indeed, paradoxical as it may appear at first sight, it is the capitalist class itself that throws the money into circulation which serves for the realisation of the surplus-value incorporated in the commodities. . . . It spends it as a means of purchase for its individual consumption.

In his analysis of the circular flow, Burchardt (1932, p. 162) came to the same conclusion. The appearance of surplus value 'does not mean much statistically. Since capitalists, as demonstrated by Marx, must fully consume their surplus value even in "simple reproduction", it constantly appears as "their" (!) power of consumption.'

Here Marx anticipates the 'Keynesian theory of distribution', which, properly speaking, can be traced back to Kalecki. 'Therefore the capitalists as a class determine by their expenditure their profits and in consequence the aggregate production' (Kalecki, 1939; 1966, p. 45). In Kaldor's words (1957, p. 267), which are almost an exact replica of Kalecki's terms, 'Capitalists as a class earn in fact what they spend, while the workers spend what they earn.' In real terms this seems to be the case, but from the monetary point of view it remains a problem, as Fritsch rightly says (1968, p. 85): 'The means of making the purchase must come from somewhere.' In essence the answer has to be that the additional means could owe their existence to falling prices, as long as the quantity of money, statistically viewed, does not expand. If the velocity of circulation of money increases, and Marx recognised the importance of this, the quantity of active money will effectively grow. What is really lacking in Marx's work is an explicit formulation of the money-creating function of the banking system, but even here he has seen the beginnings of an approach, in the analysis of credit.

In the context of simple reproduction, Marx repeatedly stresses his assumption of an identity between capitalist consumption and the sum of surplus value or the sum of profit. In the case of 'extended reproduction' we have to add to consumption net investment, i.e. the 'consumption' of additional investment goods by capitalists, though we have to allow for shifts over time. Marx has

> assumed that the sum of money which the capitalist throws into circulation to pay for his individual consumption until the first returns of his capital is exactly equal to the surplus-value which he produced and hence must turn into money. This is obviously an arbitrary assumption so far as the individual capitalist is concerned. But it must be correct when applied to the entire capitalist class if simple reproduction is assumed. . . . [It means here] that the entire surplus-value . . . is consumed unproductively. . . . A portion of the social surplus-value therefore consists of gold . . . and is thrown into circulation in order to draw products out of it. . . . Whereas one part of the capitalists constantly pumps more money out of the circulation than it pours into it, the part that produces gold constantly pumps more money into it than it takes out in means of production.   (*Capital*, II, ch. 17, pp. 340–1.)

Marx is fully aware that he is here entering the international plane, but he says that 'transferring the production of gold from one country to another produces no change whatever in the matter'.

MARX AND THE QUANTITY EQUATION

Marx comes then to the heart of the matter – namely, the fact that the existing effective quantity of money faces a greater volume of commodities. 'The other portion of money . . . is not an element of the annually produced gold, but of the mass of money previously accumulated in the country.' If there was one thing clear to Marx it is this: 'The quantity of gold necessary to realise this sum depends, in the first instance, on the rapidity of currency of the means of payment.' (*Capital*, II, ch. 17, p. 342.)

It is true that 'the fact that a number of sales take place simultaneously, and side by side, limits the extent to which coin can be replaced by the rapidity of currency' (ibid., I, ch. 3, p. 137). We can therefore assume that Marx, in mentioning the 'already accumulated mass of money within the country', did include in his calculations the velocity of circulation and its possible variations. This did not make an adequate impression; otherwise he would have arrived at a solution to his realisation problems, as the effective volume of money would, assuming that the quantity of money in the narrower sense remained constant, have undergone an increase. Here, however, Holtrop raises an objection (1933, pp. 175–6):

> The view that the velocity of circulation of money is closely connected with that of goods, and that both can experience changes only in the same direction, is one we already find in mercantalist authors and in Marx, and it can be found even in the most recent literature. This view (in so far as it concerns those changes in the velocity of circulation which are of importance for the price level) is, nevertheless, erroneous, though in the narrower sense, in which it is right, its contents represent nothing but an insignificant tautology.

Note that Holtrop explicitly ascribes this conception to Marx, whom it helped out of his dilemma with regard to the 'process of realisation'. Although the idea is not explicit in the relevant section of volume II of *Capital*, it is deducible from, for instance, the following passage in volume III (ch. 19, p. 320), 'In discussing money . . . we saw [I, ch. 3] that the movements of the mass of money circulating as means of purchase and payment depend on the metamorphosis of commodities, on the volume and velocity of this metamorphosis, which we now know to be but a phase in the entire process of reproduction.'

In opposition to this, we find the following remark (*Grundrisse*, p. 195): 'The velocity of the circulating medium can therefore substitute for the quantity of the circulating medium only up to a certain point.' For this reason, it is not quite clear whether Holtrop's reproach is really justified.

Holtrop, on the other hand, has with some hesitation listed (1933, pp. 176–8, note 1), a number of authors who are definite adherents of the thesis that increases in the volume of commodities and in the velocity of circulation run parallel. He mentions Philburn, Budge and even Schumpeter. Budge has declared (1931, pp. 250ff.) that any increase in real income, i.e. an increase in the supply of consumers' goods, comes about in such a way that these goods are successively thrown onto the market at shorter intervals than before, which speeds the circulation of money.

Behind the question asked by Holtrop, i.e. of whether, under conditions of increasing commodity production, the circulation of money becomes more rapid, hovers our modern problems of inflationary developments during times of boom. To the extent that such developments exist, for whatever reason, there arises the possibility of a 'flight into real values' impelled by fear of a depreciation in the value of money; this leads to a self-induced acceleration in the circulation of money, which in turn raises the rate of inflation and leads into a vicious circle. This is not bound to end in galloping inflation, which is conceivable only in the case of pathological developments, but may easily end in a recession, under conditions of rising prices in connexion with monopoly-induced price rigidity.

It seems that the authors Holtrop mentions, Marx among them, were not so mistaken in assuming a parallel between increases in the production of goods and velocity of circulation of money.

Fritsch thinks (1968, p. 161) that there are many correspondences between Holtrop's analysis and that of Marx, and this is certainly true with regard to the causes of the periodical release of money capital. The overall tendency towards rising prices during times of boom is referred to by Marx when he says (*Grundrisse*, p. 195), 'This much is clear, that prices are not high or low because much or little money circulates, but that much or little money circulates because prices are high or low . . . .' In *Capital* (III, ch. 28, pp. 445–6) he says,

> The velocity of circulation . . . the mass of simultaneous purchases and sales, or payments, the sum of the prices of the circulating commodities, and finally the balances of payments to be settled in the same period, determine in either case the mass of circulating money, of currency. . . . Its mass is simply determined by its function as a medium of purchase and payment.

This comes very close to the theses of the modern monetarist school: 'Friedman concludes that the demand for money is a stable function of prices and income. . . . The results of Friedman's test are impressive. The coefficient of correlation between M/P [money/price] and Y [income] is found to be 0·99, which is very high . . .' (Wrightman, 1971, p. 111, with reference to Friedman, 1959, pp. 327–51).

This similarity to the ideas expressed by Friedman, who continues the quantity-theory tradition of Fisher, may be surprising. According to Friedman, modern theory shows that with growing income money demand grows faster than income itself. This means that money must somehow or other be considered a luxury article, and that with increasing income there is a relative growth in the demand for cash. In Marxian terminology this means that there is a growing tendency towards the 'formation of hoards'. Marx's opposition to the primitive versions of the quantity theory can be explained by the fact that he put the main accent on the velocity of circulation of money, while imputing to quantity theorists the view that they were concerned only with changes in the volume of money. The same holds for the currency theory. He states unambiguously (*Grundrisse*, p. 195) 'that the velocity of the circulating money does not depend on its quantity, but that the quantity of the circulating medium depends on its velocity'. He deals with the obverse of this when he broaches the question of breakdowns in the circulation of goods through a periodical slackening in the speed with which money circulates. With this he touches upon the problem of Say's Law and the general problem of hoarding.

MARX AND THE 'CURRENCY' AND 'BANKING' SCHOOLS

In his theory of credit, Marx has aligned himself with the 'Banking School', which was engaged in a permanent controversy with the 'Currency School' in the middle of the nineteenth century. That Marx set his face against the Currency School is curious, as the latter dates back to Ricardo, who had inspired Marx and for this reason could easily be called his teacher.

The Currency School was represented above all by bankers: S. J. Lloyd, (later Lord Overstone); G. W. Norman, of the Bank of England; and Robert Torrens. They held the following thesis:

> currency (i.e., coin and notes, as distinct from bank deposits) should be regulated so as to behave like a simple specie currency. This is to say, the note issues should be controlled so that the currency acted as though it were composed entirely of specie. A limited amount of notes (well within the normal issue) could be issued without specie backing, but beyond this minimum there should be a backing of 100 per cent of specie. Then an influx of gold into the country would expand the currency by an equal amount; an efflux would contract it in the same proportion. Deposits should not be regulated at all.
>
> (Whittaker, 1947, p. 659).

Peel's Bank Charter Act of 1844–5 reflected the views of the Currency School. By this, credit creation was to be limited by tying the central bank to gold cover.

The thesis of the non-regulation of bank deposits shows that the Currency School is today, in an era of establishing minimum reserves, long out of date. The fact that Marx was opposed to this school shows his practical mind. On the other hand, the 'one hundred per cent cover clause' reminds us of many theses of the liberal 'Chicago School' of our time. Fritsch is of the opinion (1968, p. 168) that Marx opposed the Currency School because the Bank Act implied 'a measure of self-help by the capitalist mode of production with the aim . . . of avoiding the periodical reappearance of crises. . . . In this sense it was important for Marx to prove to banks their incapacity to do away with an . . . inherent regularity.'

The opposition, the Banking School, was represented above all by Thomas Tooke, John Fullarton (a former banker in India), and the founder of the London *Economist*, James Wilson.

These three men saw that bank deposits and other means of payment (such as bills of exchange) served the purpose of money. They thought it foolish to regulate currency while leaving these substitutes uncontrolled. It might have been expected that the banking school would have advocated regulating both currency and deposits, as is done now in the United States. Instead, they argued in favor of leaving both of them uncontrolled by law, trusting to ordinary banking principles – and especially to the necessity for bankers to ensure that they could meet their obligations in specie if need be – to prevent over-issue and consequent inflation of credit. (Whittaker, 1947, p. 660.)

It is certainly not the case, as Fritsch would have us believe (1968, p. 166) in his allusions to V. F. Wagner (1937, p. 445-7), that the Banking theorists had seen no danger of inflation at all. It is therefore unjust to hold against the Banking School, because of its opinion that money created by bills of exchange had to flow back to banks with a minimum of delay, the view that credit inflation was impossible. What this school really assumed was the improbability of an inflation of banknotes. In this respect, surely, it was wrong. Neisser, an author strongly influenced by Marx, showed during the 1930s that such a doctrine of the innocuousness of the extension of credit is fully founded only if the 'money created through discounting measures on the basis of commercial bills of exchange stays in circulation no longer than newly-made goods do during the process of marketing, right down to the net income receiver, and provided it effects only the necessary sales during this period' (Neisser, 1931, pp. 404ff.).

We should, however, avoid jumping to the conclusion that the Banking School entirely rejected a policy of central banking. The main thing it did was to stress that the legal reserve requirements were pitched too high. The truth of this was shown by the fact that the Bank Charter Act of 1844-5, which made no exceptions, had, owing to a financial crisis, to be suspended just a few years after its inception.

In theory the Currency School's idea was supposed to lead to the automatic functioning of the currency in the manner of the gold standard. Relative increases in price would lead to an import surplus, to a drain of gold, and to a contraction in the money supply, and with this to decreases in price and *vice versa*. In Chapter 33 of volume III of *Capital*, Marx refers to such a chain of causation.

In practice, however, private banks succeeded in creating money, for cash and later central-bank deposits served as reserve cover. The rate of reserve cover varied and as a consequence much of the automatic functioning was lost. While the Banking School was right on the principle of leaving initiatives to the discretion of the central bank, there were many aspects in which it was wrong. This is shown by the fact that in the area of regulations the ideas of the Currency School had some success. This success was attained not by statutory means, but through the application, at the central bank's own discretion, of many new instruments, concerning not only discount policy, but also, among other things, the maintenance of a minimum reserve ratio. As can be seen, the Currency School was to some extent enriched by ideas coming from the Banking School.

We should, nevertheless, refrain from identifying Marx with the Banking School. Even Fritsch concedes this (1968, p. 169): 'The fact that Marx theoretically was much too consistent to equate formally and functionally the bill of exchange with the banknote shows that we cannot speak unreservedly of Marx as a "Banking" theorist.' Moreover, he repeatedly speaks of errors and confusion among the protagonists.

It is, indeed, possible to interpret Marx as saying that the quantity of money is a function of prices, and not, as is the case in the theories of the Banking School, the reverse. On the other hand, in his writings on the importance of the velocity of circulation of money, Marx introduced an independent variability into the quantity of money and advanced a refined quantity theory, which in essence must run counter to the Banking School. In his view a banknote inflation was possible to the extent that the velocity of circulation of banknotes increased.

Fritsch has suggested, as has already been stressed, that Marx's opposition to the Currency School was in the first instance determined by the optimism this school showed with regard to business-cycle policy. It was of the opinion that banks had the potential for influencing the business cycle, a view which Marx thought to be an over-estimation. To this extent, his opposition to the theory of the Currency School was but a continuation of the polemics directed at Proudhon and his school (Darimon and others), who saw in the manipulation of banking policy the lever whereby to control cyclical developments and even to overcome capitalism. When Peel's Bank Charter Act had to be suspended, the crises that made this necessary seemed to prove Marx and the Banking School correct, but, funnily enough, this did not mean that banking policy in itself was ineffective, for these events at last allowed the central bank to have control over credit creation and to undertake policies for the revival of business. In practice it would have been impossible to take such steps on the basis of the restricted issue of notes favoured by the Currency School, which wanted to make the bank the instrument of its business-cycle policy! Appearance and reality often diverge.

Marx himself saw in the Bank Charter Act 'the arbitrary provision that the Bank may make out as many paper notes as it has gold in the treasury and 14 million more' (*Capital*, III, ch. 26, p. 433). However, the Act 'made it a principle of the Bank of England to regulate the interest rate by the quantity of bullion in its possession' (ibid., p. 431), which means that its policy was determined not from the viewpoint of cyclical control but simply by the intention to hold a reserve cover, which might offer protection against inflation but could not do so against deflation. What then followed was that the banking discount rate, still 3 to $3\frac{1}{2}\%$ in January 1847, rose to 7% in April, when the first panic broke out . . . in November to 10%. . . . The general cessation of payments caused the failure of several leading and very many medium-sized and small firms. The Bank itself was in danger due to the limitations imposed by the artful Bank Act of 1844. The government yielded to the general clamour and suspended the Bank Act on October 25. . . . Now it could throw its supply of bank-notes into circulation without hindrance. The credit of these bank-notes being in practice guaranteed by the credit of the nation, and thus unimpaired, the money stringency was thus instantly and decisively relieved. (Ibid., ch. 25, p. 408.)

Engels, who gives us this description of the events that led to the suspension of the Bank Act in 1847, only three years after its introduction, wants to show by such a statement that he himself fully appreciates the cyclical function of the bank. Marx, in attacking the Currency School, adds to this (ibid., ch. 26, p. 421),

What Overstone wished to prove is that the crisis of 1847, and the attendant high interest rate, had nothing to do with the 'quantity of money', i.e., with the regulations of the Bank Act of 1844 which he had inspired; although it was, indeed, connected with them, inasmuch as the fear of exhausting the bank reserve – a creation of Overstone – contributed a money panic to the crisis of 1847–48.

In view of these remarks it is difficult to agree with Fritsch, who explains Marx's opposition to the Currency School in terms of his aversion to monetary contracyclical policy. Rather Marx was of the opinion that the Bank Act had missed its target, as it had destroyed the opportunity of creating a contracyclical interest-rate policy and, moreover, deepened the recession, as a result of monetary panic. This is another instance of Marx's very critical and pertinent observations on events. In essence, he reproaches the school which he repudiates not so much for what it intended and for what might have been uncongenial to him personally, as on account of the fact that because of its own machinations it was not in a position to realise its declared intention – namely, the stabilisation of the business cycle. The Currency School offered a safety valve against inflation, but in the case of cyclical recessions it had to cede the field to the Banking School. Indeed, shortly after the comments cited above, Marx remarks that through high interest rates, i.e. rates which were literally forced up, 'the high profit rate would go the way of all flesh'.

On the other hand, Marx finds himself between two lines of thinking, as when, for example, he reproaches Tooke, a representative of the Banking School, for causing 'confusion' (ibid., ch. 28). The main reason for this reproach seems to lie in the apologetic attitude of the Banking School towards the function of credit. Marx reproaches Tooke above all for not seeing that 'the velocity of circulation [determines] . . . the mass of circulating money' (ibid., p. 445).

Furthermore, Marx remonstrates with Fullarton, another representative of the Banking School, for falsely distinguishing between currency and capital. While the Banking School thought it possible to restrict credit operations to commercial bills of exchange, in order to avoid the menace of inflation, Marx saw credit as having the function of extending the available sum of capital. Marx is of the opinion that within a capitalist economy the role of credit is that of an additional injection of money, which permits an increase in the velocity of circulation of money. His formulation does not say quite clearly to what extent it is a matter of the creation of additional money by way of endorsements.

As early as in his *Critique of Political Economy* Marx had shown (p. 105) that the velocity of the circulation of money was subject to variation: 'In periods of expanding credit the velocity of currency increases faster than the prices of commodities, whereas in periods of contracting credit the velocity of currency declines faster than the prices of commodities.'

Besides such a cyclical variability in the velocity of circulation, there is also, in his opinion, a secular tendency for the velocity to increase. Marx takes his point of departure from the following basic functions:

> money . . . is economised through credit in three ways. A. By dropping away entirely in a great many transactions. [Here it can be assumed that Marx had in mind the settlement of clearing-accounts, which he also mentions in other places.] B. By the accelerated circulation of the circulating medium. [Here Marx approaches the creation of money by the banking system as a whole.] This is bound up with the technique of banking. . . . C. 2 . . . On the other hand, credit helps to keep the acts of buying and selling longer apart and serves thereby as a basis for speculation. [Here the reference is to differences in settlement terms for payment and is similar to the Keynesian notion of 'finance'.]
>
> (*Capital*, III, ch. 27, pp. 435–6.)

Marx then goes on to say that credit makes it possible to have control over capital, recognising that the creation of money has to be seen as a function of the banking system.

CREDIT AND CAPITAL

In connexion with credit Marx speaks of an 'expropriation on the most enormous scale' through 'centralisation of capital'. This makes us think of the notion of forced saving. For him credit is the 'appropriation of social property by a few'. 'The credit system [forces] . . . the reproduction process . . . to its extreme limits, and is so forced because a large part of the social capital is employed by people who do not own it and who consequently tackle things quite differently from the owner'. The credit system brushes aside 'an immanent fetter and barrier to production', which is one of the characteristics of capitalist production, and it 'accelerates the material development of the productive forces and the establishment of the world-market'. (*Capital*, III, ch. 27, p. 441.)

This apotheosis of credit is basically opposed to the philosophy of the Banking theorists, who have a tendency to underestimate the consequences of bills of credit. Their theory of the constant (and, as it were, immediate) return flow of the means of exchange to the central bank tries to prove the harmlessness of the consequences. In contrast, Marx recognises the capital-creating (because centralising), concentrating power of credit. In his view, capital is in practice synonymous with discounted interest yield: 'Value of capital generally speaking, signifies precisely the rate of interest! . . . "Value of capital", as we have shown elsewhere, is never conceived otherwise in theory.' In this context he disassociates himself from the 'vulgar conception of capital as "commodities used in production"', which is the conception of the Currency theorists.

> In so far as these commodities serve as capital, their value as *capital*, as distinct from their value as *commodities*, is expressed in the profit which is derived from their productive or mercantile employment. . . . And there is no doubt that the interest rate is generally limited by the rate of profit . . . [and the theory] should tell us just how this limit is determined. And it is determined by the supply and demand of money-capital as *distinguished* from the other forms of capital. . . . It is doubtlessly true that a tacit connection exists between the supply of material capital and the supply of money-capital, and, likewise, that the demand of industrial capitalists for money-capital is determined by conditions of actual production [which nowadays we call investment]. Instead of enlightening us on this point, Norman offers us the sage opinion that the demand for money-capital is not identical with the demand for money as such; and this sagacity alone, because he, Overstone, and the other Currency prophets, constantly have pricks of conscience since they are striving to make capital out of means of circulation as such through the artificial intervention of legislation, and to raise the interest rate. (Ibid., ch. 26, p. 419.)

Here one might think that the Currency School served the interests of City financiers, while the Banking School looked after the interests of industry. Employing polemics characteristic of him, Marx calls the Currency theorists logicians of usury . . . banking lords . . . [with a] narrow-minded banker's point of view. . . . Overstone evidently thinks that the country's annual savings . . . are converted only into money-capital. But if no real accumulation, i.e., expansion of production and augmentation of the means of production, had taken place, what good would there be from the accumulation of debtor's money claims on this production? (Ibid., pp. 423–4.)

It thus becomes clear that Marx thinks that savings are created by investment, and not *vice versa*. Marx's view of the Currency School as the representative of the financial interests of the City becomes even clearer when he says (ibid., ch. 34, p. 559), 'All the following stipulations aim to raise the interest rate; that the Bank of England shall not issue notes exceeding 14 million except against gold reserve; that the banking department shall be administered as an ordinary bank. . . . And this high interest rate was precisely the purpose of the Act.'

It is not without justice that Fritsch (1968, p. 120) has called the Marxian credit theory the 'continuation of the preceding theory of capital', i.e. the theory of the circulation of capital. In general he depicts Marxian credit theory as follows (ibid., p. xiii):

In Marx's work, credit forms the integrated driving power for the centrifugal forces of the capitalist system. Credit for Marx is not just an enduring component of the system in the classical theory of harmony, for it operates in an evolutionary manner, which is synonymous for Marx with the transition of the capitalist mode of production into a centrally directed socialist economic order based on the consciousness of the members of society.

This is the reason why Fritsch attempts, 'through the integration into the system of an adequate theoretical credit perspective, to fill an obvious gap in Marx's studies'. In this he is to a large extent successful, but this cannot be elaborated upon here.

The fact that in volume II of *Capital* Marx repeatedly states that he assumes money to be only 'metallic money, excluding symbolic money . . . and credit-money' (p. 115) creates difficulties, and has contributed to the idea of him as a metallist. Despite such remarks, however, which were not eliminated by Engels as editor, Marx discusses money in the modern sense as being the basis of the credit system even within the framework of the 'simple' circular-flow process. In volume II even remarks about additional credit turn up here and there.

The basic ideas from which Marx starts are already evident in volume I of *Capital*. According to these it is necessary to finance production in advance, if we look at it from the entrepreneurial point of view: 'the surplus-value is not realised. . . . So far as individual consumption is concerned, the surplus-value is anticipated. Funds for that purpose must be advanced' (ibid., ii, ch. 17, p. 323).

To begin with, it is necessary to postulate that liquid funds have to be built up (from the firm's provision for depreciation). Marx speaks of the 'accumulation of money, a raking together of a portion of the surplus-value in the form of latent money-capital, which is not intended to function as additional active capital until later'. He then goes beyond the view of the individual capitalist, on whom, at this point, he still keeps an eye: 'with the development of capitalist production the credit system also develops'. (Ibid., p. 325.)

Repeatedly Marx speaks of 'demand for money accommodation'. Here he obviously thinks of the total effective quantity of money. In this connexion he comes very near to the description of a genuine process for the creation of book-money.

The most important passage of this kind is to be found shortly after a paragraph of which Engels says that it was partly 'unintelligible', for which reason he felt obliged to rewrite it (ibid., iii. ch. 28, p. 454). It seems that Marx was at this point particularly close to the modern theory of the creation of money. He wanted to describe 'how . . . a bank that issues notes, like the Bank of England, [can] increase the amount of money accommodation granted by it without increasing its issue of bank-notes'. He is therefore practically speaking of an 'open-market policy': 'The bank pays A notes against securities. . . . [He is then ready to make concessions to Fullarton:] A uses them to pay for bills of exchange due to B, and B deposits notes once more in the bank. This brings to a close the circulation of these notes, but the loan remains' (ibid., p. 453). Marx continues (ibid., pp. 457–8),

> Our assumption so far has been that the loans are made in notes, so that they carry with them at least a fleeting, even if instantly disappearing, increase in the issue of notes. But this is not necessary. Instead of a paper note, the bank may open a credit account for A, in which case this A, the bank's debtor, becomes its imaginary depositor. He pays his creditors with cheques on the bank, and the recipient of these cheques passes them on to his own banker, who exchanges them for the cheques outstanding against him in the clearing house. . . . or when the transactions take place without the mediation of notes by means of book credit . . . it is a peculiarity of money . . . when it serves merely to settle accounts . . . that its circulation is no more than fleeting. . . .

He adds (ibid., ch. 33, p. 522), 'We have seen previously that one and the same bank-note can constitute deposits in several banks.'

With this Marx again takes up a matter raised in the second volume of *Capital*, where he states (ch. 21, p. 497), 'these potential capitals within the credit system, by their concentration in the hands of banks, etc., become disposable [here the analogy with Cassel's notion of 'capital disposition' becomes obvious] "loanable capital", money-capital. . . .'

These and other remarks show that Marx had a clear recognition of the money-creating power of the credit system. He clearly perceives that resources which are temporarily set free in the turnover of capital feed the credit system. 'The money-capital thus released by the mere mechanism of the turnover movement . . . must play an important role as soon as the credit system develops and must at the same time form one of the latter's foundations' (ibid., ch. 15, p. 286).

The importance of this factor becomes clear when we consider that, for instance, a large part of the liquid dollar balances (including the Eurodollar market) in the modern world currency system consists of the cash reserves of large international corporations. Money of this sort, in the form of 'hot money' has had a destabilising effect wherever currency crises have occurred. It would therefore be appropriate to have a closer look at Marx's views on the world monetary situation.

40 Marx on International Monetary Problems

At the level of the world economy, Marx fully approves of the quantity theory: here, according to him, 'one can speak of the quantity of money only in so far as it concerns bullion, universal money' (*Capital*, III, ch. 33, p. 536). These and similar formulations are apt to raise the suspicion that Marx was in fact sympathetic to metallism. Nevertheless, it would be to miss the point to develop such a thesis on remarks taken out of context, for in this context Marx had in mind international and not national conditions. In many different places this thinking in international terms comes to light. It has its roots in the idea that the capitalist world forms a basic whole, and it is in this worldwide setting that the basic conception of Marxian currency theory has to be seen. Already in his *Critique of Political Economy* (pp. 149–50) it had been developed in this form:

> Money functioning as world money reverts to its original natural form. . . . Gold and silver in the sphere of international commodity circulation appear not as a means of circulation but as universal means of exchange. . . . With the development of commodity exchange between different national spheres of circulation, the function which world money fulfils as means of payment for settling international balances develops also.

In volume I of *Capital* he describes (ch. 3, p. 142) 'money of the world . . . as the universally recognised embodiment of all wealth'.

According to Marx, foreign trade helps to raise the rate of profit by means of a cheapening of raw materials and foodstuffs (ibid., III, ch. 14, p. 232). By these means it is assumed that wage increases, if they cannot be reversed, can at least be avoided, while export prices can remain at a high level. One may therefore conclude that any industrial country with access to the world market is in a position to improve its exchange situation.

Foreign demand for domestic currency remains high, while home demand for the foreign currency of raw-material suppliers remains moderate. This is the point of departure for the 'exploitation' of raw-material suppliers by means of movement in the exchange rate, reflecting a shift in the terms of trade – a shift which in the final analysis has its origin in the quasi-monopolistic situation of industrial countries (as Marx outlines in the case of Great Britain). The problem of 'exploitation' through the exchange rate has not been systematically examined by Marx or by Marxists.

In various places in his writings, Marx is on the verge of developing a theory of exchange, as for instance in the section on 'world money' in the *Critique of Political Economy*, and in the *Grundrisse*. Though regarding the whole world as a co-ordinated capitalist system, such attempts, unfortunately, come to nothing. This fiction dominates most theoretical passages of *Capital* and is relaxed only by illustrative recourse to the reality of interchange between different nations.

The problematical character of such 'world money' as developed in the *Critique* has been sketched by Marx as follows: 'gold and silver cannot comply with the demand that as money they should have an invariable value' (*Critique*, p. 155). Though he alludes to Aristotle's statement that the value of gold and silver has greater stability than the average of 'other commodities', he is sceptical of this ancient theory. He points out that the value ratio between gold and silver has undergone considerable fluctuations in the course of history: 'During the era of the Roman emperors, 15 or 16 to 1 can be taken as the rough average, although the value of silver in Rome often sank even lower . . . while Strabo's statement that an Arabian tribe gave two pounds of gold for one pound of silver is by no means incredible' (ibid., pp. 156–7). Marx's investigations into conditions in ancient times suggested that the relative scarcity of gold during the Roman Empire (in China, by contrast, the value ratio lay between 6 : 1 and 8 : 1 and remained stable for quite a long time) was caused by a continual drain of gold as a consequence of a permanent import surplus in trade with Eastern countries, whose industry was superior to that of Mediterranean countries. This comparison reminds us of the drain of gold to the USA after the Second World War, a trend which has been reversed since the mid-1950s.

Marx (*Capital*, III, ch. 28, p. 452) comes nearest to a theory of currency in his discussion of Tooke's discovery, cited by Fullarton, that 'with only one or two exceptions every remarkable fall of the exchange, followed by a drain of gold, that has occurred during the last half century, has been coincident throughout with a comparatively low state of the circulating media, and vice versa' (Fullarton, 1845, p. 121). This would suggest that a domestic scarcity of money is reflected in a depreciation of the currency of the country concerned, and this in turn implies that high interest rates go hand in hand with high prices, which, in both cases, suggests a scarcity of money, from which follows a deficit in the balance of trade and a drain of gold. It seems that the Banking School was not yet aware that there is such a thing as an influx of foreign exchange where the level of the domestic rate of interest is high.

When Marx argues that 'such drains of gold occur generally after a period of animation and speculation, as "the signal of a collapse already commenced"'', he appears to be thinking of a banking panic, such as that of 1847 or 1931. He supports the view that 'the demand for *international* media of circulation and payment differs from the demand for internal media of circulation and payment . . . and that the export of precious metal and its being thrown into international circulation is not the same as throwing notes or specie into internal circulation' (*Capital*, III, ch. 28, p. 453).

Here he wants to say that the drain of gold need not necessarily be the result of credit expansion within the country. Here an analogy arises with the drain of 'hot money' from the United States as a consequence of economic slack linked to particularly low rates of interest. This would signify that, unlike the theorists of the Banking School, Marx had already recognised that changes in the interest rate signal a drain or influx of capital.

Marx thought that variations in the exchange rate were bound to happen 'when the customary equilibrium in the interchange of products between different nations is suddenly disturbed' (ibid., I, ch. 3, p. 143). He nevertheless abstained from developing a systematic theory to explain the 'ceaseless fluctuations in the course of exchange' (ibid., p. 144). This is true even of chapter 35 of volume II of *Capital*, entitled 'Precious metals and the Rate of Exchange'. With the exception of occasional references to colonial exchange and exchange rates, there is little indication that he intended to develop an exchange theory. Here we do have a deficiency, which has still not been remedied despite many valiant attempts by his disciples.

The role of gold on the international scene Marx analysed early in his thesis on world money in the *Critique of Political Economy*, where he explains that it has the function of regulating the balance of payments. In *Capital* (III, ch. 32, p. 517) he states, 'The entire history of modern industry shows that metal would indeed be required only for the balancing of international commerce, whenever its equilibrium is momentarily disturbed, if only domestic production were organised.' In this context he prophetically speaks of 'money crises – independent of or as an intensification of actual crises'.

Marx does not think that 'reserve funds' in terms of gold are of any importance for domestic monetary circulation. For him it is obvious that 'countries in which the bourgeois form of production is developed to a certain extent, limit the hoards concentrated in the strong rooms of the banks to the minimum required for the proper performance of their peculiar functions' (ibid., I, ch. 3, p. 144).

In chapter 35 of volume III of *Capital*, Marx once again discusses inflows and outflows of gold, which he sees as only partially reflecting the import and export surpluses in Great Britain in the nineteenth century. Considering the importance of capital exports, it can be said that since the 1850s, the increase in reserves has normally played the dominant role. According to

Marx's reasoning, a drain of gold may be a token of crisis where 'an illusory prosperity is maintained only by means of credit'. Marx is right in warning the Banking theorist Wilson that a capital export is not synonymous with an export of gold. He sees capital exports in the form of surpluses of exports as the normal case – 'iron rails' instead of 'precious metal' to India. He goes on to say that

> there is a demand for Indian bills of exchange which exceeds their supply, and so the rates turn for a time against England, not because it is in debt to India, but because it has to send extraordinary sums to India. . . . [England receives from India] tribute partly for exported 'good government' and partly in the form of revenues from capital. . . . the rates of exchange are not affected when England simply consumes this tribute without exporting anything in return [i.e. if they are imported in the guise of a commodity]. . . . *it is also* evident that the rates of exchange are *not affected when it reinvests this tribute* . . . in foreign countries.

Marx contents himself with a repetition of the controversy between Wilson and Newmarch about inflows and outflows of gold and about the rate of interest. (Ibid., pp. 571, 577, 583.)

Here one might feel inclined to ask whether Marx, when he speaks of the depreciation of money ('If £1 should represent only half as much money as formerly, it would naturally be counted as 12·5 francs instead of 25 francs' – (ibid., p. 591), was anticipating Cassel's idea of purchasing-power parity. We nevertheless have to admit that in spite of the intervention of Engels, this chapter (III, ch. 35) is far from clear.

41 Marxism and the Theory of Money

The theory of money has always been something of a stepchild of Marxian theory. Bartoli regretted (1950, p. 101, note 1) that it 'was defended by Kautsky without success' and that it 'has been renounced by neo-Marxists', though discussion has not been lacking. Fritsch points out (1968, p. xii), 'The many controversies in connexion with the Marxian theory of money show that it has been rather difficult to formulate a clear and immanent critique. The example of the controversy between Kautsky and Hilferding gives some idea of the far-reaching effects of the confusion engendered by socialist and non-socialist theorists.' This controversy raged shortly before the First World War, filling whole columns of the newspaper *Neue Zeit* (1911–12), but all to little effect. For this reason Fritsch says that 'theoretically these controversies may serve only as a reference point'.

MARXIST INTERPRETATION OF THE QUANTITY EQUATION WITH THE EMPHASIS ON COMMODITIES

This controversy deals with a basic question in the theory of money and its development – namely, the problem of determining the value of money and of finding out what causes changes. Hilferding intended to blaze a new trail by coining the expression 'social circulating value'; in so doing he was not so far away from the modern view that the value of money is independent of the 'principle of cover', which was in vogue during the nineteenth century. Karl Kautsky's view, by contrast, was that of the orthodox school. In discussing this controversy, Fritsch says that, 'as it was developed by Marxian monetary theorists, it over-emphasised the influence commodities had on the value of money'.

In fact, even modern Marxist monetary theorists continually stress the importance of commodities. Pesenti, for instance, investigates the 'classical' quantity equation $M = PQ/V$ (the quantity of money = prices × the volume of commodities, over velocity of circulation of money). He is of the opinion that quantity theorists originally started from the hypothesis that both the volume of commodities and the velocity of circulation remained constant. The result is that 'the more M (the quantity of money) increases, the more P (the price level) increases, and with this there takes place a reciprocal change in the value of money to the quantity of money'. In the last resort, this theory dates back to Ricardo, who, according to Pesenti, showed that to fulfil the functions of money it is necessary to limit the quantity of money. On the other hand, Pesenti stresses that it is possible to understand the problem of money only if one is prepared to make 'the process of social production the starting point'. Only from an analysis of the production process is it possible to deduce the necessary quantity of money. (Pesenti, 1962, p. 29.)

Suzanne de Brunhoff emphasises (1967, p. 47) that in the Marxian theory there are two elements that play a major role, the hoarding of money, as a potential source of crisis, and the primacy given to production. Taking her point of departure from the Marxian 'cycle' of the transformation of money into commodities and into surplus value, she stresses that accumulation and transformation from M to M' have their origin in production and not in exchange (in the process of circulation).

The tendency to reject Hilferding's analysis can be explained by this thesis, which gives primacy to production and is highly regarded by Marxian monetary theorists. Hilferding was desirous of seeing in banking a 'powerful capitalist apparatus' forming the 'centre of the financial structure'. Contrary to this Suzanne de Brunhoff argues (1971, pp. 10, 78) that it is not possible to credit commercial banks with the role of financial control, as they are subject to stronger regulatory measures than is any other capitalist economic sector.

In her analysis she endeavours to work out the problems derived from the credit multiplier and from this the importance of a national banking policy to control the quantity of money, in the sense of a relation between a normative and an effective quantity of money. In this she takes her starting point from the work of the American authors Patinkin, and Gurley and Shaw, but she does not succeed in fully evaluating the fundamental importance that international credit creation possesses for capitalist expansion.

From a Marxist viewpoint, the creation of credit and its importance at the international level, through the existing deficits in the balance of payments of the United States, has been worked out by, above all, de Cindio, a disciple of Pesenti. In his work he demonstrates that, by way of gold, the Marxian economy can free itself from any traces of the labour-value dependence for money. He states (1962, p. 197) that gold 'has been unable to fulfil in an organic way its old exclusive role of international money' since losing this function to the dollar, but that the dollar, like any other currency system created by national measures, is the victim of an internal process through which it loses its value. De Cindio sees the possibility of a scheme to internationalise reserve funds on the lines that Keynes unsuccessfully advocated in 1944. This was wrecked by the American White Plan, which produced the International Monetary Fund and a world currency system based on the dollar – a system which de

Cindio calls the 'dollar-exchange system'. De Cindio refers to more recent plans by Triffin, and predicts that in the long run trends in the flow of international capital will be reversed. In this context he points to calculations by Jacobsson. According to these 'there will be an increase in population of 0·7 per cent (per annum) during the next forty years in Western Europe, of 1·7 per cent in the United States and of 2 per cent in the rest of the world. In relation to the United States this situation will produce a capital surplus in Europe and a capital flow from Europe to the United States' (ibid., p. 176). The question is whether this 'demographic capital-flow theory' is sufficient, in face of the problems caused by a fall in the rate of interest, by the Eurodollar market, and so on. It is not the capital market that stands in the foreground of what happens on the international scene, but problems in the money markets and in the situation of currencies.

With regard to the theory of money, which, according to von Bortkiewicz and others, is coupled with a 'theory of gold production', de Cindio's work contains certain nostalgic features. This is so when he refers to his fellow-countryman Federici, who as late as 1950 declared (p. 134), 'The great division between the theory of money and general theory, originating as it did in an epoch when it was necessary to explain value with reference to production costs, still lingers on. It has not been possible to overcome this fissure by means of the "empty box" of the marginal utility of money.'

These tendencies appear again and again in de Cindio's work – for instance, where he says, 'The essential point is that gold, having taken on the function of money, has not ceased to be a commodity, and the quantity of gold, necessary as an effective monetary means, appears in the double guise of commodity and money.' He then discusses the theses of the metallists and nominalists and gives the following opinion:

> One thing is certain: the value of the commodity gold depends on its production costs. Even those who are disinclined to accept such a fact are troubled when faced with the opposite thesis of the marginalist. . . . The debate . . . has not found an all-embracing theoretical solution and has run out of steam. As a consequence, any claims to truth have remained with [the theory of production costs]. . . . If gold is a commodity, its production must incur costs, and such costs are bound to determine its price and its normal exchange value in the long run. (De Cindio, 1962, pp. 157–8.)

Though harbouring some scepticism, de Cindo goes on to point to calculations, initiated by Cassel, of the demand for liquidity. Cassel concluded that

> the price level of 1850 was identical to that of 1910, and during the intervening period the gold stock increased by a multiple of 5·2

with an average annual growth rate of 2· per cent. From this Cassel drew the further conclusion that this increase had been necessary to secure the economic growth which had actually taken place. For the period 1938–57 (according to the IMF's *International Reserves Liquidity*, 1958) economic growth averaged about 4·6 per cent per annum (and 3·3 per cent in the case of trade). If for the period 1957–66 one assumes that foreign trade grew at a rate of 3 per cent per annum, and if one assumes no increase in reserves for countries which already have large reserves, then the additional demand for gold diminishes from $19,000 million to $8000 million, for which there is gold to hand to the value of $7000 million. The remainder has to be met from foreign exchange reserves. We have to observe that there is normally a certain amount of optimism in such calculations.   (Ibid., p. 159, note 1.)

But this last sentence of de Cindio exhibits a certain scepticism. It seems that he nourishes the same apprehensions as Triffin with regard to an eventual future scarcity of liquidity, a phenomenon which still seems to be distant, considering the flood of dollars in the 1970s, but which is none the less capable of making an appearance, in the event of a flight from the dollar. At any rate, it can be said that de Cindio's analysis is evidence that Marxist economists are interested in world currency problems. One may conjecture that stabilising as well as destabilising elements in the worldwide capitalist boom, which – prior to the "Great Recession" of 1974/5 – had been interrupted only by minor recessions since the Second World War, may have had their origin in the world currency situation. Conviction of this is gaining ground in Marxist circles, as can be seen from the work of Altvater and his collaborators Neusüss and Blank (1971).

With regard to the view that in the long run the United States will not be in a position to play, like Great Britain in the nineteenth century, the role of 'world banker', de Cindio (1962, p. 147, note 3) points to, among other things, Elliott's opinion that the idea that the dollar might take the pound's former role is probably misplaced, for the USA neither needs large-scale imports nor is under great pressure to export capital – factors which, before World War I, had rendered the pound a very readily accessible currency.

MANDEL'S MODERNISATION OF THE MARXIAN THEORY OF MONEY

It is above all Mandel in his work *Der Spätkapitalismus* (Late Capitalism), published in 1972, who has developed a modern conception of the Marxian theory of money. His conception represents a meritorious attempt to find a common denominator for the Marxian theory of money and credit, on the one hand, and the quantity theory in a dynamic form, on the other. 'It is by overcoming the dualism between the labour theory of value, which determines the value of commodities, and the quantity theory, which determines the "value of money", that Marx is enabled to develop a consistent economic theory' (Mandel, 1972, p. 373).

Mandel rejects Hilferding's attempt to derive the ' "socially necessary value of circulation" directly from the value of total products, i.e. the sum of values of all circulating commodities'. In opposing Hilferding's theories, he relies upon the refutation by Suzanne de Brunhoff, of whom he nevertheless says that she 'is as little able as Kautsky to work out the decisive features of the Marxian theory of money' (ibid., p. 374, note 9).

According to Mandel, the fundamental elements of the Marxian theory of money are to be found in his *Grundrisse*, from which (pp. 139–40) he quotes the following passage:

> The difference between price and value, between the commodity measured by the labour time whose product it is, and the product of the labour time against which it is exchanged, this difference calls for a third commodity to act as a measure in which the real exchange value of commodities is expressed. Because price is not equal to value, therefore the value-determining element – labour time – cannot be the element in which prices are expressed, because labour time would then have to express itself simultaneously as the determining and the non-determining element, as the equivalent and the non-equivalent of itself.

It was Hilferding's intention to develop his own monetary theory on the sum of values, which he divided by the velocity of circulation of money. With regard to this, Mandel says that this formula is 'of twofold emptiness: first, because the "sum of values of commodities" represents the totality of labour quantities, which can be reduced to the labour time that is socially necessary only by means of an exchange and by means of a division into different proportions'.

This first reason may be disputed, as it could be assumed that the notion of value already implies such a conversion into the average socially necessary labour time. If such a conversion is not implied, it is difficult to know what represents the 'sum of values'. Comparisons made by Marx between labour that is more, and labour that is less, productive point in this direction.

Mandel is, however, right, when he continues, 'secondly, because it is impossible to divide such a quantity of labour by the "velocity of circulation of money"; five million hours of work divided by twenty-five times per year for circulating metal money or banknotes is an empty formula'. (Mandel, 1972, p. 374.)

This controversy lays bare the difficulties arising for post-Marxian theory in applying the notion of value in the field of monetary theory. Basically this is quite understandable. In a dynamic sense the counterpart to the quantity of money, i.e. the volume of money multiplied by an (ever-changing) velocity of circulation, can, as Marx himself points out, never represent the sum of values; it can only be the product of labour, i.e. the physical volume of commodities, which the value concept does not embrace and which appears as exchange value only after multiplication.

Fundamentally this means that Mandel distinguishes sharply between a theory of value and a theory of money. All the same, he is here and there haunted by the ghost of 'the value of commodity money', which in the past did its best to give the Marxian theory of money the aspect of antiquated metallism. It has, however, to be said that in this respect Mandel limits himself to a particular function, namely that of 'world money', a function which, according to Marx, has to be fulfilled by precious metals. In Mandel's work this represents the 'first form', namely that of 'pure metal money'. The 'second form', paper money (convertible into gold) is, according to Mandel, practically 'as good as gold'. It is only to this second form that the following sentence of Mandel's could apply: 'Commodity prices always express the relationship between the value of two commodities, i.e. between a particular commodity and gold' (ibid., p. 383).

The transition from this 'second form' to a third, that of 'non-convertible paper-money at an obligatory rate' (ibid., p. 376) is to be seen as a more or less fluent process. By a simple stroke of the pen, the United States took measures to cancel convertibility into gold. In referring to a 'forced rate' Mandel contradicts himself, because it was initially his intention to set aside an explanation of the value of money in the sense of Knapp – 'through coercive measures on the part of the state'. In the final analysis, the value of money finds its expression in prices which in the long run cannot be frozen, even in the case of a successful momentary price freeze. With this statement, Mandel wants to demonstrate that, while coercive measures are of no influence whatsoever on purchasing power, such measures nevertheless do explain the acceptance of money.

RAPPROCHEMENT BETWEEN MODERN TROTSKYITE MARXISM AND MONETARISM

Mandel does not restrain himself from accepting the (tautological) quantity formula when he says (1972, p. 391), 'The increase in the quantity of money, i.e. the volume of paper money and bank deposits, is undoubtedly the direct technical cause of this dollar inflation. The quantity of money grew at a much greater rate than the volume of physical production.' He is of the opinion that his theory, which is meant to offer an 'explanation of the characteristic permanent inflations of late capitalism', had its forerunner in the 'contemporary version of the quantity theory' as we find it in the framework of the Marxian theory of money (ibid., p. 398). Here he quotes Marx's *Critique of Political Economy* (p. 119): 'where Marx points out that the quantity of bank notes is determined by the quantity of gold currency which they represent in circulation, their value being simply determined by their quantity.' Mandel is right in thinking that earlier analysts of the Marxian theory of money did not understand that Marx clearly confessed to a quantity theory, which received its 'dynamic' features from the emphasis he put on the importance of the great variability in the speed of circulation, and that he did not direct his diatribes against the quantity theory as such, but against its 'primitive' versions, which recognised only the volume of money in the narrower sense as the 'agent'. In the following passage Mandel shows that Marx did indeed recognise the full importance which an increase in the quantity of money had as a source of inflationary processes.

'While the quantity of gold in circulation depends on commodity prices, the value of paper currency in circulation depends exclusively on its own quantity. Marx refers to the state, issuing paper-money at a legal rate. He argues that 'this power of the state is deceptive, because once paper-money is drawn into circulation it cannot but obey its immanent laws.' Marx gives a numerical example which shows a five-fold increase in the quantity of money. From this he draws the conclusion: 'that commodity prices as a whole are bound to increase fifteenfold.'
(Mandel cites *Critique of Political Economy*, pp. 114–15.)

The 'difference between the Marxian . . . theory of money founded on the assumption of paper-money, and the classical or modern quantity theory' Mandel sees in the fact that,

for Marx, although he concedes a certain autonomy to the sphere of circulation – i.e. the productive sphere and demand, objectively determined by the law of value, for the means of exchange and payment are the given magnitudes – the increase in the quantity of money in relation to these magnitudes determines the decline in value of the currency unit.

Incidentally, Mandel stresses that it is a further essential trait of the Marxian theory that it treats the velocity of circulation as a variable and not as a constant magnitude. (Mandel, 1972, p. 399.)

This shows that Mandel stresses the dynamic character of the Marxian theory of money. It is not the quantity of money as such that is decisive but its counterpart, the demand for transactions – i.e. the quantity of money necessary to sell certain quantities of goods and services on the assumption of given prices – that is properly speaking the 'agent'. This may seem surprising, as earlier we came to the conclusion that the idea of a falling price level, in line with advances in productivity, is fundamental to the Marxian value concept. This would mean that the quantity of money would remain constant and yet be able to satisfy demand for a growing volume of products.

This demand for money for transactions touches on parts of the Keynesian theory of interest and money. Here we must distinguish between demand for liquidity for transactions purposes and demand for liquidity for speculative and precautionary purposes, which corresponds to the 'accumulation of wealth' or the 'hoarding principle' in Marx.

In dynamising the Marxian theory of money, Mandel argues that Marx sees the transactions demand as of pre-eminent importance, in view of the number of different stages of transaction. Hayek later took up this train of thought. Mandel sees in this aspect a unique feature distinguishing the Marxian theory from competing theories of money. Marx puts the emphasis on productive spheres and the demand derived from these. Apart from this distinction

> there are many subsidiary theses, e.g. of the stability of the velocity of circulation of money. If the latter is treated as a variable instead of as a constant, then the quantity of money ceases to be the only variable in the famous *quantity* formula $MV/T = P$ worked out by Fisher. Such a formula with two variables ceases to have any meaning at all; it expresses only an arithmetical tautology.

What Mandel tries to show here (1972, p. 399) is that Marx's opposition to the quantity theory had nothing to do with the formula itself, for it is already implicit in the reasoning of the *Critique of Political Economy*. His opposition is directed against authors who vulgarise the traditional quantity theory by neglecting particular elements such as the demand for transactions purposes and the velocity of circulation of money.

It comes near to irony that Mandel seeks to support his theses by referring to works in which the traditional quantity theory was re-surrected; we are here thinking particularly of the study by Friedman and Schwartz (1970). According to this the velocity of circulation of money shrank by 30 per cent, while the quantity of money increased by 25 per cent, during the Great Depression. With regard to this, Mandel says (1972, pp. 390–1, note 50), 'What a marvellous refutation of the orthodox "pure" quantity theory! Contrary to their assertion, the velocity of the circulation of money cannot be considered as given, and a significant increase in the quantity of money can be neutralised by a reduction of the velocity of circulation.'

Mandel recognises (ibid., p. 399, note 63) that 'the more refined versions of the quantity theory, among others that of the Chicago School . . . have given up the theory of a constant velocity of monetary circulation'. It cannot be denied that Mandel has been influenced to a certain extent by the modern theory of *Friedman*, which is built upon the Fisher approach. Thus he writes (ibid., pp. 378, 384, 398), 'There can be no doubt that there was a grain of truth in this 'orthodox' conception of money. . . . The Keynesian theory [is] true only to a certain extent. . . . To be sure there is some similarity [between Mandel's own theory and] the contemporary version of the quantity theory.' This similarity is all the more interesting as Friedman's scepticism about the efficacy of modern central-banking theory, inspired by Keynes, and of discretionary monetary and interest-rate policy makes him an ally of the Marxian theory, which expressed its scepticism of the banking-policy ideas of Proudhon's disciple Darimon (see above, ch. 37) in the same way. Sure enough, 'the decisive moment in the business cycle lies not in the quantity of money' but 'in the productive activity of capital, i.e. in the given and expected rate of profit' (Mandel, 1972, p. 399.)

THE MARXIAN ANALYSIS OF INFLATION AS OPPOSED TO MONETARISM

Mandel is of the opinion that manipulation of the quantity of money in the manner of central-banking theory is of as little use in eliminating the 'real cycle' in the capitalist system as is the recipe given by Friedman, according to which the rate of increase in the quantity of money should be kept constant over the cycle. By such means, Mandel succeeds in disentangling himself from the liberal neo-orthodox view of the Chicago School. He refers (1972, p. 399) to the fact that in the first half of 1971 Friedman and his followers had to accept to their cost that it was not possible to avoid a further stagnation of production and employment, even though a 6 per cent increase in the quantity of money had taken place.

The originality of Mandel's contribution to Marxian monetary theory rests on three points. First, it clearly shows the uniqueness of the Marxian version of the quantity theory, with its particular emphasis on the element of monetary circulation and on the 'hoarding' factor. Secondly, it shows, contrary to Hilferding and most other followers, that there is certainly a link between the Marxian idea of the business cycle and the theory of money. This is done with the implicit renunciation of the theory of value (which Hilferding puts in the foreground). Thirdly, it develops a unique, Marxist, secularly-oriented theory of inflation, which links concentration processes with modern developments in world currencies.

It is not possible here to offer a full evaluation of Mandel's contribution to the theory of business cycles, but his theoretical analysis of money presents us with one of the clearest and most complete achievements of Marxists on this subject, which had long been neglected. With these contributions Mandel has surely gone beyond the original conception of his two-volume *Traité d'Economie Marxiste*, which, though still showing strong historical and anthropological features, gives him a claim to a leading position among Marxist monetary theorists. It is most interesting to note the extent to which his theory runs parallel to 'academic' statements on the inflationary tendencies of our times.

In this context, Mandel points to a relative stability in wholesale prices in the United States between 1958 and 1964, while retail prices increased by about one-sixth. At the same time, there were above-average increases in the price of metal goods (with the exception of electrical appliances), machines and services ('above all for health and leisure'). From this and other data he draws the following conclusion (1972, p. 392):

> If we add to these series the almost uninterrupted tendency for raw-material prices to fall on the world market during the same period of time, then it is possible to determine the structure in the depreciation of money as follows. The transition from a system based on gold currency to a monetary system in which monopoly capital is able to secure the quantity of money adequate to its wants by way of bank deposits gives the large-scale concerns of late capitalism the possibility of increasing the prices of commodities sold by them in times of boom, and of keeping prices stable during times of recession under conditions of relative market control (oligopolistic competition, price-leadership). With strongly increasing labour productivity (the third technological revolution), this means an extension of the profit-margin. . . . One of the main goals of a prices policy, linked to 'administered prices', is the anticipation of sales fluctuations, i.e. the securing of profits even in times of recession. . . .

This of course would mean that the profit cycle, which for Marx and Mandel is of decisive importance, would be deprived of its effect.

A further cause of the inflationary developments of 'late capitalism' Mandel (ibid., p. 393) sees in 'realisation difficulties, which show themselves in a large increase in sales costs and consumer credit . . . [and which] are passed on to consumers. . . . The stronger the degree of monopolisation, the marginally higher are the price increases'.

In this context it is of interest to learn that Mandel, in contrast to Gillman, counts on a total shift in what appears in Marx as false costs (*faux frais*). Gillman also believes that sales costs are met out of surplus value, a remark which has been ridiculed by Joan Robinson. We have, however, to ask ourselves whether Mandel does not contradict his own earlier explanations – as, for instance, his declaration (1968, p. 211) that 'Distribution costs as a whole . . . are covered . . . by commercial capital.'

In his attempt to analyse the inflationary process from the Marxian point of view, Mandel has the help of only a few works by Marxist authors – for instance, Jourdan and Valier (1970), and works by Altvater and his pupils. Many of his arguments, however, he obtains from 'academic' economists, such as Means (1962) and Schwartzmann (1959). According to Means, 85 per cent of the overall price rise between 1953 and

1962 can be attributed to price increases in the products of highly concentrated sectors. If this is correct, one must lay at the door of the oligopolistic sectors the chief share of the social costs of inflation, in addition to the usual charge of misallocation of resources.

Here Mandel takes his point of departure from the theory of 'cost-push' inflation. He nevertheless stresses that this is correct only if there exists excess purchasing power. 'Only if there is an excess of liquidity can firms under monopoly capitalist conditions automatically pass on increases in costs to selling prices, and to consumers.'

At this point, Mandel's argument becomes obscure; he shifts his ground to the other major theory of inflation, the 'demand-pull' theory. Considering the voluminous literature on both theories, it is a pity that he does not go into the subject more deeply.

When he says that in the case of wage increases, given a constant quantity of money, 'cost increases need not, even in the absence of competition in certain industrial sectors, lead to price increases', he forgets how very precisely the Marxian theory stressed the more or less automatic adaptation of the quantity of money to the transactions needs of the economy, which in the face of wage increases would doubtless grow *via* the necessary greater liquidity – for instance, for cash balances.

After first wishing to place the responsibility for inflationary developments on the hardening of the oligopolistic structure, Mandel is paradoxically of the opinion that, 'from the theoretical point of view of money and value, the thesis of cost-push inflation is sheer nonsense'. He seems here to want to return to the Marxian theorem, according to which 'under conditions of currency stability . . . any wage increase with a given commodity output and value would have the effect of lowering profits, but would not necessarily lead to inflated prices' (Mandel, 1972, pp. 385–6). This seems to put too much weight on the *ceteris paribus* element, as the problem is just that of whether the currency (or rather its money value) will move in sympathy if entrepreneurs try to maintain their profit margins, for which they have an instrument at hand in monopolistic and oligopolistic price variability! To be sure, the Marxian argument expounded in 'Wage, Price and Profit' (*Marx/Engels, Selected Works*, 1968), on which Mandel relies, is valid only in the case of competition.

This 'contradiction' of the 'cost-push' theory of inflation is all the more surprising as Mandel's argument is built upon just these premises, and essential parts of it are derived from the theses of Jourdain and Valier (1970, pp. 56–7). Its summary treatment and its neglect of the existing literature on the subject fail to convince the reader.

There can be no doubt that the theory outlined by Mandel is not exhaustive as an explanation of modern inflationary processes. It is his main argument that in the 'modern long-wave with its stress on expansion . . . the intrinsic expenses of the state are of only secondary importance when it comes to explaining permanent inflation'. Mandel here to a large extent draws on the modified version of the theory of 'long waves' developed by Parvus, van Gelderen and Kondratieff, which we examine elsewhere. Mandel goes on to say (1972, p. 381), 'Credit extended by banks on current account to the private sector is the main source of inflation; this means credit extended for production purposes to capitalist concerns and consumer credit granted to households (primarily for the acquisition of living accommodation and durable consumer goods) . . . .'

Here Mandel joins the chorus on the debate over the destabilising effects of instalment credit (which sociologically and economically has become indispensable) and which has been in use for several decades. The present author dealt with this subject earlier (see Kühne, 1954, p. 291).

Time and again Mandel mixes together cost-push and demand-pull elements. His lapidary formulation nevertheless remains a milestone in the Marxian theory of money, which to this day has remained poor in realistic analyses. His work has to be valued more as a point of departure for further attempts in this direction than as the final word on the subject.

Mandel attempts to support his argument statistically, especially by employing United States data. He points to the fact that in the United States between 1946 and 1969 private indebtedness increased eightfold, while public indebtedness was multiplied by less than one and a half, and the gross national product by four and a half. By contrast, private indebtedness had remained practically stable between 1925 and 1945. In the case of Belgium, bank credit granted to the public sector doubled between 1962 and 1971, with the social product rising by a factor of one and a half, while bank credit extended to the private sector increased fivefold. With this Mandel wishes to prove that the source of inflationary developments must be sought in the creation of private credit. (Mandel, 1972, p. 382.)

Such an approach naturally demands a closer analysis of overall financial developments, as the different time-periods are subject to considerable fluctuations, which tend to go unheeded in a global view. The period from 1925 to 1945 is a case in point. Mandel's argument should nevertheless be of particular interest to the reader, as, in his own words, 'it is rejected by many Marxist groups, which cling obstinately to the idea that military expenditure is the only (or at least the most important) source of inflation'.

From this it can be seen that Mandel's representation is more differentiated than is the usual 'left' critique of modern capitalism, but it nevertheless needs completion through more refined investigation into the development of prices in oligopolistic capitalism, above all with regard to the role of price-fixing. Two decades ago the present author made attempts in this direction (Kühne, 1954 and 1958), but in the present work it is not possible to examine the subject more fully. The problems raised by Mandel merge into an analysis of income as well as of currency policy.

WORLD INFLATION, WORLD PRODUCTIVITY AND THE GOLD PROBLEM

Mandel, who is in any case the most persistent advocate of the utility of the value concept, undertakes the courageous attempt to use the concept to analyse the phenomenon of worldwide inflation. He uses the productivity of labour as an inverse measure for value. The more this increases, the more 'value' in its totality tends to shrink. It is, of course, problematical to reason in this way, as we show in volume II, for a more 'intensive' work performance represents a higher average social value than does a less intensive one. Mandel, however, applies the concept in the above form.

For industry and agriculture in the United States, Mandel calculates that between 1907 and 1967 there was an increase in productivity per labour hour of between 450 and 520 per cent. Mandel points out that in the other imperialist countries (this surely means leading industrial countries) the development of productivity has been roughly the same over the period as a whole: their increase in productivity was 'much smaller' between 1914 and 1940, but 'of greater importance' between 1947 and 1967. 'This means that the value of the average good produced in the imperialist countries today is only a fifth or a sixth of that before the First World War.' As the value of gold decreased by one half, 'the gold prices of goods should on the average be a third of their level in 1967'. In fact, goods prices expressed in paper dollars are three times higher than in 1907. From this it follows for Mandel (1972, p. 388) that money was devalued to a ninth of its starting value.

One has to ask whether Mandel could not have come to a more direct result by comparing the development of the volume of production and price indices, though over long periods of time considerable problems arise in the weights of the indices. It also remains an open question whether such calculations should be based on the official or on the market price of gold. One thing is certain: the quantity of 'socially necessary' labour time expended in the product of a given article in 1967 has to be much smaller than the quantity that would have been required to produce the same article in 1907.

The final conclusion that Mandel draws from this statistical exercise amounts to what was explained earlier in this book (See Chapters 12 and 13) to be the logical consequence of a concept of value thought through to its end, i.e. that the increase in production owing to competition, which Marx thought inherent in the capitalist system (despite oligopolistic elements), should properly speaking entail a sinking price level, at least where the sum of values and the sum of prices remain the same. As the value of the individual commodity declines, the price is bound to follow, for otherwise it would be impossible to maintain the equality between the sum of values and the sum of prices. Mandel does not accept such a premise. Implicitly, however, it forms the basis of his reasoning (see, in this context, ch. 17 above).

Mandel denies this premise because to him it seems that it is not compatible with capitalism.

> This devaluation of money to a ninth of its original value has to fulfil an objective function: to disguise the significant, reduced value of commodities, expressed in gold quantities, because a lasting and rapid fall in commodity prices could make the operation of a capitalist economy defective in the long run in the absence of opportunities for geographical expansion. (Mandel, 1972, p. 388.)

This statement raises a whole series of problems. Since Mandel makes the question depend on the value of gold, one could argue that a growing volume of gold (the productivity problem in gold production is of no concern here!) could spare capitalism from such a disastrous fate. Why then, we may ask, could not the same be achieved by means of 'Keynesian paper gold', 'Bancor', or Triffin's plan and other similar measures? With this we reach the point at which manipulation of the world currency serves as an elixir of life for capitalism.

Behind the question asked by Mandel hovers, furthermore, the old problem of whether a falling or rising price level is secularly favourable for growth. A falling price level is the ideal of neo-liberals, who by such measures wish to instil new life into capitalism, but it runs up against the money illusion in man, who prefers to have more money each year than to have a constant level of wages with falling prices (which cannot be accurately controlled and which affect each individual differently). Social unrest and permanent deflation are almost certainly synonymous. It is not for nothing that Röpke once observed that deflation politicians are in greater danger of being shot than inflation politicians are.

Moreover, permanent, but not, of course, galloping, inflation is certainly a good means of encouraging investment in material assets – all the more so as the owners of plants stand a good chance of fleecing their creditors to some extent. Inflation favours the industrial capitalist rather than the financier, so long as the latter does not anticipate the inflationary development by a mark-up. It is the forced savings of small savers that serve as a source of liquidity to both the proprietor and the creditor, and the small saver is being slowly expropriated. In short, Mandel may be right in his view that a long lasting deflationary development will bring capitalism to the brink of collapse. To that extent neo-liberals are bad doctors, for they would cure it to the point of death. Mandel is wrong, however, in making this problem depend on the value of gold. Revolutions do not occur because wages as expressed in gold values sink, but there will be unrest in the case of increasing money value if this means constant or even falling incomes. The decisive element is the comparison between the price index and income, not the comparison with imaginary 'gold francs', a standard that met with approval only in France in the 1920s, when the distrust engendered by frequent currency adventures led to hoarding of gold.

It is only in the framework of his theoretical analysis of the business cycle that Mandel treats the most important factor in world inflation, which simultaneously permitted 'a rapid and above-average expansion of world trade' after the Second World War.

> By way of deficits in the United States balance of payments the gold exchange standard (in reality the gold–dollar standard) functions as a vehicle guaranteeing a lasting expansion of the international means of payment. In 1958 this was happening at a rate of 4 per cent per annum. The gold-dollar standard created a system of international credit inflation, which at the same time uncovered and extended the system of 'national' credit inflation.

Here (ibid., p. 412) Mandel forgets to mention that this system in the long run threatened to destroy the independence of national central-bank policy, a fact which 'academic' economics is more and more inclined to recognise.

Here two different courses, neither of which was chosen by Mandel, may be taken in the direction of a Marxist-inspired theory of the world economy. The first is that as a result of the 'international banking function of the United States and its permanent Keynesian deficit', national monetary policy to a large extent lost its power of direction. In the event of international crises, attempts to recover national autonomy may be too late in the case of shrinkage in world trade, in new world depressions as witnessed in 1974–5. The existence of 'hot money', above all on the Eurodollar market, which compared with the footloose 'hot money' of the 1930s is of much greater dimensions, does not exclude the possibility that this phenomenon from the past could repeat itself.

THE 'SALES' THEORY AND 'SEIGNIORAGE'

The second course consists in hypothesising, in addition to a 'theory of domination' in the manner of Perroux, a theory of international exploitation through paper-dollar inflation. In a somewhat exaggerated form this would run as follows: the United States could buy up the rest of the world, one half with the newly issued dollars, which are as good as gold, and the other half with money borrowed in Europe, of which the greater portion would again consist of dollars, as Eurodollar holdings within the United States have a multiplier of 2 : 3 on the Eurodollar market, which at the international level enables the introduction of a gigantic credit-creation system.

This is, of course, an exaggerated and vulgar formulation, but one which is advanced not only by Marxists, but also by 'academic' economists, especially in France. Discussion of such theses presupposes an analysis of the conditions of world trade, and this must without doubt be done carefully if the investigator is not to be guilty of economic oversimplification.

The theory of money leads on to foreign-trade problems. The 'sales' theory has been touched upon in a book by Altvater, the leading German Marxist currency theorist. He writes (1969, pp. 67–8),

> The balance-of-payments deficits of the United States are nothing other than the acquisition of credit. . . . By such means the United States is in a position unrequitedly to import goods. It can create the general commodity, world money, with the help of which it can then buy any particular commodity, and what is even more important, it is thus able to export capital . . . [so that] United States exports of capital are loans.

Though in this context he mentions 'hierarchic effects', Altvater does not develop the idea in any way. He says only (ibid., p. 64), 'With the export of the dollar the United States underpins its economic, political and military position as a leading world power.'

The Italian Marxist and professional economist Pesenti comes nearest to such a 'dollar sales theory':

> Nowhere can a capital export which involves a deficit in the balance of payments be of long duration; a devaluation would be unavoidable. The United States is in a position to permit itself such capital exports as long as the dollar is the leading currency (monetary base). It is able to export as many paper dollars as it wishes and thereby purchase real goods. . . . The basis of creeping inflation lies in the activities of dominating monopoly capital which wants to change the ratios wage–profit and interest–profit in its favour, i.e. to keep the profit rate at a high level. . . .

According to Pesenti, 'the United States creates with the help of the dollar standard a more and more advantageous system, which makes the dollar the world currency par excellence and the basis of the (world) currency system, the more so as it can dispense with its obligation to convert the dollar into gold'. (Pesenti, 1970, pp. 627, 621–2.) This is the description of a state which in the meantime has been realised. It has been accompanied by a number of devaluations, which have had a relatively weakening effect on the 'purchasing power' of the dollar, but which have not annulled it, all the less as United States enterprises have obtained a footing in Europe and other parts of the world and are free to extend their 'dominant position' within 'dominated' countries (with the aid of credits granted by the latter).

In some modern publications it is claimed that the production of United States subsidiaries in foreign countries should be included in American domestic production. Hankel, who for many years was adviser to the Ministry of Economics in the Federal German Republic, writes (1971, pp. 127–8),

> Only such a measure would give us the true picture of the economic power of the United States. Firms inside the United States have, for instance, invested about $100,000 million in foreign countries during the last fifteen years. . . . It is to the extent of about this amount that the US balance of payments has gone into deficit. The national product of the United States is not increased by products made in foreign countries with US capital. US citizens and firms have, nevertheless, been in a position to increase their fortunes, and the export capacity of the United States has undergone strong growth through goods produced at the scene of activity in foreign markets. . . . Is it then correct to speak of chronic stagnation in the US economy and of chronic deficits on the US balance of payments? Would it not be possible to picture things differently by recording these items under different heading, such as indirect growth in the US social product, and a strengthening rather than a weakening of the US balance of payments? . . . It would be better to replace the old principle of geographical area with a more modern principle of function [in foreign-trade statistics]. In handling things in this way foreign investment by home firms would form part of their total investment activities. Thus they could be valued as a positive contribution to the national product of the country. . . .

By employing Hankel's method we should logically arrive at quite different statistics of national income and of national wealth, which would reflect the 'dominating effect' of the rich nations over poorer ones. From this side as well, the currency problem at the international plane touches upon the complex of the theory of 'exploitation'.

It seems that this complex might be mitigated by the devaluations of the dollar. Through these devaluations, however, the value of foreign investments increases, and, as these belong to big trusts, strengthens the concentration of assets inside the United States. Pesenti may be thinking along similar lines when he writes with regard to the problem of devaluation, 'If, as a result of devaluation, the diminution of monopoly capital reduces the total national capital, a sudden deflation might be the outcome, and this would decrease at a stroke wages and real interest rates, especially on the international scene. . . .' This argument cannot be applied to the case of the United States, since it is specifically addressed to the case of Great Britain. 'Monopoly capital, therefore, affects society as a whole and especially the worker and the small saver, who bear the brunt of the losses, to avoid any possible lowering of the rate of profit.' (Pesenti, 1970, pp. 621–2.)

What is lacking here is a deeper analysis of the problem. Even discussion of the 'sales' theory has been utterly neglected in the Marxist camp, which has left it mostly to 'bourgeois' journalists and 'academic' theorists. Yet the thesis has in the meantime been adopted in the Marxist-oriented daily press, as a quotation from the *Express International* shows:

> 15 August 1971 has been mourned by the bourgeois economic press as the day the gold-dollar standard died [because of the suspension of convertibility into gold]. What hinders the Federal German Republic from revaluing its currency? As US capitalists are able to buy 'hard' currencies at fixed exchange rates while offering only a 'weak' dollar, they can invest money in Europe, in the acquisition of firms, and so on. (Jeuck, 1973, p. 3.)

The theory of 'sales exploitation' of a monetary kind coincides to a certain extent with the theory of 'seigniorage' or of profits from the first use of newly minted money, as developed by the French currency theorist Kolm (1970, p. 1):

> The Americans were able to acquire goods, services and enterprises throughout the rest of the world, offering in exchange only sheets of printed paper. . . . Accordingly the United States held the same power as did the authorities in ancient times, who held the power to mint money. They issued gold and silver coins, which were of greater value than their metal content by a percentage called the 'seigniorial fee' or 'seigniorage'. There is just one difference: the rate then amounted to a few per cent, while nowadays in the case of paper money it goes up to a hundred per cent. . . .

This theory can claim Harrod as its authority. In his work *Money* (1969), he wrote (pp. 309–10),

> It does not seem quite right that to the wealth that [the USA] gains by its great productive powers there should be added 100% seigniorage profit on all the new money that the whole world needs each year. It must be remembered that the rest of the world would have to buy its dollars, which cost the Americans next to nothing to print. . . . It would be a sort of tribute, and a very large one.

In his analysis, Kolm comes to the conclusion that this thesis is relevant only in parts. It could be employed for the period shortly after the last World War, when central banks throughout the world received their initial authorisation, but it does not apply to the subsequent increase in reserves. Besides, Kolm thinks that the dollar seigniorage at that time was offset by 'Marshall Aid'; both amounted to about $15,000 million at the beginning of the 1950s. In arguing in this way, Kolm bases his opinion on the fact that foreign holders of dollars received interest on them. 'The fact that long-term credits are granted to the United States by the rest of the world and that the United States pays for them only a short-term rate of interest does not represent "seigniorage", but rather the export of services, in the form of liquidity, which that country renders to others.' (Kolm, 1970, pp. 5, 9.)

The debate, to which Marxists should contribute, must concentrate on the question of whether this service in the form of provision of liquid funds deserves the 'tribute' of which Harrod speaks.

Considering the fact that Marxists barely participated in the debate on the 'sales' theory, it is all the more astonishing that they have refrained from entering the debate on the currency problem, as here lies the key to the remarkable vitality of capitalism in the period after the Second World War, and conversely a danger for its future.

42 The International Currency System, the Expansion of International Trade and the Post-War Boom in Marxist Analysis

If, viewed from the criterion of efficiency in warding off business cycles, Keynesian fiscal policy at the national level has been problematical and monetary policy scarcely effective, with both indeed even being partly pro-cyclical, a partial Keynesianism functions at any rate with regard to the international central-banking operations of the United States. On the other hand, the balance-of-payments deficits of the United States, whatever their origins and even if they have led to variable injections of liquidity into the world economy, have permitted world trade to grow faster than production in industrial countries and have thereby supported the growth of world capitalism – although monetary factors contributed to the shrinkage of world trade in 1975, and to the slow-down in its growth 1977–8.

Despite attempts by Altvater, Mandel and Pesenti, it has to be said that Marxists have played no leading role in this debate and have offered little that is decisive. The reason for this may be that the importance of monetary policy was underestimated by Marx. This is all the more astonishing as 'academic' economists point out that here lie the real dangers for an eventual 'breakdown' of the capitalist system. In the early 1960s, long before the dollar problem reached its present acuteness, a team of currency experts, consisting of Fatemi, St Phalle and Keefe, warned (1963, pp. ii–iii) that, if rapid and effective measures were not taken to alleviate the recurrent disequilibrium in the balance of payments, the government of the USA would finally face a dollar crisis of great magnitude and be forced to employ drastic controls, that such a development would mean the downfall of the credit structure built up since the end of the war, and that, like the international credit collapse of

1931, it could very well throw the non-communist world into a serious economic depression. Shortly afterwards, Arndt asked the same question (1966, p. 10): 'Is the worldwide economic prosperity of the present free world a consequence of the liberalisation of foreign trade? And, conversely, as in the 1930 economic crisis shall we have to envisage a worldwide depression as soon as trade barriers increase in number?'

International currency problems lead to the question of why, after the Second World War, world capitalism experienced such a phenomenal boom, a boom that has been interrupted only by relatively mild recessions, until the 'Great Recession' occurred in 1974–5. Even a Marxist such as Altvater states (1969, p. 28), 'For the first time since the First World War capitalism has shown a tendency towards an enormous increase in its productive capacity.' On the basis of United Nations statistics, Hankel (1971, p. 17) sums this up in hard figures: 'world industrial production nearly tripled between 1950 and 1970, world trade rose fivefold (+ 409 per cent) and trade between industrial countries rose nearly sevenfold (+ 589 per cent)'. The question is, how to explain this gigantic post-war boom?

There are at least three answers to the question. The first is that of Shonfield, who, in his apotheosis of post-war capitalism (1965), is of the opinion that the boom was due to a combination of inner vitality on the part of the market-economy principle and of state direction, the welfare state, the control of competition and Keynesianism within leading capitalist countries. The second answer is that of Arndt, who says (1966) that the boom was caused and maintained by the removal of trade barriers throughout the world. The third answer is given by the Marxist, Altvater, who says (1969, pp. 22–8)

> integration through foreign trade, capital exports, and, especially in Western Europe, through the formation of supranational economic blocs (EEC, EFTA) would not have been possible, if the growth of production and consumption had not themselves experienced a relatively fast development . . . in comparison with other time periods in capitalist development.

He mentions a number of

> factors, which were important for demand and supply in the world economy . . . : a gigantic backlog of demand . . . wars which, though geographically limited, economically concerned the whole world (Korea, Middle-Eastern countries, Vietnam). . . . the alleged communist threat . . . [and] the consequent enormous armament expenditure . . . led to an extension of total demand. . . . Though a socialist alternative existed also in Western Europe . . . weakened competition within Western European countries was not allowed to suffer the coup de grâce, [instead] the United States had to support Western

European countries . . . [with] Marshall Aid. . . . It is important to note . . . that a far-reaching growth potential was available, . . . especially sufficient labour power . . . in the second industrial revolution.

It is surprising that in these attempts at explanation the most important factor, concerning the world's monetary system, has been utterly neglected, though each interpretation is partially true. While Keynesianism on a national scale has not been crowned by lasting effects, at least in its monetary component, and the international monetary system is subject to severe restrictions, there yet exists a sort of 'super-Keynesianism', on a world scale, the motives of which are quite different from those of contra-cyclical policy, but which is in one view responsible in large measure for the post-war boom in world capitalism. It is possible to see US military expenditure and foreign aid as a gigantic global fiscal policy that structurally underpinned the deficits in the balance of payments. These deficits, intensified by capital exports, served as a permanent source of liquidity for world trade, thus intensifying its liberalisation and supporting the world boom. The present author has attempted to analyse this elsewhere (Kühne, 1971a, pp. 733ff.)

Commentators on this subject have pointed to the inherent dangers in such a system. Thus Altvater is of the opinion (1969, p. 30) that 'on the one hand the rapid growth of capitalist production has facilitated the expansion of world trade, and on the other, has engendered in the course of the growth process divergencies that have led to crises in the economic relationships of the world'. Here the notion 'crisis' is blurred, from the Marxian point of view, and serves as a synonym for 'international currency crisis'. Moreover, it is surprising that Altvater sees in 'the lack of synchronisation' a negative factor for world capitalism, for it is known that the desynchronisation of the business cycle throughout the world has served in reality to underpin the worldwide boom (see Kühne, 1953). Mandel (1972, p. 424) sees in the 'desynchronisation of the international cycle' an 'additional mitigating effect' furthering the growth process in the world. He thinks that such a development has its origin in the political decisions of individual countries, within the framework of their business-cycle policies.

On one point there is unanimity between Marxists and non-Marxists. Altvater formulates this as follows (1969), p. 61):

Deficits in the balance of payments of the United States were a necessity in our present currency system. Otherwise it would have been impossible to create any other form of international liquidity besides gold. This means that within the international currency system the postulate of payments equilibrium and of a policy conforming to this cannot be in any way fulfilled, if the available quantity of liquidity is not to be severely reduced.

In contrast to this, non-Marxists such as Hankel (1971, p. 117) point to difficulties in defining the terms – such as payments balance, basic balance, liquidity balance, balance on official settlements. The degree of deficit varies according to the terms employed. In essence, however, Hankel agrees with Altvater's ideas on the subject, while arguing (ibid., p. 18) that here the Devil (lack of liquidity and expansion risks) is driven out by Beelzebub:

> The Bretton Woods currency system, which is at present still in existence . . . [is] a compromise . . . [which] in its strict sense has not founded an international currency order. . . . Instead there was more trust in the disciplinary influence of a dominant economy, i.e. the influence of the United States, the surplus position of which over a long time period showed strong natural features, though not willed by God for ever, and which was able to hold all other partners (especially weaker ones) in the economic world under a constant restraint to adjust themselves to a policy directed at payments' balance and stability. A constantly 'scarce' reserve-dollar, which was at no time offered in excess, would exercise a wholesome pressure on the balance of payments of partner countries. It was not realised that any constellation is unable to go on for ever, even that of a permanent excess or of equilibrium in the US balance of payments and of a supply of reserves by which inflationary tendencies in other countries were restrained rather than aggravated.

What really happened was the contrary. The dollar standard did not serve as a brake on world inflation, but acted as a motor of world inflation. Initially it supported a worldwide boom, but later it weakened the foundations, as the abundance of dollars undermined the trust set in this substitute for gold. World prosperity rests on quicksands. This is the outlook especially for the late seventies.

'Academic' experts now fear that, since the dollar does not keep down world inflation but inflames it, the system will overshoot with a subsequent collapse. On the other hand, they fear a return to national protectionism and international cartels capable of throttling world prosperity and free trade as a consequence of anti-inflationary and anti-'hot money' measures. Furthermore, they fear a worldwide collapse of currencies, as in 1931. All these factors could together unleash a new world depression (Since this account was written, the feared depression has occurred.)

TWO BASIC THESES: 'REAL' FACTORS *VERSUS* CURRENCY DESTABILISATION

The attitude of a Marxist such as Altvater is itself a paradox, for following Marxist tradition he ıs not much inclined towards this train of thought, because 'real' factors carry more weight (this recalls Marx's dislike of over-estimating monetary factors):

> The neo-Keynesian assumption of the possibility of stable and constant growth is thwarted by the currency difficulties caused by such a policy [i.e. by national attempts to regulate the business cycle]. This again makes clear that currency crises do not represent technical errors in the institutional system, but, rather, the specific expression of the permanent crisis of capitalism within the present institutional system. Capitalist crises are sparked off within the production sphere.
>
> (Altvater, 1969, p. 75.)

Altvater forgot Marx's lapidary dictum, 'Permanent crises do not exist.'

With a certain obstinacy, however, he advocates (ibid., p. 130) Marx's thesis that crises are necessary and have a purifying function in capitalism:

> Within the cyclical development of capitalism, the crisis has the function of restoring again and again the disturbed equilbrium of the economy and acting as a corrective for 'false' developments under capitalism by reviving the conditions facilitating the repeated utilisation of capital. . . . The crisis restores the disturbed equilibrium only if it can let off steam as a crisis of production, for only in this case is the cause of the crisis, the contradiction between increasing productive power and less rapidly growing power of consumption, brought to a new, transitory equilibrium.

If, indeed, the post-war prosperity of world capitalism has been due to dollar liquidity plus a free-trade revolution, it would conform to the system if the end of this dollar status also ushered in the end of an extraordinary epoch of growth for world capitalism. Surprisingly, it is Marxists who are disinclined to believe that such monetary causes can bring about such extraordinary growth and its later collapse, even though Marx himself clearly saw that the crisis was also conditioned by monetary factors.

Altvater rightly stresses (ibid.) the conflict between a nationally conceived Keynesian policy and the instability of the international economy: 'at the level of the world economy there is, as the measures to overcome the international currency crisis show, no chance whatsoever of effecting the negative strategy of avoiding crises through a positive strategy of control and of substituting this for the corrective of world economic crisis'. Whether there is a corrective to be substituted remains to be seen.

The Keynesian view is that it is possible to avoid disturbances and to maintain equilibrium, in which case the cure by crisis would be superfluous.

Furthermore, Altvater is right when he says that, 'even under the principle of the desynchronisation of development, economic recessions are created by governmental strategies of prevention, are transmitted abroad and are escalated into problems of the world economy'. In his exposition, he particularly concentrates on the situation of the Federal German Republic, of which he quite rightly says that it overcame its recession of 1966–7 by increasing its foreign-trade surplus. This picture, however, does not fit the case of countries with a long-term deficit, such as Great Britain.

At one point there is a decisive contrast. Altvater sees (ibid., pp. 133–4) the return of the international currency crisis as soon as

a sharper recession . . . arrives simultaneously in a number of important capitalist countries. . . . If the crisis, contrary to the development
of the last twenty years, does not hit one country alone but several
countries at the same time, then the problem of overcoming the crisis is
no longer a simple one as seemed to be the case during the most recent
recession in West Germany. Above all, it is to be expected that the
unstable system of the gold-exchange standard [properly speaking, the
dollar–dollar standard!] will receive such a blow that *via* the breakdown
of the international currency system even the expansionary impulses in
the world market, the prerequisite for the rapid reversal of recessive
tendencies, are rendered ineffective.

Altvater's sequence is as follows: as soon as the international business cycle is again synchronised, the international monetary crisis will threaten.

The fact is, however, that, when the world currency crisis did take place, the development of the cycle was apparently far from being synchronised. Yet, on closer examination, it becomes apparent that a certain degree of synchronisation did exist. The expansive trend in general made setbacks in the form of recessions visible in only a few countries – for instance, in 1957–8 in the USA and Britain, in 1964–5 in Italy and France, and in 1966–7 in Germany. In all other countries, the factors diminishing investment had their effect only in the form of a downswing in the 'growth cycle'. The present author tried to work out these conditions in a different framework. The analysis of the growth cycle came more and more to the fore in the analysis of the business cycle (Kühne, 1968, p. 3).

Taking into account such considerations, there is much to be said in favour of Arndt's thesis, which is diametrically opposed to that of Altvater. The rapid expansion of world trade, nourished by the abolition of trade barriers and dollar deficit-spending on an international scale, had the effect of evening out the business cycle. As soon as it is flattening out, the business cycle regains its original momentum, as prevailed in the 19th century and in the period between two World Wars. When a crisis of confidence in the dollar leads to the drying-up of the deficit on the US balance of payments or to protectionism and cartelisation in important countries engaged in world trade, or to both, the ghost of a new world crisis in the sense of Fatemi, St Phalle and Keefe was bound to appear again on the horizon – as it did in 1973–5. It seems that 'academic' economics holds a more realistic view, which is perhaps even more pessimistic than the Marxist, in so far as it sees in international currency problems an independent factor which in addition to others threatens the existence of world capitalism in its present form.

43 Say's Law and 'Hoarding'

Even if Marx tended to under-estimate elements of monetary policy, which can be explained from his controversy with Proudhon and his school, he nevertheless laid bare the foundations of the phenomenon of the business cycle, explaining it as the result of tendencies to hoard. His analysis of money problems reaches here the threshold of dynamic problems.

In connexion with the theory of the business cycle, the discussion of Say's Law is of decisive importance. The separation of purchase and sale could possibly lead to an interruption in the process of circulation, through the hoarding of money. Here the Marxian analysis comes very close to the Keynesian thesis of the liquidity trap.

In his *Grundrisse* (pp. 197–8), a decade before the appearance of the first volume of *Capital*, Marx severely criticised the basic principle of Say's Law:

> When it is said that he who sells also buys inasmuch as he buys money, and that he who buys also sells inasmuch as he sells money, then it is precisely the distinction which is overlooked, the specific distinction between commodity and money. After the economists have most splendidly shown that barter, in which both acts coincide, does not suffice for a more developed form of society and mode of production, they then suddenly look at the kind of barter which is mediated by money as if it were not so mediated, and overlook the *specific* character of this transaction. . . . In so far as purchase and sale, the two essential moments of circulation, are different to one another and separated in place and time, they by no means need to coincide.

It would therefore be correct to talk of a monetary aspect in the Marxian theory of the business cycle. Here Marx offers a direct analysis of Say's Law of markets, according to which each sale creates purchasing power, so that a loss of purchasing power as a cause of crisis is, in principle, impossible. Say's Law was given its classic formulation in Say's *Treatise on Political Economy* (1803; English edition, 1803, 1, p. 167):

> They will universally find the most extensive demand in those places where the most values are produced; because in no other places are the sole means of purchase created, i.e. values. Money performs but a

388

momentary function in this double exchange; and when the transaction is finally closed, it will always be found that one kind of produce has been exchanged for another.

In a letter to Malthus (1821, p. 402) Say gave even a more precise formulation of this thesis:

> In selling these, they exchange first their products for money; and they afterwards exchange this money for objects of consumption. Thus, it is in strict reality, with their products that they make their purchases; it is impossible for them to buy any articles whatever to a greater amount than that which they have produced either by themselves, or by means of their capitals and lands.

James Mill developed Say's ideas even further when he said (1821; 1966, pp. 328, 332),

> His will . . . to purchase, and his means of purchasing, in other words his demand, is exactly equal to the amount of what he has produced and does not mean to consume. . . . Production is the cause, and the sole cause, of demand. It never furnishes supply without furnishing demand, both at the same time, and both to an equal extent.

It is at this point that Marx's critique enters. He stresses the point that 'the person who has effected a sale, who therefore has commodities in the form of money, is not compelled to buy again and at once'. For Marx, crisis becomes imaginable as a consequence of 'purchase and sale', which are 'independent of each other and separate in time and space'.

> As Mill says, purchase is sale etc.; therefore, demand is supply and supply demand. But they also fall apart and can become independent of each other. At a given moment, the supply of all commodities can be greater than the demand for all commodities, since the demand for the *general commodity*, money, exchange-value, is greater than the demand for all particular commodities. . . .   (*Theories*, ii, pp. 509, 508, 504–5.)

Here Marx offers the possibility of the hoarding of liquid means; in other words, he speaks of a loss of effective demand.

Mill, who recognised the priority of Say, argues (1808; 1966, p. 135),

> The production of commodities creates, and is the one and universal cause which creates a market for the commodities produced . . .; the more you increase the annual produce, the more by that very act you extend the national market, the power of purchasing and the actual purchases of the nation . . .; so that a nation can never be naturally

overstocked either with capital or with commodities, as the very operation of capital makes a vent for its produce.

By this Mill denies, in principle, the possibility of pure over-production. On the other hand, he admitted that partial overproduction might exist, as did Say.

But Malthus upheld the possibility of general overproduction; Marx who despised was nevertheless in his general business cycle analysis influenced by Malthus. Furthermore, he argued that partial crises might have their origin in 'disproportionate production' leading to general crises. (Theories, ii, p. 510, 525ff,)

In the twenties, Miksch (1929) recognized that it was Marx who analyzed Malthus's vague hints in a clear-cut theory, and Spiethoff (1923; 1955) vindicated it by transforming it into a full theory of hoarding.

This will have to be explained in detail in Vol. ii of this work, in the chapters on business cycle theory.

Part IX
The Marxian Renaissance and the Transition to Dynamics

44 An Intermediate Appraisal

Our analysis has proceeded from the static to the dynamic aspects of the Marxian system. The latter have already appeared in price theory, in dynamic distribution analysis and in the dynamics of transformation of the process of concentration. All this leads into the truly dynamic area of growth and business cycles.

Marx's basic criticism of capitalism as a soulless system built on a maze of relations between dead objects prompted Croce to remind us that 'on every page of *Capital* . . . Marx's text conjures up a tone of passionate revolt and bitter satire', which finally inspired also his political activity. Croce finds this tone in the concept of surplus value, which he interprets (1900) as a moral and social phenomenon:

> Is not the interest directed to the construction of the concept of surplus value perhaps finally a moral or, if you wish, a society-inspired aspiration? Is it possible to speak of surplus value from a purely economic point of view? Does not the proletariat sell its labour power for what it is worth, taking into consideration the position it actually holds in society?

Such an ethical interpretation of the principle of labour value or surplus value has been proposed also by Lindsay and is again gaining ground.

In the view of Croce's disciple Calogero (1941; 1967, pp. 73, 74, 61, 79), this interpretation results in a recognition of the 'ethical–juridical idealism . . . of the Marxian reduction of value to labour'. But Calogero reaches the conclusion that such a reduction cannot be anything other than 'a specification of the concept of an ethical obligation which is reflected in Marx's mind, although not quite consciously'. He departs from economic analysis by arguing,

> it is clear then that we can no longer conceive [of Marxian economics] as a system organically based on this equation [value = labour]. The reduction of value to labour . . . is not an absolute principle of economic philosophy. Even if it were, it could never offer a starting point for concrete economic analysis. . . .

In this way, the applicability of the value concept is negated. Calogero then goes on to say that, on the other hand, Marx 'more or less neglected his own *a priori* schemes to concentrate his attention, in the best pages of *Capital*, on a historical analysis of the process of the concentration of capitalist wealth'.

At this juncture, the old error of interpreting Marx as purely an economic historian, if of the history of the future, crops up again. Calogero nevertheless recognises a certain workability of the Marxian system by admitting that Marx

> reports [as a historical fact] the circumstance that part of the wealth produced does not return to the worker who produced it, but is alienated and crystallises as capital. . . . This concentration . . . tends to feed on itself. Whoever manages to gain a vantage point, because he owns a larger quantity of capital, more and more approaches a monopoly situation. . . .

This form of 'renaissance' of the Marxian system conceives of it as based upon ethical considerations; undoubtedly, this has been the source of much disputation. A transition to workable economic concepts can, in this conception, be attained only *via* the concentration process.

Such an ethical–historical renaissance of the Marxian system, comes up, however, against two obstacles. First, part of the surplus value would have to be used for social purposes, as Marx pointed out in his *Critique of the Gotha Programme*. This remains true even if we agree with Joan Robinson that revolutionary conclusions might be derived from the concept of a 'supply price of capital', i.e. from the idea that part of the surplus value would need to be used to bribe capitalists to offer their capital. It will be recalled that Joan Robinson argued that such a state of affairs would justify an expropriation of capitalists in order to prevent them from holding society to ransom, since investment could be performed more cheaply without them. This is a good example of how revolutionary, economic and pragmatic considerations coalesce.

The second obstacle is to be found in Marx's own attitude, for, as Calogero notes (ibid., p. 32), he 'always declared his intention of deducing economic truth independently of any ethical tinge'.

If one wished to adopt such a preponderantly ethical and historical interpretation, one would undoubtedly, in any attempt to revive Marxian ideas, put the chief accent on distribution aspects. On the other hand, it cannot be denied that value analysis telescopes, in essence, into distribution theory. It is also true that the notion of surplus value contains some germs of workable economics, for its fixes the share of capitalists in the social product at a level given by the part of the labour force used in industries working for capitalist consumption and investment goods. The argument also holds the other way round: if one starts from von Neumann's hypothesis that workers consume their entire income (which is considered to be fodder for robots, as it were), while capitalists invest all their profits, surplus value exactly corresponds to the percentage of labour used to produce net investment, although in the next phase part of it may be used to employ additional labour from the reserve army or from a pool of pre-capitalist elements.

In this sense, we are certainly dealing with a workable renaissance of the notion of value, by which is meant that the distribution of labour among the large sectors of the economy finally determines the production of a 'surplus value', which must be conceived of as a real surplus, over and above consumption (including the replacement of assets). This is the most fruitful interpretation of the theory of value for economics. The unit of value is considered as production per head per worker, which corresponds to capital consumption plus the value added per worker which results once all labour is used optimally, taking into consideration the feasibility of mechanisation and the economies of scale which are attainable.

It cannot be denied that this sort of classical analysis is in vogue with many modern economists who are looking for an objective criterion by which to measure progress. The following quotation from Joan Robinson (1964, pp. 410ff; 1971, p. 169) neatly reproduces the Marxian value concept:

> We may postulate that, in the planned economy, consumable income is distributed as wages, and that all production can be divided into outputs of consumable commodities and capital equipment (abstracting from armaments, social services, etc., and from investment in working capital). Then, labour in the two sectors being alike, the real wage bears the same proportion to the average output per man employed in producing commodities that employment in that sector bears to total employment. (When 20 per cent of labour is otherwise employed the wage is 80 per cent of the average output of a man in the commodity sector.) It has nothing whatever to do with the marginal product of labour.

Here appears the complete contrast between the classical tradition, which interprets the surplus in Marx's sense as a macroeconomic phenomenon, i.e. as the result of the distribution of the labour force under the aforesaid conditions, and the microeconomic concept, which started from marginal-utility analysis and reached its culmination in modern neoclassical theory.

It may be asserted that a large part of the doctrines of the Cambridge School represents a revival of Marxian notions. The Marxian negation of 'commodity fetishism' is implicit in the neo-Keynesians' refusal to measure capital in money units – a method that Joan Robinson and Kaldor see as founded on circular reasoning. Joan Robinson writes (1953–4, pp. 81ff; 1971, p. 47),

> When we know the future expected rate of output associated with a

certain capital good, and expected future prices and costs, then, if we are given a rate of interest, we can value the capital good as a discounted stream of future profit which it will earn. . . . But to do so, we have to begin by taking the rate of interest as given, whereas the main purpose of the production function is to show how wages and the rate of interest (regarded as the wages of capital) are determined by technical conditions and the factor ratio. . . .

Kaldor once suggested that capital might be measured in tons of steel, but Joan Robinson saw only one way out of this dilemma: 'when we consider what addition to productive resources a given amount of accumulation makes, we must measure capital in labour units. . . . a unit of labour that was expended at a certain time in the past is more valuable today than a unit expended today, because its fruits are already ripe. . . .' This is a rehabilitation of Marx's 'socially necessary labour time', and one which agrees with the view of Keynes (1936, cited by Joan Robinson) that 'the capital in existence at any moment may be treated simply "as part of the environment in which labour works"'. Joan Robinson thus espouses the Keynesian proposition that there is a single factor of production, namely labour.

There remains the problem of how to measure interest, which is applied to gauge the difference between the 'more valuable' work done in the past and the efforts of living labour 'expended today'. Here again, Joan Robinson follows Marx's path, defending him against Böhm-Bawerk. In accord with Pietranera, she denies (1953–4; 1971, pp. 54–5) that a positive rate of interest can be explained by the generally prevailing 'higher valuation of present goods': 'Whether it was positive or negative would depend upon whether spendthrifts or prudent family men happened to predominate in the community. There is no *a priori* presumption in favour of a positive rate. Thus, the rate of interest cannot be accounted for as the "cost of waiting"'. At this point she directly returns to Marx's 'social monopoly in the means of production':

> The reason why there is always a demand for loans at a positive rate of interest, in an economy where there is property in the means of production and means of production are scarce, is that finance expended now can be used to employ labour in productive processes which will yield a surplus in the future over costs of production. Interest is positive because profits are positive.

Here the Cambridge School attaches itself to the theory of distribution, which has been dubbed by Preiser as the 'theory of class monopoly' and which has been developed not only by that author, but also by Graziadei and Kalecki, in the footsteps of Marx. Marx's 'institutionalised class struggle' finds its expression in the vast literature dealing with the conflict between trade unions and employers, a good deal of which may be traced back to the analysis of bilateral monopoly. It may be no accident that one of the principal authorities on this problem is a Marxist, the French economist Denis (1943).

In spite of the analogies between the modern capital and interest theory and the distribution analysis of the Cambridge School and the Marxian system, a number of questions remain open and it is only recently that solutions to these have been indicated. There is first of all the problem of how to measure 'values'. Here there is the objection of Marchal and Lecaillon that 'socially necessary labour time', which is subject to a process of permanent shrinkage (discontinuous in the course of time), simply does not offer a good yardstick. Meek in particular has emphasised that there should be no confusion here with the imputation theorem, which attributes the whole of value added to the single factor 'labour'. This theorem, as Calogero has aptly said, is simply an equation 'value = labour time' and cannot be considered as a fundamental deduction of Marxian economics. Rather, it must be seen as a premise of Marx's system and as a symbol of the revolutionary's interest in the ethical and political aspects. In this context, we may quote Bharawaj's statement (1963, pp. 1450–4) that the 'efforts, notably by Ricardo and Marx, to discover an invariant yardstick to measure value . . . [were] unsuccessful'.

Here Sraffa's neo-Ricardian experiment is relevant. He introduces (1960, p. 24) as a yardstick a 'composite commodity', 'which consists of the same commodities (combined in the same proportions) as does the aggregate of its own means of production – in other words, such that both product and means of production are quantities of the selfsame composite commodity'. This notion takes up Ricardo's famous 'corn' example. Sraffa's method introduces the notion of 'dated labour' and relates yesterday's labour, which is more valuable because it is already embodied in finished products, to labour expended today. Sraffa thus determines the 'surplus' 'within the framework of the physical, non-human world of technology' and simultaneously exposes the impossibility of measuring capital without first analysing distribution and determining the rate of profit, although it is true that he does not give us a theory of distribution in the proper sense of the term. (Bharawaj, 1963, pp. 1450, 1453.)

It is true that even Marxists contest the question of whether Marx himself provided such a theory, and it cannot be denied that Marx 'left open the question of how the rate of exploitation is determined. He himself viewed it in terms of the balance of class forces', as Bhaduri has pointed out (1969, pp. 532ff.; 1971, p. 258). Here we find another analogy with Sraffa, who indicates that the profit rate is exogenously given. Marx wanted, at any rate, to analyse possible changes in the rate of surplus value within the framework of his system. As Cole asserted, and as the present volume tries to show, in the last resort the value theory is to be considered in its entirety, in the context of an analysis of Marxian wage and distribution theory, as a macroeconomic distribution concept, which is seen here as entirely relevant.

Kalecki coined the notion of the 'degree of monopoly', which is derived from the Marxian rate of surplus value, and leads us *via* distribution theory to the problems of competition and concentration. Marx himself fought shy of the term 'monopoly'. He distinguished 'natural', 'artificial' and 'accidental' (i.e. 'temporary') monopolies, and he wanted to exclude these terms from the central area of his theorising. Nevertheless, he was not fully conscious of the fact that in his dynamic price analysis he analysed nothing other than what he had already called, in *The Poverty of Philosophy*, 'competing monopolies', for his dynamic price analysis is undoubtedly based upon the oligopoly concept. Without going as far as de Cindio, who wants to transform the theory of value into a formula for price calculation, it can be said that innovations and monopolistic vantage positions are synonymous.

Marx's price theory is primarily concerned with long-run costs, though the demand aspect is implicit in the notion of 'socially necessary labour time'. This long-run price analysis is confirmed in modern studies such as Lombardini's (1971, p. 343): 'In a competitive system with free entry, prices . . . are independent of the level and of the distribution of final demand. Modifications in final demand cause only changes in the number of firms in different branches of industry.' Whereas in Marx's work the dependence of demand on income distribution looms large, modern Marxists stress the possibilities of influencing and manipulating demand through advertising, the costs of which largely determine consumption.

Within the framework of the theory of concentration two points are of a decisive importance. Lombardini (ibid., pp. 63–4, 111) has emphasised the first:

> Marx is the only economist who has imagined as one of the possible consequences of competition a complete transformation of the entire system. . . . He puts the accent upon the radical transformation of the capitalist structure. . . . And since the days of Marx the study of the relationship between the development of the forces of production and that of the entire economic system has not shown much progress.

The second problem, that of the repercussions of such a transformation of the structure on the stability of the whole system – which leads us to consider the growth process and its problems – has of necessity been only partially and sporadically touched upon in this volume. Marx was one of the first economists to treat this problem comprehensively, and he also combined the dynamic aspects of growth with the business cycle, which, in his view, was endogenous to capitalist development. Here, his analysis of monetary phenomena and of effective demand, as represented in his criticism of "Say's Law", appears surprisingly 'Keynesian'.

These dynamic aspects undoubtedly represent the essence of the Marxian system. They are dealt with chiefly in the second volume of this work.

Index